SOMETHING LIKE TREASON

DISLOYAL AMERICAN SOLDIERS & THE PLOT TO BRING WORLD WAR II HOME

WILLIAM SONN

SUNBURY
PRESS

Mechanicsburg, PA USA

Published by Sunbury Press, Inc.
Mechanicsburg, PA USA

SUNBURY
P R E S S
www.sunburypress.com

For information about special discounts for bulk purchases, please contact Sunbury Press Orders Dept. at (855) 338-8359 or orders@sunburypress.com.

To request one of our authors for speaking engagements or book signings, please contact Sunbury Press Publicity Dept. at publicity@sunburypress.com.

FIRST SUNBURY PRESS EDITION: August 2021

Set in Adobe Garamond | Interior design by Crystal Devine | Cover by Darleen Sedjro | Edited by Lawrence Knorr.

Publisher's Cataloging-in-Publication Data
Names: Sonn, William, author.
Title: Something like treason : disloyal American soldiers & the plot to bring World War II home / William Sonn.
Description: First trade paperback edition. | Mechanicsburg, PA : Sunbury Press, 2021.
Summary : A disloyal group of American soldiers, stashed, abused, and seething in a remote camp in Colorado, conspire to war against their own country. At their head: the only soldier convicted of treason in the U.S. during World War II. And then their fates take an only-in-America turn.
Identifiers: ISBN : 978-1-62006-509-9 (softcover).
Subjects: HISTORY / Military / World War II | HISTORY / Social History | POLITICAL SCIENCE / Political Ideologies / Fascism & Totalitarianism.

Product of the United States of America
0 1 1 2 3 5 8 13 21 34 55

Continue the Enlightenment!

For Goldie, Ike, Jonah, and Saphira, my favorite quartet

CONTENTS

ABBREVIATIONS

HC   Dale H Maple Research Collection. MSS 2261, History
      Colorado. Denver
      and
      Colorado and Dale H Maple Collection MSS 1589
      History Colorado. Denver, Colorado.

FF   file folder

FBIM Federal Bureau of Investigation file materials (in HC);
      FBI records from the Department of Justice archives.

C   Correspondence (in HC)

NARA National Archives Records Center

SIX YEARS LATER

Six years later, when he got home again, Dale Maple was 30 and not very famous anymore. No press, no jostle greeted the bus as it pulled into San Diego's terminal on October 10th, 1950. After two long days of traveling—1,558 miles from Kansas through Oklahoma, New Mexico, Arizona, and across California—he wasn't all that presentable anyway. Not too long before, during his heyday in San Diego and in Cambridge and beyond, he'd been a genius, a glorious pianist, a prodigiously talented linguist, and a gifted student of most of the physical sciences and all the liberal arts. As a teen and then a college student, he'd confidently told the adults who flocked to him he was going to be a diplomat, a chemist, a concert pianist, or maybe an internationally known linguist. Few doubted it was all within his reach. But things go awry for young men during wartime.

So far, Maple's most notable adult deed had been to conspire with a handful of scorned soldiers to bomb communications and transportation hubs, attack military posts and make war against and within the United States of America. Of all the things he could have been, he was now the only American soldier convicted on home soil of the military's version of treason during World War II.

All his confederates—he called them the Inner Circle—had been like him: sons of the middle and upper-middle class fated to first test the quickening currents of American adult life during one of the world's great storms. All were smart, most of them well-educated, and several of them disoriented not only by the mind-boggling roar of global war but the often-confounding bureaucracy of the burgeoning U.S. military. All were soon swept over the war's falls and against its rocks, abused and then bewildered and alienated and primed to retaliate.

He stepped off the bus into a placid, 71-degree San Diego day, a re-shaped world and a seemingly foreign society that was now growing richer and more powerful than any in human history. Average family income in 1950 was $3,300, already up 27% from $2,595 in 1945. Even fear had a new dimension: Russia had busted the U.S.'s monopoly in nuclear weapons the year before, and Americans suddenly were living under a whole new kind of threat.

American citizens had an impressive 25 million cars in 1950, but that was about to grow to 67 million by 1958. Television was taking off. Sets that were $500 in 1949 became sets that cost $200 in 1953. By the decade's end, 90% of American homes had at least one of them.

The war seemingly was slowly but surely upending America's version of Abraham Maslow's Hierarchy of Needs, the ranking of humans' five psychological needs. As Maple stepped off the bus, more and more Americans' access to food, clean water, warmth, clothing, and sleep—the foundation of basic physiological needs, according to Maslow—was steadily expanding. They worked and lived in different places (two-thirds of industrial construction during the coming decade would take place outside of cities, with suburban residential accounting for 75% of total construction). Their understandings of security, both personal and national, were morphing in the ominous new atomic age. So were love and belonging, and how we defined accomplishment.

And for the relatively secure American castes in 1950, the times promised a sunny era of opportunity, honest government, and, after decades of tumult and Depression and mourning, stability. That was new, too.

A couple of decades later, there was a good argument to be made that Maslow's whole pyramid of needs had been nearly flipped over. Self-fulfillment was often more important than, say, accomplishment.

On the day of Maple's arrival, fresh, gentle 8-mile-per-hour breezes blew in off the Pacific. The day seemed safe from any of October's often-punishing autumnal weather events, especially the brutal Santa Ana winds that blasted scorching desert temperatures, fire, and, it was said, portents of distress and intimations of madness from the east. For now, the winds were quiet.

For the would-be traitors and Nazis Maple had once claimed to lead, however, the quiet could be menacing. Job prospects for ex-cons were not good. An era of retribution flourished in 1950. The FBI was arresting collaborators, even people like Maple just freed from years of military confinement. Their new sentences were often harsher than the military ones they'd already served. The month Maple's bus pulled into San Diego, U.S. Attorney General J. Howard McGrath published guidelines for "Communist-action" groups to register and reveal its members, finances, leaders' associates, and more under the new Subversive Activities Control Act. The same year, Sen. Joseph McCarthy spectacularly claimed there were 200-some "communists" in the U.S. Department of State. Though the numbers he gave changed from press interview to interview, he dramatically accelerated a "Second Red Scare" (the first was in 1917-1920). Politicians were already accusing and attacking those who they deemed too tepid in their support of the war or too open-minded about alternative ideologies. Maple qualified on both counts. Employers, under pressure, were firing or rejecting the accused simply for being accused. Innocents suffered. How all this would affect Maple's disloyal, just-released confederates—hardly innocent— was, if nothing else, a curious social experiment. How quickly can the wartime villains of one national delirium, the visceral hated of Japanese and Germans, be obscured by the next national delirium.

At first, most of the tainted men of the Inner Circle were making uncharacteristically wise choices. They were scattering as unobtrusively as possible to Pennsylvania, Michigan, Ohio, New Jersey, and Illinois. Another was in Argentina.

Maple would be the most recent of them to try to blend in, although blending in had never been his strong suit. Six years before, he was intent on forging a notorious path to wartime Berlin and returning home with the tools and training of the Third Reich to blow up parts of the United States. Even now, in 1950, his professional sights were immodest. His keepers had warned him post-prison prospects for convicted traitors—even smart ones—were generally limited to hardscrabble jobs at best. Should he manage to stay out of jail, no self-respecting school or company or agency was going to hire him.[1] But he had been steadily raising his expectations for a future magically free of the consequences of his own actions. He aimed to be a pioneer of new teaching methods for slow learners. a mathematician, a psychiatrist with an academic appointment, and, in his off-hours, a pianist with a local symphony. The odds against realizing such jailbird ambitions, much less in the changed United States, were absurdly long.

In San Diego that day, his father was at the terminal; a gruff man, a realist, an engineer. Next to him was a stranger, official-looking. A woman was there, too; likely the new arrival's as-yet-unmet stepmother. She was something else that had changed since the day he'd disappeared.

PART ONE

ESCAPE

CHAPTER 1

WHERE IS HE?

They last saw Dale Maple—listed at 5'10" tall, 168 lb., with brown hair and fair complexion—early on February 15th, 1944, at a place called Camp Hale high in the mountains of Colorado. He'd played piano for a few friends at a rental house a mile from camp the night before, which was hardly unusual. They drank beer and sang and, weaving a little, made it back to the barracks in time for curfew.

In the morning, he stopped at the bunk of his buddy Theo Leonhard holding something in his hand. It was his Army ID bracelet. He asked Leonhard to keep it for him.

Leonhard who knew Maple to be strangely theatrical at times, took it and added he had to get to work, which for him that day was at the dump at the edge of camp. But Maple, talkative, followed him to the dump. "Well," he volunteered, "I don't think I'm going to be around for a while." Leonhard had "a pretty fair idea" Maple was headed to Denver to keep a promise to defend another mate awaiting court-martial. It was as peculiar to Leonhard as the ID bracelet, to be sure. Maple, he knew, had neither a furlough to travel to Denver nor a shred of legal training.

Trucks, full of garbage and ash, were arriving at the dump, and Leonhard, who directed the truck traffic there, had to go. Maple walked away.

No one noticed at first. The 15,000 other soldiers in the vicinity were busy with the tense, miserable business of preparing to join the war's stupendous planetary carnage in China, Southeast Asia, Russia, Africa, and, not least, Italy. They belonged to the legendary 10th Mountain Division and soon would find themselves north of the once-lovely Monte Cassino. The hilltop abbey, built in 529, was by then a heavily fortified German observation post blocking the way to Rome and would take three months to overrun. Twenty thousand Germans would be wounded or killed in the process. There would be 55,000 Allied casualties. The men would then throw themselves against the Germans' massive Gothic Line, built by slaves and mostly hidden within the 7,000-foot Apennines Mountain range that stretches across the width of northern Italy. They'd inch toward a rock-hard 10-mile belt of concrete gun pits and trenches nearly immune to aerial attack and crawl beneath interlocking fire from 2,376 machine-gun nests and 479 anti-tank, mortar, and assault gun positions. While under fire, they'd have to cut through parts of 120,000 yards of barbed wire. If they made it over the Apennines, the men from Camp Hale were supposed to secure the Po River Valley and draw some German troops away from their defensive positions in western Europe. The mission: increase the odds of success for what the men believed to be an imminent and probably even bloodier Allied invasion of France.

Sgt. Alexander V. Altman, the man formally entrusted to keep an eye on Maple, was distracted. Ordered to spend his morning at the camp dentist and finally freed around mid-day Altman, a 34-year-old Russian immigrant, quickly grabbed lunch to hustle back to camp. The place was less than ideal. Called "Camp Hell" and "Camp Hole" by many, his posting was a hastily assembled, frigid training camp set 9,300 feet above sea level. Its 1,000-some wooden buildings were heated by small coal stoves that incessantly pumped ash into what had recently been a pristine alpine valley. Two loud, soot-belching locomotives pulled trains past the camp up over 10,424-foot Tennessee Pass several times a day, thickening the smog. On days like February 15th Hale was often under a winter temperature inversion, which kept a heavy shroud of coal haze low over the camp, sometimes at head height. Not far from the small town of Pando, Colorado, many of Hale's soldiers dubbed the resulting persistent cough "the Pando hack." Some called it the camp song.

The air was marginally cleaner about five miles from camp, where most of Altman's men were doing sawmill duty that day. They cut trees and sawed wood in a cold winter forest shade. Dirty and dangerous even on nicer days, sawmill duty was "the least desirable detail in camp," a War Department Board of Inquiry would later note.[1]

Altman's job wasn't easy, even in better conditions. Maple and the 200-some men he helped monitor were pariahs among the U.S. Army's 7.9 million soldiers. Maple, Leonhard, and their mates shared Camp Hale with the illustrious

10th but were separately part of a secretly organized, much-shunned misfit unit called the 620 Engineer General Service Company. In the 16 months since the unit was formed, the men had become increasingly difficult for Altman and the other officers to control. By now, it operated in a constant hum of administrative chaos and seething hostility.

Altman had nervously left Corporal Paul Kissman, "the First Aid man," in charge at the sawmill for the morning. Much to the disappointment of the officers who liked him, Kissman lately had become a friend of some of the unit's most vocal complainers.

At slightly after 1 P.M., Altman got to his men laboring in the forest and asked the once-trusted Kissman if all the men had reported for duty earlier in the day.[2]

"Flitsch," Kissman replied.

Altman wasn't surprised. Pvt. Flitsch was a notably nervous man who, the previous month, had abruptly run amuck, knocked out windows in one of the unit's barracks with a fire extinguisher, raced outside, and then flung himself into the shallow stream that ran through the camp. His absence on February 15th was not all that unusual.[3]

But Altman, who no longer had faith in anything his men told him, took Kissman's duty roster to check for himself. Kissman's math was wrong. The headcount was still off by one. Who?

"Maple," Kissman said. Maple was on sick call.

Maple's absence was worrisome. Everything about Private First-Class Dale Maple was worrisome. Harvard '41, *magna cum laude*, he was a hyper-active complainer known to deliver impromptu lectures in the barracks about German Oswald Spengler's brooding *Decline of the West,* a favorite of Nazi philosophers. He was perhaps the brightest, most capable, and most truculent of the often-insufferable misfits in Altman's 620th

———

Maple was hardly the only smart—or resentful or alienated or elaborately educated or astringent—man in Altman's unit. A secret Military Intelligence effort had thrown him into a misfit group with a Columbia dropout and black sheep son of an internationally known statistician, an Oxford-trained mechanical engineer, a political science doctoral candidate from the University of Texas, and still others who had once "said or [done] something subversive prior to their induction."

The men, however, need not have done anything wrong. An allegation—of some manner of retrospectively dubious speech, behavior, assembly, travel, of being born in a foreign land, communicating or singing in a foreign language—frequently was enough for them to be tagged for a "special organization" like the 620th. There were at least five of them; two in Colorado, one each in Missouri, Texas, and Tennessee. "Mere suspicion," the War Department wrote in its October 1942 order creating the unit, "was sufficient" for transfer into one of the forsaken units. Most of the suspects in the 620th were German- or Italian-born, although there was a complement of American-born U.S. soldiers like Maple and Kissman. Many of the foreign-born were not yet U.S. citizens.[4]

Someone at some point before the war had written or guessed that each of them was untrustworthy, "deviant" (meaning gay to those in authority), communist, an isolationist, an America-Firster, born in the "wrong" country, a German sympathizer, or some other kind of undesirable that the War Department, having mistakenly inducted them in its rush to build an army in 1941 and '42, didn't otherwise know what to do with. Some of the 620ers, it was true, were simply cowardly, stoking suspicion to stay put and avoid combat. "A subversive word a day keeps the foxhole away," one mantra had it.[5]

Nevertheless, most had joined the Army as loyal soldiers and were shocked and humiliated to find themselves in a unit like the 620th. The Army never acknowledged that the company was, in essence, a holding pen for undesirables. But the men of the 620th caught on quickly. By now—not least since Maple had arrived to lead them—even the men who had entered the military anxious to fight for the U.S. were behaving the way the Army perceived them.

So Altman was not about to take Kissman's or anyone's word about where the notorious Dale Maple was. He turned his Jeep back to camp to find him. He'd look in the barracks first and then, perhaps, among battle-hardened German POWs interned a couple of buildings away at Camp Hale's stockade.

———

Altman, Maple and their comrades had arrived at Hale one night about two months before, in December 1943. Reality bent the first morning. They awoke to two Army of the Reich soldiers walking between their bunks. As the enemies calmly passed by, word quickly spread among the 620's sympathizers that two real flesh-and-blood German soldiers were among them in Colorado U.S.A. and settling down, it seemed, to work on a boiler. The rest of the soldiers of the 620th rushed to the scene. All disarmed by order of the Army, they gawked. In

German, they asked the strangers who they were, how they got there, what was going on.

And in German, the enemy soldiers explained they were part of a detachment of thousands of robust, disciplined members of Germany's elite, unprecedentedly mobile Afrika Korps that earlier in the war had conquered most of northern Africa at lightning speed.[6]

At Camp Hale, the Germans were already famous for their smart, chest-out marching and bravado singing to and from their POW work duties. They remained a sharply military, defiant, inventive lot. They engineered small stills in their barracks that produced schnapps brewed from fruit secreted from the stockade mess. The prisoners sold the schnapps they didn't drink to Hale's civilian workers. At Camp Bullis, Texas, where still another detachment of captured Afrika Korps troops was held, the Germans built what one U.S. serviceman stationed there later called "an awesome swimming pool out of rocks that was still used when we went there." The Germans at Camp Hale were also widely noted for playing soccer shirtless in the winter mountain cold.

Some at Hale, including at least five of the 200 Women's Army Corps soldiers stationed there, were smitten. The women sent the prisoners romantic notes, and there were rumors of what one WAC soldier reported was "an interesting arrangement worked out in the mattress warehouses." It was, she added drily, "an experiment in international goodwill." The peace initiative had other adherents. A major's wife purportedly was having an affair with one of the prisoners. Another POW shared a love letter a WAC had sent him. "She loves a German, and she would like to ask him to stay here," the POW's GI friend reported to his barracks mates, "but she don't think he would." The prisoner also revealed that "several WACs were in contact with the prisoners and would bring them anything they wanted."[7]

In the months since the enemy soldiers first walked by their bunks, Maple, Leonhard, and the 620th's grumbling German sympathizers also had fallen for the POWs. "It is hard to explain our emotional reaction to these German soldiers," said one of them, a veteran of what he considered Army discrimination, segregation, surveillance, punishment, and abuse. "When they marched by our barracks for the first time, singing their German songs—almost all of us were outside to look at them." Maple, a third-generation Californian of British and Scottish heritage who had never been outside the continental United States, re-imagined his ancestry. "Many of the men in our company broke down and wept when they saw these men, our brothers and cousins, men of our blood and our way of life."[8]

The men brought the dashing prisoners candy and cigarettes. They tried to make friends, although many of the Germans initially proved standoffish. "These men distrusted us because they had been told by their guards that we were renegades from Germany, who had left to escape military service," a German-born member of the 620th recalled. "That hurt." But they persisted and, by the day Maple himself disappeared, had visited the prisoners' barracks often. As relationships warmed—one 620er, also born in Germany, began by inquiring if any of his long-lost brothers or cousins were among the prisoners—they sometimes exchanged uniforms with the prisoners, knocked back schnapps, and gossiped in German. They wanted to know about the prisoners' triumphant Panzer dash across northern Africa, the tank General Erwin Rommel, women, daily life in Germany.

The fawning over the prisoners made Altman and the 620th's other officers, who had been humiliating their men for 16 months, still more disgusted with the men. The unit's new commander, a 1st Lt. Leroy Wilson, piled restrictions on them. Despite putting them and the POWs together for work—on that February 15th, many prisoners were also on sawmill duty, working near the 620th men—he forbade fraternization. Defying the order carried heavy punishment. He soon impoverished Leonhard for saying "*guten tag*" to a POW, cutting his wages by two-thirds for three months.

The men weren't to speak German or Italian anymore. Wilson turned off their barracks lights before the rest of the camp went dark. He banned them from living off the base, a common practice at many units. They were not allowed to carry weapons at any time. Then one day, he abruptly ordered the men who had cars to sell them immediately or put them in "dead storage," meaning far away. "I asked [Wilson] if there was any particular reason," one GI remembered. "He just said, 'You are in the 620th, and that is all.'" The men, many of them enlistees, were not soldiers anymore, Wilson told them upon arriving at Hale. They were just a labor battalion.

If that didn't work, the Army had made it clear in other ways that they were not like other soldiers. One sergeant, responding to a fresh recruit's question about why they didn't have the same career paths as others, screamed that "none of the 620 Nazi bastards should have more than a PFC ranking." Another sergeant addressed them only as "Nazi bastards" when he called them to formation. Fritz Siering, a German-born anti-Nazi who had fearfully fled his homeland seven years before getting trapped in the 620th, was greeted on his first day in the company by an officer giving him the Nazi salute. "I escaped 3,000 miles from that, and then they should greet me with 'Heil Hitler.' I thought, 'what is this?' I was greatly disappointed." Maple also was put in his place at his arrival at the unit. Delivering laundry to the supply room, he joked that it was so cold that all they needed to do to freeze the germs was hang the laundry outside. "They ought to hang you guys and freeze all of you," the supply sergeant replied.

Physical abuse followed. One officer "in a drunken rage" humiliated two of the men, ordering them to stand among 30 of their mates and "to give the Nazi salute and shout, 'Heil Hitler.'" Another officer once repeatedly hit another soldier over the head with a flashlight, and when the man cried out, the officer had him court-martialed for making a disturbance. After Wilson issued his English-only order, "an Italian immigrant who spoke no other language than Italian tried to explain this fact to the officer." In response, "the Italian was prosecuted for disobeying the order and sentenced to three months' confinement at hard labor." One of the stockade guards threatened to lynch them.[9]

By February 15th, the threat was credible. Other soldiers frequently jumped the 620ers in the dark. "In addition to engaging the American turncoats in acrimonious debate at the service club," one 10th Mountain Division vet wrote years later, his mates "occasionally vented their anger by beating up on some of the same soldiers." It was a sport. Shouting and then scuffles had become common at camp events, not least at weekly forums where officers held what were supposed to discuss civic-minded inquiries into "Fascism in America" and "What to Do with Germany After the War." During the latter discussion, one Austrian émigré in the 10th Mountain Division suggested stringing up all the Germans who had supported Hitler. Maple objected. He maintained that using the Austrian's logic, if the war happened to go the Nazis' way, the Germans would be justified in hanging all 27.3 million Americans who had voted for Franklin Roosevelt in the 1940 election.

For arguments like that, Maple was already notorious at camp—as he had been as a college student—for his admiration of German culture, philosophy, and economics. The Army and the Roosevelt Administration, he contended, were blinded by "questionable" reports of German atrocities. They were too coarse to appreciate the German genius for science, organization, social benefit, for art, its economic miracles, its promotion of national strength, and its principled devotion to order. The Nazis' refinements, he said, were merely the latest in a millennium of German advances, as much a flowering of its heritage of accomplishment as religious skepticism and Beethoven and Kant. Germany had always led these advances. The rest of the world eventually caught up, sometimes against its will.[10]

———————

All the men, "first-aid man" Kissman said, resented "being distrusted and placed in a labor group when so many were highly skilled." Kissman himself, an Erie, Pennsylvania native, hoped to become an eye doctor someday but, without prospects of promotion, meaningful duty, or even returning to his barracks safely, dug ditches with his mates. They did trash detail repaired tents, washed clothes, sewed camouflage netting, skinned mules, and sawed wood. They got six-month disciplinary sentences when others drew only reprimands for the same offenses. Only the "stool pigeons" among them got high ratings. The Army followed them when they left camp and hid microphones in their barracks at their first posting at Fort Meade in South Dakota. They were confident the same thing was happening at Hale. Worse yet: officers and other soldiers beat and abused them without consequence. The men especially despised Wilson. A former milk-wagon driver from Texas, Wilson was "a sneering, contemptuous misfit of an officer," one of the company's men stewed well after the war.

Altman believed and Kissman knew their patience was wearing dangerously thin. "The porcupine's only defense is its quills," Kissman explained. "We were marked men, and our quills rose higher." Maple, dispensing with metaphors, called it "active hostility." He had good reason. Officers found excuses to make his life particularly difficult. "Of all the men in the organization," one of his mates later recalled, "he was discriminated against by the officers more than any other since his intelligence and education were so much superior to theirs that they were inclined to compensate for their intellectual inferiority by making life as hard as possible for him. He was constantly given the dirtiest jobs available."[11]

By February 15th, simple insubordination was no longer sufficient. Some turned overtly antagonistic not only toward their officers, the other soldiers at Hale, and the war, but toward the United States. A self-described "inner circle" had begun to plot: first protest, then defiance, desertion, sabotage, and finally, rebellion.

By their third month at Hale, a few were using their furloughs to try to organize nothing less than a national uprising of other shunned units like theirs. They'd take over their camps by force of arms. They'd demand either better treatment, dismissal from the Army, transportation to Germany, or all three.

At least one conspirator reserved the honor of killing Altman first. Others targeted the sergeant who tampered with their mail. Among other sins, Wilson bullied them into buying war bonds. For that and other reasons, he, too, was a target.[12]

Maple, more impulsive than most, had become driven. He and his group, he said, had some weapons. They had maps. They had estimates of troop strength levels at other camps. Kissman, for one, was certain they were about to blow.

———

Altman rushed first to the orderly room, but Maple was not there. He was "not in the barracks or latrines or day room" either.

Altman was getting panicky when a messenger arrived. There had been a sudden change at the German prisoner stockade, and the stockade commander was ordered to drop everything. He was to get to Trinidad, Colorado, where German prisoners had tunneled out of a larger POW camp two months before. A new officer was taking over the German prisoners at Hale, and he needed Altman in his office right away.[13]

———

At that moment, Private Dale Maple was a mile away, crouching in about 1" of crusty snow on the stony shoulder of U.S. 24, next to what had once been a cream-colored sedan; a 1934 Reo "Flying Cloud." It was new to Maple; he'd bought it only days before on the strength of a test drive of a few blocks. Now, when another vehicle drove by, he innocently rose and pretended to be fixing a flat tire.

"*Guten morgen.*" Two men were behind him.

They were in the coats and blue shirts the prisoners of war wore. One regarded Maple skeptically. All he knew was that he was supposed to meet someone pretending to fix a flat. The car man—Maple—had already changed from his own normal camp wear, which looked the same as the one the two men wore, save for a "PW," for prisoner of war, on its back and seat.

Maple shook their hands. In German, he asked where the others were. There were supposed to be three more.

In German, they told him the others couldn't come. They handed Maple a passport. It belonged to another prisoner back at the stockade.

In German, Maple shooed them into the Reo, and they took off, heading south.[14]

CHAPTER 2

AN IMMENSE, STAGED LIE
OF A PLACE

At the edge of a vast valley of wartime-depleted ranches and farms just below the looming, saw-toothed Collegiate Peaks, they rattled 60 miles along the Arkansas River down U.S. 24 toward the town of Salida, Colorado. Maple knew the road well. He and Kissman, a relatively new acquaintance, had hitchhiked their way to Salida three days before. Their first stop in Salida that day had been at Crews-Biggs Mercantile, where Maple had wandered around the tables before settling on a ladies' yellow sweater (size: large), a ladies' hat, and what he thought was a "very pretty" scarf. Kissman, surprised, pulled Maple aside to ask what he needed with women's clothes. "Skip it," Maple replied.

Watching him, the store's owner figured Maple was buying gifts for the upcoming Valentine's Day and wanted to do something special for a soldier. "I asked him if he wanted it wrapped for Valentine, and he says, 'no.' So I says, 'I will just put it in a box.'"

Maple next led Kissman down the street to buy "a civilian hat, on the dark side," at Golden Rule Merchandise. Just before closing, they were at the town's hardware store where Maple took some fishing line, a pack of hooks, seven buckshot sinkers, and some .22-gauge cartridges up to the register. "I told him I had very few but was glad to accommodate a soldier," the clerk recalled. "Naturally, I was interested in hunting and fishing and attempted to give the boys a few good fishing points."

They finished their Saturday with dinner before repairing to a boarding house room, where they drank and "talked about guys at the camp." They grabbed breakfast on Sunday morning at the USO before going to look at cars over at the Y&R Garage.

The Y&R's main business was auto repair, but T.R. O'Haver, the garage owner, sold used ones on the side when he happened to get some. On that Sunday, February 13th, he had two: a Ford Coupe and the 1934 Reo Flying Cloud sedan, which had belonged to O'Haver's recently deceased neighbor. Maple was drawn to the bigger Reo, which was parked snugly against a wall behind the Ford. "I didn't care to get it out unless they had the money to pay for it," O'Haver said later. He wanted $250 for it (plus $5 sales tax). The soldier promptly flashed a substantial wad of cash. They drove the car around "a few blocks," bought it, and agreed to return the next day, Monday, February 14th, to pick up new license tags and an "A book" of wartime gas ration coupons.[1]

Maple didn't show up on Monday, though he called that evening. He got O'Haver's sister, who was minding the office at the moment. He'd been delayed but swore he'd arrive the next day, Tuesday, February 15th.

———

At about 3 P.M. on Tuesday, Fritz Owen, a railroad switchman, was moonlighting at the Y&R when the soldier appeared. "He told me he had purchased a car, which I did not know of, and he said: 'I am supposed to have some license tags here.' I said, 'I do not know anything about it.' I looked behind the desk, and I seen the license laying there and took them and seen they was made out to Mr. Maple."

Out the window, Owen saw the Reo parked down the block. He recognized it; he had always thought it kind of beaten up. He couldn't tell for sure, but it looked like there were two or three people in it. Soldiers.

"We're in sort of a hurry." Maple was impatient. He was on furlough, he said, and couldn't waste time. He wanted the tags and the Reo documents and to get on his way.[2]

They wheeled away, heading north for a bit to Highway 285, then east and south into what soon became a long, slow night in a dark car. When they spoke, it was in German. *Unteroffizier* (Sergeant) Earhard Schwichtenberg, 25, preferred to ride in the passenger seat. *Stabwachtenmeister* (or staff sergeant) Heinrich Kikilius, the older (33) and quieter of the two, was in the back. Both foreigners thought they knew where they were going. It was an article of faith among the prisoners as well as the "Inner Circle" of the 620th that there was an "underground railroad" through Mexico, Peru, Argentina, and finally, across the Atlantic back to Germany. The Germans assumed they were heading there.

For the moment, the Germans themselves were lost in this endless night and this vast country. To some German prisoners, the United States was an immense, staged lie of a place. Upon being transported through the country on their way to confinement, many professed shock at how the Americans had covered up the savage devastation the Luftwaffe reportedly had visited on U.S. cities. The newspaper and radio reports of sensational American and Russian victories only made the rich, fantastic, funhouse mirror exaggerations and deceptions more disorienting. Both of Maple's passengers had been captured by the British in northern Africa in a May 1943 battle that, for all they knew and despite what their probably mendacious captors claimed, may well have ended with another miraculous German victory. It was the last they had seen of the real world. Other prisoners had confided to other witnesses they had to believe the war was going well out there. Reports from the 78 POW camps scattered around the country in 1944 said the bulk of German prisoners were still confident of victory or, if the Reich's complete triumph was denied, that a stalemate and an honorable peace was in the offing. They had seen the Reich's power.[3]

Back at camp, the men of the 620th buzzed. Neither Friedrich Siering nor the other men knew that prisoners are also missing, but "the whole company was talking about [Maple's disappearance]," wondering what Maple was doing. Siering guessed that "He might have been going to Washington to clear things up about the 620th, and he might be back in a couple of days." Most guessed he was in Denver, pretending to be a lawyer at their mate's court-martial.

Kissman, "kind of excited," got back to the 620th's barracks. He had news: "He is on his way."

Kissman was fresh from meeting Captain A.F. Collar, filling in while Wilson was in Omaha for a meeting that day. Collar had asked what Kissman knew about Maple, now officially absent without leave. Kissman, in turn, went short on specifics, pleasant but vague. He said he wasn't surprised that Private Maple was missing. He didn't know Maple well, but he knew Maple, like just about every one of the 200-some members of the dispirited, desperate 620th, had frequently threatened to go "over the hill."

Leonhard piped up. Maple had said "goodbye" to him that morning at the camp's ash pit.[4]

Theo Leonhard, called "The Professor" around camp, was a flat-nosed, acne-scarred, often-brusque intellectual from an all-German small town in Texas about 80 miles west of Austin. A University of Texas doctoral student

in his pre-Army days, he and Maple were two of the group's most vocal malcontents. Together, they were the nucleus of the unit's "inner circle" of the
once-patriotic plotters. Even those who started the war vaguely pro-German
had, by the time they arrived at Hale, become rabidly pro-German. Their plans
had escalated. A Private Eric Bell Hotelling, late of Columbia University and
son of an internationally known statistician, would recruit the men at other
camps. At a pre-arranged signal, the misfits at the various camps would fling
open prisoners' gates, storm the camp armories, arm themselves, take each of
the camps by surprise, and dedicate themselves to interrupting the American
war effort on U.S. soil. Maple had taken charge of arranging to disrupt and
destroy as much communication, rail, and motor transportation as they could.
With material support from Germany, his crew would blow up "all vulnerable
communications centers in the United States simultaneously." Maple figured he
needed about 150 like-minded men to pull off the sabotage of bridges, rail ter-
minals and junctions, and signal block systems he'd targeted in Dallas, Omaha,
St. Louis, and Salt Lake City.

If they had to flee, an FBI agent's memo later reported, "they all had agreed
to fight to the last man and not permit capture."[5]

The two Germans rode in darkness, a stranger at the wheel, across an alien
landscape, some of it mountainous and threatening, some of it flat and seemingly featureless. The vehicle had looked substantial enough in the daylight.
There were vents on the right side of the auto's nose, with small swept-back
pieces of metal to present a not-altogether convincing illusion of flight and
speed. It started and changed gears by pulling a long handle out from beside the
steering wheel and twisting it from one position to another. Amid the wartime
rubber shortage, tires like the Flying Cloud's were a rarity. It still had a white
wall. As the night wore on, however, the muscular-looking Reo began to rattle
and get louder.

They did not talk much. Before the war, the taciturn Kikilius was a farmer
in East Prussia, married, with two children, and was, as one observer later described him, "the motion picture villain Nazi-type . . . heavy set, sharp, clipped
sentences, scowl, and uncooperative. Schwichtenberg was completely under
his control. Schwichtenberg was a nice-looking young fellow who, when away
from Kikilius, wanted to be friendly and talked quite a bit."

Schwichtenberg offered a few stories about the war in Africa "just to make
conversation." He had been "a laboratory worker in the milk establishment" in

Elbing, in West Prussia. His father had died in 1928; his mother, he hoped, was still alive there, although he had no way of knowing. He had two sisters and two brothers until "one of them fell in France." He had been in the German Army for five years, was captured the previous May with the surrender of the Afrika Korps, and after a four-week journey from Africa, had landed in the U.S. in August 1943. He'd been at Camp Hale since September.

But the conversation soon ran out during the drive, which was stretching on and on. Tension rose as Maple resisted giving up the wheel. He finally let Schwichtenberg drive, but after a half-hour got antsy and slipped back into the driver's seat himself.

About 35 miles from Espanola, New Mexico, where the Rio Grande River intersects with U.S. Highway 285, one of the Reo's precious tires went flat. The men, weary, fetched the lone spare and mounted it. But the exhausted fugitives already had some 270 often-twisting road miles on them since leaving camp. Near the dawn of Wednesday, February 16th, 1944, they agreed to park safely off the two-lane highway and bed down in the car. They also decided to take a significant risk later in the day. They'd drive into Espanola and civilization in broad daylight to get their flat tire fixed.[6] They were 350 miles from Mexico and a long way from South America.

CHAPTER 3

PANIC

Day broke in Colorado and 2nd Lt. R. L. Dawson, who had hurriedly inherited command of Camp Hale's prisoner of war "side camp" the day before, got his first real look at the Afrika Korps veterans. (The larger "main" POW camp was in Trinidad, Colorado, about 180 miles from Camp Hale). He watched them assemble at 7:40 to go to work and pause at the gate guards as they filed out. They netted 10 cents a day doing assigned menial tasks around the camp, often working with men from the 620th.

The guards took a formal count of them every Thursday, but as the prisoners left the stockade this Wednesday morning, they gave only their names and their work detail group. Morning checkouts and evening check-ins like this usually took about 20 minutes. Someone would check the names against a master list of prisoners later in the day.

Something was wrong.

"In the process of checking the work details," he later explained, "it was brought to my attention that there was two prisoners of war that was absent without leave." On the job for less than 24 hours, "I had no way of knowing at that time exactly who they were by name, rank, and serial number."

Alarmed, Dawson and his men broke to search the premises. It was not unlikely that a prisoner had simply left the stockade for work early, gone for a stroll on his own, or was lolling behind on his cot. But no one was in the prisoner barracks. Dawson sent word to poll the work details out on duty.

The survey came back two prisoners short, and Dawson, still more worried, ordered his men back into the stockade. This time, they "tore the walls out." They found the still, the stored schnapps, a big "pyramidal tent," a pup tent, skis, snowshoes, U.S. military fur coats and uniforms, and a pair of WAC underwear.

Three and a half fruitless hours later, an aide gave Dawson two names missing from the morning count: a Schwichtenberg and a Kikilius. It was then, almost 24 hours after the two had slipped out of captivity that Dawson delivered the disturbing news to the camp intelligence officer. It was not a good first day in a new job.

The intelligence officer jumped on the phone and wired local law enforcement officials while Dawson and his men rechecked the stockade. "During the afternoon, along in the evening, I made another search as the parties came in. I double-checked them in by name, and then at the evening count, which takes place at 5:50, we checked them again.[1]

It was 6:30 P.M. on February 16th, twenty minutes after the evening check-in ended., when a Major Ross of the Provost Marshal Office, the head of Camp Hale's military police, called D. Milton Ladd* of the FBI's Domestic Intelligence Division in Washington. Two prisoners, he reported, had escaped.

In the mess hall, Siering stopped Leonhard in the mess hall to ask a question. "I said, 'Professor, was something fishy about Maple? He must have taken some prisoners along.' He said, 'I don't think so, Fritz.'" Siering brought up the mysterious car Maple had shown up with two days before, and then there were some rucksacks Maple had asked him to store at his rented house. "But [Leonhard] said, 'Don't worry, don't say anything, and everything will be all right.' And we split."[2]

Capt. Collar, still filling in for Wilson, thought something smelled fishy, too, and sent for Kissman again. Had Kissman heard anything more about the AWOL Maple, and did he know about any escaped prisoners?

"No," Kissman replied. Then he helpfully added that, in their grumblings about deserting, some of his mates had indeed fantasized about taking prisoners with them.[3]

Collar, a soldier himself, knew soldiers always groused. Even going AWOL, moreover, was not uncommon. The soldiers typically returned quickly, and both motivations and injuries were resolved quietly. Prisoner trouble also was not unusual. Many prisoners of war tried to escape; their captors expected

---

* Ladd had a storied career at the FBI. W. Mark Felt, the FBI executive who in the 1970s anonymously guided *Washington Post* reporters in their reporting of the Watergate scandal said, "Much of the Bureau's success in combating German espionage and sabotage [during World War II] was due to his effective leadership." Ladd was later involved in the Alger Hiss and Rosenberg spy cases. He died in a July 1960 auto accident in Sanford, Florida, while campaigning for Congress.

it, and many of the prisoners themselves considered it a duty. By then, military routines for handling escapes were already firmly in place. At Trinidad, the state's largest (and now-overcrowded POW stockade), some 13 German officers recently had snuck out one-by-one through a 150-foot tunnel that stretched from the German officers' compound barracks to a point 60 feet beyond the camp's perimeter. Some 20 prisoners had dug the thing during the prior month, moving the dirt in small increments to the "cellar" beneath the floorboards. After all that industry, however, each escapee was recaptured within five days. Some arrests didn't take that long.* One German soldier, who had cleverly altered his German motorcycle jacket to resemble an American Army jacket, had been picked up almost immediately on the nearby Trinidad train station platform on suspicion of being an American deserter.[4]

But the combination of an AWOL American soldier with escaped German POWs was a far more urgent kind of crisis, increasing the prisoners' odds of success. Not least, it raised the specter not just of desertion but treason in the ranks of the United States Army. Collar, worried, hurriedly dismissed Kissman. He ran to tell Intelligence Officer Ross the startling news that an American soldier may be helping the escapees.

———

A mere 10 minutes after first reporting that two German prisoners were missing, Hale's Provost Marshall called the FBI's Ladd back. Ladd immediately shot the news up the FBI's hierarchy. "A private went AWOL at the same time that the prisoners escaped," he reported, "and it is believed that there might be some connection between his leaving and the prisoners escaping."

While Ladd made calls to more agents, Camp Hale's Ross worked the military chain. He wired the Army's Intelligence Branch at the 620's headquarters in Omaha. "A member of the captioned War Department' special organization'," he wrote, "was AWOL."

Speculations spread. The FBI's Denver office called Washington headquarters: two POWs were missing, adding there was even a "possibility that a private in the 620th engineers helped them get away."

The missing private, they now confirmed, was Dale H Maple, A.S.N. 11048476 of the 620 Engineer General Service Company. He was, Ladd added in his next rushed memo, a "Harvard graduate—well educated—American

---

* The troubles at and occasional escapes from Trinidad persisted. Shortly after Maple Schwichtenberg and Kikilius fled, prisoners at Trinidad stole two revolvers and a carbine from a U.S. guard. A subsequent search for the guns unearthed a prisoner cache of crude weapons made out of old razor blades and pieces of wood.

citizen—home is in San Diego, California and the address of his father is Route 3, Box 451, San Diego 7, California, telephone 0743." He had sandy hair "thin on top," hazel eyes, "scar on chin," and a "heavy build." He was last seen "wearing a Class A uniform with a dark green shirt. Apparently left in automobile."

At 6:50 P.M.—about an hour after confirming that the two POWs were missing—the FBI notified its offices in El Paso, Oklahoma City, Dallas, San Antonio, Salt Lake City, Butte, and San Diego and, most importantly, Director J. Edgar Hoover. It described the escaped prisoners and added that they "may have escaped with PFC Dale Maple." Maple is "known to be pro-Nazi and to speak German fluently although an American citizen." The recipients should alert local radio, newspapers, and police agencies to the prisoners' escape.

Agents, however, "suggest no mention be made of association with Pvt. Maple." It might cause panic.[5]

At that moment, Kissman was at Camp Hale's PX, discussing Maple's chances over coffee with two friends from the 620th. All three were unaware that POWs had escaped or, until Kissman told his tablemates about Maple's Reo purchase, that Maple had a car. They debated the odds that the Reo would hold up and guessed where Maple might be heading. Leonhard, remembering the Maple had once quizzed him about Mexico, guessed he was heading to El Paso, some 18 to 20 hours away. Perhaps belatedly, Kissman later recalled, "we discussed us being implicated."[6]

Ten hours later, in the pre-dawn morning of Thursday, February 17th, the Flying Cloud finally sputtered and quit on its way up a mild grade. The gloom was complete. Stranded in a dark, cold rain about 15 miles from the town of Columbus, New Mexico, the fugitives were some 17 tantalizing miles from Mexico.

Beyond the border would be Puerto Palomas, then in a day or so, a friendly German who would get them to Mexico City. There, they would change some 20,000 francs they had into pesos. In the southern Mexican city of Tuxtla, they would approach a secretive German family that lived quietly on a lake and, according to whispers back at Hale, was connected to German agents in Panama and Colombia. In Colombia, at last, would be a George Albert of Kaiser Textile Mills, reputedly a high-ranking Nazi agent with a way to get them to Germany.[7]

In the wretched New Mexico night, the fugitives argued about whether to abandon the Reo and camp on the wet ground somewhere out of sight. Perhaps they could make it the rest of the way on foot.

At about 1:30 A.M., a car approached.

Sgt. John H. Breen of the U.S. Customs Patrol and his partner were off duty, on their way to Columbus for work, when they saw the Reo, its hood up. "A man in front of the car as we drove up flagged us down," Breen recalled. "He asked if I would give him a push." Breen noted Colorado license tags 31-702 and thought he saw somebody in the back seat. "It was awful dark." Middle of the desert; overcast; no moon. Someone else was in the front passenger seat. "It appeared to be a woman in the front seat with a baby. There was something tied around her head," maybe a scarf.

The Reo had no radio, and the fugitives had no way of knowing what—if anything—was in the news about them. The chances were good, however, that the official car that pulled up behind them had a radio.

Breen, a 24-year veteran of the Customs Patrol, had seen his share of bootleggers, refugees, and innocents stranded in the middle of the night on this desert road. This group, in an old car, could have been anything, and he was unsure about giving them a push. Aside from the danger, Breen was driving a 1942 Buick and worried about what could happen to the bumper of his lower-slung car when it engaged with the older, broader, boxier Reo. He walked around the back of the Reo to see what could be done. The figure in the back seat appeared to twist around to watch him.

This family looked like it needed help.

"We pushed them about 100 yards, and the car finally started," Breen later recalled. "The driver stuck his hand out and kept waving us to go around." Breen and his partner, however, ignored the insistent waving and stayed behind them. The Reo had no lights. It was a danger to others. It looked like it could break down again at any moment.

Slowly, they went "about seven or eight miles" until Breen finally ran out of patience. "Then we went around his car. After we passed the car, they turned on a dim light. We went on. That was the last we saw of the car that night."[8]

———

The fugitives, doubtless relieved to be rid of uniformed men creeping behind them, could not urge much more out of the car. The Reo continued to cough and labor up the road until Maple pulled it over to the side of the road again, this time for good. Maple, Schwichtenberg, and Kikilius took their sacks—they all had Afrika Korps packs from the stockade—and carried them out of sight from the highway and into the New Mexico desert to sleep.

Maple's pack was especially heavy, filled with compasses, a hunting knife, mosquito nets, riding boots, some cooking equipment, a .22 caliber rifle, and, not least, a .38 Colt revolver Kissman had bought for him at a Denver hock shop. Leonhard had once suggested such things as necessary to survive in Mexico. The professor claimed to know a lot about the country. He had a yen to chuck it all someday to study Mexican archeology.

Maple thought Leonhard "something of a 'Kunze,'" after Gerhard Wilhelm Kunze, the U.S. citizen who was the former leader of and propagandist for the German-American Bund. Maple, in fact, was now following a path Kunze himself had cut not all that long before when he tried to escape through Mexico. Kunze made it as far as the fishing village of Boca Del Rio in June 1942, where authorities arrested him and seized the 20-foot launch and 200 liters of gasoline he had marshaled to get him to Germany. As the fugitives felt their way through the desert, Kunze was in the second year of a 15-year prison sentence for espionage and for violating the Selective Service Act.[9]

Maple and his passengers, now road-worn and wet in the dark desert and at risk of an even greater punishment than Kunze's, struggled to keep their confidence up. They'd try to make it on foot. Maple, sick of his heavy load, ditched some of his pack's contents.

CHAPTER 4

A COLLECTION OF REBELS

As Dale Maple, Kikilius and Schwichtenberg neared the border, Eric Hotelling—a tall, thin, blond, barely mustachioed 19-year-old lapsed Columbia student—was just back at Camp Hale from a recruiting trip. He'd been to Camp Carson in Colorado Springs, 90 miles south of Denver, looking for soldiers as disaffected and alienated as the men of the 620th. Someday, he told the Carson GIs, they could join the rebel force he and his Camp Hale brethren were organizing.

Young Hotelling was "definitely peculiar," even to his comrades. "A real Nazi in point of view." He was not just pro-Nazi but anti-Semitic. (Many of the pro-German soldiers in the 620th contended that being pro-German did not necessarily mean they were anti-Semitic.)

Hotelling, too, was smart. A mate marveled at how he could "pull out words so long that you'd have to carry a dictionary around to understand." He was also notable in the 620th for his "long, funny stride, as if his joints were stiff," and a fondness for ice cream and champagne.

Camp Carson was home to some 9,000 POWs and the 338th, a general service unit supposedly as disaffected as the 620th. Carson was just one likely recruiting ground for the guerilla army Hotelling envisioned. The 620 conspirators each claimed to know potential rebels at their previous postings at Fort Leonard Wood in Missouri, at Indiantown Gap in Pennsylvania, Fort Blanding in Florida, Camp Shelby in Mississippi, and Camp Maxey in Texas. They, in turn, would pass along the news to sympathetic soldiers they knew.

Hotelling had been at it for more than a month, but his recruiting had not yet taken off. In January, he had gone to Denver on a pass with Kissman, and while Kissman went shopping for items Maple would need to survive in the Mexican desert, Hotelling met a group of soldiers from Carson. The most likely recruit of the pro-German Camp Carson soldiers, he'd heard, was once a member of the German American Bund that met at Camp Norland, N.J. The soldier—a quartermaster—didn't show up in Denver, but Hotelling pressed ahead, trying to charm the quartermaster's buddies who did make the trip. At the city's Hotel Standish, Hotelling pressed them about troop numbers at Carson, pledged to visit Carson in a few weeks, and asked for the names of "reliable" soldiers who Hotelling should "talk to" when he got there.

One of the Camp Carson buddies (his name is redacted from FBI files) stopped him. "It's hard for me to understand for someone to be so interested in the military personnel of any Army camp," said the soldier, who himself had been active in the Bund before the war. Until a few minutes before, he thought himself merely on a weekend pass to Denver to run personal errands, go to the USO War Center and meet a couple of Hale soldiers for kicks.

"Why the notebook?" he asked.

"It is well to know," Hotelling replied conspiratorially.

The Carson men subsequently went to dinner, stayed at a fellow soldier's house in Denver, and went back to Colorado Springs in the morning, still loyal members of the U.S. Army.[1]

Hotelling kept trying. He met more Camp Carson soldiers on another trip to Denver on February 6th. Bringing his next group of potential recruits up to his hotel room, he uncorked some wine and dramatically opened his suitcase to reveal small Nazi banners and a miniature Italian flag. One of the recruits had seen similar ones for sale near the German American Bund headquarters in Yorkville, New York. Encouraged by finding an apparently like-minded fellow, Hotelling then described a vast command structure in waiting.

"There was an inner group, another group outside of that one, and still another group involved [in the planned uprising]," one of the Carson soldiers later told Army investigators. Hotelling was, with Maple and Leonhard and unnamed others, in the Inner Circle. And if the soldier wanted to let him "know anything," he should communicate through letters to one of Hotelling's compatriots in the 620th at Camp Hale.

The pitch didn't work. Back in Colorado Springs, the worried Carson soldier shared the news with a buddy, Pvt. Paul M. Ochojski. "We agreed that any such type of [plan] was idiotic and possibly playing with dynamite and that it might be misunderstood by Army authorities."[2]

Still, Hotelling pressed on. On February 14th, the day before Maple planned to desert, Hotelling was back at Carson. He had come to see the quartermaster who purportedly was the most pro-German of the Camp Carson group. The quartermaster, however, was on duty. Hotelling cooled his heels until about 1 P.M. when he told another Camp Carson soldier about an "escape plan" brewing up at Hale.

He hustled three of the Carson soldiers into a "secret meeting," where the agenda stayed stubbornly pacific. They shared a meal and looked at photos Hotelling had taken at the previous get-togethers in Denver. But time was short, and Hotelling's bus left at about 2:30. He got back to Hale that night, just in time to see Maple's new Reo.[3]

———

While Hotelling was recruiting rebels in January and February, the increasingly worried Maple was finalizing plans for getting to Germany or at least getting out. His notion had once been grander: mass desertion from Camp Hale. "Wouldn't it be spectacular," Maple mused to Kissman one day, "if we could take prisoners with us?"

Maple had told Hotelling about it on January 29th and then moved into the prisoners' stockade for three days to find POWs to come with him. Maple would have Leonhard get a furlough to go to Mexico, seemingly to study an archeological site. In the meantime, Maple and another deserting member of the Inner Circle would spring a total of 10 prisoners from Hale. In two cars, they'd flee to Mexico and beyond. Sooner or later, they'd get help from the Reich—more men, more materials—to disrupt the American war effort from inside the U.S.

Like all plans, Maple's kept fraying. Most damaging, Leonhard quit. He had seriously considered going with Maple but deserting with POWs was too much. "I at that time made a statement that, if there is any prisoner of war escape out of this camp, I don't want anything to do with it." Leonhard told Maple, "I think it's foolish and, secondly, I just don't think it would gain anybody anything and just don't think it would succeed."

Leonhard, however, considered the resourceful Maple a close and not unamusing friend. He was admirably "action-oriented," sharp, and smart. When Maple asked him what someone needed to survive in the Mexican landscape, Leonhard, who as it turned out had never been to Mexico, gave him a list of items to take with him. (Leonhard's knowledge of the place derived from a single 1936 college archeology trip that, thanks to "an obscure but disagreeable Mexican consular official," Leonhard ultimately didn't go on.)

He had other suggestions. Maple, The Professor later told investigators, "did ask me this: 'how large a group of people do you think could remain rather inconspicuous across the border, assuming they were not Mexicans, of course?" Leonhard replied, "I think almost any non-Mexican causes some attention down there." Maple also "asked me further whether I knew anything about Central America, whether it would be difficult for [Maple] to go all the way through Mexico down into Central America." Leonhard advised that it would.[4]

———

Without Leonhard, Maple still needed at least one car. For transportation, Maple and his mates always turned first to Fritz Siering. Siering still had his car, a prized possession he'd bought in Chicago and a symbol, he once thought, of how much better life in the United States was than in Germany.

At Hale, Siering had put his new wife Ana up in a rented house in nearby Red Cliff and had won a reprieve from the order to sell the car because she shared the house with the very pregnant wife of another soldier. Siering had pleaded that they would need the car to get to the doctor when the baby came. In the meantime, the men of the 620th were forever asking to borrow it. The 5'4", 27-year-old German immigrant was kind-hearted and often gave his mates rides, but he would not lend the car to anyone. Maple had already asked him once. He had wanted it for a trip to Denver, he'd said, but Siering had refused and didn't have the time or inclination to drive him there himself.

Now, after his sojourn in the prisoners' stockade, Maple asked again. He needed it, he explained, for a three-day furlough. Siering, who, after eight years in the U.S., still spoke with a heavy accent and had trouble understanding English, was confused.

"He wanted to take the car and go to Columbus. I am not so familiar with the United States—state Columbus or city Columbus." It would be Columbus, New Mexico, Maple explained. And then, Siering recalled, "he says he wanted to meet somebody; he wanted to go to Germany, and, of course, I thought it was a joke. Who wants to go to Germany in wartime?"

And, even if Maple got to Columbus, how would Siering get his car back?

Maple, apparently off the top of his head, said Hotelling would meet him in Columbus and drive it back. Siering refused again. He didn't lend his car to anybody.[5]

———

But time was growing short. Worried that the 620th would soon be transferred far from the much-admired Afrika Korps, he would lose his chance to pull off a "spectacular" prisoner escape and the opportunity to recruit the hardened, battle-tested veterans of the Afrika Korps into his guerilla army. He had to act soon. And he needed a car.

From Hale's public phone, he called his mother on the East Coast and his father on the West. Harvard, he told them, was pestering him to pay off a student loan. Could they help him?

A few days later, on the morning of February 12th, Maple asked Siering for a shorter ride, this time "to the dumps to pick something up." Siering, an accommodating man, readily agreed. He watched as Maple "went out of the car, and he went on the edge where they put all the ashes and stuff like that. He went down there. . . ."

Maple emerged with a large box, about a foot wide, a foot deep, and five feet long. In it were "packs, like the ski troopers have," Afrika Korps rucksacks. "At first, I said to him, I said, 'Dale, what do you want to do with them?" Then he said to me, 'You wait and see.'"[6]

It was later that day that Maple asked Kissman to go with him to Salida. They'd go shopping, have some fun. Kissman was a little surprised and a bit flattered that Maple, who had never shown much interest in him, asked him. They went out to Route 24 and began hitchhiking about mid-day.

Leonhard didn't learn about the Reo until Maple brought it back from Salida the next afternoon. He assumed the extravagant purchase was just the stubborn, oppositional Maple's way of testing Authority's will to enforce the recent, insulting ban on 620 members owning cars. Everybody despised the rule. "They believed they had the right to require a man to sell some of his property," Leonhard said.

"I did it for spite," Maple told Siering when he showed up, unbidden, on the 13th at Siering's door with his new Reo. He asked to park it there for the night.[7] Siering, the agreeable man, was happy to help.

CHAPTER 5

JEWISH REFUGEES,
SEEKING FREEDOM

And now, in a cold predawn New Mexican desert of February 17th, 1944, Dale Maple was on foot, ditching the heaviest contents of his pack. He could console himself that, if things were on track back at Camp Hale, the stockade officers would only now be making their detailed weekly count of the individual prisoners and just deducing that two were missing.

A few hours later, between 7 and 8 in the morning, Breen and his partner were on their way back from Columbus to their office 30 miles away in Deming. They saw the Reo pulled over on the right-hand side of the highway. They stopped to inspect it. It was abandoned.[1]

By then, the combined forces of the FBI, the Army, and state and local police had mobilized, hunting for Maple and his companions. By the daylight morning hours of Thursday, the 17th, Utah had issued a statewide alert for two escaped German prisoners of war. Word that an Army man might be involved had leaked. The *Salt Lake Tribune* reported a Private Dale Maple "may be in company with the war prisoners." Wire service stories about the German escapees, although not always the American soldier apparently with them, appeared in newspapers nationwide.

The FBI's Boston agents hustled to Newport, Rhode Island, and Maple's mother's house. Divorced from Maple's father in September 1939, Mae Harris Maple had moved from San Diego to Rhode Island to be near a niece and her son, Dale, a short distance away at Harvard. She remarried in 1941 and was now Mae Scoville—Mrs. Edwin W. Scoville—looking after her new husband's shop while he served as a sheet metal worker at the Navy's torpedo station out in Newport's harbor. They made and worked on torpedoes there; the most significant challenges then were keeping them at an even depth after firing and making sure they didn't explode prematurely. Between a mother and proximity to a weapons facility, it was, in any case, a likely destination for an AWOL, pro-German fugitive looking to commit sabotage or get classified information.

In San Diego, the FBI was at the door of L.G. Everett Maple, Dale Maple's 47-year-old father. He worked at the National Iron Works, which, prospering during wartime, had recently expanded into building barges for the military. Dale told Kissman his father was "an executive" and gave Kissman the impression L.G. Maple was "quite wealthy." (He'd told others his father was in the Army and, still others, the Navy.) L.G. Maple was, in fact, a division manager at the company, which would soon become National Steel and Shipbuilding, a joint venture of two large construction and steel corporations. L.G. was doing as well as his growing employer, already comfortably supporting Ruth, his new wife. His son's education expenses were essentially off his shoulders, and the boy's future clearly was bright.

Dale, he told the agents on his front stoop, had been giving public piano recitals since the age of seven and got a one-year scholarship to Harvard at age 16. The boy had an "incandescent mind," sang beautifully in choirs, surfed, was an accomplished swimmer, and graduated first in his high school class of 1,500. He was a wizard with languages and a persuasive debater. The elder Maple still expected the boy would become a great and famous scientist.

There had been some worries: young Dale had been a little too friendly with some "very pro-German" locals. The mother of one of them had called repeatedly to find out when Dale was coming home from college. L.G. had been "very concerned about the interest" the woman was showing, Questioning Dale's loyalty, however, never occurred to him. If Dale was mixed up with escaping German POWs, his father said, they had to be forcing him to help them. And if the two Germans showed up in San Diego with Dale—who was surely their captive—L.G. assured the FBI he would shoot the Germans.[2]

FBI and military intelligence officers in Denver, Omaha, Butte, Oklahoma City, Kansas City, El Paso, Dallas, San Antonio, and elsewhere had fanned out, hunting for the men, identifying friends and associates, reviewing files.

In El Paso, Special Agent in Charge Delf Albert Bryce—also known as D.A. Bryce, "Jelly" Bryce, and "Quick Draw" Bryce—was among them.

Bryce, 38, was one of the FBI's most famous agents. He first caught law enforcement's eye as a youth at a pistol shooting contest in Oklahoma City, where he "put six shots no bigger than a silver dollar into an envelope stuck in a tree." The city's new reform-minded police chief supposedly hired him on the spot.

Legend stuck to him. Other accounts said it was a card instead of an envelope, that he was not that young, and that he wasn't hired on the spot. Both legend and fact, however, had coalesced into a fearsome reputation. It included killing a robber his first day on the job and two more before his first year was finished. He killed still more men after joining the FBI in 1934, then in its gangster war days and learning how to mythologize its agents. None too accurately, he was tied to the capture or pursuit of Mad Dog Coll, the infamous Machine Gun Kelly, and the nationally reviled Vern Miller, the Al Capone gunner who was part of the massacre of six police officers at Kansas City's Union Station in 1933. Bryce was more certainly in the group that tracked down and killed Wilbur Underhill, a man said to enjoy shooting an officer "just to see him kick."

The agent was indeed a lightning-fast draw. Legend had it that he could "drop a silver dollar from shoulder height, draw his pistol and drill the coin with a bullet before it reached waist level." One of the agency's most colorful hunters – his "Jelly" nickname was derived from "Jelly Bean," 1920s slang for a sharp dresser. An interviewer once asked him if he ever aimed to bring a criminal back alive instead of killing him. He didn't. "I'm more interested in bringing me back alive," he responded. Before he retired, he would be involved in 19 shoot-outs. He'd have 17 notches on the custom ivory-handled Smith & Wesson .44 Special he carried.[3]

By 1944, Bryce and his men in west Texas also kept their eyes on the nearby border for escaped war prisoners. Their El Paso base was itself home to a POW encampment at Fort Bliss while Texas, desperate for farm labor, had successfully lobbied Washington to place a total of 33 POW camps in the state. Security was tight for the 3,000 prisoners at Fort Bliss, but rules and privileges at many of the state's other stockades and branch camps were lax. Some were known as "The Fritz Ritz."

At El Paso's Coliseum branch camp—more casual than even the porous stockade area at Camp Hale—some prisoners had nearly free rein. The 1,000 Italians at Coliseum "swam in the Washington Park pool, attended Mass, consumed record amounts of beer, and chatted with girls at the fences." To stop women from tossing romantic notes wrapped around stones to the prisoners, El Paso passed an ordinance forbidding loitering near camps or throwing objects into them. Despite the supposedly luxe camp reputations, an estimated 21 German POWs tried to escape from the Texas camps during the war.* Even as word arrived about two escapees from Camp Hale on February 17th, Bryce and his men were busy searching for four German POWs who had just walked away from a worksite in Amarillo.[4]

———

At about 2 P.M. that day, Paul Kissman knocked again on Captain Collar's door at Camp Hale. He had more news: he knew that Maple had deserted and that Maple had indeed hinted that he was going to take some prisoners with him.

There was more. Kissman told Collar about the previous weekend's trip to Salida and his surprise that the stand-offish Maple had asked him to come with him. He told about Maple's purchases of women's clothes and a car. He said most of the men hated the 620th generally and Lt. Leroy Wilson, Collar's superior, specifically.

And one more thing: he knew with some certainty where Maple and the prisoners were going. First, Mexico. Then Germany.

Why, the incredulous Collar asked, hadn't Kissman told him about Salida and Mexico before, on the day of the escape, on Tuesday, or even on Wednesday when he'd been in Collar's office a second time?

"To cover for Maple," Kissman replied reasonably. Now, however, he wanted him caught.

Collar hurriedly relayed Kissman's news about Mexico to Military Intelligence, which sent it to the FBI, which flashed its agent near the Mexican border, "Quick-draw" Jelly Bryce.

———

It was ten days later when Collar, Curran of Army Intelligence, and Wilson, still stupefied, had Kissman in custody and got to ask him about his timing and motivation. "If you wanted him caught," Curran wondered, "why didn't you say something earlier?"

"To allow . . . for a speedier conviction," Kissman patiently explained. He'd planned it that way. Waiting three days to talk gave Maple and the Germans

---

* All the escapees were re-captured within three weeks. In one notable case, a German POW had sneaked away from his farm work through a field, and almost immediately called for his guards' help when a bull chased him up a tree.

time to get out of the country. "To cross the border in Mexico would [result in] a certain conviction, and it was my idea that they should be allowed to cross the border [before helping authorities find them]."

"What grounds," Curran asked, "do you have [to believe] that a conviction would be strengthened by apprehension of fugitives in a foreign country rather than over short distances from the military reservation at Camp Hale, Colorado?"

The answer was simple, at least to Kissman. The fugitives' "intentions should be more obvious if they had crossed the border than if they had merely been seeking refuge within the United States." And a sensational international capture and conviction would shine enough light on the unfair treatment of the men of the 620th that the Army would be shamed into letting the men serve with more dignity. In a statement he wrote for his interrogators, Kissman explained the example would persuade the more rebellious men of the 620th—all on the verge of riot, he reiterated—to reconsider before they invited more of the humiliating wrath of the War Department and spoiled everyone's reputations forever.

"Knowing of Maple's intentions, I let him go through with it with Full [sic] intention of reporting him at the logical time. . . . This to save others, for from his example or something similar, was the only way of circumventing trouble! This may sound like something out of a fairy book, but I assure you every word is true." Kissman meant no harm to his country. "My ideals may be radical, but they do not include treason."[5]

"Did the possibility occur to you," one of his interrogators asked, "that your delay in reporting the offense was very likely to result in failure to apprehend the fugitives, which would defeat the purpose entirely which you have set?"

"No, sir," Kissman replied. [6]

———

Around the same twilight of February 17th, as Bryce and his other pursuers accelerated their search, Dale Maple woke his fellow refugees and led them farther into the desert.

In darkness, they finally touched on the edge of the town of Columbus, New Mexico, filled four canteens with water, and walked another two miles west to avoid detection before heading south in the night toward the border. They hiked another five slow miles before settling down in the desert again to sleep. Maple guessed they were in Mexico by then. "When or how we crossed we did not know," Schwichtenberg was to recall, "at least Kikilius and I didn't" [7]

They laid low and stayed out of sight until about three the next after-noon—Friday the 18th—before heading off again. They were looking for Casas Grandes, a small town where Maple hoped to get their first helping hand. He was reasonably sure they were close. He had a compass and the .38 Colt revolver Kissman had bought for him. Schwichtenberg carried it now. Maple himself carried the .22 rifle and the ammunition he'd bought in Salida. They had had three and a half days of hard travel by then, sleeping in the car and on the ground. They were exhausted.[8]

They trudged on another 90 minutes when, on a dirt road near a town called Old Palomas, they heard a car approach. One of them stuck out his thumb to hitch a ride. The car slowed but did not stop until it was beyond them. Then the driver got out, holding a shotgun.

He had a badge of some sort. "*Pasaporte?*" The three men shook their heads. The armed man, who did not speak English, made it clear he wanted them to wait for something.

Schwichtenberg inched backward toward the side of the road, thinking about running.

In pidgin Spanish, Maple told the man with the shotgun that they had come to Mexico to look for work.

Behind his back, Schwichtenberg dropped the revolver into the brush. Be-ing found with a gun meant the death penalty for POWs.

An old Ford with two men pulled up. The man with the shotgun indicated the three stragglers should climb in, and one of the men in the Ford introduced himself as able to speak both English and Spanish. He would be the interpreter, he said. The man who'd been holding them, he explained, was Customs In-spector Medardo Martinez Mejia. Maple, who actually was fluent in Spanish, asked him to tell the Inspector again that they were only looking for work. But Martinez again asked for their passports. Maple, who had another prisoner's German passport in his pack, explained they didn't have passports. In that case, Martinez would take them to the Customs House in Palomas.

At the Customs House at about 6 P.M., in sight of the U.S. Customs House across the border, Martinez called his boss to report the curiosity: he had found "three strangers or foreigners in the uniform of soldiers." The news quickly lured Chief Customs Inspector Jose Magnana Zaragoza from his house, a sick-bed, and six kids to the office.

He arrived to find one of strangers, seemingly the leader, wearing "a uni-form or suit . . . badly disheveled or unshaven, somewhat of a beard, a black hat, shoes or half-boots up to about here." He took care to describe again the leader's "dark grey or black felt hat." The others wore dark blue wool pants "commonly used in field labor," quite dirty, and dark blue shirts. Through the interpreter, the Customs chief asked their names. He couldn't pronounce the one beginning with "S." Another was Heinrich Kikilius. The third, the apparent leader, was Eduard Mueller.[9]

What, the chief asked, was their destination. One of the men explained they were going to Casas Grandes. Then it was on to Tuxtla in the state of Chiapas "to embark to go possibly to Germany."

Magnana, who didn't know English or German, was sure he had misunderstood.

Worse yet, "I was sick, and I could not write," Magnana later recalled. He decided to "send [the men] to Señor Bates."[10]

———

William Bates' desk was about 100 yards away, across the border at the U.S. Customs House in New Mexico. It was an unusual posting for him. Bates, an Immigration and Naturalization Service inspector, usually worked out of El Paso. But on that night, he was in New Mexico on the lookout for the Amarillo escapees when Magnana, his peer on the other side of the border, called to say, "he had three fellows over there whom they thought were Americans, and they were not able to talk to them . . ." He asked Bates to come over "to see who and what they were."

In a nod to the international border between them, Bates signed out a government car, grabbed a partner, and, holding the proper paperwork, made the short drive to the Mexican Customs Building. The three strangers were just inside the door, in the foyer.

One called Eduard Mueller explained in a slight, cultivated German accent that they were Jewish refugees from Europe, seeking freedom.

Bates was dubious. "We talked to them some time," he would recall. The conversation was in English, mostly with Mueller, while Bates's partner "inspected all of the equipment they had with them and the baggage and some little flags they had with them."

In the end, he "finally decided they were three of the German prisoners who had escaped from Amarillo." Bates informed Magnana, "we would receive them if they wanted to turn them back to the United States."

Magnana, agreeable, formally made "a record to proceed with their deportation . . . to the United States."

Bates and his partner loaded the Amarillo suspects into the government car for the short drive back to the U.S. Customs House, where the fugitives saw a disabled Reo in the parking lot, found abandoned and towed there the day before.

Bates put the three in a room and called the El Paso office of the Federal Bureau of Investigation. He had the three Germans from Amarillo in custody. Special Agent in Charge D.A. Bryce congratulated him and promised to send some men out to secure the captives. Bryce would follow the next day to question the escapees himself.[11]

PART TWO

INFIDELITY

CHAPTER 6

THE GRAD SCHOOL PLOT OF 1940-1941

Quick-Draw Jelly Bryce thought "the sun rose and set on J. Edgar Hoover," and was wearing a double-breasted suit and snap-brim hat—both Hoover favorites—when he arrived in New Mexico on the afternoon of February 19th, 1944. He had spent the morning on the phone and reading the telexes shooting between FBI offices, so as he arrived at the Las Cruces jail, he already suspected the escapees were not from Texas. He had a healthy suspicion, too, that one of them wasn't a POW or even German.[1]

He'd gleaned the curious background of Dale H. Maple from the flurry of FBI messages, many from the Bureau's Maple file. It had been tracking—and dropping—him on and off for the four years since student Maple had manufactured a storm of controversy at Harvard and, by his own account, began a determined effort to muddy his name.

The file reached back to 1940 when, Maple liked to believe, his pro-German views had not been all that unusual in the United States. Nationalist and right-wing populism was robust and loud. Depending on who was doing the counting, 10,000-to-25,000 Americans were dues-paying members of the German American Bund. The Bund had held a big, alarming Nuremberg-style rally at Madison Square Garden the previous year. On Long Island, a planned German Gardens community in Yaphank had streets named after Goebbels, Goering, and Hitler and held a Bund rally of its own. The Bund ran summer camps for kids near Windham, New York.

In its zeal to keep the U.S. out of Germany's military way, its activities overlapped with many Americans' hopes to stay out of another European war. "According to the public opinion poll of *Fortune* magazine—noted for its accuracy—approximately 73 percent of the American public disfavored becoming involved in the war even if Germany should be victorious, and Germany seemed well on the road to victory," Maple would recall. He wrongly equated aversion to the war to sympathy for the Reich. But he could accurately say that at the time "it was no more un-American to be pro-German than it was to be pro-British. This was not our war."[2]

His view, in fact, was not unusual even on the Harvard campus. Student and faculty opinion at the time, according to a lengthy student history of Harvard's pre-war views published in 1942, was primarily divided not into pro- and anti-Nazi groups but groups for and against U.S. intervention in the war in Europe.* When Germany invaded Poland in 1939, "the most definite apparent reaction was a burst of isolationist feeling, a great surging cry: 'Stay out of the war!' That was, of course, the predominant feeling in the nation at that time."[3]

Powerful isolationist and anti-Semitic voices were in full throat in the United States. Leading them was the glamorous aviator Charles Lindbergh, who remained beloved enough in May 1940 to get radio time to address the nation. He maintained the only danger to America was if the United States sought to meddle in the affairs of foreign countries. He discounted Germany's threat to the U.S. "No foreign navy," he said, "will dare to approach within bombing range of our coasts." He warned that Franklin Roosevelt's increasingly hostile acts toward Germany (FDR had just gotten Congress to approve the constitutionally questionable $7 billion "Lend-Lease" agreement with Britain) would result in "neither friendship nor peace." Already personally awarded medals by Adolph Hitler, Lindbergh later referred to Jews as "other people" and was sure that "leaders of the Jewish race are not American in interests and viewpoints." He blamed Jews in the media for trying to lure the U.S. into war and urged Americans to "strike down these elements of personal profit and foreign interest."

The tactics were not subtle. American democracy, a home-grown fascist group called The Silver Shirts maintained, was "strictly kosher." It needed to be replaced—by force if necessary—by the efficient National Socialist model. Industrialist Henry Ford distributed 100,000 copies of "The Protocols of the Elders of Zion," the wholly made-up Jewish "secret plot" to take over the world,

---

* Harvard President James Bryant Conant was an ardent interventionist. On a May 1940 national radio broadcast, he urged that "we must re-arm at once."

and authored a book called *The International Jew.* Just four months after coming to power in 1933, Hitler had sent Robert Pape to Los Angeles to recruit Americans (mostly unemployed German Americans who had served in World War I) to build an often-martial Nazi presence in Los Angeles. Using cash from abroad literally hand-delivered at L.A. docks, they infiltrated German American social clubs, opened bookstores and beer gardens, and held meetings to instruct recruits in the advances of the Aryan nation across the sea.

Pape and his successors' goals, in conjunction with other Friends of New Germany and then Bund groups in American cities, included the overthrow of the U.S. government and joining a worldwide Reich of people "of German blood." They argued that German Americans—in the intra-war period, about a quarter of the U.S. population—were actively discriminated against, especially as "war hysteria" mounted toward the end of the 1930s. Indeed, as Hitler announced and enforced a brief boycott of Jewish businesses and goods in Germany, Jewish groups called for a boycott of German goods. German propaganda minister Josef Goebbels added that if the American boycott continued, a newer and meaner boycott of European Jews would last "until German Jewry has been annihilated."

The American Nazi groups, in turn, added a boycott of American Jewish businesses. Understanding the power of spectacle, they marched through cities lined by large crowds frozen in the Nazi salute in celebration of Hitler's birthday, the Munich accords, and other "holidays." They trained youth and willing adults in Nazi ideology and tactics at camps not only in New York but Pennsylvania, New Jersey, Pennsylvania, and Wisconsin. In Los Angeles, they at one point plotted the simultaneous kidnapping and public hanging of "the ten most famous Jews in Los Angeles."* Public brawls were common. One busy night in Milwaukee in 1938, for example, Bundists participated in two simultaneous street riots, fighting a mélange of Jewish, anti-Bund German Americans and leftist protestors.[4]

In that thickened climate, Maple did not yet think of himself as a Nazi, at least not one who "knew the full meaning of the term." By that, he meant he had not yet come to appreciate National Socialism fully. The horrific stories of bankrupting and wrenching German Jews from their German Christian neighbors, homes, and families were, he figured, as credible as the fabulist World War I propaganda about German soldiers raping Belgian nuns.

---

* The targeted Jews included Al Jolson, Samuel Goldwyn, Jack Benny, James Cagney, Charlie Chaplin and William Wyler, among others.

His real affinity, Maple said, was for German culture and accomplishment. Adolf Hitler himself wasn't the founding object of Maple's affections. But around a bridge table during his fourth year at Cambridge, Maple, like thousands of American sympathizers, was apt to point out that the dictator had lifted Germany very far and astoundingly fast. Germany's economic success under the Nazis, they could legitimately argue, was far greater than the United States under Franklin Roosevelt.[5]

In 1933, Germany was dismembered and destitute, with six-to-seven million unemployed. By 1938, it could brag of full employment. Gross weekly earnings were up 21 percent, while the cost of living had risen only seven percent. Decades later, the British historian Niall Ferguson would write that German worker (at least the heterosexual, Gentile ones) "were better off in real as well as nominal terms" than other European workers during the latter years of the 1930s. The birth rate had risen, which he saw as an index of confidence and optimism.

Hitler had done it with massive public borrowing not just for military spending but for railroads, canals, the Autobahn network of highways, and other infrastructure work. He stimulated private industry with tax rebates and consumer spending with low-interest marriage loans to help young couples get started. To assure a helpful distribution of wealth, Hitler put modest caps on profits and introduced progressive taxation. He subsidized theater, built athletic fields, and—by reclaiming the Rhineland lost in the Treaty of Versailles, hosting the 1936 Olympics, and allying with Mussolini's Italy—created what another pair of historians called a "spectacular rise in power and prestige" in just a few years.

The future, Hitler promised, would be a return to glorious German advances in science, medicine, education, and art. Once freed from the "bacillus" of certain political, religious, and degenerate "parasites," his land would rise to new heights of order, safety, and prosperity. There'd be cars for all the people—Volkswagens—and houses filled with conveniences invented by German scientists. A united Germany would reshape civilization and, soon enough, spread it throughout the world. And the heavens. Adolph Hitler foresaw gleaming German cities and mineral mines on the moon.

"The misery of our people is horrible to behold!" he had speechified in 1933. "Along with the hungry, unemployed millions of industrial workers, there is the impoverishment of the whole middle class and the artisans. If this collapse finally also finishes off the German farmers, we will face a catastrophe of incalculable dimension. For that would not just be the collapse of a nation, but of a 2000-year-old inheritance of some of the greatest achievements of human culture and civilization." By the time Maple started paying attention in 1938, Hitler bragged his party "overcame chaos in Germany, restored order, enormously raised production in all fields of our nation's economy, by strenuous efforts produced substitutes for numerous materials that we lack, encouraged new inventions, developed traffic, caused mighty roads to be built and canals to be dug, called into being gigantic factories and at the same time endeavored to further the education and culture of our people for the development of our social community."

He had won. "I succeeded in finding useful work once more for the whole of the seven million unemployed, who so touched our hearts, in keeping the German farmer on his soil despite all difficulties, and in saving the land itself for him, in restoring a prosperous German trade, and in promoting traffic to the utmost."

"What did the Fuhrer give you?" one party propaganda pamphlet asked.

The Fuhrer gave you work. Number of workers and salaried employees:
    1932 – 11.5 million
    1938 – over 19 million

The Fuhrer gave you bread. Income of workers, salaried employees, and civil servants:
    1932 – 26 million Reichsmarks
    1937 – 39.5 million Reichsmarks

The Fuhrer gave you homes. New home construction:
    1932 – 159,000 new homes
    1937 – 340,000 new homes [6]

Meanwhile, the United States' experiment in stimulating growth—also through public financing—during the same period had flagged. Orderly decision-making (or even Order) is not a hallmark of a functioning representative government, and the American president operated in a tripartite constitutional republic. Independent institutions still debated and compromised Executive initiatives, including public financing. Instead of expanding the money supply as some economists prescribed for the United States (and Hitler simply ordered in Germany), the Federal Reserve independently decided to pull it back. The Supreme Court and Congress then undid much of the Roosevelt Administration's version of economic stimulus. (The former Ford employee Fritz Julius Kuhn, head of the German American Bund, unmindful of The New Deal's similarities to the Nazis' fiscal recovery programs, called it "The Jew Deal.")

Whatever the reasons, the United States thus had collapsed again into recession in 1937 and 1938. Unemployment, which had been falling, ballooned to 19 percent. "The recession of 1937-38 is sometimes called 'the recession within the Depression,'" economist Douglas Irwin wrote. "It came at a time when the recovery from the Great Depression was far from complete, and the unemployment rate was still very high. In fact, it was a disastrous setback to the recovery. Real [gross domestic product] fell 11 percent, and industrial production fell 32 percent, making it the third-worst U.S. recession in the 20th century (after 1929-32 and 1920-21)."[7]

The comparative misery was not lost on some. In Erie, Pennsylvania, Paul Kissman's father worked for a railroad, and Paul "was able to get a pass, and I had spent considerable time visiting various parts of the United States during the Depression around 1932 and 1933." Looking for work, "I had visited Detroit and seen people in breadlines and people that appeared to be ill-fed. I felt that in a land of plenty like the United States, there was something wrong with the system that would permit this condition to exist." Out of work again in 1939, Kissman got a letter from a German family he had known in Erie reporting that booming Germany had plenty of jobs. After a harrowing journey—he was on a ship that was impounded in Rotterdam when Germany invaded Poland on September 1st, 1939—he made it to Germany on September 21st and promptly found work in a textile factory and then a kitchen equipment company near Leipzig.

He got back to the U.S. in March 1940. "I had observed how National Socialism worked in Germany and was of the firm belief it was a good thing for Germany, although food was rationed, people were apparently well-fed and that everything seemed quite clean and well-kept." He saw "no Jewish persecutions although I know they existed and were deplored. I did not see any starvations." On balance, he subsequently told Army investigators, "previous to my entry into the service [in October 1941] I had leanings toward Socialism."[8]

Germany, moreover, was on an awesome military roll, a seemingly invincible force not seen on the continent since Napoleon. It was everywhere. As its armies sliced through opponents, its vanguards in 1940 were at the center of turmoil in Colombia, Uruguay, Mexico, Chile, Argentina, and the Panama Canal Zone. They built U-boat fueling stations in the Caribbean. They backed a coup in Afghanistan.

And they were on the move in the United States. In May, Atlanta police arrested a 54-year-old mystery man carrying suspicious sketches of rail and gas lines. The FBI arrested a father-and-son duo in Paris, Texas, with maps of industrial targets. In October, an executive told a congressional committee about ongoing sabotage of Navy and merchant marine ships under repair at his Chester, Pa., shipyard. He'd found wads of torn-up t-shirts stuffed into newly installed gears, rendering them dysfunctional. He'd discovered 63 lengths of deliberately slashed hose intended to carry potentially explosive mixtures of acetylene, oxygen, and propane through one ship. "Such gases," the executive explained, "could fill the hold of a ship and be ignited by a spark, blowing up the vessel." To some, such revelations sounded like the rise of an ingenious, committed, ubiquitous, inevitable, and dynamic new military and political force. Kissman, like Maple, was willing to overlook or even disbelieve its cruelties.

Leonhard, then a pro-German grad student, followed the shipyard executive to the congressional committee's witness stand. He argued the relentless advances of 1940 probably were a product of Germany's superior new politics.

Eric Hotelling was an undergrad at Columbia University, loudly arguing the same thing. Even louder, he insisted on playing the *Horst-Wessel-Lied*, the Nazi anthem, from his dorm room decorated with swastikas, a picture of Hitler, and a map of London highlighting places the Nazis had successfully bombed.

Germany's rise, Maple himself argued, reflected not just the superiority of dictatorships but the weakness of democracies.[9]

"This was a time," one of Maple's Harvard classmates recalled of 1940 and 1941, "when Germany was doing so masterfully in Poland while the democratic nations vacillated between indecision and despair. I can remember 'bull sessions' that lasted into the early morning hours on the fateful progress of the war in Europe with most of us maintaining an isolationist point of view; or a cynical, disillusioned one (that our world was collapsing and no one was doing a thing about it) while Dale held forth at great length on the need for action: for sharp, definitive moves as with a rapier: cutting through opposition and forcing your will upon the mass as an army general (or a dictator) might."[10]

Maple's view was out-of-step on campus mostly in a matter of degrees, according to the essays in Maple's Class of 1941 yearbook. By graduation in June 1941, a yearbook writer claimed, "the great majority of all the undergraduates seemed to share three ideas: we wanted to see Germany defeated; we didn't want to go to war, and we were pretty sure that we would go to war." In general, "disagreement (with one of these opinions) cropped up only in the question of emphasis."[11]

At Harvard, the Anglo-Scottish descendant Maple, who still considered himself only a "cultural German," was making some "sharp, definitive moves" of his own. He attended a Halloween party at school dressed as Hitler and positioned a bust of Hitler on his desk in his room at Harvard's Dunster House.

The posturing seemed out-of-character for the often-withdrawn Maple. His house supervisor at Dunster House thought him a "peculiar, very quiet individual who never spoke to her unless she asked him a question . . . He wouldn't even say 'good morning.'" His room "was always clean, always neat." Maple, another acquaintance said, was "a rather quiet individual, excellent character, level-headed, emotional and capable." A hall-mate at Dunster who, as a pro-interventionist campus activist, had a very different view of what had become of German culture, thought Maple "friendly" and "sensitive," funny, and a paragon of "modesty, generosity and good manners." Another described him as a "quiet individual who kept to himself, was of the effeminate type and not athletically inclined." He was, yet another said, "the type of individual who would much prefer a book to the companionship of other people . . . he did not seem to care for dances, shows, or the average amusements that young people indulge in." Those who claimed to know him best cited an overweening sensitive side as well. His mother once found the young Maple "weeping" next to the family piano and rushed to find out what was wrong. "It's just so beautiful," he said of the piece he had just finished practicing. His hours at Harvard were consumed by Glee Club, the German club, Harvard's Reserve Officer Training Corps (ROTC) unit, and the Boylston Chemical Club, for which he served as treasurer.[12]

He was also detached, a snob, oppositional, and something of a jerk. "He is a very good student, but he is not very well-liked," reported an FBI agent who was soon tracking the ever-more active pro-German, 20-year-old Maple. High school classmates in San Diego reviled him. "The other students called him 'a brain' and were not too friendly toward him on account of his superiority in music and public-school work," his San Diego music teacher said. Edwin Self, a classmate at San Diego High skilled at snark, added, "A world history instructor, who later was committed to an insane asylum, virtually worshipped the boy."

Self, anyway, was most offended by Maple's apparent homosexuality. At a class assembly, "Dale came on after a particularly engaging and extremely popular girl dancer who had bought the house down. When he walked out on the stage . . . the audience broke into a loud, derogatory guffaw, for Dale didn't walk like the average high school kid. He seemed to be bent, or rather curved backward in the middle, like some skinny half-moon. He had a horrible slouch, and he had one of those mincing, self-conscious walks which are taken to mean that the guy is not one of the gang. He looked exactly as the student body wanted this pale, studious, brilliant grind to look—a queer ugly duckling of a sissy."[13]

He fared about the same, generally absent the homophobia, at Harvard. A bridge partner at Dunster House read his diffidence as a "superiority complex." His resident advisor later described him as "a very intelligent, but a rather thwarted and unhappy boy." To another FBI informant, Maple was a "fairly brilliant, misguided young man" who was "emotionally unstable." Another classmate who had known him since Maple arrived at Harvard at age 17 diagnosed him as "very badly adjusted and was the type who had a chip on his shoulder who would put it right back on if it was knocked off." In the spring of 1940, the classmate added, he developed "a case of political measles."[14]

Maple then turned contagious at *Verein Turmwachter*, Harvard's German Club. Amid the war threats of 1940, faculty advisor James Hawkes was at pains to divorce the club—made up of students of German culture and language—from anything remotely political. He carefully avoided anything that might invite wartime-like censorship or threaten the German department's academic freedom. It was not an idle fear. Because they were pressured or simply intolerant, many similarly worried college administrators had turned into ideological, budget-slashing, punitive censors after the Soviet Union signed a non-aggression pact with the German government in 1939. City College of New York barred Earl Browder, general secretary of the Communist Party in the U.S., from a campus panel of both isolationists and interventionalists. At about the same time, Yale's president, acting in the name of academic freedom, had intervened to overcome last-minute American Legion objections to a similar forum in New Haven. The same City College administrators then surrendered to the Episcopal Church and the Knights of Columbus pressure to prevent mathematician and pacifist Bertrand Russell from joining its faculty. A Columbia professor, meanwhile, organized an investigation of Columbia colleagues who belonged to an American Federation of Teachers local. The professor suspected it was pro-Nazi.[15]

Harvard's German Club was thus "desperate to keep its nose clean in connection with German political theory." Whatever was going on in Germany, the club's president claimed in that year's yearbook, was very different from what was going on in Harvard's German Club. Its 60 members, he swore, "have kept alive at Harvard the liberal spirit and traditions of German student life at a time when these things have been suppressed in Germany."

Associating with things German grew ever riskier as Europe's war grew even uglier. By spring, 1940 the entire continent had fallen into barbarism. Germany had divvied up Poland with the Soviet Union, invaded Luxembourg and Belgium, carpet-bombed Rotterdam, and accepted the defeat of the Netherlands. It was sinking scores of British ships, moving into Norway and, by June, nearing Paris. At the end of June, it would begin bombing England's citizenry. Unbeknownst to most of the world, Hitler and Goring had appointed Reinhard Heydrich, already having earned a reputation as "The Butcher of Prague," to coordinate the historically horrific solution to the "Jewish Question." The world already knew about Nazi cruelties like rousting Jews and stealing their homes, banning them from professional jobs, enforcing boycotts of their businesses, revoking their voting rights, and forbidding them to work in any capacity in politics, industry, and education. The existence of concentration camps for political rivals and "undesirables"—gays, Roma, people the party diagnosed as "mentally deficient"—was already the subject of much news coverage. There were rumors of buildings dedicated to killing the mentally ill. Although it refused to take them in, the world definitively knew of the flight of some 304,000 newly impoverished German Jews, stripped of their assets before being allowed to leave. Most notorious of all was the state's "Night of Broken Glass" when mobs, acting with the S.S., destroyed Jewish-owned stores and synagogues and, in some instances, kidnapped men, women, and children into civilian basement "jails' for torture.

The hard-to-believe news invited a response even in the still-isolationist U.S. The Roosevelt Administration's reactions to the fantastic violence were politically fraught and carefully measured. But there were material responses. The United States had already forbidden companies engaged in interstate commerce to employ members of the German American Bund. In his radio "fireside chat" in May, Roosevelt publicly warned, "We must and will deal vigorously" with the threat from other nations and proposed to increase military spending. On other campuses, anti-German sentiments had led to declining club memberships and, worse, the crackdowns on academic freedom. At Harvard, the German Club's Hawkes was determined to avoid the same fate.[16]

But then, at one of the club's final meetings of the 1939-1940 school year, club treasurer Dale Maple spoke up.

The German Club, he warned, was falling behind. It should be studying modern German and fascist literature, even if it meant not studying the classics. A hot debate ensued.

And as the meeting prepared to adjourn with the club's traditional singing of German folk songs, Maple insisted it was time for the music to become modern, too. He began to sing the *Horst-Wessel-Lied*, and then *Deutschland uber Alles*, insisting over Hawke's objections that his fellow club members join him.[17]

This, Maple later swore, was nothing more than an intrigue to wheedle his way into graduate school. It was perhaps his first crackpot scheme, although not the last to quickly blow up in his face. This one rested on a dream to start graduate work in comparative philology, the study of ancient languages and literature, after graduation from Harvard in June 1941. He aimed to do so, moreover, at the University of Berlin, which he considered the world's leading philology program. He was interested especially in Hittite languages, and Berlin's collection was supposedly the largest.[18]

He could not, however, ask his busy father to foot the bill. "My only hope was to obtain some assistance from the University of Berlin," he explained. "It was necessary, however, to support such a request with something more than my excellent scholastic record at Harvard. A scholarship from the University of Berlin would, in effect, be a subsidy from the German government, and the German government would subsidize an American only if it had reasonable assurance of some return on its investment . . . I was an admirer of Mendelssohn as well as Wagner, of Heine as well as Goethe. [But] a reputation as a political sympathizer was necessary. I had no such reputation and certainly no such sympathies. I decided to acquire the reputation."

So, Dale Maple set out to make a name for himself as another American Nazi sympathizer. He'd do it by disrupting Harvard's German club and putting a bust of Hitler on his dorm room desk.[19]

When the German Club reconvened in the fall of 1940, one of its first decisions was to demand that the disruptive Maple resign. Maple, seeking publicity but not banishment, replied with an unapologetic but peace-seeking letter. He wrote that separating the study of German culture from German political thought "is impossible." In his letter to German Club President George Farwell, he added that "my unqualified support of the present German state is well known to you and to other members of the University," Still, "I shall be happy to remain in the discharge of my duties" if his continued membership wouldn't embarrass the club.[20]

To Maple's surprise, club leaders held their ground. Angry, he marched to the offices of *The Harvard Crimson*, the school newspaper, ready with an inflammatory statement about what he charged was the German Club's intellectual cowardice. Julian Sobin of the *Crimson*'s Executive Committee was also a German Club leader and knew Maple well. They lived in the same house and were in ROTC together. Maple, Sobin thought, suffered from a "predominant inferiority complex" and would go to extremes to attract attention. Thinking Maple was going too far, Sobin tried to talk him out of the pro-Nazi language as well as publicizing his expulsion. It would damage the club and especially Maple's increasingly shaky reputation. Maple didn't seem to care.

"Because of his intense belief in Adolf Hitler and his methods of government by dictatorship clashes irreconcilably with the tenets of the *Verein Turmwachter*, Harvard's German Club, Dale H. Maple '41 formally resigned from the Club last week," the *Crimson* eventually reported. "Making no secret of his unlimited support of the Third Reich, Maple stated his belief yesterday that the best of all possible methods of government is totalitarian. 'Even a bad dictatorship is better than a good democracy,' he claimed."[21]

If his goal was infamy, he hit it. Maple's name had been in the *Crimson* three previous times in four years; twice appearing among small-print names of scholarship recipients. His third and most notable appearance had been on May 4th, 1938, during his freshman year, when the paper had published a short piece called "Yardling Gets 13 Hearts." "With the odds 50,000,000-to-1 against him," the article read, "Dale H. Maple '41, of Stoughton Hall, was dealt a perfect bridge hand last night, 13 hearts."[*][22]

In the tradition of intemperate interviewees everywhere, Maple later groused that "the *Crimson* chose to highlight the more spectacular language of [his German Club] resignation." Nevertheless, his plan started working. "I could now at least prove that I was politically as well as culturally a German sympathizer." Maple's father called to urge him to disavow the statements before his reputation soured beyond redemption. Maple thought that doing so, however, meant he'd "say goodbye" to any chance of a Berlin scholarship.

Shortly after the *Crimson* article appeared, *Time* magazine followed up on October 28th with an article in its Education section called "Making of a Nazi." All he had wanted was some obscure fascist *bona fides*, Maple later mourned,

---

* The odds in this case had been shortened, for Ev Graham, a bridge partner and classmate, had secretly stacked the cards before they were dealt. The excited players—all ignorant of Graham's stunt—called the; *Crimson*, which sent a reporter and photographer over to record the miracle. The *Crimson* and the *Boston American* both published stories about it. Graham didn't confess his prank to the other bridge partners until after the *Crimson* reporters left. They, in turn, held their tongues as the papers made the bridge hand famous.

"but I had ended by convincing the whole press that I was the recognized Nazi leader of Boston."[23]

Lt. Col. Henry D. Jay, who commanded Harvard's ROTC unit, saw the *Time* piece and kicked him out of the unit, publicly saying that "Maple was not fit material for an officer." Privately, Jay later told the FBI that Maple "showed traits of character and an unbalanced mind. Possibly psycho."[24]

Then the *New York Times*, reliably covering all things Harvard, took notice. "Dale H. Maple, 20, Harvard sophomore who recently was quoted by the *Harvard Crimson* as expressing admiration for dictators, left the Reserve Officers Training Corps today."[25]

"The first fruit of this notoriety was bitter," Maple said. He had enrolled in ROTC—which trains school-aged civilians to become commissioned officers in the military—back in high school in San Diego and continued it throughout his Harvard career. A friend remembered, probably with exaggeration, that "most of the time . . . [Maple] was to be seen in his ROTC uniform, which he wore even on non-drill days." He enjoyed military theory, had learned about guns, admired military strategy, and had an affinity for its orderly, disciplined life. He maintained he would have applied to West Point if a childhood series of ear operations had not disqualified him physically.[26]

Not least, the expulsion and the dust-up in the *Crimson* caught the FBI's eye. One of the next disturbing entries in Maple's file, which would soon reach many hundreds of pages, reports that student Maple had recently reached out to contact Dr. Herbert Wilhelm Scholz,* the notorious German consul in Boston.[27]

———

According to his press assistant Scholz, then 34, was "a six-foot, hefty, blond young Nazi socialite." Before coming to Boston in 1938, he was secretary and effectively second in command at the German Embassy in Washington. He was "a great favorite with Washington society, especially with the ladies, many of whom thought him 'so handsome, so charming,'" one newspaper reported. Ambassador Hans Luther went home in 1937, and his successor, Hans-Heinrich Dieckhoff, was soon recalled amid the precipitous decline in relations with Germany after *Kristallnacht* in November 1938. But Scholz stayed, reassigned to New Orleans and then Boston. Once there, he promptly moved the consulate

---

* Maple first tried to contact Scholz in November 1940. In 1946, the FBI found file cards from Scholz's long-closed consulate. One read, "Dale H. Maple, Dunster House J 52, Harvard Univ., Cambridge Mass., 11/40: Request for interview with consul."

from a "dowdy" downtown office to "a handsome brick home" on Beacon Hill, where he was known to "discretely" entertain "Boston's Brahmin elect."[28]

Besides charming people, Dr. Scholz (his doctorate was in economics) was an energetic Gestapo agent. He ran a spy network and helped finance front groups like The Welfare Association of Boston and The Christian Front and their local leaders, the Moran brothers. Francis, one of the brothers, was an insurance man whose goal, he once wrote, was to "kill all the Jews." (The FBI had broken up the Front's New York chapter in January 1940, just as the gang was preparing to launch *Kristallnacht*-type terrorist attacks against "communists and Jews"). Scholz was "a close personal friend of Heinrich Himmler" and a member of (and later an *oberfuhrer* in) the Gestapo. He was later implicated, much like Maple and Leonhard and Hotelling would be, in a conspiracy with 30 Americans to set up a rival Nazi government in the U.S. His 31-year-old wife Lieselotte (or Lilo) was also a spy, frequently as a courier from Boston to London to Berlin. (Her father was "factory director" at I.G. Farben, the German chemical giant that used—and used up—slave labor at Auschwitz. He was tried at Nuremberg after the war.) [29]

Scholz's active espionage network was staffed in part by students like Maple, Leonhard, and Hotelling. One was William Colepaugh, an MIT dropout from toney Nitanic, Connecticut, who, like Maple, "admired the thoroughness of the German military." While at MIT, Colepaugh, like Maple, "attempted to gain attention by evidencing strong pro-German statements." He also began visiting and drinking with the beached crew of the *Pauline Friederich*, a German tanker stuck in neutral Boston's port while it hid from British warships. He soon got to know Scholz, who, at about the same time Maple began his flirtation with Scholz, invited him to a Hitler birthday celebration at the consulate in April 1941. Soon, too, Scholz got the young man to Buenos Aires, where Colepaugh's pro-Nazi mother back in Connecticut bragged he was "setting up radio broadcasting stations for the German government." Mrs. Colepaugh, Colepaugh's biographer noted, was "not a stable person" and had many outsized estimates of her family's importance to the Nazi regime. But Colepaugh did eventually get to spy school in The Hague, then occupied by the Germans, to learn firearms and get espionage training. He was next sent with another agent via U-boat to be put ashore on a cold, snowy night on the coast of Maine.* Their mission was called Operation Elster. They were to build a radio and transmit technical information about the Allied war effort back to Germany.[30]

---

* Colepaugh eventually drank away his spy adventure, leaving his partner in the lurch and without ever building any radio stations in the U.S. He ended up a print shop owner in Pennsylvania.

Scholz also tried to recruit a Harvard student who, the FBI believed, was 21-year-old Leonhard Sausman, "large and blond." Sausman* lived with his family in Boston, had been in school in Germany, and, an FBI agent maintained, was a member of Hitler *Jugend*. The FBI considered the group "one step before admission to the S.S. Elite Guard." Sausman also knew Dale Maple. The FBI contended he exerted "considerable influence" on Maple's views and theories at Harvard.

So it was in the spring of 1941 that Maple knocked on Herbert Scholz's consular door, hoping that "the head men of the German government in the United States" could help get him into the University of Berlin. "I was received quite cordially," he recalled. Scholz was "somewhat noncommittal" but suggested Maple return[31]

———

Soon, "different individuals" began contacting him. The contacts, Maple swore, "were entirely innocuous," although, in the retelling, they sounded more sinister than harmless. One visitor's "last name was 'James' from Lexington or Concord." This James was "rather elderly" and was missing four fingers on one of his hands. A newly converted Catholic, Maple didn't like him because he was anti-Semitic and anti-Catholic, but he nevertheless saw him "two or three times" and visited his home. Despite the multiple visits, Maple was never able to recall James's first name, location, occupation, or conversations. Scholz, he figured, was using James and the other innocuous visitors to keep an eye on him.

Maple soon applied for a passport to study "Comparative Philology and Biochemical Sciences" in Berlin. And Scholz had a surprise for him: he'd arranged a summer tour of Germany. Maple would depart on June 23rd, 1941, soon after his Harvard graduation. (In his commencement address that year, university President James B. Conant presciently warned students they were graduating into an age of doubt "when any interpretation of human conduct which is not stated in terms of selfishness, greed, and lust is regarded in many circles with suspicions.") Scholz booked Maple on a Spanish ship, and, different from most innocent summer trips, he'd travel with a false name, visa, and passport. "If given an opportunity," Maple learned, "we would attend a German sabotage school near Hamburg." [32]

---

* Maple and the handful of Germanophiles on campus readily pronounced and spelled each other's' names to sound more German. Sausman, for example, was actually John Leland Sosman, son of a Boston-area physician. Sosman himself subsequently entered the Army in the medical corps.

Then the world intervened. On June 13th, the Roosevelt Administration froze German and Italian assets in the United States. Two days later, Italy froze U.S. funds in that country. The next day, the U.S. ordered both Germany and Italy to close their 24 consulates by July 10th, 1941. They could keep their Washington embassies open, but several consuls—in particular the German consul in San Francisco, who was once Hitler's adjutant—had indulged in "improper and unwarranted" activities inimical to the United States' welfare. The Boston consul, according to a local politician quoted in the *Boston Globe*, was "along with the one in San Francisco, regarded as one of the two American hotbeds of Nazi propaganda and activity." Their activities included "breaking down national morale and easing the road of conquest." It was, the *New York Times* reported, "another way of saying fifth column activities." Senator Lester Hill of Alabama approved. "These consular offices have been nothing more nor less than regional headquarters for the German Gestapo."[33]

The order ticketed some 171 German officials and agents, including Scholz, for departure. Scholz himself initially refused to comment and then blandly told the *Times*, "I don't know what I will do or when the consulate will be closed . . . I have been in this country seven years now, but if orders came, I would be forced to leave and return to Germany."[34] He had five employees, all of whom would leave with him.

———

Maple's trip was off. Though he was unaware of it, the University of Berlin was no longer much of a philology center anyway. The Hittite materials Maple claimed to seek were at the National Museum in Berlin, not the university, and the museum did not allow grad students to have access to them. Moreover, the university's philology department had been thoroughly politicized; its Jewish faculty purged, its language curriculum larded with bogus racial theories, and its most famous professor already retired.

But the trip's cancellation left the new graduate Maple bereft, and he slumped back to San Diego to live with and work near his father for the summer. He had a job at Ryan Aircraft, but before his first day, "I received notice that my services could not be used." Saddled with his hard-earned pro-Nazi notoriety, he suspected that "military intelligence had not approved" of his working at a defense contractor.

He took it as proof of America's moral bankruptcy. It was shameful that in a free country like the United States, "a simple statement of opinion"— meaning his *Harvard Crimson* statement of "unqualified support" for the Hitler regime—"should, ten months later, be made the basis of denial of employment. I could only hope that with the passage of time, suspicion against me would be relaxed."[35]

Unsure what else to do, he enrolled in a post-graduate program at Harvard, and moved back into Dunster House in September. At about the same time, in Ukraine, just-arrived German officers rounded up and marched almost 34,000 Jews to the edges of a ravine near Kyiv. During the next two days, they methodically shot them before, with a bulldozer, burying the piles of bodies. Maple, meanwhile, filled his time with a research fellowship back in Cambridge to study microphone and headset performance in inclement and noisy conditions* and applied a second time for a passport. He said it was to go to Berlin, where this time he hoped to become a foreign correspondent for American newspapers. But he failed to find a paper to hire him and didn't get the passport. He felt stuck.

On Sunday morning, December 7th, 1941, much changed. The Japanese attack on Pearl Harbor was "a great shock" to him, although for reasons different from most Americans. War with Germany now looked inevitable—the U.S. and Germany would almost simultaneously declare war on each other on December 11th—and "I was then left in the position of being in a country at war with a country whose ideals I wished to uphold." Before the casualties in Hawaii were counted, Maple also saw an opportunity. If he could get to Berlin before war was officially declared, he figured he could be interned there for the duration and, in the process, complete his studies. "Of course, I could not believe this fantasy—could not actually desire its realization—but on that day of despair, it seemed to offer at least a measure of security."[36]

Whatever his reasons, he "called the German Embassy that Sunday afternoon. My conversation lasted perhaps fifteen seconds. I referred to Dr. Scholz and asked if there were any possibility of going to Germany with the diplomatic staff. I was told simply that it was too late." Still deaf to the callousness of trying to leverage the drowned humans and twisted metal in Hawaii into hitching a ride to Berlin, Maple did later concede this last stab was a "desperate act, an act of hysteria."[37]

The FBI, monitoring him as well as everything vaguely German, thought it threatening. The Bureau on that day was already busily rounding up people on the list of possible subversives Director Hoover had been compiling since

---

* The study appeared to be related to military needs, much as his work would have been at defense contractor Ryan Aircraft. Harvard itself was knee-deep in war-related work before Pearl Harbor. War Department projects included research on explosives, radio electronics and military medicine.

1939. Starting in the evening of December 7th, Hoover's men arrested 1,002 German resident aliens, 169 Italian resident aliens, and 1,370 Japanese resident aliens. They also brought in 19 American citizens of "German extraction," two of Italian descent, and 22 of "Japanese extraction" during the next four days.* Inaccurate newspaper reports had Japanese planes over San Francisco, Japanese submarines off Los Angeles, and Japanese spies throughout the West Coast. Alarmed, the government began rounding up another 110,000-to-120,000 American citizens guilty of being of Japanese ancestry. It forced them to sell their homes and property and, in the now-infamous forced migration, transported them to internment camps.[38]

And Maple lost his job. When he returned to campus after Christmas break, the Cambridge lab told him he couldn't have his microphone job back. "This was defense research," he later said, "and orders came from Washington, barring my further participation in it."[39]

And then he got a new idea.

"I realized immediately: I must become a member of the armed forces."[40]

---

* Director Hoover had started an index of people to be detained in the event of war in 1939, and those arrested in December 1941 were put in a "Custodial Detention Program." Attorney General Francis Biddle, Hoover's boss, ruled in 1943 that "The evidence used for the purpose of making the classifications was inadequate; the standards applied to the evidence for the purpose of making the classifications were defective; and finally, the notion that it is possible to make a valid determination as to how dangerous a person is in the abstract and without reference to time, environment, and other relevant circumstances, is impractical, unwise, and dangerous." He told Hoover to end it. Hoover essentially ignored the order, and re-established it under a new name, The Security Index. It was maintained until 1971.

CHAPTER 7

"HIS MAD CAREER"

At about 1 P.M. at the Dona Ana County Jail in Las Cruces, New Mexico, on Saturday, February 19th, 1944, Special Agent D.A. Bryce was anxious to start interrogating Erhard Schwichtenberg, Heinrich Kikilius, and, most urgently, the dubious Eduard Mueller. The Bureau's German-language translator, however, was still on his way from Los Angeles. Bryce, impatient, couldn't wait any longer. He went directly to Mueller's cell.

Mueller snapped to attention when Bryce entered. He bowed from the waist and gave the Nazi salute. He said, "Heil Hitler."

Bryce, following FBI protocol, showed him his credentials and explained his official capacity. Mueller, following military protocol, nodded curtly, formally accepting the sharpshooting agent's credentials.

Before they began, he asked for the agent's forbearance. It was going to be difficult for him to converse in English. He cautioned that, while he had attended English schools, it had been some time since he used that language.

Bryce told him to do his best.[1]

His name, the prisoner reported "with a distinct German accent," was Eduard Mueller, Army of The Reich. Until four days before, on February 15th, 1944, he had been a prisoner of war interned at Camp Hale, Colorado. His American captors gave him serial number 7-WG-34158.

More or less unbidden, Mueller unspooled "his life's history." He told stories about his family in Germany and described how he, as a member of the Afrika Korps, had been captured in Africa. He helpfully provided times and locations of where he had served. For another 35 minutes, he described his brothers, sisters, and jobs he held before the war[2]

At last, Bryce interrupted him. He had two things to show him.

One was a telex from FBI headquarters in Washington, D.C., which had run the prisoner's fingerprints through its files.

805 Rtr13 Rr
i 17 U U

The prints matched one Dale H. Maple.

He added that Camp Hale prisoner Eduard Mueller, formerly of the Reich's Afrika Korps, was still in Colorado wearing a different serial number. The serial number 7-WG-34158 did not appear to be a real one.[3]

Across the table Maple, "very much disturbed," began to cry. Composing himself, the prisoner admitted he was Pfc. Dale H. Maple, A.S.N. 11048476. And he wanted to tell Bryce and eventually the world a terrible story about the kidnapping of American soldiers. There was oppression within the ranks of the United States Army. Repression and suppression, too. His was the victims' revenge. Now they were ready to plant bombs, commit treason and contribute as much as they could, including their lives, to the preserve the German Reich.[4]

Bryce stopped him again. This case had just gotten bigger than desertion, bigger even than a prisoner escape. It was mutiny, sabotage, a war against the United States.

The interview needed to pause. Maple should "lie down and rest awhile." Bryce had work to do.

First, he called U.S. Attorney Howard Houk in Santa Fe. He told Houk he had the fugitive Maple in custody and that Maple had confessed to aiding the POWs and planning something worse. He advised Houk to charge the soldier with treason.

He hung up and called the FBI's Denver field office to report Maple's capture. The Denver Special Agent in Charge should "keep this matter quiet" for now. It had become a treason case, and treason cases were sensitive.

They were also valuable. As another agent, R.H. Cunningham, put it in another telex that night, "if a treason case could be made, the Bureau would receive excellent publicity."[5]

At Houk's direction, Maple was charged with treason and placed under $100,000 bond (about $1.4 million today). Houk, also alive to the publicity and political opportunity, ordered Maple and the real Germans sent to the Albuquerque County Jail, closer to Houk's office.[6]

Bryce thought the five-hour trip from Las Cruces to Albuquerque could be dangerous. Others could be involved. Rescue attempts were possible. Fearing the worst, he asked D. Milton "Mickey" Ladd of the FBI's Domestic Intelligence Division for permission to use necessary "restraining devices on these escaped prisoners in transporting them." Even though he knew by then that Mueller was Maple, an American citizen, Ladd told Bryce to do what was necessary "despite the provision of the Geneva treaty."[7]

———

Maple, Schwichtenberg, Kikilius, Bryce, and the guards' 200-mile trip through the lengthening New Mexico evening went without a rescue attempt. They found Houk waiting at the Albuquerque jail with a news photographer, ready to publicly walk Maple, wearing his dark hat, into custody. Houk got in a quote for the next day's papers and said the photo would be proof that the GI suffered no injury during his capture or the ride from Las Cruces. When off-stage, he called a doctor to come to examine and attest to Maple's physical condition and state of mind. It could come in handy if the accused traitor claimed insanity someday. The physician got there at 11:55 P.M. on February 19th.[8]

Jelly Bryce, back at the jail in the morning, informed the prisoner that he didn't have to make a statement and that staying quiet wouldn't be held against him. But Maple shrugged it off. He was "very willing," even anxious, to talk. Bryce asked one question before Maple launched a 90-minute monologue about how an innocent lover of German culture purposefully became an emphatic, action-oriented, and putatively dangerous Nazi. Bryce broke in to ask if he had been a member of the German American Bund. Maple dismissed the Bund as kids' stuff; beneath him. "I believe the real subversive underground was separate from the Bund." The Bund was "merely a front to attract attention."

Getting into the University of Berlin, he admitted, was also a front, mere cover for his daring fascist victory work. "I intended to remain in Germany and was discussing the possibility of entering a sabotage school at Hamburg and returning to the United States as a sabotage agent." He implicated someone else: his classmate Leonhard Sausman was going to supply contacts in Germany for him.[9]

But he halted abruptly. He wanted to switch to writing.

"They wanted a story," he would soon tell his mother. "And I gave them one."[10]

Before the prisoner could change his mind, Bryce got Maple a typewriter, some paper, and some carbon paper to make a copy. So, as Bryce and two other agents paced nearby, Maple spent most of Sunday, February 20th, in his cell, typing. He was producing an explanation of how he become a linguistically talented, musically gifted, *magna cum laude* pro-German Ivy League graduate who conspired to sabotage the war effort and, ultimately, desert with two prisoners of war before returning to wage guerilla war. His plans, one of Bryce's superiors said upon reading the statement, were "shocks" against the United States.

He began the story like an autobiography, starting with a highly accomplished childhood that was comfortable despite ongoing "disharmony" between his parents. He described piano recitals, valedictory high school grades, his Harvard scholarship award, his political pedigree ("I was always known as a political dissenter"), and, at last, his evolution as a committed Nazi. Now, by exposing the abuses in the 620th, Dale Maple was also standing bravely for justice for his fellow American soldiers.[11]

The story was not altogether verifiable. Maple was not, for example, widely known as a dissenter or even as politically aware in his school days. One of his teachers remembered Maple's paper about a summer trip to Germany with his mother. It was neither true, political, nor even very good. "I disapproved of excessive adolescent snobbishness . . . Maple was not, as I recall, at all popular or noted for his political views." Maple's high school German language teacher thought the boy terrifically smart and facile with languages, but "I have sometimes wondered to what degree I might have been responsible for Dale's 'bizarre' performances later. I am sure he never heard from me any favorable comments on Hitler in those earlier days of his mad career." Even after he got to Harvard, the dean of the Department of Semitic Languages and History, "had no idea he was a Nazi."

Maple's versions of his life story would change over time cleverly, radically, or ludicrously, and sometimes all three. He once said he changed his majors at Harvard to please his parents. (His mother favored history; his father, chemistry). Then, first for Scholz and then for D.A. Bryce, he said he changed his major because Authority victimized him. His dreams of a career in diplomacy vanished, he said, because "the university would not let him express his opinions."[12]

Typing his story in Albuquerque, he recounted hitting bottom. The German Club and his beloved ROTC ostracized him. His philology and Hamburg sabotage dreams had been smashed. The aircraft company in San Diego barred him from a promised summer job. His sullied reputation cost him his defense research job in Cambridge after Pearl Harbor. It was apparent, he wrote for Bryce, that the FBI and the War Department had taken his grad school kabuki dances with fascism far too seriously.

"I saw then," he wrote, "that I was to find no employment until the question of my loyalty was cleared up. In order to clear this matter up once and for all, I joined the Army voluntarily."

He had tried the Navy first, which cited a childhood ear condition and turned him down. The Army accepted him the next day, on February 22nd, 1942. He took the oath and was sent immediately to nearby Fort Devens, which on that day was being outfitted with tents for what the *New York Times* reported was "New England's only concentration camp." The camp would house some 800 of the male aliens the FBI had been rounding up since the evening of December 7th. [13]

He was resigned, he wrote, to being a good American soldier and was not thinking about turning against the United States. "I took the [loyalty] oath without reservation" on his enlistment day. "My attitude toward the United States had always been not that I wished to see her defeated, or her form of Government changed, but simply that Germany must not be destroyed." He took the oath, moreover, with ambitious post-war plans in mind. "I felt that any part I might have had in destroying Germany by joining the Army would be more than offset by the influence I might be able to exert in peace-time."[14]

There may have been more to his abrupt exit from Cambridge and enlistment than hoping to shape the postwar world, repairing what had become his toxic reputation or even finding some characteristically convoluted way to get a job after the war. Harvard's library, it seems, had discovered some of its Slavic language texts were missing. The university sent someone (the FBI redacted the name) to search Maple's room, where they found neither the books nor Maple. The resident advisor hadn't seen him. The searcher gave up. But several days later, an anonymous package arrived at the library. It bore a postmark from "New Bedford, Massachusetts," a short distance from Newport, Rhode Island, where Maple's mother lived. The books were in it.* Then, a few days after the package arrived, Maple's mother herself showed up at Dunster House

---

* The books' provenance remained something of a mystery, and Maple claimed he was innocent. "The matter of the books has been a puzzle to me ever since it was first mentioned. I am completely in the dark . . ." After his final exams in June 1941, "I packed up and left rather suddenly. I had some six or eight books checked out (Spengler, Spinoza, Kant and several other philosophers). I gave the books to a fellow at [the] grad school of [business] administration to return for me." The library sent him a notice during the summer, and upon returning to campus in the fall he found the books had been returned. The library had already bought a replacement for the Spengler book. Maple paid for the replacement plus "a nominal fine" of a not-so-nominal $100 (about $1,100 at this writing). He said knew nothing about the Slavic languages books the arrived mysteriously in early 1942. Separately Robert Pfeiffer, then head of Harvard's Department of Semitic Languages and History, had no recollection of any difficulties Maple had with the library.

to clean out her son's room. It was the first the advisor, Maple's housemates, and Harvard knew that Maple was not returning.[15]

Whatever the reason, he officially withdrew from Harvard on March 10th. By then, Maple had been at the Field Artillery Replacement Center at Fort Bragg, North Carolina, for seven days.

Maple liked the Army. He was comfortable at Fort Bragg and with the familiar ROTC-like structure to the days. He met some Harvard classmates who had been in ROTC with him and didn't even mind that a sergeant made no secret about keeping him under constant surveillance. Maple figured he deserved it, and it "certainly didn't arouse my resentment." The scrutiny would help prove his loyalty and, inevitably, his fitness for his newest goal: overseas duty.[16]

The War Department's Counter-Intelligence Corps (CIC) began watching him his first day at Fort Bragg. Its investigation wasn't unusual. The CIC routinely conducted "thousands of personnel investigations" of new arrivals, probing local police and FBI records, employment and educational backgrounds, and soldiers' associations. One of the personal associations was Julian Sobin, former German Club member, *Crimson* staffer, and Harvard ROTC soldier who had once tried to talk Maple out of giving the *Crimson* his pro-dictatorship statement. Sobin, now a lieutenant at the base, told the CIC, "I have never believed Maple was sincere in his notions of the greatness of the German state."

After 60 days of surveillance, the CIC agreed. Maple, the lead investigator concluded, had had "Pre-Nazi ideas" as a student, but that they "were only those of a college boy and that upon reaching maturity he has completely changed his views on Fascism in general." [17]

Not everyone was so understanding. In June, shortly after the CIC wrapped up its forgiving investigation at Fort Bragg, the agent in charge at the FBI's Atlanta field office received a report from South Carolina. It deemed Maple "not desirable for enlistment in the armed forces of the United States or for employment in any national defense project . . . the District Intelligence Office at Charleston has received information on the Subject, which would indicate he is not so desirable." Director Hoover assigned his Savannah office to look into the Charleston report, which apparently referred to the June 1940 *Time* article about Maple. In August 1942, five months after Maple's arrival at Fort Bragg, the Savannah office reported it had found nothing except that Maple was a boor. "The entire attitude of Subject is prompted by a sense of hostility. . . . A manifestation of immaturity by a young man who appreciated his own virtues and who constantly liked to be against many things when [it] results in bringing Subject to the attention of others." It quoted a CIC officer who said Maple had ". . . a contradictory spirit and the typical egotism of a young man."

At Fort Bragg, meanwhile, the "contradictory spirit" himself had by then entirely morphed into a cooperative, even happy soldier. Maple sincerely found the work and training stimulating. He requested parachute training, then glider pilot training, and then to be groomed for intelligence work. His testing and training scores were good, some of them excellent. "My military record was absolutely impeccable," he'd write in his statement for Bryce, and he was soon promoted to corporal. "I was not particularly pleased with this assignment, for I had desired combat duty." But he was on his best behavior and accepted it. His request for glider pilot training would surely come through soon. [18]

It didn't. After six long months of silence, "I felt that such a transfer had probably been disapproved," Maple told Bryce. But he had another idea: he asked to be demoted to private and transferred to a combat unit. That request, anyway, was granted, and Maple was sent to Fort George G. Meade in Maryland for further training on October 17th, 1942.

The War Department memo that came with him was neither alarming nor very helpful. The probing at Fort Bragg had gleaned "no positive information . . . either to indicate the subject has disavowed his Nazi sympathies or that he still actively adheres to them." Thus, vaguely reassured, his superiors made him an instructor in the radio school, which he also cooperatively accepted as a prelude to overseas duty. Maple was "quiet, soft-spoken, with an aloof personality," one fellow soldier later reported and spent most of his time at the radio school. But his superiors rated him "one of the top men" there. Maple wrote one of his old ROTC buddies that he was so pleased with Army life that he wanted to make it a career.[19]

Still, the Counter-Intelligence Corps watched him. Two investigators continued interviewing soldiers at Fort Meade. When they interviewed Maple, they let him know—apparently to Maple's surprise—that the government had a record of his Pearl Harbor Day phone call to the German Embassy in Washington. When they interviewed other GIs who knew him, they heard a lot about his homosexuality. An unnamed private complained to his superior one evening that "the two lovebirds [Maple and another soldier] are at it again." A sergeant [also unnamed in the report] "went downstairs in the barracks and found MAPLE and [name redacted] lying on a bed with their arms around each other in an intimate manner." The private's superior passed it on to the CIC.

"According to [name redacted], Maple is disliked by his associates because he is thought to be perverted."

"Maple," the CIC investigators' report noted, "was observed in an embrace with [name redacted], although no one observed SUBJECT actually kiss him. When they play with each other, they caress each other's bodies and gently tap one another." Another soldier said Maple "is disliked by his associates because of his haughty personality and because he is rumored to be a homosexual . . ." Yet another said Maple would "be an outstanding soldier if he were more of a man." Maple, he complained, would not go out with girls and made only a "token pouty appearance at a dance."

The same soldier "stated that he has no reason to question Maple's loyalty." Another reported Maple was "a good speaker." And he was ready for combat. His orders were cut, and he had packed to serve as a casualty replacement in the African campaign.

———

"By January [1943], I was ready to be shipped to Africa, but the shipping orders were suddenly canceled," he wrote his mother. "This much I do know. It's something very extraordinary, and it is not a shipment overseas. I am going to the 1367th Service Unit at Indiantown Gap, Penn. That might mean almost anything, though. There are 7 of us going on special orders, and I am the only one in the 76th Division . . . The transfer has all [Battalion Headquarters] in an uproar since no one knows what it's all about."[20]

He stayed at Indiantown Gap only a week before being put on a train headed west. "From that time on," he explained as Bryce looked over his shoulder in faraway Albuquerque, "my treatment by the Army became increasingly peculiar."[21]

CHAPTER 8

SHANGHAI CAMP

Life turned "peculiar" for other soldiers, too. At Camp Blanding, Florida, 26-year-old Paul Kissman had been in the Medical Corps for nearly two years. He was a happy man. His Army work had him thinking about going to college and into some sort of postwar medical career, maybe ophthalmology. A high school grad with two years of correspondence school courses under his belt, he was born to a German father and an American mother. He grew up loving music, studied piano and voice extensively, and had sung with dozens of choirs and groups back home in Erie, Pennsylvania. In his church choir, he was a powerful tenor soloist.

Among the secular groups, he sang with were German clubs, where members of the German American Bund were among his acquaintances. More concerning, he was a member of the Kauffhauser Bund, and at a public occasion, he reportedly refused to sing "God Bless America." His explanation was, "America has never done anything for me." And, looking for work in 1939, Kissman had taken the kitchen equipment job in Germany for six months, where he came to admire the economic dynamism of the new German government and, after his short stay in Germany, lean toward socialism as the best way to organize a nation. He also developed a weakness for evidence-free racial theories and was particularly antagonistic toward the Japanese as much for what he thought was their disregard for life as for their imperial aggression. "The white race is committing suicide," he later wrote of the war in Europe. He was particularly anxious to finish his training, join his brother, then serving with the Army Transport Corps in the South Pacific, and, as he later put it, take on "The Yellow Peril." The goal would be "the re-creation of a United White Race."

Then the Army took his gun away and sent him to South Dakota.[1]

Pfc. Fritz Siering's Army career had been peculiar from the start. A German merchant seaman afraid that his anti-Nazi views would get his family in trouble, Siering had jumped ship in New York in 1936. Before fleeing, he had been a member of "the *Arbeitsbund*, which is similar to the Hitler Youth. I had to belong to it to work." It was for those reasons that he stole into the United States, and he "wouldn't go back to Germany unless the Nazi government gets overthrown." He eventually found himself married and earning a good living in Chicago but, tired of looking over his shoulder as an illegal alien, tried to become a U.S. citizen in 1940.

Nevertheless, after seeming to permit him to start the citizenship process, the Immigration Service soon ordered him deported. It then deferred his expulsion because Germany was already at war, and the law forbid deportations to war zones. Two years later, the Selective Service ordered Siering, still in limbo, to report to the Chicago draft board, where he thought he'd struck another deal: He'd agree to serve if the government dropped the deportation order. Although the Second War Powers Act of March 1942 had reduced naturalization standards for aliens serving in the armed forces, Siering's deportation order was still in force on induction day in November 1942. He was ordered to get in line and take the matter up with his eventual commanding officer. Sent to Camp Grant, Illinois, his new superior said he'd look into the matter but never did. Seven months later, in June 1943, Siering was still waiting as he trained for the Medical Corps, still at Camp Grant. He had established a "satisfactory record" when the Army abruptly took his gun away and sent him, too, to South Dakota.[2]

Theo Leonhard was, like Siering, officially still a German citizen but had been in the United States since the age of 11 with his mother and father, a Lutheran minister. Growing up in a tight, well-established, and peaceful German community in the west Texas hill country, he was active in politics and a regular speaker at the town's annual festival. He got to know the young Lyndon Johnson, whose parents' home until Johnson was five was "right across the river from [Leonhard father's] church." (The rest of Johnson's childhood and teenage years were in Johnson City, 13 miles to the east). With a good education, job, and future—Leonhard had been a political science instructor at the University of Texas, where he was working toward a doctorate—he had volunteered for the Army in 1940, before the war. He liked his adopted nation, "which impressed me with its greatness, and it did not take me long to develop a love for this country." He also liked his duty with the 40th Division Artillery. "I was in every way treated as an American soldier, although I was not and am not an American citizen. There was no discrimination against me whatsoever." And "when that division got ready to go overseas in the summer of '42, I was packed and ready to go like any other soldier."

Rabidly anti-French (the French had expelled his family from their Alsace home in 1919), Leonhard also had a habit of contacting German officials working in the western hemisphere. One was Edgar von Spiegel, the German consul in New Orleans, a former submarine commander in World War I who by 1940 was suspected of pointing German submarines toward merchant ships in the Gulf of Mexico on their way to England. Another was Ernst Wendler, who succeeded von Spiegel. And another was Gerhard Wilhelm Kunze, then head of the German American Bund. Back in 1936, another was Adolf Hitler himself, to whom Leonhard had sent a letter.

Hitler never replied, but Leonhard told his fellow graduate students at Texas that he was waiting for materials "from German officials" for his thesis, which was to be called "Present Foreign Relations between the United States and Germany." He had, moreover, come to admire the Nazi regime's diplomatic and economic accomplishments. While on choral trips with his undergraduate Southwestern University choir, he addressed "young people" about Germany's virtues. He "traveled a considerable amount," a military investigator noted, and "always seemed to have funds. [He] spoke to young Germans' meetings in central and south Texas." He also name-dropped. He told how, as a nine-year-old in Nuremberg, before his parents emigrated to the United States, he'd seen Hitler, Goering, and right-wing General Erich Ludendorff at the Deutcherhof Hotel. "He was sometimes given the Nazi salute by young people and at one time exchanged the Nazi salute with the German consul before the student body at Southwestern University," the FBI reported.

Rep. Martin Dies, the chairman of the House Un-American Activities Committee, also took notice. He called Leonhard to testify as part of his committee's investigation of the German American Bund. He asked Leonhard, by then in the Army, why he had once signed a letter to the editor of the *Texas Herold* with "Heil Hitler." "Probably as a joke," Leonhard explained. "My interest in Hitler is more or less academic."

For such reasons, Leonhard was abruptly called to his commanding officer's desk one day in 1942 and ordered to South Dakota.[3]

It was happening elsewhere—staff Sgt. Menke Drewes, a German immigrant with a master's in mechanical engineering from Hanover University and a year at Oxford, was on assignment in Detroit at the Ever Ready Power Company. He was studying how to adapt diesel electrical power units for broader use by the U.S. Army and Navy and the Australian Army. A former National Guard soldier, he was naturalized in June 1936. Since being inducted in May 1941, he had the second-highest scores in his class in command and leadership. He had visited his parents in Germany in 1938. Upon turning 28, he declined an age-limit discharge from the U.S. Army. It "was my duty as an American citizen, due to the emergency existing, that I stay." In November 1942, out of touch with and not knowing if his parents back in Germany were still alive, he was suddenly recalled from Detroit and sent to South Dakota.[4]

Not least, the new immigrant Fritz Leuth was "at liberty under fifty dollars deportation bond, and was ordered into the Army," one fellow soldier said. "He refused to take the oath and was sent from the induction center to Ft. Jay military prison, then transferred to" South Dakota.[5]

All told, the United States government was shifting thousands of soldiers and civilians with German and Italian surnames not only from place to place but from freedom to some form of close control. Aside from the administration's uprooting of Japanese Americans from their homes and properties to internment camps in Wyoming, Colorado, Idaho, Utah, Arizona, California, and Arkansas, the FBI rounded up a total of 4,800 German, Japanese, and Italian alien residents in just the two weeks after December 7, 1941. Before that, on the day in 1939 that the German Army invaded Poland, Franklin Roosevelt created a Special War Problems Division within the State Department to identify, among others, still more resident aliens who he might someday exchange for Americans imprisoned in Asia and Europe. The State Department and Immigration and Naturalization Service began taking these aliens into custody soon after the outbreak of hostilities. Most were sent to an arid internment camp near the Mexican border at Crystal City, Texas. After a 15-minute "hearing," the alien resident and his or her family—many of the children and spouses were American-born—were moved into barracks-like buildings. There, they awaited an uncertain future in Japan and Germany if they were, as the administration hoped, eventually exchanged for American hostages overseas. Thirty-one thousand two hundred and seventy-five resident aliens ended up behind 10-foot barbed wire fences at what many came to call the "kidnap camp" in Crystal City.[6]

The Army's "peculiar" plan specifically for Maple, Kissman, Hotelling, and the other soldiers had been hatched at the end of December 1942, years after many of them had enlisted. "Measures will shortly be instituted by this office," a War Department memo to the CIC read, "to remove SUBJECT [Maple from Fort Meade, Maryland]. Until removal, it is requested [that] observation and mail interception, if feasible, be maintained." It then began the "subsidiary investigation" to determine Maple's loyalty that centered on his sexuality.

The "subsidiary investigation" quickly determined that Maple qualified for the 620th, one of the Army's mysterious new "special organizations." There were least five of them, all reserved for men the Army suspected either might become or already were disloyal. To house the 620th, the War Department chose a small, remote, nearly abandoned, and easily monitored camp in South Dakota.

So, in March 1943, Maple found himself with Kissman, Siering, Leonhard, Drewes, Hotelling, and about 170 other suspected subversives at South Dakota's Camp Meade. All were shocked. "The outfits," Maple wrote from the Albuquerque jail, "are non-combatant outfits and . . . were used to garnish camouflage nets—work which we considered to be outside the province of a soldier."

It was worse than that. They were guilty by association. "These units are composed, as nearly as I have been able to ascertain, of persons who by reason of nationality are of questionable loyalty to the United States. I was shipped to such a 'Subversive Unit' without any charges having been placed against me[7]

"I'd be happy if I could be sure of saying where I am right now," Maple wrote his mother a little more than a week after being sent to South Dakota. It wasn't entirely horrible. "As you probably know, the Black Hills . . . are very beautiful, and we have a little village all to ourselves. It's hardly a part of the Army at all. And the food is the best I've ever seen in a mess hall." Of his new unit's members, he later noted that "some were university instructors, some were professional men, some were laborers. Some had been in the Army for nine years, some three months. Some had literally been taken off a troop train and sent here. There was one common denominator: all were under suspicion. None were available for combat duty. All were to be strictly watched."

Leonhard had arrived at the camp the day after Thanksgiving, 1942, and, "It took me just one hour to know to what kind of an outfit I had been assigned to." Almost everyone had a German or Italian accent. One resident in nearby Sturgis told him it was an "alien concentration camp." One of the first people Leonhard asked described the unit as "semi-honorable internment camp." It was boring as well. There was little for the men to do, so fort commanders invented menial work for them.

Maple soon shared the growing anger. In a letter to a former classmate at Fort Bragg, he called Meade a "shanghai camp" and the 620th a "shanghai unit." He "was very disgusted and hurt at the fact that he was 'shanghaied' to be with soldiers of questionable loyalty," his former classmate recalled. [8]

"If one is taken out of a line company where all your former comrades are that you trained with and learned to fight with," Menke Drewes explained, "then one does get disgusted."[9]

Kissman's bile first rose when he got his mail "glued together badly." There were the microphones in the barracks. On furlough in Chicago, "I was followed for about three days constantly, and my hotel room was entered . . . about noon the second day, upon arrival at the Palmer House, by a person professing to be the assistant manager and a person professing to be a rug inspector. My room was examined while I was there, and everything was looked at except the rug."

They followed him on a furlough home to Erie, Pa., too, although he wasn't aware of it. He returned to Meade to resume digging ditches, doing laundry, and carting coal and wood. Maple's duties included building a fireplace in the former officers' quarters, re-weaving helmet nets, finishing a new tennis court for the officers, and pulling weeds and transplanting trees when it warmed up. It was, Kissman said, "a terrific let-down to be put into an outfit where I was doing absolutely nothing for myself or my country. My country seeming not to trust me made me, even more, let down. Naturally, my spirit was somewhat broken."[10]

Their reputations were sullied, too. "It got known at home and caused my parents considerable embarrassment and caused me embarrassment when I went home because people could not understand why I was in the 620th unless I committed some serious crime," Leonhard said. "I was never charged with anything. I was never given an explanation. I was never told why I was in there; that I had done anything, or there was anything in my papers warranting distrust in the line of duty in the Army of the United States."

Maple, as was his habit, dressed the despair up. "'*Dole et décor est pro patria mori,*' the poet announced 1900 years ago, 'Sweet and proper it is to die for one's native land.' It is not, therefore, to be accepted with complacency when, on the *ipse dixit* of an unknown accuser, Americans, either native-born or naturalized, are deprived of this right."

His humiliation was universal. One sergeant "left no stone unturned to make things as rigid as possible," Leonhard said. "Certain members of the cadre of our company took great delight in shoving us around, barking at us, making us do menial work with a vengeance."

"Even worse," Hotelling confirmed, "was the brutal, provocative, and incompetent conduct of the persons placed in charge of [us]. For the most part, these men were misfits who were disqualified from any other sort of military duty for mental or moral reasons." The indignities were constant, including public dress-downs, random punishments for offenses like speaking in their native tongues, and, not least, occasional beatings. Even the pranks others played on them were mean and dangerous. On a field exercise, after a day of building a new campsite, the men settled in on a "very cold, late in December" night. While the men slept, an "officer went around and cut all the ropes . . . and [collapsed] the tents on the men sleeping in them, destroying much government property and endangering many lives.

Their despair deepened. "I had hoped . . . to free myself from all suspicion and be able to utilize the training I had received in ROTC. It was now evident that I had not been successful," Maple said. His name, thanks to his association with the 620th, "would become even more defiled." A lifetime of isolation and under-employment was ahead.[11]

They went through channels, searching for ways to get out. Kissman had his parents come from Pennsylvania to vouch for him and help get him transferred to a combat unit. Soon after they met, Maple and Leonhard discussed "possibly approaching people of influence on the outside to act for us." University instructor Leonhard thought maybe former neighbor Lyndon Johnson, then in his third term as a congressman, might help. He also suggested writing to "certain prominent columnists and ask[ing] them to help us to get relief." They'd try Westbrook Pegler and other doggedly anti-Roosevelt, often anti-Semitic writers.

When that didn't work, they turned to provoking their keepers. Forbidden to speak either German or Italian in camp, they thought to speak nothing but German or Italian. The expected overblown retaliation from their violent officers, they figured, would bring cleansing publicity to the unit's injustices.[12] That didn't work, either.

They considered simply leaving. "One of the men in the camp and I discussed the possibility of absenting ourselves from the 620th and reappearing on the battlefront in a front-line outfit," Maple recalled. He also "wrote to one of my close friends in Africa, asking him to try and persuade his company commander to requisition me."

But each idea failed or faded, and their desperation grew. Being assigned to an outfit like the 620th was bad enough, but the inability to get a better one was the final straw, Maple later told Jelly Bryce. He was now thoroughly alienated from both the Army and the country. "Since the offices of the United States showed by their actions that under no circumstances would they trust me, I did no longer feel I was justified in serving them loyally.

By then, Leonhard also "no longer felt I had any legal, moral or ethical obligations to the Army."

Their attention turned fully to helping Germany and if it would help the Reich, damaging America. "In this unit, I met many men who were as enthusiastic in their love of Germany as I," Maple explained. "We consequently began to organize our outfit and as many of the other outfits of similar nature as we could contact, with the view of sabotage and other subversive action . . . I may say that I had no intention of remaining in the United States after a cessation of hostilities," he told Bryce, "but only of going to Germany as rapidly as possible." His dusty plan to use his postwar influence for good was, like his Grad School plot, forgotten.[13]

Hotelling changed the spelling of his first name to a more Germanic "Erich" at Camp Meade. Maple adopted a slight German accent and cut his hair close on the sides in the style of German soldiers. He told everybody that his parents were German nationals and concocted a story about a trip to Germany.* He dropped tantalizing hints to his equally alienated new mates about his secret, dangerous relationship with Herbert Scholz, the Gestapo spy who had run the Boston consulate. His goal now, he said, was to befriend the 620 "radicals" like Leonhard and Hotelling.[14]

Some of the company's radicals already knew each other. Five of them had attended German American Bund rallies together at Camp Norland, New Jersey.† Hotelling had spent time in Yorkville, the Manhattan area that was home

---

* Maple had concocted stories about traveling to and living in Germany before. A teacher at San Diego High School recalled reading some of Maple's student writing "about a trip to Europe he had taken with his mother." The teacher, one Harry Jones, thought, "American Express ads [describing foreign lands] were better than his [essay]." The trip had never occurred. The teacher recalls being "rebuked for my lack of judgment when Maple was accepted at Harvard. Maple may have also told his ROTC mates a similar story. Henry D. Jay, who as ROTC commander kicked Maple out of Harvard's ROTC and went on to become a brigadier general during the war, years later opined that "I understand that his parents were divorced and that his mother had taken him to Germany and that he attended German schools under the 'Nazi' regime."[121]

† The five who knew each other from Bund rallies were Kurt F. Schoen, Robert G. Bischoff, Otto Idelberger Jr, Robert Roser, Wilhelm Poehlmann. Gerhard Spieler, who was then stationed at Camp Carson, Colorado, eventually joined them. The Bund and the Klan regularly held meetings at Camp Norland.

to the Bund, and where not a few brown-shirt marches regularly went down 86th Street. In the 1930s, a local Yorkville group tried to boycott local Jewish businesses. Hotelling was still a subscriber to the Bund's newspaper and on the mailing list of the German Library of Information in New York. Known to each other before the war or not, "the German boys in the company soon drew together," gathering for "regular German beer parties" where both politics and resentment were frequent topics, Leonhard wrote. Hotelling managed to join the "German boys." As such, they were one of the few functioning social groups in the camp. They did discuss defiance, although at the start, "The general consensus was that probably we could do little now but could bring the matter up after the war."

On a weekend in April 1943, nine of them headed off to the Old-Style Bar in Deadwood, some 15 miles from Meade. Maple had been in the 620th for less than a month but tagged along. The newcomer, no shrinking violet, readily dove into the thick of trading stories about abrupt transfers and resentments over their apparent banishment from the regular Army and any sort of military dignity. He mused about sterner retaliation, and the participants, perhaps a bit drunk, didn't disagree. They designated the outspoken, articulate newcomer as the leader of what they dramatically decided to call The Committee of Nine.

One of the Nine, Staff Sgt. Drewes found a more remote place for their meetings and soon became the group's organizing center. He arranged for them to spend weekends at Rim Rock Lodge 26 miles from camp in Spearfish Canyon in South Dakota. They'd rent the whole Lodge for $40 a month for all the weekends through the summer, plus $2 for every soldier beyond the agreed-upon number who visited. It was "purely a place to go over the week-end," Drewes swore. "It was less expensive than hanging around the bars in Deadwood," where most saloons had roulette wheels and available prostitutes. He got Arthur Luck, another member of the 620th, to put up the first $40. And the Lodge itself was perfect. It was done up in an apple-cheeked German theme that had to otherwise look provocative in 1943 America, with un-ironic posters bidding "Welcome to Germany" and heralding "Germany The Land of Music" and "Summer in Germany."[15]

Most of the soldiers who visited Rim Rock that summer came for fun. They typically arrived after duty on Saturday and returned to camp Sunday night. In the interim, they drank, fished, hiked, cooked, and sang German songs. Corporal John F. Schumacher remembered it as "a recreation group in the mountains" and visited twice. "Food and beverages were served. Then everybody was talking, singing, and just having a good time." T/5 Frank X. Hofmann went once, was charged $5 (well over the real $2 cost per "extra" soldier) and believed "the group running the lodge were doing so solely for their own entertainment plus what money they could pick up on the side by entertaining guests." He never went back.

But grousing and "political" talk were constant even among the merry-makers, and there were hints of weightier discussions going on elsewhere on the site. Someone asked Schumacher, for example, if he was interested in joining "a closer group to work out details which I would be informed on later on." But he wasn't interested and never learned what kind of "details" the group was discussing. At first, Maple would recall, "we were interested not in the military defeat of the United States, but rather in the termination of what we considered to be an unjustified and undesirable war and in the preservation of Germany."

Some of the proposed details were high-minded. "We should form an organization," Private Carl Chiaramida, one of the more moderate malcontents in the "closer group," said in one Rim Rock discussion. They could "keep it alive after the war is over without necessarily helping the Axis against America or America against the Axis, but in the post-war, promote better relations between the three countries, Germany, Italy, and America." But even that idea, made during a war, seemed risky to the Rim Rock outsiders he tried to recruit. Chiaramida, "told me they were trying to organize those people from different languages. I stopped him right there," Eugene Ricci, another of the Italian speakers assigned to the 620th, said. "I told him he had better stay away from those boys."

"Those boys'" whisperings, meanwhile, were escalating beyond improving international relations. "Many of the members were against the New Deal and expressed a desire to see a better government in the United States. Many of them were sympathetic with the German government," Arthur Luck would recall. The question was: how to create "a German type of government" in the United States? "One way is by educating the people. Another method was by force. Those are the only two that I know of . . . I myself suggested the education of the people, but as for force, I don't know who suggested that out there.[16]

It required further discussion, of course. As conspirators seem wont to do, they reorganized their committee again. Among a marginally bigger group of planners, Leonhard, Maple, Luck, and Hotelling—according to some, Kissman and Drewes participated—formed a smaller and more "reliable" group of men. They'd be "intelligent" and "reliable" enough to plan and carry out more concrete havoc. The planners alternatively dubbed themselves "The Inner Circle" or "Executive Committee."

Even Chiaramida, the moderate, urged the group to quit talking and be "more active." Hotelling had an idea: they should contact similarly alienated men at the Army's other "special organization" camps. Maybe, he said, they could organize simultaneous, newsworthy protests at other camps. Maple's thinking also was evolving. Since no one was going to let them out of the 620th anyway and since the whole enterprise of opposing what Maple considered the planet's only effective government was a tragic historical mistake, maybe they should aim higher. Why not, Maple began to think, try to "disrupt the internal economics and morale of the country to such an extent that further participation in the war would be impossible." Hotelling signed on. And the other camps wouldn't just protest; they'd mutiny. He volunteered to contact men in the other special organizations to execute a "plan of armed uprising" and coalesce into what was now going to be a "guerilla army operating on United States soil."[17]

The military was listening in at Rim Rock. In a November 4, 1943 report called "Subversive Meetings, Rim Rock Lodge, Spearfish Canyon, S. Dak," the Counter-Intelligence Corps (CIC) reported that Maple now favored "organized sabotage." Leonhard "was principally concerned with getting discharged from the Army, attracting public attention to this 'special organization,' and detecting 'stool pigeons' in the company." He and Drewes regularly tested company newcomers to find out just how sympathetic they were to the German government and if they could be trusted. Drewes was particularly interested in "what my ideas were and things like that," one new arrival later told an investigator.[18]

The CIC picked up statements like "we should take over Fort Meade," "blow up the country," and "let's go back to Germany." Drewes noted they'd need a short-wave radio to contact Germany for support. Arthur Luck, who later swore to investigators that he favored revolution by education, was heard "want[ing] to change the United States Government by force." They'd use weapons, another [unnamed] conspirator said, "furnished by [sympathetic] officers at Fort Meade." Or they'd storm the armory.

Drewes later described the plans as "jocular;" the remarks were made "only jokingly." They were the kind of complaints and boasts, he swore to the investigators who later interrogated him, that every soldier made when things didn't go as planned, which in the Army, he explained, was most of the time.[19]

CHAPTER 9

MUTINY

It may be that Menke Drewes didn't take the talk seriously. He happened to be in a particularly good mood that summer, falling in love with the organist and musical director of a traveling theater troupe playing nearby. But others of the Rim Rock conspirators that summer truly yearned for action.

Itching for action or perhaps just drunk, Maple and another (unnamed) soldier stole an auto on July 15th from in front of a hotel in Deadwood. They drove it to Boulder Canyon, where, somehow, they wrecked it. The sheriff initially charged Maple with grand larceny, but after some unknown intervention from the civilian "transient" who owned the car, a judge reduced it to "tampering with an automobile without the owner's consent." Maple paid $50 (about $700 at this writing) to repair the car damage, plus court costs and was sentenced to 30 days in jail. Behind bars, he relied on time-honored ways of hiding misdeeds from one's parents. "Sorry that I haven't written for so long now," he sweetly wrote his mother a few days before his release date of August 14th, 1943, "but I seem always to be busy even when I'm doing nothing." [1]

There'd been a disappointment while Maple was behind bars. The Inner Circle either had asked Arthur Luck or Luck had volunteered to see if he could find someone to finance its increasingly ambitious plans. Luck, from Detroit, had led the men of Rim Rock Lodge to believe he knew Charles Lindbergh, Henry Ford, and Father Charles Coughlin, the popular anti-Semitic radio priest who led The Christian Front. Luck promised to contact them during his upcoming furlough to visit family in Michigan. He'd ask how they "felt about the present government, and if they were in discord with it to what means they would go to change the present political party."

But he didn't. Upon returning to South Dakota, he explained that those people probably already knew all the pro-Axis groups in the land, and "I felt rather foolish even to mention anything to these men." He didn't know them anyway, he confessed. He'd met Coughlin, "although . . . he would probably not remember me. I have been next to Henry Ford many times. But he does not know me. As for Charles Lindbergh, I don't remember ever seeing him."[2]

Maple, meanwhile, had developed contingency plans. One fallback was to escape "this persecution by seeking refuge in South America." Just desert. Don't come back. Better yet, they'd all desert. A big, public mass escape of U.S. soldiers would expose the Army's shanghai units and cause massive embarrassment. Hotelling recalled that, by September 1943, Maple's "idea was to go with several members of the 620th as a protest against conditions in the camp."

Once out, his first step was to depose Drewes, the leader of the Rim Rock retreats. Drewes had sinned. He had let an officer at Meade know about their weekends, potentially (and in actuality, as it turned out) jeopardizing their secrecy. In Maple's mind, it made Drewes too "inefficient" to lead them any longer. He called a "political" meeting of his own in a Sturgis bar and, reminiscent of Hitler's famous 1923 meeting in a Munich beer hall, offered his vision. There was no limit to what the companies like the 620th scattered around the country could accomplish if they all acted under one "high command," much like the German Army's. If he ran it, he'd start the mayhem with simultaneous bombings throughout the country. He soon bought a Rand McNally map of the western United States and carefully marked the spots he'd destroy.

His Drewes coup complete, he insisted they change their name back to The Committee of Nine, which had been dropped when the love tossed Drewes had moved the activities up to the Rim Rock Lodge. There was no room for drinking or singing this time. Maple, Leonhard, and Pvt. Hugo Opton rented an apartment in Deadwood for their subsequent Committee meetings. Opton made it up there one October day, aiming to clean the apartment but finding two "large maps of the coast of Mexico." They were "detailed." They showed coastal currents and depths. Next to them was a roster of more than 600 soldiers' names. There were checkmarks next to forty of the names. The checked ones, Leonhard told Opton back at Camp Meade, were "fellows in the outfit that they considered trustworthy for any occasion that they might have reason to call on them." [3]

Months later—in November—21-year-old Eric Hotelling was on furlough in bucolic Mountain Lakes, New Jersey. At the time, the New York suburb, set around man-made lakes, placidly abided by a rarely spoken agreement to keep

Jews, Black people, Latinos, and Catholics from buying its real estate. It was also home to Hotelling's father, his stepmother, his sister, and his half-siblings. He got home anxious to show them that the family's black sheep should be taken seriously. He had reason to feel good. Mobilizing his Army was moving slowly, but it was actually moving. The Inner Circle's plans were evolving nicely, and if he did say so himself, were pretty innovative.

Hotelling's father was an outlier among Mountain Lakes' prejudices. He was an internationally known Economics professor at Columbia, head of the Roosevelt Administration's war-related Statistical Research Group, author of oft-cited academic works on advanced mathematics and game theory and, not least, one of the first to apply statistics to the study of national economies. (Nobel Prize-winning economist Milton Friedman was said to be an admirer). Both he and his second wife Susan were famously liberal mainstays and classic academics. Each month, they held salons in Mountain Lakes for the professor's academic colleagues, "refugees from Europe and students from India." Two admiring scientists later eulogized the professor as having "none of the prejudices then still common" and possessing "human and liberty-loving sympathies [that] made him a bitter opponent of Hitler and an early advocate of intervention in World War II."[4]

Harold Hotelling had long thought Eric—who he had named after his storied mentor, the numbers theory originator and science fiction writer Eric Temple Bell—somewhat troubled. The boy was smart enough. He was energetic, did some community theater, and grew up the oldest in a house with a sister and the three children his father and stepmother had. (Hotelling's mother, Floy, had died when he was nine. Harold and Susan Hotelling, a former statistics student at Columbia, married two years later). But Eric had had a rocky time as an undergraduate at Columbia. First, there were the incidents at his dorm: tacking swastikas and a picture of Hitler on his wall next to a map showing areas of London the Luftwaffe had bombed; blaring the *Horst-Wessel-Lied*, the Nazi anthem, on his phonograph each night. His references to the Reich were constant, and he was not above insulting fellow students who disagreed with him. His dorm hall supervisor recalled his classmates "believed him 'a little crazy.'"

For a while, the Hotellings wrote off Eric's behavior at Columbia, his attending Nazi rallies and his rejoicing in German military victories as some sort of youthful rebellion. But tensions rose in the dorm, where his hall-mates "were inclined to be amused up to Pearl Harbor, at which time he would have been in danger if he had not ceased to occupy his room." He dropped out of school and, as it happened, came up with the same solution to a darkened reputation that Maple had concocted up in Massachusetts: he enlisted. He first joined the National Guard and, when that didn't work out, the Army. On April 23rd—barely two weeks after Eric enlisted—the Bureau's New York office had gotten a call about young Hotelling's "un-American" and "vociferous" support of Nazi doctrine. The call had come from "someone from Mountain Lakes," home to Professor and Mrs. Harold Hotelling.[5]

More red flags: On April 30th, 1942, a week after the call from New Jersey, Eric was handcuffed on a New York street, arrested for disorderly conduct. Still a wisp of a figure—6'1", 151 pounds, pale blonde hair and mustache, blue eyes—one report called it "annoying female pedestrians; touching them on outside of various parts of their bodies." Another called it "molesting a young woman." He served 30 days at Rikers Island. Both father and stepmother took the news hard. Concerns about him spread. In July, Columbia Dean Nicholas M. McKnight, surprised to learn that the troublesome dropout Hotelling was in the armed forces and carrying a gun, also asked the FBI to investigate the former student who "had given evidence of very strong Nazi tendencies." In October 1942, yet another Columbia administrator wrote the Bureau, suggesting it contact another Columbia dean, who had more information.

A year later, by fall, 1943, the Hotellings' youthful rebellion theory about their son momentarily looked good. Eric's latest letters home had been without their characteristic politics.

———

Their optimism was short-lived. On November 19th, 1943, Susan Hotelling called the FBI again. Eric, she whispered to an agent at the Newark FBI office, was home on furlough from some godforsaken post full of fascist sympathizers in South Dakota. He had arrived more boastful and adamant than ever. She was concerned. Earlier that day, he had confided that he and some confederates were planning something big. He boasted they were "in constant communication" with Nazi sympathizers based in Yorkville as well as other Army camps. They didn't do it through the mail or by telephone, Eric noted. They were too smart for that. They knew they were being watched. Instead, they communicated through relatives and "personal visits." It was one of the reasons he came home on his furlough. He was "scheduled to meet and deliver a message to an unknown person believed to reside somewhere on East 83rd Street, New York City" at 9 A.M. on Tuesday, November 23rd, 1943.[6]

She feared the worst and needed help. If someone from the FBI would call her the night before the meeting, she could relay details about what train Eric was taking to the rendezvous so that agents could follow him. In the meantime, they should interview Professor Hotelling and three of his Columbia colleagues for more.

Separately, the elder Hotelling pulled no punches. Eric was pro-Nazi. The agent found that "he considered his son to be subversive." Professor Hotelling blamed Eric's conversion on a former German tutor, and he was deeply embarrassed. As for the boy's plans, he knew little. At 8:22 P.M. the night before Eric's assignation, a Newark field agent called Mrs. Hotelling for the information. "She talked rather evasive as though her son were there. Suggested he call Professor Hotelling at the home of Mrs. Charles Norman Shephard in New York City." The professor, also "talking evasively," had the name of a doctor Eric might be going to contact and an address: 1026 Second Ave.

Eric left the Hotelling house at 7:20 A.M. on November 23rd, bound first for his meeting and, his furlough almost over, then back to his co-conspirators at Camp Meade in South Dakota. An FBI agent from the Newark office followed him to the railroad station, where the private checked two blue duffel bags and a suitcase through to Rapid City, Iowa, before boarding the train to Hoboken and then Manhattan. He was, the agent noted, carrying one brown overnight bag and a parcel covered with brown paper. The agent ran across two Military Intelligence men following Eric Hotelling that morning, too. Together they watched him enter 1026 Second Avenue. He emerged without the parcel. While the Military Intelligence officers followed Hotelling onto his train west, the FBI agent left to find out just who lived in the dwelling on Second Avenue[7]

And a week later, in early December 1943, soon after Hotelling got back to South Dakota and the War Department got its disturbing report about the treasonous talk at the meetings at the Rim Rock, the whole company was told to pack. They were being transferred to Camp Hale.

It was then that, with the fresh subversion report in hand, 1st Lt. Leroy Wilson the 620th's new commanding officer, warned the men about their new, tougher day. Their labor would be harder, and the rules enforced. Cars, off-site living, and speaking in their native tongues were all forbidden. And they'd wear blue work uniforms, different from all the other soldiers at camp except the singing, marching, robust German prisoners of war.

The new humiliations hardly banked the men's resentments and having actual and unbowed German soldiers living two barracks buildings away emboldened at least some of them still closer to action. The California-born Maple was as smitten as the German-born 620ers. "The effect of these fellow-countrymen [the Germans] was enormous," he told Bryce. They cemented the unit's radicals' identity as American enemies. "And why should it not have? We were dressed in the same blue fatigues as the prisoners and in a great many instances on the same details." Maple, with some exaggeration, claimed that by then, "approximately every man in the 620th Engineers entertained definite pro-Nazi ideas and possessed the same desire . . . to the sabotage of the war effort, and if possible, were anxious to engage in espionage activities on behalf of Germany."[8]

Hotelling hit the road, recruiting in Denver and Colorado Springs. At Hale, defiance of Wilson's new rules became epidemic. Against orders, the conspirators talked with the prisoners, exchanged notes with them, and brought gifts and cigarettes to them. The latrine became a favored place for the prisoners and U.S. soldiers to trade with each other. The American soldiers began to think still bigger. Wilhelm Poehlmann of the 620th asked to borrow Siering's car (parked off-site in nearby Red Cliff with Siering's wife) to use to go "on a vacation trip" with a prisoner named Waldman. Siering said "no," but it gave Leonhard an idea for a special New Year's celebration.

On New Year's Eve, 1943, prisoner Erhard Schwichtenberg walked unmolested past the guard at the stockade's gate and, following Leonhard's instructions, went down to a spot by U.S. 24. As promised, a car soon showed up. The driver was Fritz Siering, who had the prisoner get in and drove them both to Red Cliff to pick up Siering's wife. They then went off to celebrate the holiday in the nearby towns of Minturn and Eagle. In Eagle Schwichtenberg, wearing an American private's blouse and overcoat that Leonhard had loaned him, checked in as "Fred Ball" at the Montgomery Hotel that night. In the morning, the Sierings, with prisoner in tow, went to take in a movie in Glenwood Springs before heading back to Eagle to meet Leonhard in the evening. The next day they visited the towns of Rifle and Glenwood, where, driving through a residential area of the town, Siering asked Schwichtenberg, "now do you believe we can live better here?" They finally wound back to Camp Hale at about 10 P.M. on January 2nd. Schwichtenberg, weary, spent the night in Siering's car in Red Cliff. In the morning, he changed from his borrowed U.S. uniform and calmly walked into camp to rejoin his work unit.[9]

Schwichtenberg's New Year's holiday quickly became a legend among the men, many of whom were fixated on a new outrage: The Army had heaped more abuse on the unfortunate Fritz Leuth. Leuth—in various records, his name also was spelled Leuck and Loock—was a defecting German seaman who had been interned on Ellis Island with his wife. Uncertain with English, he signed a paper that he initially thought was an application for United States citizenship. It turned out to be an induction paper, on which he'd thought to cross out the word "not" in the sentence, "I do not object to service in the Armed Forces of the United States." Confused, he abruptly found himself swearing a half-understood oath of allegiance to the U.S. Army before his wife set him straight. He objected but agreed to serve if it was within the United States and only if the Army released his wife from internment on Ellis Island. The Army, nodding in agreement, shipped Leuth to the 620th and transferred his wife from New York, not to freedom, but the internment camp at Crystal City, Texas.

Stuck in Colorado, Leuth felt betrayed. He insisted on being discharged and sent to Crystal City to be with his wife, but Wilson shrugged his demand off.

Then, during one of the unit's first weeks at Camp Hale in December 1943, Maple pulled him aside with some questionable advice. Leuth, he suggested, should get himself arrested and get a trial. A trial would be the best path to being freed and reunited with his wife. All would be well; Maple himself would be his lawyer.

Thus assured, the desperate new recruit refused to leave his bunk. He declined to leave the barracks, to go to work, or participate in any way with the unit until the Army met his demands. And then, as best as his mates could tell, he "disappeared."

———

The Army, in fact, had spirited him to Denver for a court-martial, charged with refusing to obey a direct order. After finding out about it, Maple, Leuth's putative attorney, marched to Lt. Wilson's office to request a furlough to Denver to fulfill his legal obligations. Wilson was not amused. Maple, who had what was considered one of Hale's better work assignments—as an electrician—was suddenly transferred to the sawmill, one of the worst. Maple had "every reason to believe it was a form of punishment for my interest and activity in the . . . case.[10]

Now outraged, Maple resolved to go to Denver to represent Leuth anyway. He also thought of a way to make his pet plan—the mass desertion of
620ers—even more embarrassing to the Army. "Wouldn't it be a sensational
thing if some of the prisoners were to escape from here while the company
was stationed here?" he asked Leonhard. As January 1944 wore on, apparently
worried about "stool pigeons," he shared only incomplete scraps of his amended
plots—liberating Leuth and prisoners, setting up a pipeline to Germany—with
his Inner Circle. He'd have Siering and Kissman play key roles, for example,
though they never learned much about what he was planning.

Siering's role was to be a dupe, to lend him his car. With a second (and as-
yet un-recruited) group of deserters and escapees in another car, Maple would
drive it to Mexico. Leonhard, meanwhile, would get a furlough, meet Maple
and the Germans at the border. Either Leonhard or maybe Hotelling would
drive Siering's car back to Camp Hale. Since he couldn't figure out where to get
a second car, Maple eventually pared the caravan down to one.

"When we moved to Camp Hale, and we became associated with the PWs,"
Eric Hotelling recalled, "his idea [to desert with a mass of 620 members] un-
derwent a change." Maple's focus had shifted to maximizing the Army's embarrassment. "No one else in the 620th would agree to go with him or believe his
plan had any chance of success, so he decided to take several POWs with him.
His chief motive . . . was that the mere desertion of a few soldiers would pass
unnoticed by the public, where the concerted escape of American soldiers with
German PWs would cause a great scandal (which it actually did) and would
bring about an exposure of and an end to the odious 620th organizations."[11]

Leonhard agreed that including the prisoners would be get a lot of attention. At least it would at lead "somebody in the War Department to realize the
impossibility of placing the 620th as next-door neighbors to German prisoners." But it was also unrealistic, and he dismissed it as just more "big talk . . .
I pointed out the absurdity of such plans," he later wrote, and "Maple often
became peeved at me . . ."[12]

Both Maple and Hotelling dismissed the doubters and kept planning.
Maple wrote a shopping list of things Leonhard said he'd need to survive in
northern Mexico and requested another furlough to go to Denver to fill it.
Wilson denied the request. So, he asked Kissman and Pvt. Maurer, themselves
heading to Denver on a furlough with Hotelling and others, to shop for him.
When Kissman saw a gun on the shopping list, he figured Maple was about to
do something big, although he wasn't sure what it was.

Meanwhile, on January 29th, Maple began three days of visits to Camp Hale's POW compound, "visiting German prisoners and perfecting plans."[13]

Hotelling said Maple "approached four PWs whom he considered especially useful for his plan by means of knowledge of Spanish or Portuguese, contacts in South America, ability to speak English without an accent, drive a car, sail a boat, and otherwise assist in the plan." In retrospect, Hotelling contended Maple had changed his plans while visiting the stockade. The embarrassing mass desertion would proceed, but Hotelling believed Maple had decided not to go on to Germany. "His idea was to reach South America and then to settle down in a new country under assumed names and begin new lives. He did not plan to go to Germany or to help the PWs get there, so then we would in no way be aiding the enemy or impeding the American war effort. It cannot be too strongly emphasized that he harbored no hostile intentions toward this country," Hotelling, himself on thin legal ice, wrote carefully. "[A]nd his chief motive in thus sacrificing himself was his drive to end a very great and un-American injustice."[14]

Nevertheless, in an interview a few weeks later, Maple insisted he aimed to get to high-ranking Nazis abroad and then enlist the substantial German support he'd need to carry out his sabotage plans.

Hotelling's plans also were solidifying throughout January, expanding his enlistment targets to the German POWs at Hale and Camp Carson (and, next, Fort Leonard Wood in Missouri) in his mutiny. He planned to start firing in late spring 1944. He would "seize arms, free and arm the German prisoners of war, 'take over' Camp Hale by force of arms, and then take to the hills and wage guerilla warfare. The goal was to divert American troops from their regular war duties and create a 'shuttle system' to get the German POWs home." Fresh German ammunition would replace them. "Similar plans, but much more phantastic [sic] in their implications, were forwarded by Pvt. Hotelling," Leonhard marveled. "He conceived of an idea of being a second Marshal Tito and operate like Tito's Serb guerillas" who were then successfully harrying Axis occupiers in the Balkans. Hotelling's targets, however, would be American troops. "He talked with utter abandon of armies of thousands of men which would suddenly be formed and then begin operations.[15]

Hotelling made two recruiting trips to Denver—one with Kissman, who shopped for Maple's still-secret escape plan—and two to Camp Carson in

Colorado Springs. In his barracks at Camp Hale, he wrote up detailed notes about troop strengths at numerous Army installations. He had written out "a plan for six armies to assemble at various points in the United States and march to designated objectives." He had outlines and time frames for more recruiting and propaganda. The plan, an Army lawyer later reflected, "was rather complete in detail."[16]

PART THREE

NOOSE

CHAPTER 10

"THE BIGGEST CASE OF IT'S TIME"

Less than a week after Hotelling's second trip to Camp Carson, Special Agent D.A. Bryce was at the Albuquerque jail listening to Dale Maple describing the mutiny and rebellion plans. When Bryce asked him if others were involved, Maple dropped a bombshell. He named Hotelling, Leonhard, Kissman, and Siering. They weren't alone. There were, he said, 34 other members of the 620th involved in the putative uprising.

Bryce was shocked. This was more than a startling breakdown in military discipline and morale. It was more than the escape of two German POWs. It was a broad conspiracy that posed a grave threat to the war effort and national security.

He ordered Maple to stop again.

Bryce's case had just gotten crowded and thrown into a complex legal cul-de-sac. Suddenly everything—legally and, not least, publicly—needed to be re-thought. Bryce and District Attorney Houk's treason charges against Maple covered acts of war against the government and giving aid and comfort to an enemy. "Aid and comfort," in turn, specifically meant giving arms, troops, transportation, shelter, or classified information to the enemy. Maple had undoubtedly given the enemy transportation, shelter, and even the use of some guns. For all Bryce and Houk knew, there was classified information involved, and now it sounded like some U.S. troops were essentially enlisting in the German army. The penalties included a minimum of five years in prison and a fine for each count or, cumulatively, death. In the meantime, a treason trial like that would generate sensational, career-changing publicity for both Houk and the FBI.[1]

But with Maple pulling additional military men into the conspiracy, a struggle over who would get to try Maple and his Inner Circle loomed. The military would surely try to take over the case. Legally, the military's procedures and even definitions of "treason" were different for soldiers than for civilians. In the military, treason was aiding the enemy in the field, which was not where Maple and the others committed their subversive acts. And though the Army's punishments would be essentially the same as the ones a civil court might mete out—civil authorities tended to end such cases with electrocution, military authorities with hanging—the legal claims would come out of different sets of laws. If the Army won jurisdiction over the case, the governing codes would be the military's Articles of War. Aiding and "relieving" the enemy during a battle was covered by the military's Article of War 75. The articles that might apply to Private First-Class Maple's off-field escapades would probably be the 58th—which covered desertion—and the 81st, which covered "relieving, corresponding with or aiding the enemy." Just as important to New Mexican politicians and the FBI, such a case would be heard by uniformed officers in a closed court-martial far from the nation's press. The "excellent publicity" the FBI sought, in particular, would be muted, if reported at all. In 1944 the Bureau, moreover, was in something of a dry spell. Its last sensational publicity and budget-enhancing success in its domestic wartime counterintelligence was in 1942.*

The Bureau had lately had a hard time holding onto domestic spy cases, which had a dispiriting record of running into similar jurisdictional and judicial challenges. The military was regularly seizing the cases, credit, publicity, and gaining the reputation as the nation's leading domestic counterintelligence force.

The Bureau's troubles began even as it turned its attention from gangsters to espionage and sabotage again in 1936 when Secretary of State Cordell Hull asked it to start looking for foreign agents on U.S. soil. A 1939 directive from President Roosevelt explicitly added "subversives" to its jurisdiction, and in 1940—about the time Dale Maple, Eric Hotelling, and Theo Leonhard were forging their pro-German reputations at Harvard, Columbia, and Texas—the Smith Act outlawed advocating the violent overthrow of the government.

---

* Its record in Central and South America, however, was "a great piece of work," according to Adolf Berle of the State Department. It broke up a number of German spy rings and prevented a German group from taking over the government in Bolivia, which supplied one of the essential minerals the U.S. needed for steelmaking.

Though that law first aimed at supposedly revolutionary labor union members, it also got the FBI firmly into the treason and espionage business.[2]

Its first efforts under its refreshed responsibilities were an investigative comedy. In February 1938, British Intelligence tipped off the Army, which tipped off the State Department, which tipped off the New York Police Department that a naturalized American citizen named Guenther Rumrich was a spy. Rumrich, it seems, had been posing as no less a personage than Cordell Hull to get blank U.S. passports, which he then passed on to the 18 Nazi agents he managed in the United States. Unsure who should investigate after the New York police made the arrest, the War and State departments forced it on an unwilling FBI Director J. Edgar Hoover. Hoover thought (accurately, as it turned out) the case already compromised by jurisdictional confusion and lazy police work but dutifully assigned it to Special Agent Leon Turrou, who proceeded to compromise it further.

Turrou started with a lot of advantages. Rumrich had already confessed and named the 18 Nazi agents working with him and for the Abwehr (the German secret service). Turrou had their addresses.

He looked them up and proceeded to interview them. After each interview, however, he helpfully informed the spies that they'd soon have to talk to a grand jury. He then resigned from the Bureau and signed contracts with the *New York Post*, Warner Brothers, and Random House to write articles, a movie, and a book about his spy ring-busting exploits.* He gave lectures. He made radio appearances.

———

Turrou's revelations transfixed the nation. The press coverage was constant. The *New York Times* called the former agent's case "A Spy Thriller—in Real Life," complete with "clerks and soldiers, beautiful women, British Secret Service men, army and navy intelligence offices . . . G-men, State Department agents, newspaper reports, German seamen, Yorkville residents, etc." One historian said the publicity did nothing less than awaken many in isolationist North America to "Hitler's commitment to offensive action against the United States" and ignite "a Fifth Column scare."

Meanwhile, all but three of the spies and their higher-ranking managers, mindful of Turrou's post-interview warnings that they were soon to be subpoenaed, quickly fled the country. Turrou's investigative grandstanding was

---

* The movie, released in 1939, was "Confessions of a Nazi Spy." It starred Paul Lukas as the Rumrich-based villain and Edward G. Robinson as "the G-man who smashed to Nazi spy ring."

not only unprofessional but fatal to the legal case. Thanks to compromised evidence, the remaining spies drew seemingly modest sentences ranging from two to six years. The FBI was genuinely embarrassed. Turrou was retroactively fired, in part for being "motivated by profit and fame."

Thus, the mortified FBI began making itself into a skilled counterintelligence unit. It involved training agents in spy and sabotage investigative techniques, corroborative testimony, and the use of new technologies.[3]

But the Bureau's next big counterintelligence case—its spectacular 1940 break-up of a Christian Front terrorist attack in New York—ended with no convictions after the court determined the FBI had used evidence gathered from illegal wiretaps.

The new training, however, came in handy in 1941, when the FBI broke its most sensational domestic espionage case of the war. One agent called it "the most outstanding case in Bureau history." As of this writing, it remains the biggest espionage case in American history.

———

The Abwehr's record of industrial espionage in the United States dated back to 1927, six years before Hitler came to power. By 1937, four years after Hitler's rise, the Abwehr had more spies, all moving far more aggressively. In that year, they delivered the "most important military secret project under development" in the United States—plans for a new bomb-siting technology—to the Wehrmacht's chief of military intelligence.[4]

Spying apparently was not always hard during those years before "the Fifth Column Scare." Legend had it that the monocle-wearing Frederick (Fritz) Duquesne—the Nazi regime's reigning American "spymaster"—once called up Grumman Aircraft Engineering to request plans and photos of a new technology it was developing, saying he needed them for lectures. Grumman obligingly sent them to him, signed with "warm regards."[5]

The game had changed by 1939. New Yorker William G. Sebold, a naturalized American of German birth, was in Germany visiting his mother when the German government, aware that he used to work in an American aircraft factory, pulled him off the street. It threatened to kill him unless he spied for Nazi Germany when he got back to the States. Sebold, shaken, went directly to the U.S. Consulate in Cologne to alert the consul to the encounter and his dilemma. When he docked on February 8, 1940—not long before Maple disrupted his Harvard German Club—the FBI was there to meet him and enlist him as a double agent.

He proved to be a brave and effective one. His work eventually led to Duquesne, a network of 33 spies working on American soil, and a Long Island radio station devoted to sending coded ship movement information to Hamburg. Hamburg, in turn, used it to direct U-boats to their targets. On one busy day in June 1941, some 250 FBI agents fanned out to arrest the 33 agents, almost half of whom quickly pleaded guilty. Duquesne was convicted and sentenced to 16 years.* In all, the courts issued sentences that totaled more than 300 years. They included 12 years for one Lilly Stein, described by an FBI agent as "a good-looking nymphomaniac" who was exceedingly close to a U.S. diplomat, had once attempted to seduce Sebold, and was often seen in certain nightclubs prowling for men with industrial secrets. Upon being arrested in the June 28th raid, she allegedly attempted to bargain her way back to freedom by propositioning the arresting FBI agent.[6]

Otherwise, the Bureau's domestic counterintelligence work sometimes seemed cursed. About a year later, in 1942, the FBI did foil two groups of German saboteurs, but almost despite itself.

In the dark morning hours of June 13th, a 39-year-old naturalized American citizen named George John Dasch led a group of four terrorists off a U-boat and onto the south shore of Long Island. Six days later, another U-boat dropped eight more saboteurs, this time on shore at Ponte Vedra Beach, Florida. In a venture much like the one Maple was to plan, the two groups aimed to blow up hydroelectric plants, railroad switching facilities and bridges, water supply systems, Jewish-owned department stores, and, not least, railroad station locker rooms and restrooms. The goals were to cause maximum panic and an advantageous fear of Nazi power. They got onshore with the requisite munitions and, in total, some $171,000 in small bills to set up fake identities and pay their way to Cincinnati, where the two groups would meet on July 4th to blow up locks along the Ohio River.[7]

Their plot—called Operation Pastorius—began to fray almost immediately. Just after midnight on June 13th, a Coast Guardsman patrolling the beach near Amagansett, Long Island, saw four men struggling to beach a large rubber raft. He also saw what looked like the outline of a U-boat about 125 yards offshore. Asked what they were doing, one of the men said they were going into

---

* Upon conviction in 1941, Duquesne was sent to the Leavenworth Penitentiary but was transferred in 1945 to the U.S. Medical Center for Federal Prisoners in Springfield, Mo. due to "failing physical and mental health." He was released, again due to ill health, in 1954. Herman Lang, a member of Duquesne's ring, was sentenced to 18 years in prison, and was deported to Germany in 1950.

the night to fish. Another offered the Guardsman $260 to keep quiet. Another said something in German to one of his raft-mates. The unarmed Guardsman, figuring it was the safest thing to do, took the money and went directly back to report the strangers to the Coast Guard station two miles away. In daylight, a team returned to the beach, found munitions, insidious poison technologies (one in the shape of a pen and pencil set), and a German uniform in boxes buried in the sand. By the afternoon, they had let the FBI know.

The Coast Guard's alert initially confused Washington. For all anyone knew, more submarines were landing more saboteurs all along the East Coast. The saboteurs, moreover, could well be the advance parties of a full-scale invasion. Hoover and Attorney General Francis Biddle, his boss, could of course let the War Department know but would run the risk of massive troop movements igniting an ultimately damaging national invasion panic. They could also keep it quietly away from the War Department, fighting a war and emerging as something of a competitor in counterintelligence, and let the FBI investigate further. They chose the latter.

Meanwhile, John Dasch, the crew's leader, and Ernest Burger, a member of his team, were having an awkward talk. Hiding out in New York City the next evening, they admitted that they both "deplored the Gestapo." The dam broken, they agreed they "hated Hitler" and hoped the United States would win the war. Burger, for one, had been in a concentration camp for 17 months for criticizing the party. It was an incident hard to forgive. They both revealed they'd volunteered for the mission only to get out of Germany. Burger proposed that they quit the conspiracy, take the money, and try to melt into the American masses. Dasch refused, figuring life in the United States eventually would be easier if they turned themselves in and helped the FBI catch their fellow raft-mates and a second group about to land in Florida. They'd be patriots, heroes, and probably set up for life. Burger agreed and that night Dasch, excited, called the FBI's New York Office.

His name, he conspiratorially told the skeptical agent who picked up the phone, was "Pastorius." He told the agent he'd led a group of German saboteurs intent on wreaking havoc on the United States. They had poison-pen and pencil sets, dynamite disguised as lumps of coal, fuses, timing devices, sulfuric acid, money, and pre-selected targets.

The agent on the phone, still unaware of the Coast Guard's discovery of the prior morning, was in no mood for jokes. "Yesterday, Napoleon called," he said, and hung up.

Exasperated, Dasch left the next morning for FBI headquarters in Washington to tell and re-tell his fantastic story, for he was shuttled from office to dismissive office. He was about to be ushered out of the office of D.M. Ladd of the Bureau's Domestic Intelligence Division when, frustrated and desperate to be taken seriously, he grabbed the suitcase he'd brought. He popped it open and dumped $84,000 in German sabotage money onto Ladd's floor. It got Ladd's attention, and Dasch finally got in to see J. Edgar Hoover. Over the next eight days, Dasch provided names, locations, plans, secrets of the Nazis' sabotage school, U-boat capabilities, and, not least, the existence of a previously secret German submarine base. The FBI soon arrested all the saboteurs. One was in Chicago, where he had told his family everything and had used part of his sabotage money to propose to his pregnant girlfriend. [8]

Their arrests caused a brief sensation in the press. "FBI Captures 8 German Agents Landed by Subs," the *New York Daily News* reported on June 29th, 1942. At his press conference, Hoover stayed brilliantly coy in answering questions about how the Bureau broke the case. In giving no hint of how the FBI first nearly drove Dasch away and had the suspects handed to it, he gave the impression the Bureau had done sophisticated counter-espionage work. In his memoir, Attorney General Biddle recalled that "Mr. Hoover, as the United Press put it, declined to comment on whether or not FBI agents had infiltrated into not only the Gestapo but also the High Command, or whether he watched the saboteurs land." [9]

Biddle and the Roosevelt Administration were nervous. They feared that an open civil trial in federal court would expose Hoover's—and the Administration's—reluctance to let Dasch turn himself in. Secretary of War Henry Stimson and Attorney General Biddle scrambled for ways to conduct an open civil trial—a sentinel principle of American justice—while keeping the FBI's missteps under wraps. A relatively new voice in wartime affairs—Major General Myron C. Cramer, the Judge Advocate General and thus the Army's top lawyer, recently charged with overseeing all military justice proceedings—noted another problem. Cramer, who would play a pivotal role in Dale Maple's fate, noted open court rules of evidence would also make a sabotage conviction difficult. The best they could hope for was a conviction for a lesser charge of conspiracy, which would carry a maximum sentence of only three years. "The maximum permissible punishment [for sabotage]," he advised, "would be less than is desirable to impose."

His solution: move the trial to a military court. But Biddle's lawyers protested and correctly pointed out the case didn't legally fit a military court. Military courts exist to try members of the armed forces, and the would-be saboteurs were not formally members of even the German armed forces. Some of the saboteurs, moreover, were U.S. citizens.

Cramer and Biddle came up with another idea. Roosevelt would concoct a semi-secret "military commission." The defendants' legal standing could be fudged enough to allow a sabotage charge, and, under military law, their sentences could be harsher. On July 2nd, 1942, Roosevelt then appointed Cramer and Biddle as co-prosecutors in a secret military tribunal to try the eight German saboteurs.[10]

The tribunal began hearing testimony on July 8th, and on August 1st found all eight guilty of "attempting to commit sabotage, espionage and other hostile acts." Six of them were electrocuted in Washington a week later, on August 8th. Burger and Dasch—who expected to be treated as heroes—were also sentenced to death. Their punishments, however, were reduced; Burger's to life imprisonment, Dasch's to 30 years.

It was not until November 1945, after the war, that the full story would begin to leak out. Attorney General Tom Clark, who had replaced Biddle, gave the investigation story to *Newsweek*, and Hoover, who chalked up one of his first reasons to personally dislike Clark, grew nervous that the Bureau's questionable investigative prowess in the case would be exposed. He asked but didn't convince *Newsweek* to make changes in Clark's version before it was published. Desperate, Hoover then produced a press release casting the FBI in a heroic light while diminishing the importance of Dasch's voluntary surrender and the information Dasch gave.

He had it in the morning papers before *Newsweek* hit the newsstands. When the *New York Times* published its version of the *Newsweek* story, now old, it buried it on page 10. Hoover yanked more attention from *Newsweek's* FBI story in other ways. A few days later, *Life* magazine ran a time-lapse photo spread of D.A. Bryce manfully drawing on and plugging a silver dollar dropped from shoulder height.[11]

But now, in February 1944, Special Agent Bryce had another big, dramatic reputation-burnishing sabotage case. He knew cases like this one—an espionage trial perilously close to the jurisdictional bog between civil and military law—could suffer the publicity-snuffing fate of the Dasch trial. The FBI looked into more than 19,000 domestic espionage and sabotage cases during World War II, and in the overwhelming majority, found false leads and harvested little more than more information for its mountainous, ever-burgeoning files. This one had solid leads and plentiful evidence. But to harvest it, Bryce would have to find a way to keep it in civil court.

He called Edward Tamm at about 3 P.M. on Saturday, February 19th. He had news, and some of it was great. Dale Maple had "just typed out his own statement." Bryce had merely asked Maple for a brief story of his life up until his arrest in Mexico, and Maple unspooled a damning six-page, single-spaced tome, complete with dramatic explanations of each provocative move Maple had made since 1940. He had also implicated 30-some other soldiers. And it expanded beyond the Army, too. "The soldiers' relatives and families are utilized in their espionage and sabotage activities."

Maple, Bryce reported, was already arraigned, behind bars, held on a $100,000 bail, and destined for a grand jury the week of March 6th.

Tamm hung up to buck the news up the hierarchy. "Mr. Bryce," he told fellow FBI executive Ladd, "is of the opinion that this is the biggest case of its kind that we have handled."

But Tamm worried the Bureau could lose this one, too. "We probably won't have jurisdiction since Maple implicated 38 [sic] Army men, except for the part where the work was carried on through [civilians and] relatives."[12]

———

At midnight, hours after hearing the FBI had captured Maple "a guy with a tommy gun kicked in the door" of the 620th's barracks at Camp Hale. Armed M.P.s poured in behind him and hustled 14 men, including Leonhard, Otto Idelberger Jr., and Hotelling, away. They took Leonhard to the guardhouse and handcuffed his right wrist to his left ankle. At dawn, they moved him and Kissman to the Lake County Jail in nearby Leadville in case violent mates in the 620th would try to free them.

Later in the day, Bryce got a call from Major Ross of Military Intelligence at Camp Hale. Ross had interviewed Leonhard, "who is allegedly first assistant to Maple." Leonhard hadn't said much yet, just described the epidemic disaffection within the 620th. He did volunteer that he'd heard some "ridiculous" talk among the men about a revolution. None of it led anywhere yet. Ross was "curious as to what Maple was talking about" in Albuquerque.

With that, Bryce knew the Army was moving in on the case, and the jurisdictional fight began. He dissembled. The sensational revelations he'd just described to his superiors went unmentioned. Maple, Bryce said, had been "just giving his background up until the time he entered Harvard."

Sooner or later, of course, the military was going to find out what Bryce already knew: that this looked like a full-blown conspiracy to commit treason, mutiny, and sabotage. Legally, soldiers who committed a crime within the U.S. were subject to punishment by either civilian or military courts. In practice, however, over-stretched civilian authorities often just ceded the cases to the Armed Forces. Bryce wasn't about to cede the Bureau's biggest, splashiest intelligence case in two years.

Tamm, his superior, agreed. He conceded to Hoover that investigating 38 soldiers "fundamentally" belonged to the Army. The FBI, however, could still play a role., "[Maple's] statement that their activities are carried on through relatives, etc. establishes a certain amount of civilian participation, which gives us some interest and at least joint operation."[13]

Hoover, Ladd, and Tamm prepared to settle for a "joint operation," shared with the military, if they had to. It might not be public, but Roosevelt would know about it, and that could help in other ways. Since early 1942, Director Hoover had been fighting one of his ongoing turf battles with the military and other federal agencies over espionage and sabotage cases.

His main jurisdictional adversary of 1944 was William "Wild Bill" Donovan, head of the Office of Strategic Services (OSS). (The OSS would, after some detours, evolve into the Central Intelligence Agency after the war).

———

To Hoover, the stakes were which agency—and which director—would oversee all U.S. intelligence efforts. Roosevelt created the OSS initially to stop the constant hissing and clawing between Hoover and General Sherman Miles, head of Army Intelligence, over the same prize.

The president was "exasperated by the intransigence and narrow-minded bickering of Miles and Hoover, [and] decided that an integrated strategic intelligence was long overdue," one historian of the era later wrote. In 1940, he had tried to split the responsibilities up geographically. The FBI got the western hemisphere, while the OSS would do the spying in the theaters of war. The Army's Military Intelligence Division (MID) and the Office of Naval Intelligence (ONI) would cover everywhere and everyone else.

The bureaucratic peace did not hold for long. In 1943, Military Intelligence's Baltimore unit, for example, unilaterally expanded its mission beyond foreigners' espionage to "foresee, report and, if possible, prevent" sedition and "racial unrest." In Boston, MID had an informant nested in the NAACP. From Governor's Island in New York, it undertook investigating "Communists, African Americans, pacifists, and labor groups." In Atlanta, it tracked Black U.S. servicemen for a while. Looking for instigators of racial unrest—generally meaning Black, not white, protesters—it surveilled a Ba'hai reading room in Mississippi. In 1945, its agents were at a "Constitutionalist" meeting in Detroit to hear a resolution to deport all Jews within five years and to sterilize any who were still around in six.

Donovan quickly placed agents in FBI territory in Central and South America and, not least, the United States. He repeatedly pressured Roosevelt to give him the still-broader jurisdiction. Even on February 20th, as the captives waited cuffed wrist to ankle, Donovan was preparing to propose a super-agency to control all worldwide intelligence gathering, including the work of the FBI, the MID, and the ONI. Donovan, as the proposal's author, volunteered to head it.

The FBI, meanwhile, had infiltrated the OSS's territories and energetically set up ways to embarrass Donovan. Hoover's FBI, tipped off by its spies inside both the OSS and the Spanish legation, once arranged to interrupt an OSS burglary of the Spanish Embassy. It allowed Hoover to report the illegal break-in—and Donovan's jurisdictional violation—directly to the president. (Apparently unknown to the Roosevelt or Donovan, the FBI had previously done its own "bag jobs"—break-ins—at the Spanish embassy).

Hoover also did everything he could to block visas for Donovan's employees, shut out Donovan's supporters (including Britain's MI6) from American intelligence, and plant bills in Congress to circumscribe Donovan's scope of practice. Just a week before his agents were concocting ways to keep the 620th case—on February 12th—Hoover had delivered what he believed was a direct hit on Donovan. He called Harry Hopkins, FDR's close advisor, Attorney General Francis Biddle, and Adm. William Leahy, head of the Joint Chiefs of Staff, together. He helpfully pointed out that Donovan had committed a grievous diplomatic sin. Without telling anyone or any authority to do so, Donovan had unilaterally cut a porous, unapproved deal with the NKVD, the Soviet Union's secret police.[14]

Under it, the NKVD would open an office in Washington in exchange for an OSS office in Moscow. The two agencies would share information, although there was no requirement to use it exclusively against the Axis powers. And even before the idea—much less the agreement—got to Roosevelt's desk, Donovan was turning over "documents, special equipment, secret intelligence . . ." to the Soviets. He fed valuable material—including insights into the secret American initiative to build an atomic bomb—to what was already an elaborate Soviet espionage program operating in the United States and Mexico. "Few categories of intelligence or equipment were withheld." Hoover thought he had the keys to Donovan's final bureaucratic defeat.[15]

And then came the promise of sealing it with a significant publicity splash. And even if a less public joint prosecution would serve to impress only Roosevelt, Bryce's spectacular treason case—30-some men and their families and friends preparing to open a domestic front in the war—could well put Hoover over the top in his jurisdictional turf war with the OSS. What remained for a fantastic double victory was to secure a leading role in the Maple case.

His men acted accordingly. On February 18th, the same day Bryce heard about Eduard Mueller's capture in Mexico, he warned the FBI's Denver field office not to issue a press release. Bryce, Ladd noted in a memo to himself, "wanted to keep this matter quiet and work on the angle of treason involving the private, who they think may be identical with Eduard Mueller."

The next morning, Bryce told Ladd he intended to hold on to the prisoner, no matter what. His first task: keep Maple out of a military brig. "If he [Maple] were turned over to the Army, it might be difficult to secure his custody at a later date should it be decided to prosecute." Ladd agreed and "instructed him to retain custody of Maple pending the [subsequent] interview with him and the presentation of the facts to the United States Attorney."[16]

U.S. Attorney Houk also was fully invested in keeping what would be a politically compelling, high-profile treason case. Houk told Bryce that he was "willing to go to D.C." to keep it.[17]

On Sunday, February 20, Houk got a call from a H.B. White "of some Army unit at Omaha." White was, in reality, Lt. Col H.B. White, chief of the Intelligence Branch, Security & Intelligence Division of the 7th Service Command. He determined that both Maple and his statement were to be turned over to the Army right away. The Provost General, who oversaw investigations and incarcerations for the Army, would make it an order.

Houk stuck to the plan. He told White he was going to hold on to the prisoner. He did agree to send over the statement, although only a copy.[18]

A few minutes later, Tamm, the number three man at the FBI, called General Clayton Bissell, head of the military's G-2, to try to shoo the Army away. Maple, he assured the general, was something short of a real soldier and probably not subject to real Army jurisdiction. He told Bissell "that Maple is quite a colorful character; that we investigated him in 1940 when he was thrown out of the ROTC unit at Harvard because of his pro-Nazi sympathies; that he is an intellectual who tried to go back to Germany in 1941 before we got into the War." Maple, he added, was safely in custody in Albuquerque, "where he has unfolded a story of an espionage-sabotage ring . . . Maple alleges they have plans to blow up railroad bridges, sabotage communication centers, etc." Civilian targets, all. He might be insane. The FBI was still "unable to determine whether Maple is crazy or whether he is talking facts."

Bissell didn't bite. Whether or not he was making it all up, Maple and his confederates were sworn-in soldiers. They were the Army's to prosecute. "This is something which could probably be better pursued by the Army," he said and ordered Tamm to tell Bryce and Houk to back off.[19]

About 20 minutes later, at 6:05 pm. Bissell called Tamm back, livid. He'd just found out that someone had told newspapers about the treason charge—the civil version to be tried in a civilian court—as well as Maple's identity. It must have leaked the previous day, on Saturday, February 19th, because it was in all the Sunday papers. And it must have happened soon after Maple had finished typing and reading his statement to the FBI. Bissell, Tamm told Hoover, "wants no more publicity."[20]

Bryce, in turn, was grudgingly becoming resigned to at least sharing control over the case. He mildly groused that he had no confidence in the Intelligence officer up at Hale. "If he's in charge of the case, this is as far as it will ever go." But in fact, White and J. M. Curran of Military Intelligence at Omaha headquarters were already on their way to New Mexico to take Maple and the prisoners into custody.

"There's no use in wasting any time talking to Maple," Lt. Col. White advised Tamm. "The case is already made."[21] The military's jurisdiction over military personnel, Tamm finally advised Hoover was probably unassailable. The FBI was out.

U.S. District Attorney Howard Houk was not taking it well. "At the request of the Attorney General of the United States, I am compelled to release custody of Maple to General Clemmons of the Seventh Service Command," he told reporters. It was a shame. "Had I tried this individual, the death penalty would have been asked."[22]

The Army, in the persons of White and Curran, arrived in Albuquerque on February 23rd and agreed to let Bryce sit in on their initial interviews with Maple, Schwichtenberg, and Kikilius.

With Bryce doing the interviewing, Maple helpfully repeated his most inflammatory statements: about going to sabotage school in Hamburg and coming back as a saboteur; Leonhard and Sausman furnishing contacts for him in Germany; about the original plan for ten men and two cars to escape and pledging "to fight to the last man." Moreover, "I personally undertook the complete disruption of all railroad and motor transportation in the United States . . . Men would be located throughout the United States, and at a given signal at a specific time, all would be destroyed with explosives . . ."[23]

The two Army officers, now entirely in control, shipped Schwichtenberg and Kikilius off to another POW stockade at Camp Phillips, Kansas, the next day. And on the next day, February 25th, ten days after Maple and the Germans slipped out of Hale, the civilian treason complaint against Maple was officially dismissed "by direction of the Attorney General."

Maple followed his former passengers out of town the same day. With a military guard, he was transferred to the U.S. Disciplinary Barracks at Fort Leavenworth, Kansas. He arrived on the 27th with some clothes, a copy of the Albuquerque Tribune of February 21st, a pocketknife, a ring with a swastika on it, a "brown leather folder containing 4-photos of German soldiers," and some 3,440 francs. He would stay there until his court-martial. The military's charges were not yet filed, but they would undoubtedly be capital ones.

His co-conspirators—Leonhard, Kissman, Hotelling, Siering, and maybe even Opton, Nobis, Idelberger, and others—would follow him to Kansas in a few weeks for trials of their own. Frederick Maurer, who Kissman had asked to choose and hand over the money for the gun for Maple, had already agreed to become a witness against his former mates.[24]

D.A. "Jelly" Bryce headed back to his home office of El Paso for the moment, his case and a chance to add to the FBI legend seemingly flickering.[25]

CHAPTER 11

THE DESIGNED-TO-FAIL PLOT OF 1944

Maple's father was furious when he heard about it. He instructed the first reporter to show up at his San Diego home that the Germans surely had forced his son to drive them to Mexico. "A man will do strange things with a knife in his back." Or at his head. Dale had been radicalized. "The Army made a Nazi of my boy."[1]

The elder Maple was known as a tough, obstreperous, and sometimes angry man. He could hold a grudge. Years earlier, he had supposedly resolved a bitter fight with his brother by permanently changing his name from the original British "Mapel" to "Maple." His father was the city marshal in Colton, California, and one of his brothers, Ralph, was a Colton police officer "shot down in cold blood without warning" in the line of duty in 1916.* By the late 1940s, L.G. Maple "hated" J. Edgar Hoover, *Time* magazine, and columnist Walter Winchell. As a forceful leader "of some kind of structural iron company," L.G., Dale's priest in San Diego would recall, "is not exactly a sissy." His former wife—a Baptist herself—remembered him as bitterly anti-Catholic. After a couple of months to think about his son's predicament, he would narrow the blame for his son's actions to the Army's personnel office. "The person to blame for the entire unfortunate incident was the Army officer who had transferred Dale to a German prison campus when they knew his attitude toward the German people."[2]

Maple's mother suspected a different problem. Her boy's high school tutor once told her "that no one brain could stand what Dale was trying to cram

---

* The killer was a long-time Colton resident who'd begun drinking heavily after his wife's death, and had been on a 10-day binge when, apparently unprovoked, he shot L.G. Maple's brother.

into it." The tutor "was anxious" about the effect four years at Harvard without the moderating influence his mother would have on Dale. Keeping an eye on him was one reason that she moved from California to Rhode Island, 66 miles from Harvard. She saw her son almost every weekend for his first three years at Harvard. Indeed, Dale's troubles mounted as their paths diverged.

Mae Scoville (she had remarried in 1941) had no inkling of Dale's Nazi sympathies until the day at the beginning of his senior year when she picked up the paper to read that her son was something of a Nazi. "I immediately went off duty [she was working at a nursing home at the time] and went to Harvard to find out about it." She said she spent five days on campus interviewing people. In the end, "I was assured it was nothing but a campus squabble and that Dale was all right."[3]

His father was angry, his mother mystified, and, as military investigators surrounded him, Maple himself was worried. Something had gone wrong. He was supposed to tried in a civilian court. Being a military prisoner was not supposed to happen.

—————

So, in Kansas, he changed his tune.

The insurrection talks at Rim Rock Lodge, his secret meetings in Deadwood, his identifying sabotage targets and estimating the resources he'd need to attack them, his recruiting first of fellow 620ers and then of German POWs to desert with him, his desertion and surreptitious flight through the night, and his attempts to deceive Mexican and then U.S. customs officials were never meant to succeed. He told the Army men interrogating him that he was trying all along to get into a civil court.

Once in open court, he'd reveal that he had carefully designed everything to fail: the shopping trips to Denver and Salida; his stockade visits; memorizing the real Eduard Mueller's German life and family; storing packs in the camp dump; helping POWs escape. And when it all failed, he would dramatically reveal the motive behind it all at his big, sensational, widely publicized, civil trial.

His motive, he swore now, was only to expose the un-American activities of the Army and its brutal "special organizations" of misfit soldiers. He never intended to commit sabotage or conduct a guerilla war against the United States military. All he wanted was to let the public know about the cruel 620th, a patriotic goal.

"I saw in [helping the prisoners escape] the means of getting the desired public attention. If I placed myself in such a position that [if] a charge of treason were entered against me, the press, recalling all their former statements about me, would undoubtedly react violently. Then, while I controlled this limelight of publicity, I could turn it from myself to the 620 Engineers . . ."

America, he figured, would rise and demand the abolition of the 620th and the other "special organizations." Leonhard, Hotelling, Kissman, Siering, and all his co-conspirators still in uniform would be freed. He, too, would be free to "continue to serve my country. I have so great confidence in the ultimate judgment and justice of the American people that I was willing to take the risk." He had figured there were two keys to the plan. First, he must look like a traitor again. "Second, the escape must obviously not succeed too well."[4]

Which, he told his interrogators, is why he had tried hard to get caught. He reviewed the evidence: He had used the Camp Hale telephone, probably tapped, as much as possible. He used it, moreover, to contact his parents to wire him money to buy the Reo and get supplies. When he got the money, he showed the receipt to Wilson, his commanding officer. Seeing it, Wilson should have known some sort of trouble was on the horizon. He told "everyone" he was going to buy a car, hoping it would get back to Wilson. He used the camp telephone again to call car dealers. He even took a witness from the unit, the loquacious Kissman, when he went to buy it. He used his own name when he finally purchased the Reo in Salida. "I was certain that [after all these calls] I would be subjected to even closer observation."

On February 15th, escape day, he let himself be seen carrying off one of the prisoner's packs and picked a time in broad daylight to meet the Germans. "I was certain that, if I should reach Salida, I would be apprehended. I did not expect, however, to reach even Salida." Before leaving Hale, he drove the car, "which was well loaded and which had a cardboard packing carton tied to the trunk rack, down to the intersection by the M.P. gate, made a U-turn and then another" as one of the prisoners came down an embankment. His description of the morning didn't align with Schwichtenberg's or Kikilius's, but Maple maintained that, even with the enemies on board, "I approached the M.P. gate once more and passed it. The man on duty eyed us curiously but made no attempt to stop us."

They'd surely get him in Salida when he picked up the license. But, again, no MPs there. "I had no choice but to go further. If my plan were to succeed, it was necessary that the escape appear genuine." Going straight to the police, he figured, would not have generated enough publicity to suit his purposes. So, he kept going.

When they had tire trouble in Deming, he claimed he tried to attract attention by driving on the rim for a while. "If nothing else . . . the rattle of the steel rim on the concrete would, I thought," draw attention. "The police of Deming were, unfortunately, un-obligingly unobservant. No one noticed our noisy presence."

When the Reo's engine gave out, leaving the fugitives stuck on the road, "I saw a large car coming down the road. I stopped it, hoping it would contain border officials." His wish came true, but they, too, were too blind to arrest them. He tried walking with the prisoners "in daylight straight into" Columbus on their way to the border, but Authority presented "nothing to prevent our crossing."

And when finally apprehended in Mexico, "I offered no resistance." He did not, however, immediately confess. "It was imperative that I avoid a premature disclosure of my intentions, lest they be thwarted by the imposition of an official censorship."[5]

His next idea was to give Bryce and the FBI a wildly exaggerated version of his Nazi sympathies. When civilian jurors examined it in open court, they would have surely understood his flight was "a final, spectacular press-gaining attempt. If I had been tried in civilian court, as I expected to at that time, the trial would have been open."[6] His message would finally get to the right ears, and all the 620ers would be freed to serve their nation.

Elsewhere at the Disciplinary Barracks, Eric Bell Hotelling was also changing his story. Like Maple, Hotelling had "an exceptionally high I.Q." and a checkered past. Moreover, investigators' doubts about him had deepened since his arrest. In their interviews with witnesses and Hotelling's comrades, they got a fuller idea of his bellicose visions.

In his bunk, investigators found plans for armed conflict dating at least back to September 1943. He had collected estimates of troop strengths at other Army camps, maps, written battle plans, kept records of his recruiting forays, and, among other pieces of evidence, had a patch of Navy code he'd been trying to decipher. He kept adding to the stash and revising it after the 620th's transfer to Camp Hale in December. It was there that he got the idea to recruit battle-hardened German soldiers into his guerilla force.

On his recruiting trips, he assured the soldiers at Camp Carson that German prisoners would fight by their side. He told them he already had the uniforms and furlough papers they'd need. Army investigators had learned of his detailed plans for deploying the armies he was recruiting. He had a protocol that the disaffected soldiers at Carson could use to get closer contact with and to sign up more POWs. Together, they would continue a "violent revolution" even after the war and get the U.S. a stronger government.

Some, like his Columbia dorm-mates before Pearl Harbor, maintained they'd always thought him a nut. "How is Hotelling?" a Camp Carson soldier once asked Pvt. Otto Idelberger Jr. after one of Hotelling's Denver recruiting trips. "Just as crazy as ever?" By the time Maple was caught and his suspected conspirators were rounded up, Idelberger, a former member of the Bund whose talk at Rim Rock and Sturgis had been as threatening as Hotelling's, decided he thought him loopy, too. "Well, personally," he told Military Intelligence (MI), "I think [Hotelling] is a crackpot, a grown child."

Camp Hale mate Wilhelm Poehlmann, who had given Leonhard the idea for the New Year's excursion with Schwichtenberg, concurred. He is "scholastically brilliant," he conceded to MI during his interview. "He seemed to be well-read . . . He recited some rather difficult English ballads. However . . . I believe he is suffering from delusions of grandeur." [7]

But on the Ides of March 1944, about a month after Maple deserted, Hotelling disavowed everything. He swore that Maple's accusations that he was part of some "inner circle" were untrue. Other than listen to Maple's apparently idle talk about deserting, he had nothing to do with any escape.

He did confess that he sympathized with "the geographic and ethnic views of the German government, but denied he is pro-German." Asked about arming the POWs, his plans to have the "special organizations" take over military camps and have six armies meet to wage "guerilla warfare" from the Colorado mountains in the Spring of 1944, Hotelling said it was a misunderstanding. "Hotelling," his interrogator's notes say, "denies any intention to start a mutiny and claims that he was merely making preparations for a 'defensive organization' to protect the Pro-German members of his Company in the event of mob violence or a Communist-inspired revolution in the United States . . . Subject Hotelling admits that he failed to inform any of his listeners that his plan was defensive in nature[8]

—•—

They started questioning Kissman about 20 miles away from Hale in the jail at Leadville, Colorado. There and in Kansas, Kissman maintained that he opposed Maple's plan all along and had always been on the Army's side. He reminded his interrogators that it was his tip about Mexico that led to Maple's capture. "His capture was made possible by information I volunteered, and my testimony will condemn him . . . Yes, I knew about his leaving and protested violently to no avail."

He knew, too, that he would "also be condemned because of my beforehand knowledge and my delaying the volunteering of such information." But he had reckoned the Army would crack down even harder on the 620th if Maple got away. "That so many should suffer for one man's stupidity is regrettable beyond words, and I believe I could save so much suffering [for the men of the 620th] and still be responsible for Maple's arrest." He understood his delay in reporting Maple's desertion might now bring him the death penalty, but there were other, heavenly, awards awaiting the righteous. "I accept only the Almighty's judgment, and however I am punished by man, a greater judgment awaits me far beyond the reach of any mortal. He (God Almighty) do I fear, and He alone."[9]

———

The thoroughly disgusted Leonhard, alone among his mates, maintained his defiance throughout his interrogation. On February 24, while Maple was still in Albuquerque and about to be shipped to Leavenworth, Leonhard told his interviewers he had felt no duty to share his knowledge of anyone's plans, including Maple's. Asked if he felt he owed any allegiance to the U.S. government, he replied, "No, sir, I honestly do not." Asked if he owed allegiance to the German Reich, he replied, "I do now." His interrogators then asked if he hadn't reported the wild conspiracies boiling around him because he didn't want to do anything to harm the Reich, he said, "No, sir, that would not be correct."

"What," Capt. Curran of MI asked him, "would be the correct assumption?"

"The correct assumption would be that I just didn't care," Leonhard said. "I didn't give a darn about anything."[10]

He did still care about getting out of the 620th and, if given a chance, retaliating against the Army. While Maple and Hotelling pursued their schemes, Leonhard had broadened his focus to include going to the Swiss Legation in Washington, D.C. on his next furlough. He'd get the Swiss to ask the German government to help free him because "a number of German citizens were being retained in the American army against their will." He, Fritz Siering, and Fritz Leuth were not the only ones.

But Leonhard told his interrogators that he'd also tried to create another option for himself. In case Maple or his escapees did make it all the way back to Germany, Leonhard slipped Schwichtenberg a letter the night before they fled. It explained Leonhard was staying behind at Hale "to keep the group loyal to Germany." Then he asked Schwichtenberg to contact several high-ranking Nazi officials—the former German consul in New Orleans and a "Doctor

Neumann"—Leonhard knew. He would await their instructions for subversive activities he could do for them. "I asked in that letter to tell my story to German intelligence and to tell them that as a German citizen I would be at their disposal, that I was willing in every way to do my duties as a German. I asked specifically that their agents contact me."

Leonhard became only more aggressive and committed to the cause as the military justice system moved toward considering a noose for him. Among other tactics, he ultimately sued the Army, claiming it had illegally inducted him.

The hot rumor of the moment was that the Army was going to reduce its charges against Hotelling to "conduct prejudicial to military service." If true, he would likely get a light sentence and soon be freed.[11]

To Leonhard, it was opportunity. A few weeks later, he sent Hotelling a long set of instructions for continuing the struggle after he got out.

"Eric," Leonhard wrote, "I feel I have a wonderful chance with you free." He and Hotelling should keep communicating, but they had to be careful. Hotelling, Leonhard said, should sign his notes to Leonhard as "Lake." He should send them only in the afternoons and only when specific guards were on duty. Leonhard's replies would be on page 50 of an otherwise innocent book or in the back pocket of some magazine he'd send.

And once Hotelling got out, he was to get in touch "with our reliable men in the 620th. Get some steam behind them! Tell them that I rely on their loyalty!" Their first task: get Leonhard out. Hotelling himself was to contact the conservative McCormick-owned papers (meaning the *Washington Star* and *Chicago Tribune*) and "memorize this name: Congressman Lyndon Johnson . . . He is a friend of mine (or was) and I want you to give him the entire story if anything worse than internment happens to me. He is close to Roosevelt and can get me clemency, and I expect no less from him . . ." Hotelling should also contact Burton Wheeler, the once-isolationist and still anti-FDR senator from Montana. "Don't hesitate to tell them that we were implicated in the [prisoner of war] escape, but tell them why . . . And Eric—go strong on the story of Fritz [Siering] and myself as loyal Germans being forced to serve against our own country, etc., etc. . . . So Eric, Keep [sic] at it. Contact also Swiss authorities. And get the necessary 620 to help you . . ."

If their former mates were reluctant, Hotelling should make it an order. Leonhard recommended giving the order on the "authority vested in me as a ranking member of the Gestapo section of the S.S. (I am a *Standortenfuhrer* SS, corresponds to full Col. in German army and I receive full courtesies by German Army officers who know my rank.) Use this information only if absolutely necessary."[12]

Leonhard's actual Gestapo affiliation apparently started and ended with that one sentence in his secret letter to Hotelling, which the Army eventually intercepted on June 26th, 1944, and never delivered to the inmate.* (Prison officials also routinely intercepted the other incarcerated Camp Hale soldiers' notes.) Clyde Tolson, the FBI's second-in-command, judged Leonhard's letter as one of the "most bizarre documents in the entire case. . . . This communication was regarded as ridiculous . . ."[13]

———————

In his cramped cell at the Disciplinary Barracks, Maple's understanding of his role in the war, like Leonhard's, also ballooned. He greeted Kissman's arrival at the Disciplinary Barracks in early March with an equally fantastic jailhouse note.

"Yes," he confessed to the new inmate he'd swept into suspicion, "I'm mixed up with a bunch of Germans (a lot of Italians and Americans too), and I've helped more than 2 men escape. I haven't seen what the papers say, but I was picked up in Mexico with 2 Prisoners of War."

He added that he and a distant, unnamed crew were still busy changing history, positioning themselves to deny Franklin Roosevelt a fourth presidential term. "Right now, I think most of the gang in New York are working to get the right men elected when election comes around."

He ignored the possibility that he'd be dead by the November election. The military held some 1.7 million courts-martial during World War II, or about a third of all criminal cases heard in the United States from December 1941 through August 1945, when the war ended. The military convicted 21,000 soldiers of desertion and gave death sentences to 49 of them. Most of the death sentences, moreover, were in 1944.

But Maple was confident. In fact, he suspected the Army would not even try him. "They have me here because they think I know a lot about German activities in this country, and they want to pump me," he bragged to Kissman. "They know they can't prove anything, and that's why they don't want to try me. I was over the hill 4 days, and I can beat a charge of desertion."

To his mother, he was reassuring, kind, and just as enamored with his fantasies. "I certainly hope you haven't been unduly worried by whatever the newspapers may have been printing," he wrote her. "You know how that sort of thing usually goes. I think I told you once by phone from New York that I

———

* Bernard Ladon, then a military court official, recalled, "While they were incarcerated at Leavenworth, I permitted them, unknown to each other, to pass notes back and forth; all of which were intercepted, photostatted (SIC) and then delivered . . ."

might be doing some strange things, so please don't worry yourself sick now."
As for the frightening plots he'd outlined in his statement for Bryce, her son
assured her they were simply part of his grand plan to embarrass the Army.[14]

His prosecutors, however, were taking his emphatic protestations of Nazi
sympathy, his Harvard disruptions, his contacts with Herman Scholz, his conspiracies to sabotage communication and help for prisoners of war, as well as his
actual desertion and escape with prisoners far more seriously. They spent much
of March 1944 interviewing Leonhard, Kissman, Siering, Schwichtenberg,
Kikilius, and the 34 other members of the 620th Maple had named as being in
the plot to open a second German front within the United States.

Back at Camp Hale, investigators were quickly learning that Maple's contention
that he led a committed group of American guerillas was news to the putative
guerillas themselves. In interview after interview, the accused mutineers swore
they were mystified that anyone had mentioned them, much less named as
members of a treasonous cabal.

The majority said they had done little more than visit Rim Rock and some
that they'd never visited at all. A few who admitted to being there didn't recall
even seeing Maple there. Others had fallen out of touch. Chiaramida and Mazza
lost even incidental contact with "the Germans" in the unit after Italy surrendered in September 1943. "Both Chiaramida and Mazza," the captain who
spent March at Camp Hale interviewing almost all the people Maple had named
reported, "fell out with the German element of the camp because of certain
derogatory statements made by the Germans against the Italians." The gang, in
fact, shrank. Julius Kogelman,* who the Army once recorded at Rim Rock as
saying he "absolutely refused to fight any enemy of the United States," was gone,
transferred to a regular unit serving in Hawaii.*[15] Drewes, in love, "lost interest"
and had abruptly "realized there was a purpose for that company . . ." He had
married just outside Camp Hale in January and was now intent on saving money

---

* Kogelman 's transfer was especially surprising to some. During the summer of 1943, in a Camp Meade
  discussion about several 620ers being court-martialed for speaking out against the United States, Pvt.
  Hugo Opton recalled Kogelman "suggested it might be a good idea for the company to go down to
  the guardhouse one time and release these men by force, and also to disarm the MP guards." He was
  transferred out of the 620th in November 1943. Others also were able to accomplish the transfers that
  Leonhard, Maple and Kissman pursued so adamantly. Indeed, the very day after Maple and the Germans
  slipped out of camp, Pvt. Arno H Zickmantel and T/5 Frank Heidt were transferred to units in California
  preparing for combat in the Pacific. In the next week, Pfc. Ernesto Carcone and Pvt. Jack Del Gatto were
  transferred to infantry units preparing to go overseas.

for a house for after the war. With those things in mind, he said, "one can't be going around doing foolish things."[16]

And in Kansas, Maple was characteristically wrong about the Army's intentions. The Army was formalizing charges against him even as he sent his grandiose notes to Kissman and his mother. The charges were grave: desertion under Article of War 58; aiding, harboring, and protecting two escaped prisoners of war under Article of War 81; and conspiracy under Article of War 96. The court-martial would start the next month, on April 17th, 1944, at the Disciplinary Barracks.

The Army planned to charge Leonhard with assisting Maple in aiding and harboring the prisoners (Article of War 81), for conspiracy (covered under Article of War 96) and, because of the letter he gave to Schwichtenberg just before the escape, for "corresponding with and giving intelligence to the enemy." That, it claimed, also violated Article of War 81.

They'd charge Siering with harboring Schwichtenberg on their New Year's jaunt, assisting Maple, and conspiracy. Kissman and Hotelling were to be tried in the coming months for assisting Maple and conspiracy.

Prisoner of war Schwichtenberg, with his status as both a POW and an enemy alien, had asked the Judge Advocate to reconsider the espionage charge against him, which stemmed from having Leonhard's letter and the New Year's incident.

"Maple's plan for sabotaging communication systems and transportation did not progress beyond the discussion stage," the Seventh Service Command's lead investigator conceded in his summary of his March interrogations. "However, it is apparent that Subjects had formed a well-organized group, potentially very dangerous, and were attempting to organize similar groups in other 'special organizations.' . . . [They] are known to have taken steps to organize an 'Inner Circle' in the 358th Q.M. Service Company [at Fort Carson] . . . and to have had slight connections with the 525th Q.M. Service Co "at Fort Leonard Wood.[17]

With that, the corrective might of the United States Army, having helped to reverse the tide of a world war, wheeled toward Dale Maple. It would deal with him first. Maple was ready. He sent another note to Kissman's cell:

> Paul: Trial on April 17. Will use abused Americanism angle. Will reveal sabotage plans, etc. Pass word to others: We'll lay it on thick.

The prosecutors who intercepted the note chose not to forward it.[18]

CHAPTER 12

IN COURT

The main entrance to the United States Disciplinary Barracks at Fort Leavenworth, Kansas, was an arched doorway set in a three-story reception and office building of mustard-colored stucco, beige stone, and brick. Called "The Castle" or "Little Top," the complex itself overlooked a cemetery for about 280 prisoners who had died while in the facility sometime during the prior 70 years and gone unclaimed.

By April 17th, the Army had Maple, Leonhard, Kissman, Hotelling, and Siering quarantined within Little Top's 600,000 square feet of painted gray metal and stolid concrete for well more than a month. Their cells were narrow one-bed alcoves of approximately 8 feet by 6 feet by 10 feet. Their beds consisted of thin mattresses set on top of three-or-four-foot-high concrete rectangles. They had a toilet and a three-inch-thick concrete shelf built into the wall, equally gray. Guards watched over them from a fortified rotunda at the intersection of the echoing cell block buildings. Isolated, the prisoners of the 620th couldn't see much from their cells. Kissman caught a glimpse of Maple but saw none of his other mates during the weeks leading up to the trial.

Mae Scoville, Maple's mother, has been in town for about a week. Maple's father was still on his way, enduring what would be a rushed 1600-mile, 39-hour drive from San Diego. He was trying to stay awake on only three hours rest to get to Kansas on time.[1]

He hadn't arrived by the day of the trial when a soldier diverted Mae Scoville from the courtroom to an adjacent room. She was, she learned, to stay there until and unless she was called to testify next door.

In the court-martial room next door, eleven Army officers filed in to serve as the jury and arranged themselves in a semi-circle of chairs that faced two tables;

one for the prosecution and one for the defense. There was also a chair for a witness. The officers—high-ranking for what would be an important treason case—included a major general, a brigadier general, six full colonels, and three lieutenant colonels. Facing Maple were the "law member" or "military judge" of the court, a non-voting judge who would rule on procedural questions as they arose. A trial judge advocate and assistant trial judge advocate were Maple's prosecutors. They expected to call 26 witnesses and offer about a dozen exhibits that would include the receipt for the Reo from the Y&R Garage, the yellow scarf that Maple bought on his Salida shopping trip, and the statement Maple typed for D.A. Bryce in the Albuquerque jail.

The Army assigned two inexperienced men to defend Maple: 2nd Lt. William Fleischaker—described as "a graduate lawyer"—and Major Rinold L. Ohman, another Harvard man who wasn't a lawyer "but had some experience in court-martial matters."

And then there was William Humphrey Biddle, a Leavenworth, Kansas civilian lawyer recruited and paid for by Maple's father. The lawyer had been a captain in the Army's Judge Advocate General Department during World War I and had tried court-martial cases in both Europe and the United States.[2]

Biddle's first meetings with his new client were puzzling. Maple appeared to be remarkably detached. "If he did sense the seriousness of the charges against him and the penalty which might be imposed—death—he did not outwardly show it." Biddle, then 51, warned his client "that he could expect the extreme penalty. We were engaged in a war, and tension was pretty high, and . . . no sympathy could be expected from any source." Maple didn't adapt. "I cannot say he exhibited any particular form of nervousness during the trial."[3]

Biddle's warning had heft. In the nation's third year of a brutal two-front war, the military had not been shy about avenging transgressions. In 1944 alone, it would put some 39 of its soldiers to death; 19 by hanging, one by firing squad. (The remaining 19 had no method of death listed in what had become the Army's annual Execution Report). The Executive Branch turned vengeful as well. On the day Maple's court-martial began in Kansas, 40 reporters were crowding into a federal courtroom in Washington, D.C. It was the beginning of a sensational sedition trial of some 30 isolationists, Bund members (including Gerhard Kunze, the former Bund leader), members of the Christian right, war critics, and Klansmen. All were accused of conspiring to promote insubordination in the armed forces. Like the men of the 620th, many were perfectly law-abiding citizens who were now having their speech equated with disloyalty.

But President Roosevelt, on the cusp of a campaign for an unprecedented fourth term in office, was determined to mute the relentless political criticisms of his war policies. It nevertheless hadn't been easy to dig up a charge that would fit the entire colorful assortment of civilian critics. He'd had to convene three grand juries to secure enough indictments. Attorney General Francis Biddle (not related to Maple's lawyer) had tried to dissuade him, but FDR "was not much interested . . . in the constitutional right to criticize the government in wartime." The trial would soon become known as The Great Sedition Trial of 1944* and a troubling echo of Stalin's infamous show-trial disposals of his political opponents.[4]

In Kansas that day, Maple's accusers began by solemnly reading the charges. The Army had dropped an initial conspiracy charge in favor of more provable crimes that, in turn, carried more severe penalties. They included desertion, a violation of the 58th Article of War. The second charge was relieving "the enemy . . . by furnishing, affording, and providing certain escaped Prisoners of War and members of the Army of the German Reich, at war with the United States of America . . . with automotive transportation and other articles and things of value . . ." He also "knowingly harbor[ed] and protect[ed] escaped German Prisoners of War . . . who were then being sought as fugitives from Side Camp No. 1, Prisoner of War Camp, Trinidad Colorado, located at Camp Hale, Colorado . . ."

Both those acts, if proven, violated the 81st Article of War. Both, though unrelated to the Inner Circle's plans for sabotage and guerilla war, were capital offenses.[5]

— • —

The Army rarely used the hammer-blow 81st Article, the military equivalent of treason in civilian courts.† Actual convictions under it would always include the death penalty. The assertion that Maple violated it by aiding the enemy outside of a theater of war was even rarer. Out of almost eight million Army personnel

---

* The trial soon devolved into a circus-like atmosphere with the government unable to prove intent to interfere with the war and the defense presenting strong constitutional rights. It ended in a mistrial months later, in November, 1944. It was never re-tried.

† The Army was careful to distinguish between treason charges (aiding the enemy on the battlefield) and its Article 81 charges (aiding and abetting the enemy elsewhere). Court martial procedures emphasized "The term 'treason' should not be used" in Article 81 trials.

by war's end, fewer than ten were charged with aiding the enemy. Those would soon include Leonhard, Kissman, and Siering.

Arrest on Article 58, the desertion charge, was the more conventional offense. During World War II, some 15,000 Army soldiers would be convicted of it.

After hearing the charges, Maple's lawyers, who barely knew each other or the defendant, requested that Maple's parents be allowed in the closed courtroom as spectators after all. Both would soon testify but wanted to be with their son as the government debated whether to put him to death. Biddle claimed barring them would be the first time in American history that any court had kept a defendant's parents away. The judges were unsure and agreed to take the question under advisement. Then Maple's lawyers asked for more time to prepare. It has been 62 eventful days since Maple, Schwichtenberg, and Kikilius disappeared from Camp Hale. The lawyers themselves—not all of them had law degrees—had been on the case for mere days in some instances. The court agreed to recess for a week to allow them to prepare and gaveled the day's session closed a mere hour after it had begun.

They returned on April 24th to hear the court rule Maple's parents could not observe the trial in the courtroom. Both mother and father would soon be testifying as character witnesses, and witnesses in any proceeding were prohibited from hearing other witnesses on the stand. So, as one reporter subsequently put it, Maple's parents "who had not spoken since [their divorce in] 1938 sat together in strained anxiety in a tiny anteroom off the trial chamber, wondering what was happening to their son next door."[6]

Next door, the proceedings were getting strange. Maple "has muscled aside his lawyers and taken over the lead in his own defense," an FBI observer cabled his superiors. One of the defendant's first moves as an amateur attorney was to ask to have his father, also not a lawyer, recognized as one of his attorneys. The judges denied the request, but as testimony began, the younger Maple kept the lead. "Maple is doing all the cross-examining" of the prosecution witnesses, the FBI observer reported. His appointed attorneys "take very little part in the trial." Attorney Biddle, L.G. Maple later maintained, "was afraid of Dale. Dale snowed him under with technical questions."[7]

The prosecution's first witness was 2nd Lt. Dawson, who had assumed command over Hale's POW stockade the day Maple and his prisoners left camp. During the next three days of testimony, more witnesses essentially corroborated the facts and timeline of both the prosecutors' version and Maple's statements to Bryce and the Army. Leonhard, the vendors from Salida, Sgt. Altman, Kissman, Siering, the customs officials who arrested the escapees in Mexico and finally New Mexico, Bryce, and, at last, the stern, stiff German prisoners themselves came to the stand. Asked to swear, to tell the truth, Schwichtenberg, speaking through an interpreter, noted, "It is prohibited for us to swear in the country of the enemy." Asked to elaborate, he pledged, "I will tell the truth." His other replies were similarly dry and unhelpful.

Kikilius was resolutely opaque. He evaded saying even how long he'd been in the German Army. He answered most of the prosecution's questions by referring to the statements he'd already made during the investigation that had followed his recapture. Asked where and when he'd met Maple, he said, "Well, I don't know that anymore now. It is probably also in the testimony." The prosecution accommodatingly produced the statement Kikilius had given in March and showed him where his answers to the question were. "Now, having refreshed your memory," the lawyer asked, "will you tell the court from your own recollection just what occurred on or about February 15th this year and following?" He remained stony. "I can't explain. It is best to read it, and, anyway, I have a headache." The prosecutor, defeated, returned to his seat.[8]

Kikilius was the final prosecution witness, and Maple opened his defense by putting his star witness—Dale Maple—on the stand.

Prompted by Biddle's softball questions, he recounted a seemingly idyllic childhood of horseback riding, surfing, swimming, and being "regarded as one of the better student pianists." He detailed his sterling academic performance, capped by his graduation from Harvard, *magna cum laude.*

Biddle, hoping to underline the accomplishment, pointed out that "*magna cum laude* means, of course, 'with the highest praise.'"

His punctilious client corrected him. "'With high praise."

Maple then unspooled his amended version of his desertion and aid to the enemy. In it, he was no longer the aggrieved grad school applicant or the emphatic Nazi on his way to Germany with two POWs and, ultimately, to be a saboteur within the United States. Now, per his undelivered note, he laid the "Americanism" angle on thick. He was, he told the court, the hero hoping to do something so outrageous that it would generate enough publicity and civilian outcry to get the Army to disband the 620th and let him get into an American combat unit to help win the war.

His prosecutors were not about to let these latest explanations of his behavior go unchallenged. They quoted from the inflammatory and entirely different statement Maple gave D.A. Bryce in Albuquerque on February 20th. They asked him about his plan to go to sabotage school in Germany and, among other threats in the document, his hopes to disrupt the American war effort by blowing up strategic transportation and communication hubs.

Maple dismissed it all. It was a ruse to attract attention to the civil treason trial he'd expected, attended by reporters from far and wide. Upon hearing the real story, they would stoke the ire of an American public that frowned on unfairness.

As proof, he repeated the ways he tried to get caught: the presumably bugged phone calls, the cash receipts, the "public" purchase of the Reo, dawdling with the New Mexico customs official, the supposed daylight visit to Columbus and, not least, his peaceful surrender to arrest.

"*Acta exterior indicant interior secrata*," he told the court. "' Acts indicate intentions,' as the learned judge advocate will probably affirm . . ."

His mother took the stand next. Prompted to describe Maple's character and sterling education, she dutifully reported how talented, sensitive, and accomplished he was in school, going off to Harvard in 1937.

Maple stopped her. "I would like to clear up one point. You say that I, the accused, entered Harvard in 1937," he said, demonstrating just the kind of mastery of detail that made him an academic superstar. "Would you reconsider that, please? With what class did the accused graduate?"

"1941," his mother testified.

"And how long was he there?" he asks, leading his mother like she was a child in math class.

"Four years," she said.

"September 1936, I believe is correct," he said, causing his mother some embarrassment while clarifying a detail that, in truth, offered no additional clarity to the proceedings. Satisfied, he instructed his mother to continue her testimony.[9]

She did, although without noting that her son was wrong. Maple's high school diploma, as well as his certificates of "Excellence," "Life Membership in the California Scholarship Federation Chapter 18," of Merit, and of "The Wayne Gridley Simmons Scholarship Prize," were all dated June 18th, 1937. That would put the start of his Harvard career into the fall of 1937.[10]

Maple's mother reported she was currently a "housewife." She and L.G. Everett Maple, her first husband, married on July 20th, 1915, setting up house in Colton, California, before moving to San Diego in 1918. Dale, their only child, was born in 1920. They doted on the boy. But she added that the home was not a happy one.

"There had been domestic difficulties?" Biddle asked, sensing some evidence that circumstances might have driven him to treason.

"Yes."

"For how long?"

"Ten or fifteen years," she said, which would cover just about the entirety of Dale Maple's life before he left for Harvard at age 17. [11]

L.G. Maple was next. He identified himself as a division manager at National Steel and Shipbuilding in San Diego, where he oversaw the company's machine shop and sheet metal foundry. Then he stopped. "I prepared a little thing here to kind of refresh my memory," he said, pulling some papers out of his jacket. "I have been under somewhat of a strain here, not only weeks but months."

Reading from the papers, he praised his son's intellect and energy. The young man had always been smart, fastidious, and precise. When L.G. asked the young Maple, "if he wanted to go to a show, he'd say 'no.' If I asked for an explanation, he would say, 'well, you just asked me to go, and I thought that was all you wanted to know. What else should I have said? You did not ask me why.'" Equating that variety of exasperating conversation with brilliance seemed to be a given for both the elder and younger Maple.

Even "as a boy, he was always brutally frank and honest that sometimes it was painful . . . Whatever he has done has always been done to the extreme, never halfway or with moderation, always plunge into the most difficult task." The result was often excellence. More times than not, Dale would "emerge with top honors." Dale, he believed, was "a most unusual man." He had "the mind of almost a genius, a mind that grasps the knowledge of the deepest science almost with the reading of the printed word, a brain capable of absorbing knowledge at a rate almost unbelievable." He had mastered shorthand by the age of 16. In high school, he was writing papers about bullet trajectories and the monetary system. The latter paper, Maple's father boasted, attracted the attention of Harvard President James B. Conant. On a visit to San Diego, Conant hosted Dale for dinner at the Harvard Club and, impressed by the boy's current ambition to become ambassador to England someday, made sure Maple got a one-year scholarship. "His imagination would build anything."

The son, acting as the lawyer, asked his father about the son's mental condition.

"The mind is unbalanced," L.G. Maple testified. Whether Dale Maple was surprised by the answer is not recorded, but L.G. remained adamant. "It is just absolutely not balanced. The judgment—his judgment is just not developed;

overly educated, terrific drive in one direction only. Never having had occasion to come to Earth, as you might say, or work things out as we, in the struggle of today, have to do, the mind has never been developed along that line at all." [12]

With character references like that, it became apparent to Dale Maple, now both lawyer and defendant, that his defense was foundering. He asked for a pause in the proceedings. He was, he tells the court, changing his plea. Now, he was "not guilty by reason of insanity."

Lawyers, both Maple's and the Army's, were stricken. Amid a certain scrambling, the court quickly gaveled itself adjourned, recessing to call in the psychiatrists who had evaluated the defendant since his arrest. [13]

In the 1940s, in what was then the infant study of terrorism, much of the professional understanding was based on psychoanalytic theory. The traitor, it posited, was a narcissist or hated his or her parents. But most traitors and even terrorists "are not 'psychopaths,'" more modern examinations eventually concluded. "Histories of childhood abuse and trauma and themes of perceived injustice and humiliation often are prominent in terrorist biographies, but do not really help to explain terrorism," a summary report of terrorist research by the University of South Florida's Psychology of Terrorism Initiative found. Instead, these aggressors share a need for identity and a need for belonging. They tend to focus on others' mistrust of them, competition, and, not least, a culture's unfairness toward them as threats to their existence. [14]

Dale Maple, as it happened, fit the outsider profile nicely. A gay man in 1944, he certainly experienced the social unfairness, prejudice, mistrust, and ostracism that characterized much of straight America's treatment of lesbians and homosexuals at the time.

A sense of belonging could not have come easily to him. His college, as well as his high school peers, had often derided his mannerisms, his social unease, his dress, and the way he occasionally tried to separate himself from the herd by affecting indifference toward all that was around him. "Maple always impressed me as a rather effeminate person without many friends and more or less harmless because he wasn't the type of person to impress anyone," a Harvard classmate would say. "I still don't believe he would impress anyone, but I was wrong about him being harmless." They laughed at his odd, self-conscious walk. "He had a peculiar walk," another Harvard classmate would say. "He slouched; his knees bent strangely. An un-rhythmic walk, with a short step and then a long one." And he came to cultivate his "otherness." He was oppositional, irritating, regularly taking views and stances vividly out-of-favor with his surroundings.

Maple's conversion to Catholicism, his mother maintained, was born of a love of Latin and the church's "spectacle and robes." But something else was at play. Maple's father was bitterly anti-Catholic at the time, and a Maple family friend thought, "he probably joined the Catholic Church for the same reason that he 'heiled' Hitler. He thought it daring and bad. He had been brought up in an environment where the Catholic Church was unpopular. Had he been brought up in a Catholic atmosphere, he would or should have turned Pentecostalist."

A former Harvard classmate later agreed. Maple's college-era isolationism was "a reaction against his father," who Maple led his classmates and several professors alternately to believe was either a Navy captain or an Army colonel. If it was hostility toward L.G. Maple, it was hostility toward a papered-over image of L.G. Maple (who had been rejected by the Army in 1941 because he had flat feet) that the complicated Dale Maple had made up.[15]

———

When court resumed on May 7, 1944, a short parade of doctors took turns parsing Maple's sanity, if not the reasons for his unpopularity. Erwin S. Chappel, a Medical Corps captain and the psychiatrist attached to the Disciplinary Barracks, had met with Maple twice before. From the witness chair, he read his report: there was "no evidence of psychosis" and "no distortion of reality." The private was "of a very superior intelligence," with an I.Q. of 152 and an appropriate mental age of 22. "He is neat and tidy, quite cooperative . . . no unusual postures, mannerisms, or abnormal facial expressions noted, except for a somewhat bland smile, even when discussing things of utmost gravity to him."

Yes, there were oddities: "This individual shows no concern for the outcome of the impending court-martial. He shows definite poverty of emotional tone, does not appreciate the seriousness of his military delinquency, and has no remorse." In fact, "he shows no understanding of the discrepancy between his intellectual reasoning and the emotional poverty and lack of identification with his native country . . . He considers himself a 'professional soldier,' but he does not appreciate the inconsistency in violating his oath by escaping in the company of German prisoners of war."[16]

But by any recognized clinical definition of insanity, Chappell concluded Dale Maple was sane.

Maple rose to cross-examine him. He recounted his arrival at Camp Meade in South Dakota. There was nothing normal about an American-born man who "spoke English with a German accent; had his hair clipped short; told the other soldiers that his name was Mapel and that his parents were born in Europe, and even invented trips made to Europe to convince the other soldiers that he was not a *bona fide* American and hence justly belonged to the unit which consisted mostly of subversive people of foreign extraction."

Would the doctor consider that "losing contact with reality?"

"Well," Chappell said, "we might compare it to an actor in a play. He assumed a role for a certain time, yet when the show was over, going back to his normal self."

Major Thomas I. Metzger, the ranking surgeon at Fort Leavenworth, came next. He'd met the defendant "four or five times" before the trial, and Metzger, who was not a psychiatrist, was direct. "It is my judgment that he is sane."

Maple tried a variety of the same questions on him as he had with Chappel. "Doctor," he asked, "are people sane on some subjects and insane on others?"

"No, I wouldn't say that."

"Well, a person might be sane and still be a Jack the Ripper; he is insane when he sees a woman, and he is going to cut her up. He is insane on that subject, and he can't control it. He is insane on that subject and sane on everything else."

Metzger was unmoved. "I wouldn't say that was a case of insanity. That is a case of misjudged temper."

Prosecutor Bernard Ladon stood. Holding the record of Maple's arrest on February 19th, he quoted U.S. Attorney Houk as "having in mind that Maple might pretend insanity or some other form of mental aberration or might say that he had been injured physically since his capture." To make sure that didn't happen, Houk had a physician put Maple through an immediate two-hour exam when Bryce brought Maple to Albuquerque around midnight on February 19th. The doctor found him in good physical and emotional health.

On the stand, his parents had talked about him being "nervous" and "sensitive" and "unbalanced," but more psychiatrists come forward to offer more clinical definitions. All testified that, while Maple was not the most attractive of personalities, his sanity seemed intact. The problem wasn't mental competence, said one. It was his coldness.

"The ability to say things without feeling them is very much vicious if it is combined with a person who has the kind of intellect the accused has. The leaders of the Nazi party have the same kind of ability. They are the kind of people who will rationalize things but not feel them, aren't they?" [17]

———

At a court-martial, the military jurors in the room do not have to reach a unanimous vote in most cases. Only two-thirds of them were needed to convict; any lower percentage ended in acquittal. Few military trials ended in hung juries. A unanimous verdict, however, was required for death penalty cases like Maple's. In civilian courts, a sentencing hearing and maybe even a pre-sentencing report happened before the accused learned his or her punishment. At a court-martial, the impact of a crime on a victim or a unit's discipline and morale, the soldier's performance record, and any mitigating circumstances determine the sentence. [18]

Jurors announced they had reached a verdict on May 8th, 1944. But before determining the penalty, they wanted to know if Dale Maple had had any prior criminal convictions.

To Biddle, there could be no more ominous question. A court inquired about previous convictions was "a sure sign of a finding of guilty." Hearing (erroneously) that Maple had never been in jail before, the jurors recessed again to determine a sentence. Watching them leave the room, Biddle was sure they would return with an extreme one. [19]

CHAPTER 13

TANGLED WEBS THEY WEAVE

A mere half-hour later, the men determining Dale H Maple's fate filed back into the trial chamber in Leavenworth, Kansas.

Everyone but the defendant and his lawyers sat as the president of the court announced that it had not bought Maple's shape-shifting explanations. The court, in effect, said it didn't care if he favored or pretended to favor fascism. The law was uninterested in why he flirted or pretended to flirt with going to sabotage school in Hamburg or why he planned or seemed to plan attacks on American targets. It didn't matter if he intended to defect or fake defecting to one of history's cruelest regimes or if he tried to disappear or tried to get caught after he helped two enemy soldiers escape.

Whatever his motives, mistakes, or fantasies, the court ruled he had violated the 58th and 81st Articles of War. He had deserted his post in wartime. He had impeded the war effort. He had aided and relieved the enemy.

The judges, however, did not announce the punishment, at least out loud. As was the custom in a closed court-martial, especially ones involving capital punishment, Maple's actual sentence would stay secret until a separate Board of Review examined the proceedings behind the scenes. In the next weeks or months, one or two military men would read the trial record, the findings, and the sentence that the court-martial jury had secretly recommended: death by hanging. They would decide if the trial had been fair, the evidence persuasive, and the judging had been done well. After some undetermined length of time, they'd announce their decision and, not least, decide if the court-martial's recommended punishment should be carried out.

Biddle, Maple's lawyer, was sure how it would end. This, he reminded both the defendant and his family, was a brutalized world unlikely—and in some ways unable—to show mercy. A total of 405,399 Americans would be killed during the war, robbing them and the society of their futures and leaving dark holes in their survivors' lives. Those who weren't mourning family members who would never come home again realistically feared heartbreaking telegrams that might arrive at any moment. To end the suffering and breathtaking, implausible violence around them, jurors often gave in to vengeance.

"I felt certain that he had been sentenced to hang," Biddle said, "and I so told Maple right at that time." Having watched his detached client for a month and heard the testimony about his carefully distant and indifferent manner, Biddle was not surprised by Maple's outward reaction. "I cannot say that he showed any emotion or excitement."

Disheartened, the lawyer left the courtroom to console Maple's mother and, after that, to call Maple's father in San Diego. "I told him what I thought the sentence was and urged him to do all he could as a father to use his influence to have the sentence commuted or modified."[1]

And then there was silence. Courts-martial do not tell the defendant, much less the defendant's parents and lawyers, who was on the Board of Review, where it was meeting or if it already had met.

The lawyer Biddle warned all the Maples, however, to be prepared. The military's punishments, when they came, were exacted quickly, often within days after the Board of Review reported its findings. Maple might well be hanged soon, any day.

Offstage, the Army had already disposed of many of the other supposedly troublesome men of the 620th. Much evidence surrounding them apparently felt soft. (The records of the Army's legal decisions in most of these cases are either lost or destroyed). Upon questioning Drewes, Rudolph Nobis, Chiaramida, Hugo Opton, Idelberger, Maurer, Poehlmann, and dozens of others all maintained Maple's allegations confounded them. They swore they had not known they were part of an organized conspiracy. Those who heard the threats and talk of sabotage and mutiny had shrugged them off as little more than hot air and frustration.

But they were once—and still were—suspected of disloyalty. By casually and probably falsely including them in a conspiracy to commit treason, Maple had grievously stained their military reputations. The options for what to do with them were limited. "It couldn't spread them around [the Army] for fear of infecting other units," one clemency expert of the day pointed out. Discharging them wouldn't work, either. "As civilians, they might carry through their sabotage, and interning them might not be secure enough."[2]

The Army's solution was to "reorganize" the 620th. Adroitly sidestepping the kind of public awareness of the abuse that the Inner Circle had hoped for, the War Department proposed a reorganization "of certain units" on February 26th. On March 1st, it issued two General Orders. One disbanded the 620th.

"They actually didn't break up the 620 Engineers after the trouble," contended Rudolph Nobis, one of the soldiers on Maple's list of putative traitors. "What they did do [was] change the name of it."

The second General Order then created a larger unit for a variety of strange soldiers, and on March 9th changed the 620th into "Company A" of the newly formed 1800th Engineers Service Battalion. On the same day, the Army quietly transferred Nobis and the other former members of the 620th to the 1800's new encampment in rural Belt Buckle, Tennessee, well out of public view.

They joined a bigger and equally motley collection of unwanted soldiers. In Tennessee, the innocents as well as the malcontents of the old 620th were paired with a "B Company" made up of Japanese-, German- and Italian-born Americans and American residents. Groups of overtly political inductees—soldiers who either once or still belonged to the America First Committee, the Christian Front, or the Ku Klux Klan—were in "C Company."

By any name, the Tennessee units were worse than the original misfit outfits. "Conditions, as they were in the 620th, were bad but nothing compared to conditions as existed afterward," Nobis recalled. "Things really became tough. Most of the food was terrible, and not enough to go around." The men had to pool their money to buy eggs to eat from nearby farmers. In view of Hotelling's recruiting forays, visiting other military camps without permission was forbidden. Worse yet, many of the officers from the 620th transferred with the men and remained as "sadistic" as ever. Tensions with local civilians were taut and occasionally violent. "There were a few fights with civilians," Nobis reported. "One civilian stabbed a German at a bar; then one of the Japs . . . picked up the stabber and, while he still had the knife, tossed him neatly, via jujitsu, through a glass door."

The work was no more soldierly—perhaps dirtier—than in Colorado. The Army had them repairing fences and roads and digging out hog ponds. It would soon move them to Mississippi for yet more menial work and then on to flood control work in Arkansas. With a final name change to the 5000th Quartermaster Company, at least 10 of the men were sent overseas in 1945 to dig up dead American soldiers for shipment back home.[3]

While the Army moved its men around, Maple, Leonhard, Kissman, Siering, and Hotelling watched spring turn toward summer, 1944, from inside the Fort Leavenworth Disciplinary Barracks. Their daily life was probably better than for those in the 1800th, where the men were hungry, lacked many basic comforts, and did more physical labor.

Still, in Kansas, the Camp Hale prisoners were tightly confined and generally isolated from others. Maple himself was quarantined with much time to ponder the genuine prospect of being hanged someday soon. He waited for word. He got no visitors.

To his former mates, not hearing from him was unnerving. They'd last heard of Maple in March and early April when he was making ever-escalating claims about helping other prisoners escape and influencing elections. He was still vigorously bragging that he was a tested Nazi and still insisted he led a dangerous force of 30-some Camp Hale soldiers.

As far as they knew, he still held to his promise to swear to his mates' bellicose guilt at their courts-martial. All of them, he'd say, were intent on opening a new theater of war on U.S. soil.

In May, reading a summary of evidence for his upcoming court-martial, Fritz Siering was alarmed. Maple was going to testify that he, as well as Leonhard and Kissman, were active rebels, part of the escape and the mutiny plans. Siering—who in truth had known nothing of Maple's plans and never took what little he did know seriously—panicked.[4]

And it could happen soon. Siering's, Leonhard's, and Kissman's joint court-martial was supposed to start on June 12th. None of them yet knew of the new, marginally more pacific stories Maple had offered at his April court-martial. They did know that Maple had since been found guilty and was, according to scuttlebutt, probably headed to the gallows. It was certainly possible that, with nothing left to lose, the unpredictable Maple would, in fact, testify they were also saboteurs. They, too, would be put to death.

Siering, still struggling with English, and Leonhard mounted a quick, last-ditch effort to avoid a trial altogether. On June 10th, two days before their court-martial was to convene, they filed for a writ of habeas corpus.

Their maneuver formally asked a civil court in Wichita "to determine whether or not [each prisoner] is illegally restrained of his liberty" by the Army.

They were still German citizens, they said. Officially, they were classified as "enemy aliens" and thus had been improperly inducted in the first place. Now they were being wrongly held.

Both Siering and Leonhard had, in fact, tried to become citizens, though the reasons the government had rejected them differed.

Siering, like someone out of the Book of Job, had repeatedly failed to convince Authority that he loved America enough. Still afraid that the Nazi government would punish his family back in Germany for his anti-Hitler feelings, Fritz Siering had essentially been on the run since fleeing Germany and illegally jumping from a German merchant ship in New York harbor in 1936. For years, he kept a wary eye out for both U.S. immigration officials and German agents who might kidnap and spirit him back to Germany. To be safe, he often used a fake name—Rottman—as he dodged in and out of kitchen and mechanic jobs in Philadelphia, back in New York, and, finally, in Chicago.

But hiding was hard. Hoping to finally "get my papers legalized," he nervously went to the immigration office in Chicago in 1939 "to tell my story." He was by then a 22-year-old married man (though soon divorced) using his real name again, paying taxes and holding down a good job at Keene Manufacturing where, according to his lawyer, he "earned quite a bit." At the immigration office, he was "asked if I desired to stay in this country, I said 'yes.'" Encouraged and looking forward to being naturalized soon, he paid an attorney $180 (about $3,200 today) to help him prepare for and earn his citizenship.

His optimism was premature. Several weeks later, immigration agents showed up at his door and, armed with the information Siering had volunteered to them, served him with a warrant for his illegal 1936 entry into the United States. He was arrested and ordered deported. Siering's boss rushed to vouch and post bond for him, and, as it happened, the agency deferred the deportation. Germany was already at war, and the U.S. in those days did not send refugees back into war zones. Siering would be allowed to stay in the country until Germany was at peace.[5]

And a few weeks after that, in 1940, the new Selective Service Act required him and all men his age to register for the draft. About a year later, the draft board changed his classification from 4-C—a citizen of Germany and thus an "enemy alien" ineligible to be drafted—to 1-A.

"I was eager to get my citizenship papers. After fourteen days, I got my notice and I went to the immigration authorities, and I told them I was going to service [sic] in the United States Army. I would be glad if they would disregard the deportation charges," he recalled. They seemed to agree. "I signed a statement that I do not object to service in the United States Army." In return, "they had promised they would drop the deportation charge."

But the Army was not the Immigration and Naturalization Service, and it told Siering so when he got to the draft center. He learned "they had nothing to do with [immigration]. They told me I had come illegally into the country in violation of immigration laws and that they could not do anything [about dropping the deportation order].[6]

"Certainly, I was a little bitter that they had not dropped the charges." It was time to take a stand. He (correctly) said he could not take the oath because, while registered as an enemy alien, he was not legally permitted to swear allegiance to a different country.

Somewhat flummoxed, the officer "said I had to take that up with someone else" after he was processed and assigned to a unit. For now, Siering should just line up with the other new soldiers.

Siering refused and stepped to one side. He did not physically resist, however, and he was herded with all the other inductees into buses to start their service to the United States of America.

They took him to Camp Grant in Illinois, where, per instructions, Siering took his case to his commanding officer. "They first promised me that they would make me a citizen, and then they drafted me as a German citizen," he told him. The commanding officer, in turn, promised "he would look into it." Siering "heard nothing further from him."

He tried again after his transfer to the 620th at Camp Meade in South Dakota. Telling his new commanding officer his story, he added that if the U.S. didn't want him as a citizen, he should be dismissed from the Army and interned as an enemy alien. Again, "no action was taken upon his request."

As his June 1944 court-martial approached, Siering remained classified as an enemy alien, still longed for citizenship, and now believed the American government had bamboozled him. He maintained that everything about his draft and induction was illegal.[7]

Theo Leonhard's quest for citizenship was no less frustrating. He had flirted with naturalization three times. He didn't follow through on his first attempt, made while he was in college in 1936. The government lost his second application in 1941 and never acted on it. His third, in 1942, was overtly denied, although his Army superior neglected to tell him about it for over a year. As required by the Alien Registration Act of 1940 and then a presidential proclamation Leonhard, like Siering, had twice registered as a German citizen, once just before induction in 1940 and again in 1942 in Los Angeles. That left him, he now said, not only as an alien but, again like Siering, legally an enemy alien.

So, two days before their joint court-martial was to start, Leonhard and Siering jointly sued for their writ of habeas corpus. They contended that enemy aliens didn't belong in an Army unit and certainly not an Army prison. The military had improperly inducted them and thus had no legal jurisdiction over them. The government, moreover, was confining them for violating military rules they had no obligation to follow.

The suit, formally Leonhard v. Eley (Col. William S. Eley was then the Disciplinary Barracks' commander), would take a 16-month journey through the courts. Its first impact, as Siering and Leonhard hoped, was to make the Army drop its plan to try both Siering and Leonhard on June 12th, pending a ruling on their request for the writ of habeas corpus. [8]

That left Paul Kissman on his own in the Barracks trial room, facing an arc of Army brass still looking to resolve the remainder of the Maple mess as quickly and quietly as possible.

Kissman, to some, was the most sympathetic of the Camp Hale prisoners. "My impressions of them, individually and collectively," recalled Bernard Ladon, the trial judge advocate in both Maple's and Kissman's proceedings, "were that they were educated fools, egotistical to the Nth degree, and possessed of little or no common sense." He thought Leonhard, in particular, a "dyed-in-the-wool Nazi." Of them all, Paul A. Kissman was "the most sincere."

Over six feet tall and 170 pounds, Kissman—good vision but "poor" dental health—had been at the Disciplinary Barracks since the beginning weeks of March. To his jailers at the nearby Leavenworth Penitentiary, he appeared "to be highly intelligent. He was very polite and courteous during the [admissions] interview but did not care to discuss his case . . . He had never been in trouble before." His mother told his investigators that Paul was "a Christian boy." She said, "his behavior was always exemplary until his present difficulty." She had "no idea what might have influenced him to react as he did."[9]

He ultimately sat in the same chair Maple had occupied the previous month, before the same semi-circle of chairs in the same dingy room. Kissman, his prosecutors charged, bought the .38 and supplies for Maple, failed to report Maple's unauthorized absence, and then lied about it. The Army contended those actions, as much as Leonhard's and Siering's and Maple's, also violated the Article of War 81 that prohibited "relieving the enemy." It added that Kissman's delivery of the gun and supplies amounted to "knowingly assisting the said Maple to desert." "Failing to report and falsely reporting" Maple's absence violated the 59th Article of War.

To prove it Ladon, the prosecutor, called many of the same witnesses he had called for Maple: 2nd Lt. Robert L. Dawson of the POW stockade at Hale, Sgt. Altman, one of the Salida merchants, customs official William F. Bates and Capt. Curran of Military Intelligence, who first interviewed Kissman at the Leadville, Colorado jail on February 24th. Ladon also called Pvt. Frederick T. Maurer, who had gone to Denver with Kissman on February 7th, eight days before Maple deserted. Working from Maple's shopping list and spending the $50 Maple had given him, Kissman and Maurer went to stores and hock shops to buy clothing and other supplies. When they got to the gun store, however, Kissman said he didn't know much about handguns. He had Maurer, who did know about them, choose and buy the .38 for Maple. One of the exhibits at Kissman's trial was the gun receipt made out to a "John Graham," the fake name Maurer used that day. "John Graham" had handed the newly purchased gun to Kissman, who, in turn, committed the crime of handing it to Maple back at Camp Hale.[10]

———

After Ladon's arguments, Kissman's lawyers countered with witnesses and statements praising the defendant's character. There was a friend he'd had since grammar school, an "old friend and neighbor," a county welfare worker from Pennsylvania, and a schoolteacher who had known Paul in Erie all his life. His brother, a chief military engineer then posted somewhere in the Pacific, sent a testimonial about Paul's patriotism. His lawyers presented his military records (spotless) from Camp Blanding, Florida, where he had been posted before the 620th, and supporting statements from former officers at Blanding and Fort Lee, Virginia. Three officers—including Lt. Leroy Wilson's predecessor as commanding officer—from the 620th pitched in complimentary statements. Among other exhibits, there were Military Intelligence reports from surveillance of him during furloughs in Chicago in March 1943 and Erie in November 1943. "On the whole," the report said, "Subject's conduct was exemplary."

Letters were read. "I proved a loyal, helpful, industrious, and trustworthy soldier from October 22nd, 1941 [the date of his induction] till now," he had written his parents upon his abrupt transfer into the 620th in November 1942. "I am still the same person as I was from October 22nd, 1941 till now, yet here I am, thrown in a semi-concentration camp, which is all one can say for it. I'm an American and would defend my country to the last drop of blood." Kissman's lawyers read more letters about his parents' efforts to find out why their son was being punished and how they could help get him, like his brothers, into a combat unit.

Kissman took the stand and talked about his educational interests, his love of singing, his work history, his trip to and quick return from Germany in 1939 and early 1940, and how much he liked his medical corps training.

It was true, he said in his statement, that upon returning to the United States, "there were many phases of National Socialism which I thought was working marvelously for the German people, which could not be adopted in the United States." His lawyer's questions led him to describe the disaffection and coercion in the 620th and, trickier still, to explain how first aiding and then betraying Dale Maple would help his mates.

"Learning of Maple's plans, I protested as did everyone else who knew about his plans . . . Maple persisted, and finally, I conceived the idea that by sacrificing Maple, I could save the entire Company. After his capture, the example set would show the more radical members of the Company that it doesn't pay to go against authority, and thus insurance against radicalism would be provided. I allowed time enough before volunteering information to show motives, *e.g.,* the object for making the escape, destination for the group, and the design of the escape."

On the stand, he claimed his crazy plan had succeeded. "The results of the case have been the transfer of the 620th as a group to another camp, the establishment of the 620th as the 1800th Engineers Organization, Company A." Unaware of his former mates' continued woes, "I am led to believe [the unit] is now directly connected with the War Effort, which is an entire change from the former status . . ."

Ladon then rose. Did Kissman know a Joseph Brockmeyer and a Walter Sneller?

They were childhood friends from Erie, Kissman replied.

Did he know that both had been convicted of conspiracy to aid draft evasion?

He did not.

Did he know that both had been active in the German American Bund?

Kissman did know that but quickly added that he had never been a Bund member. He belonged only to the Siebenbuerger Singing Club, a local civic organization. "Judge Evans, judge of our court," and the judge's wife, who sang solo soprano, were also members. As for off-stage pursuits, Kissman's overriding interest at the time was chemistry, not politics. He'd had a lab in his parents' basement and didn't go to college because he believed all the other courses would distract him from chemistry. He took two years of correspondence courses in chemistry instead.

Ladon next produced a newspaper photo of Brockmeyer, Sneller, and Paul Kissman in front of a theater in Erie in 1938. The theater marquee behind them advertised "Confessions of a Nazi Spy," the night's feature film (and the Hollywood adaptation of the former FBI agent Leon Turrou's book). The newspaper caption reported the three were handing out fliers warning the picture would damage U.S.-German relations.

Yes, Kissman allowed, that was him in the photo. He had handed out leaflets and later even brought a small swastika flag back from Germany as a souvenir for Brockmeyer. But all that had happened in peacetime, before Germany was an enemy of the United States. His gift of a flag was a perfectly legal and understandable act of generosity toward a friend in those days. Everybody in town, he recalled, knew about his sympathies. (Indeed, though Ladon didn't realize it, during one public ceremony in Erie, Kissman had made a point of refusing to sing "God Bless America" because "America has never done anything for me.")

He hadn't been shy about any of it, and Erie's community was not noticeably put off by it. Given his impending 1939 trip to Germany, for example, New Castle High School's German Club had invited him to lecture the class. He "stressed the importance of German as a language and some characteristics of the German people."

But Kissman's youthful, outwardly naïve affection for the German Reich mattered greatly to the men acting as jurors in the room in 1944. Within hours, on June 13th, they came back with their verdict:

Paul Kissman had indeed bought supplies for and delivered a gun to Dale Maple and had known of Maple's plan to desert at least 24 hours before it unfolded. Then he failed to report Maple's absence on February 15th and lied—by both commission and omission—to at least two superior officers (Altman and Collar) about Dale Maple. The sins amounted to violations of Articles of War 81 and 59. The president of the court, per protocol, announced that the findings and sentence would not be made public until a Board of Review approved the proceedings.

Kissman knew the standard punishment for his offenses was a long—perhaps life—imprisonment at hard labor, dishonorable discharge, and forfeiture of all military pay then and about to become due. Behind closed doors, the court had already suggested a prison term of 25 years. His sentence, regardless of what a Board of Review ultimately decided when and how it would end, would begin immediately.[11]

———

Still, Maple waited as Army brass reviewed his trial and, not least, considered the jury's still-secret recommendation that he be put to death. His first reviewers were Lt. Col. Bernard R. Brown of the Judge Advocate General Department and then Brown's superior (a colonel whose name on the surviving records is illegible), who would review Brown's initial opinion. Officially, their job was to examine the court's jurisdictional claims on Maple, whether there was enough evidence to sustain the court's findings, the quality of Maple's legal representation, and, not least, Maple's sanity.

Brown concluded the case was well-tried. The court's findings were "overwhelmingly sustained by the record of the trial," and the "Accused's protestations of his honorable motives are patently not true." Maple's actions, moreover, probably fit civil courts' definition of treason, but not the military's. Military courts could level treason charges, which were covered by Article of War 75, but they were intended to punish "misbehavior before the enemy (in the field)."

Maple's misbehavior did aim at violence against the United States, but it wasn't on the battlefield. In military terms, the convictable charges were desertion and "relieving the enemy," which to Brown also meant to "assist, furnish, supply" the enemy. There was plentiful evidence. "More than 300 pages of record irrefutably point to the fact that [the] accused knowingly planned his flight." He had "laid elaborate plans," furnished a car, outfitted both himself and his passengers with supplies, and had carefully prepared to pass himself off as Eduard Mueller.

"Even if an intolerable disciplinary situation existed" in the 620th, Brown added, deserting and aiding "two enemy prisoners of war is not the proper method of inviting the attention of the War Department."

"The [death] sentence [recommendation], though severe, is legal," he added. "Acts comparable to treason have been shown. I know of no legal reason to recommend mitigation in either the findings or the [death] sentence."

Brown's superior agreed, though at first seemed to reconsider hanging the prisoner. The strange, awkward prisoner, he said, might have some redeeming qualities worth saving. Maple, after all, had enlisted without waiting to be drafted. His military record before being transferred to the 620th was "without a blemish." His superiors had trusted him to become an instructor, and Maple had shown a commitment to the war effort by asking at one point to be demoted from corporal so he could join a combat unit.

But, when weighed against the seriousness of the case, those qualities were not enough. Brown's superior ultimately agreed with the recommendation to hang the defendant.

The reviews climbed up the remote, invisible chain of command through the summer and into the fall of 1944. Meanwhile, Maple remained under "close custody" in the Disciplinary Barracks. His father waited for some sort of word in San Diego; his mother in Newport, Rhode Island.

As she waited, Maple's mother petitioned the Disciplinary Barracks for some extra time to visit in September for Dale's birthday, should he still be alive by then.[12]

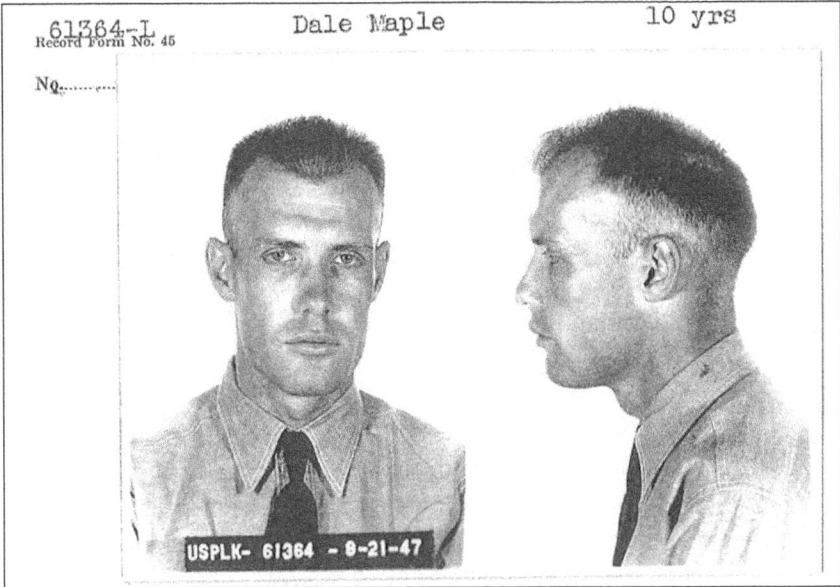

Dale H Maple at Leavenworth Penitentiary

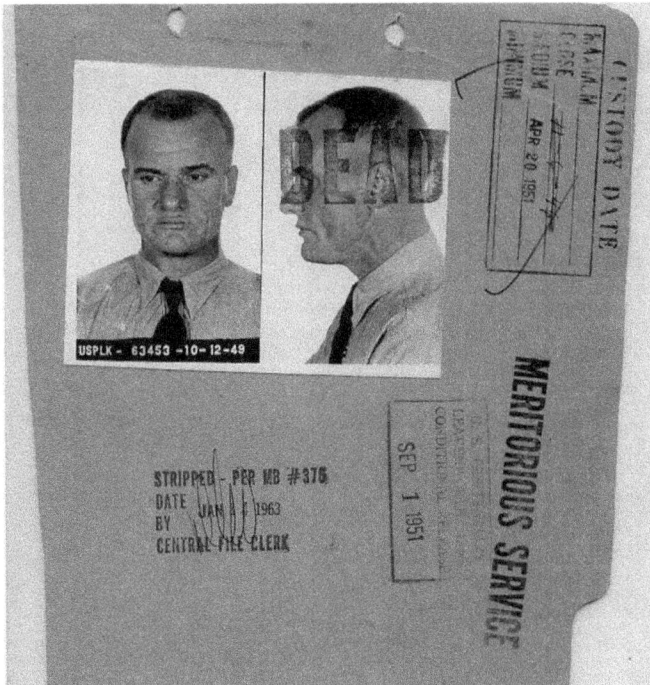

Theophil Leonhard, "the professor's" prison file

Paul Kissman at Leavenworth Penitentiary

APPOINTMENT — Eric B. Hotelling, Ph.D., has been appointed vice-president, technical research and development for Yoo-Hoo Chocolate Beverage Corporation, Carlstadt. Prior to joining Yoo-Hoo, Dr. Hotelling was associated with Stein-Hall & Co. as technical director for all plants in North America plus overseas installations.

Eric Bell Hotelling, 1972

Trying for a scholarship in Berlin, in Cambridge Maple put a Hitler bust in his room, disrupted a campus club meeting to show he sympathized with the Reich. He told The Harvard Crimson a bad dictatorship was superior to a good democracy.

Germany's Boston consul ran a network of spies, some of them students at area colleges, from the consulate. He welcomed Maple in his quest to get to Berlin in 1941.

Breadlines during the Depression moved Kissman toward sympathy with the Reich which was relatively prosperous by 1938.

Marching through New York. Like many other Americans, all four misfits admired Germany's new military might, "efficient" dictatorship and a recovery from the Depression that outstripped the U.S.'s during the 1930s.

DETAILS OF WAC-NAZI NOTES ARE WITHHELD

CAMP HALE, Colo., March 10.—(UP)—Col. John Chase, commanding officer at Camp Hale, disclosed today that three WACS stationed at the mountain center have been found guilty at court-martial of writing notes to German war prisoners interned nearby.

Camp Hale Soldier Is Caught in Mexico With 2 Escaped Nazis

FBI Agents in Colorado On Alert for Prisoners

DENVER—(INS)—FBI agents in Colorado, Utah, New Mexico, Arizona, Nevada and California were on the alert today for two escaped Nazi prisoners of war and an AWOL army private who may have engineered their escape.

Army officials called in the FBI after the escape of the war prisoners Erhard Schwichtenberg, 24, and Henrich Kikillus, 32, which coincided with the disappearance of

Private Accused of Treason Sought to Join German Army

"MOST PROMISING."

MUST GET WAGE APPROVAL

Maple's Dad Won't Talk About Arrest

Hale Officers Suspected Maple As Pro-German

Rocky Mountain News

8 CAMP HALE SOLDIERS HELD IN NAZI ESCAPES

Sensational Friendship Story Involves 5 WACS

Military Trial for Dale Maple

ALBUQUERQUE, N. M., Feb. 22 (UP)—Pvt. Dale Maple, who is accused of aiding two Germans war prisoners in an escape attempt, will be turned over to military authorities for prosecution, United States Attorney Howard Houk said tonight. Mr. Houk said the Harvard University graduate, previously charged with treason by civil authorities, would be placed in the custody of the Seventh Service Command and face a similar charge at court martial.

Manhunt. Newspapers across the country covered the escape, although WACs' rumored sexual dalliances with the POWs at Hale ("an interesting experiment in international good will in the mattress warehouses") drew their attention first. (Courtesy Elizabeth Fowler)

As the war's tide turned, the U.S. put thousands of captured German soldiers into an estimated 700 camps around the country. These were the major ones.

Aided Germans

Dale H. Maple,
Helped Prisoners Escape.

SCHWICHTENBERG.   KIKILLUS.

The F.B.I. arrested Dale Maple, 23, a U. S. army pri-

From left: Dale Maple and the two German POWs who fled with him, Sgt. Erhard Schwichtenberg and Sgt. Heinrich Kikilius, who fled with him.

Maple (left) with his pursuer D.A. "Jelly" Bryce, the sharp-shooting FBI agent who "thought the sun rose and set on" J. Edgar Hoover, down to copying his business attire.

Will Jersey Soft Drink Bridge The Nutrition Gap?

By BOB DUBILL
Associated Press Writer

CARLSTADT, N.J. (AP) — A company called Yoo Hoo is convinced it can bridge the nutrition gap in America and abroad with a soft drink.

The firm is establishing franchises in 17 foreign na-

of protein and, more specifically, a shortage of animal protein," Dr. Eric Hotelling, vice president of research and technology of the Yoo Hoo Beverage Chocolate Corp., testified before a Senate committee on nutrition and human needs.

Hotelling said a plant that was started in Cypress last year to produce 1,500 cases a day was expanded in June to produce 3,000 cases a day because of demand. Expansion is also scheduled for a plant in Libya.

The Yoo Hoo beverage company was launched in a

ERIC HOTELLING

roll detect cited

GOP harps: Hotelling is a loser

NEW TERRITORY — Dr. Eric B. Hotelling, left, senior vice president of international operations for Yoo-Hoo Beverage Co., Carlstadt, and Albacine Dove, general manager of the Freetown Provincial Co. of Sierra Leone, review franchise territory in African countries.

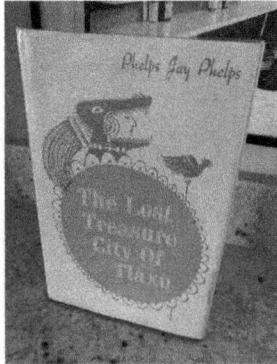

Phelps Jay Phelps

The Lost Treasure City of Tlaxo

The Herald-News: I notice that Dr. Eric Hotelling has again been quoted in reference to his function (for a time) as chairman of the Citizens' Advisory Committee to the Kinnelon Board of Education. It is obvious that Dr. Hotelling's disenchantment stems from the fact that he was unable to interject into his lengthy introduction to the final report some points which were discussed in committee and completely rejected. There was no indication of objection on his part prior to this incident.

No one else voiced dissatisfaction with relationships with the administration or experienced difficulty in obtaining information. I feel sure others would speak up at this time if there had been such difficulties. Others were, in fact, much more directly involved in obtaining specific information than was Dr. Hotelling.

Criticism has been leveled at the fact that there was an educator on the committee. This educator was happy to serve and I cannot agree that a single educator on such a committee is undesirable. In fact, I felt I was able to understand and to help others understand what Dr. Hotelling has referred to as "an overabundance of glittering generalities". I'm sorry Dr. Hotelling was unable to comprehend these concepts and programs. He speaks from a very weak position. It is a shame he is so vocal.

RICHARD W. TEWS
331 Brookvale Road, Kinnelon.

KINNELON — The qualifications of Dr. Eric B. Hotelling continue to be the dominating issue in the Republican party primary election here to nominate two candidates for the Borough Council.

Postwar successes. All the Army misfits did well in postwar America, especially Hotelling. He owned 42 patents, held top executive positions, traveled the world, had bruising fights with other Republicans over local New Jersey politics and, with a pen name plucked from an early railroad baron, self-published his "thriller," replete with cringe-worthy racist and misogynistic plot points.

PART FOUR

DESERTS, JUST AND OTHERWISE

CHAPTER 14

ON THE SCAFFOLD

One hundred and seventy miles away, in Omaha, the noose around Dale Maple's neck tightened. Major General C.H. Danielson, the Seventh Service Command's new commanding officer, voted to hang him. "In the foregoing case of Private First-Class Dale Maple, Company A, 1800th Engineering Service Battalion," Danielson wrote in his May 24th order, "the sentence ('To be hanged by the neck until dead') is approved."[1]

Danielson, per protocol, then sent Maple's death penalty file on to the Army's top lawyer, the formidable Major General Myron C. Cramer.

Cramer, a Wesleyan University and Harvard Law grad, was a military power. He'd served on the Mexican border and in Europe before and during World War I, taught at West Point, run the Army's judicial system in the Philippines, and since 1941 had headed the War Department's burgeoning Judge Advocate General Department. As such, he'd tackled Supreme Court-level wartime decisions about military control over companies that supplied critical war materials. His cases also involved deciding whose national law to apply when United Nations' rules conflicted and which U.S. departments' interests in the massive enterprise of a global war should take precedence when they met.

Another of Cramer's knotty jobs was to approve or disapprove the punishments handed out by his Judge Advocate General Department, which ran the Army's courts-martial. He was no softie. After the war, he would go on to become the sole American judge on the 11-nation war crimes trials of Japanese leaders. All told, that panel convicted 5,000 Japanese and executed more than 900. During the war, Cramer was the one who revived a dusty "military commission" solution with Attorney General Biddle to try and punish the eight German saboteurs of 1942. Such commissions had been left unused since the

Civil War. (During the Civil War, the Supreme Court had stopped an offended officer from organizing a military commission to prosecute a lawyer who, not unlike the disloyal Maple, had spoken up for the enemy Confederacy in unionist Indiana). Eighty years later, Cramer used the commission to impose a death sentence on the Germans who had arrived secretly by U-boat to blow up—again like Maple hoped to do—factories and train stations.

Cramer had not softened since. Through June of 1944, he already had written the final approvals in six of the 45 capital punishment cases his staff had won. He would decide Maple's case personally, too. It would be the weightiest and probably binding opinion in determining if "the findings are sufficient to justify the penalty." [2]

From Cramer, military death sentences went to the secretary of war and then to the president for what was often a rubber stamp agreement. Secretary of War Henry Stimson, busy running the largest organization in American history, typically took his reviewers' recommendation. Roosevelt, busy with supply chains, dying Americans, allies, politics, and (most recently) new illness, was also short of the time needed to pick through a court record. He, in turn, typically took the secretary's advice.

Wartime mercy, especially in capital cases like Maple's, was rare enough in the military to become legendary. During the Civil War, General Joseph Hooker sent President Lincoln an envelope with the cases of 55 convicted deserters, all sentenced to die. Lincoln, not bothering to open the envelope, wrote "Pardoned" on the envelope's face and returned it unread to the general. But many leaders before and since, regardless of their personal feelings, believed extreme punishment was essential to military discipline in the terrifying crucible of war.

In the year 1944, as lawyer Biddle kept warning, few were inclined toward mercy anyway. Roosevelt, Cramer, and Stimson were to approve the death penalty for 39 American soldiers that year. Roosevelt himself commuted only ten sentences in '44, the fewest since he took office in 1933. The Army was to execute 148 men from 1941 through 1950. It had executed none in the 1930s. It would impose the death penalty on ten in the 1950s.

And just as Maple's file reached Cramer in October 1944, U.S. soldier Eddie Slovik was in a stockade in France for deserting. Admitting he was "too scared" to serve as a rifleman on the front lines, he walked to the rear and gave a note to an enlisted cook. "I, Pvt. Eddie D. Slovik, 36896415, confess to the desertion of the United States Army. At the time of my desertion, we were in Albuff [Elbeuf] in France. I came to Albuff as a replacement." The Army sentenced him to death, and General Dwight Eisenhower denied his appeal for leniency. Two months later, in January 1945, Slovik was executed.[3]

Maple, still marking time in Kansas, did his best to keep his worries from his mother. Ten days after his trial ended, he wrote her an elegiac letter about the season budding outside his concrete home. "In some ways, it's a pity you didn't stay a day or two longer," he wrote on May 17th. "Summer arrived quite suddenly, and we haven't had any rain since you left. The trees are that brilliant green which they show only in early summer, and everything is very pleasant." He pondered switching from breeding Chow dogs—a family avocation for years—to Afghans.

"This is a postwar objective," he said as if he would ever emerge from the Disciplinary Barracks alive. He sent her recipes, worried about the Red Sox, and mused about how he'd celebrate after the war with friends from North Africa and Sicily. As summer 1944 became fall, he wrote her about his disappointment over Roosevelt's defeat of Thomas Dewey in the presidential election. "Well, Dewey put up a better fight than anyone else ever has against that man. I, too, am very happy over [Massachusetts] Gov. [Leverett] Saltonstall's success [in being elected to the U.S. Senate]. He is everything that a senator should be, and then some. The old New England families can still show their worth, can't they?" And at movie night at the Disciplinary Barracks, he saw the movie "Show Business." Star Joan Davis was "certainly a scream."

Much of this was for his mother's benefit. In one letter, she mourned that "it looks bad." He affected nonchalance in reply. "Well," he wrote back, "I can only die once."

But for all his chipper talk and grandiosity, he was frightened. The news arrived on December 6th. "Well, this is the day I've been dreading more than anything else," he wrote his mother. "Of course, we both knew that the sentence would have to be revealed sooner or later, and I think we both had a pretty good idea what it would be . . ."[4]

———————

Maple's crimes, Cramer wrote, were "despicable." They included his "open" advocacy of National Socialism, his attempt to get to Germany after Pearl Harbor, his sabotage planning, his desertion, and his aid to the German prisoners. Not least, "his actions both before and since the commission of the offenses effectively refute" his claims that he acted to benefit the men of the 620th.

"There appears little in the record other than the accused's youth to suggest mitigation."

Then, a surprise. "I believe, however, that under all the circumstances justice does not require this young man's life and that the ends of justice will better be served by sparing his life so that he may live to see the destruction of tyranny, the triumph of the ideals against which he sought to align himself, and the final victory of that freedom he so grossly abused.

"I recommend that the sentence be confirmed, but that it be commuted to dishonorable discharge, forfeiture of all pay and allowances due or to become due, and confinement at hard labor for life, that the United States Penitentiary, Leavenworth, Kansas, be designated as the place of confinement, and that the sentence as thus modified be carried into execution. The Secretary of War concurs in my recommendation."[5]

Cramer's recommendation then went to the president. In November, Roosevelt made Maple the 10th commutation of his year of rare commutations.

> In the foregoing case of Private First Class Dale Maple (11048476), Company A, 1800th Engineer General Service Battalion, the sentence is confirmed but commuted to dishonorable discharge, forfeiture of all pay and allowances due or to become due, and confinement at hard labor for the term of his natural life. As thus modified, the sentence will be carried into execution.
> Franklin D Roosevelt
> The White House
> Nov 15, 1944[6]

Maple was staggered. Realistically or not, he had done his best not to listen to his lawyer's warnings and remained hopeful the Army would change its mind, overturn his conviction or slap him on the wrist. When word finally arrived, however, he was shaken by the reality of spending the rest of his life behind bars.

"Of course, it could have been worse, I suppose: The President might have approved the original sentence," he wrote his mother in a sad, unusually depressed letter on the day he got the news. Perhaps, he said, "it won't be as long as it sounds? Natural life is a long time, though." Before mailing it to her in Rhode Island, he added a somewhat brighter postscript: "I feel better now that I've had dinner and a breath of air. It was a bit of a shock, you know, but I'm over that now. 'I'll live to 108 and turn into an old grey mule.'"[7]

They came for him that same night of December 6th, 1944, soon after he finished the letter to his mother and a year and three days since he and the rest of the 620th had arrived at Camp Hale. Guards manacled him, took him from his cell at the United States Disciplinary Barracks, and drove him six miles through the dark to the forbidding, massive U.S. Penitentiary at Leavenworth. It was to be his home for the remainder of his life. He arrived wearing a shirt, trousers, coat, overcoat, and cap that, his transfer documents noted, were to be returned to the Disciplinary Barracks as soon as possible.

Maple was exhausted. "He listens to and answers questions with only a fairly well-concealed boredom," the prison official who did his admission interview wrote. "Of course . . . he is tired of it all." He was "quiet, well-poised, and well-controlled." On his face, there was "no evidence of shame nor any contrite feeling. In some ways, it may be said that his attitude is entirely inexplainable [sic] to this examiner."

He "still believes the National Socialist Party was the only kind of a force that could save Europe, and he believes that Hitler had the right kind of government . . . and . . . that we should have left this alone for Hitler to do so." He "does disagree with the Nazi campaign against the Jews if they are as anti-Semitic as reported."[8]

Word spread quickly. "President Commutes Death Sentence Given Deserter," the Associated Press reported on December 7th. Newspapers across the country picked it up, including in Washington, D.C., Maple's hometown of San Diego, near his mother's home in Rhode Island, and, not least, in Tennessee, where his old mates now in the 1800th were stationed.

Even his comrades were "astonished by the lack of severity of the sentence," one said. Still assigned to an often-abusive "special organization" and under conditions that even Maple's Board of Review said were "fertile soil for disloyalty," some of his trapped former mates reportedly concluded, "Maple must have been cooperating with the FBI all along."

Others thought his changed sentence was a sign of the country losing its nerve. The reporter who would soon try to make Maple famous was disgusted. "The general gutlessness of America," he wrote in a note to himself while researching his story, "has created the no-capital-punishment tradition."

Still, others attributed his escape from the gallows to privilege. "I believe that Maple's sentence was commuted from the death penalty to life imprisonment because of his father's long and satisfactory military record," a former Harvard classmate guessed. At Harvard, Maple had claimed L.G. Maple, among other fictitious military references, was a high-ranking officer. [9]

Secret conspiracies or influence-peddling aside, Maple's new sentence might also be seen as evidence of something more. Fatigue was evident in Washington D.C., where "The Great Sedition Trial" reached a deflated, anti-climactic end just days before Maple got word of Cramer's mercy. Begun in April on the same day as Maple's court-martial, the mass trial of more than a score of isolationist, conservative, racist, and anti-Semitic critics of the Roosevelt administration had ground on and on. The trial itself had become an embarrassment. Within a month of its start, the government's case already looked thin, primarily based on a questionable constitutional argument that criticism of the Roosevelt Administration amounted to sedition. Government lawyers repeatedly backed into almost comic legal quagmires trying to find something in the law to agree with them. The press widely mocked the whole enterprise. Public sentiment had turned toward the not-very-sympathetic defendants. And when the 65-year-old judge in the case died of a heart attack and a mistrial was declared, there was no one in the judicial system with the time, heart, or budget to re-try it.

And some military crime, now increasingly viewed through victors' eyes, was also beginning to look smaller and less significant than it had just a short time before. Disciplinarian Cramer's commuting of Maple's death sentence differed dramatically from his dogged insistence in 1942 on executing the eight German saboteurs, two of whom turned the whole group in and none of whom actually sabotaged anything. One military justice specialist familiar with both events pointed out that "by the time we get to Maple, it's pretty clear that we're going to win the war. We could kill this guy, but it's probably not worth it. In the end, he didn't really damage security."[10]

CHAPTER 15

FIRST DRIPS FROM A
FROZEN HEART

Paul Kissman, who the military now listed with some literary license as a "paint sprayer" in civilian life, followed Maple from the Disciplinary Barracks to the same forbidding penitentiary at Leavenworth a few days later. On December 13th, General Court-Martial Order No. 1994 officially ended Kissman's service to his country. He was now a dishonorably discharged soldier, denied whatever money the War Department still owed him, and set to spend the next 25 years of his life behind bars. He'd be 54 if or when he got out.

His term began in the prison's intake office, where he signed the standard set of papers. He was "courteous," his Admission Summary noted, as he designated where to send his belongings if he died in prison and agreed to have his mail opened. He named five "authorized correspondents:" his parents, his two brothers, and Mrs. L.B. Pratt, "a friend" from Jacksonville, Florida. Kissman reported he had no money or property to be put in safekeeping, although he was not altogether poor. His mother estimated his inheritance from his parents' estate would "probably total about $12,000" someday. At the time, a new house in unincarcerated America cost about $4,600. The average wage was $2,400 a year.[1]

Kissman then changed into prison garb and, with Maple somewhere nearby, began life in a 4½' x 9' cell. Separately, he and Maple each had a cot, a washbasin, a commode, a shelf for books, a broom, toilet paper, cleaning powder, hangers, and a rod on which to hang their clothes. A locker with a dial lock for valuables was attached to their beds.

Those first days and for years to come, a bell woke them at 7 A.M., and they had 15 minutes to wash up and clean their cells before marching to the cafeteria. Talking was forbidden while waiting for food. Maple and Kissman barely spoke to each other even when they had the chance, a fellow prisoner recalled. Once they got their food, they could talk but couldn't go back for seconds. No one—including Kissman, a heavy smoker—could smoke. They had 20 minutes to finish before marching back to their cells and reporting for prison work at eight. Each day they worked until 11:30; washed up; ate; indulged in some kind of "recreation" from 12:20-to-1 P.M.; worked or attended short school classes or went into the yard until 4:30; ate at five; and counted off.

Summer would prove to be the worst. To prisoners, Leavenworth was "the Hot House," stifling without air conditioning in the Kansas heat and humidity. During the worst winter weather, they would generally be confined indoors. They could listen to the radio as long as they had headphones. They bathed and changed their clothes twice a week. They kept their heads down to avoid beatings and rapes. There were church services and a movie on Sundays and holidays.[2]

The once-voluble Kissman became "somewhat introverted," though his supervisors graded his work at the prison hospital as good. Otherwise, he would attract administrators' attention only rarely during the next two years. He once requested a transfer from Kansas to the federal prison at Lewisburg, Pennsylvania, to be closer to his family. His family—his father (a retired railroad engineer in ill health), mother, and brothers (both of them back from the war)—was able to muster only one trip to Kansas a year. But the Bureau of Prisons denied his transfer request, although his lone black mark in prison was minor. He had borrowed a book from another inmate—a violation—and then altered the registration number of the book to conceal the transaction. He got 30 days of restrictions.

Overall, his adjustment to prison life was "excellent." His supervisors, much as the officers of the 620th once had, came to like him. They admired his genuine interest in his work as an "eye, ear, nose, and throat" technician in the infirmary. Just 12 months into his 25-year slog, they proclaimed him already "reformed." At his first annual progress report in December 1945, they claimed he "now realizes his error in being disloyal to his country."

And, having spared Maple's life, the War Department began to forgive Kissman, too. His keepers denied his transfer to Pennsylvania in part because the Army found him to be "restorable material"—meaning he could be returned to active duty one day—and that it would be easier to re-activate him from Leavenworth than from Lewisburg.[3]

Then, just four months after Japan surrendered, his jailers shortened his term by 60%, from 25 years to 10. With luck, Paul Kissman—convicted contributor to mutinous Inner Circle planning, desertion, and rebellion—could be paroled as soon as October 1947.

Five months later, it loosened some more: in April 1946, just a few months after his first annual progress report, the Classification Committee that reviewed prisoners' behavior shortened his sentence once more, this time to eight years. His possible parole date moved up, too.

And it was happening elsewhere. Back in February 1944, on the day they learned that Dale Maple and the Germans were not only missing but probably together, Camp Hale's MPs stormed into Eric Hotelling's barracks. They rousted him from his bunk, already knowing about his suspicious behavior before and after inducting him.

They knew about his apparent failure to register for the draft. They had the CIC's records of his disturbing and dangerous talk at Camp Meade. They believed he was close to the fugitive Maple. Then, in his bunk, they found "considerable documentary evidence" of the mutiny plans for six armies of freed German POWs and pro-German American soldiers to meet at various points in the U.S. His rebels would then to march to "designated objectives." There were records of troop strengths at "numerous Army installations" and from his recruiting trips to Denver and Camp Carson. His notes included plans to create a "shuttle system" back to Europe for the prisoners his army would free. The escaped Germans would replenish the Army of the Reich and, upon return, supply Hotelling's guerrilla force in the Rocky Mountains. Then there was the patch of Navy code in his papers.

Hustled off to the brig, Hotelling swore he had simply found the patch in his barracks' day room. The MPs thought his notes suggested he had been trying to decipher the code.

Military Intelligence spent the next weeks interrogating more than 30 other Camp Carson and Camp Hale soldiers, and none in the surviving interrogation records thought Hotelling's notes and the documents were mere idle musings. His mates nearly unanimously thought Hotelling was promoting violence.

An FBI memo summarized the case against him. He had "aided escape of German prisoners of war; . . . actively planned and attempted to recruit other pro-Nazi American soldiers into an organization to mutiny against the U.S. Army, seize control of western Army bases, arm German prisoners of war, and after that hide in the hills for guerilla warfare. Subject collected information regarding other Army units from fellow American soldiers. Subject attempted to decipher an intercepted U.S. Navy code, which he claimed he had found." He looked like the Inner Circle's conspiratorial center. When the FBI arrested Maple in New Mexico the very next day, the Army quickly connected the dots and sent Hotelling to the Disciplinary Barracks to be court-martialed along with Maple, Leonhard, Kissman, and Siering.[4]

Hotelling, for his part, denied "any intention to start a mutiny." Yes, he had been "sympathetic" to communicating with other disaffected soldiers at Camp Carson and Fort Leonard Wood, where "the same legal problems existed." But, far from organizing a guerilla army, he swore he had been interested in forming only a "defensive organization" to "protect pro-German members of the Company" in case of a communist uprising in the United States.

His prison interrogator was amused. "Hotelling," he noted wryly, "failed to inform any of his listeners that his plan was defensive in nature."

At the Disciplinary Barracks at Fort Leavenworth Bernard Ladon, assigned to prosecute Hotelling for the Army, was convinced that given time, Hotelling would have put some parts of his plan into action. "Strange as it may seem, those men were very serious, and while I admit that their ideas were so fantastic . . . they were in dead earnest and believed they could disrupt communications . . ." Upon spending an afternoon interviewing the accused, "he explained to me in detail their plan of attack and sabotage. They even had a T/O [take-off or attack time] for their army . . . and it was rather complete in detail."

Late in the afternoon of the long day of questioning, Ladon asked Hotelling how he'd "supply his guerilla army once it got back to the mountains. His answer was a blank expression, and I started laughing. They had planned on guns, ammunition supplies, and everything but the main thing a soldier needs, and that is food."[5]

Ladon and the Army thus formally charged him with big, capital crimes: complicity in helping the POWs escape and, even darker, violating Article of War 66: mutiny and sedition. Soldiers guilty of mutiny and sedition "shall suffer death or such other punishment as a court-martial may direct."

—•—

His prospects, given the physical evidence, looked dim. But something happened.[6]

Records surrounding Hotelling's Special Court-Martial Order No. 38 were lost to a fire at the National Archives at St. Louis and, with them, an explanation of how the case against Eric Hotelling fell apart.

Perhaps it was witness testimony. The same mates from the 620th who thought him radical and potentially violent also almost universally hastened to tell investigators that he was hard to take seriously. They regarded Hotelling "as a crackpot," an FBI agent reported. A Camp Carson soldier who Hotelling tried to recruit for his mutiny thought him "batty." Leonhard thought him delusional. "He talked with utter abandon of armies of thousands of men which would suddenly be formed and then begin operations," Leonhard mused to his own Army interrogator.[7]

Whatever the reasons, by the time Hotelling entered the trial room at the Disciplinary Barracks in July, he faced relatively minor accusations under Article of War 96. His remaining charges: he had registered at a Denver hotel under a fake name on a recruiting trip to Camp Carson in January 1944. On another recruiting foray in Denver, he displayed "flags, banners bearing Nazi symbols [and] emblems of enemy power while soldiers of the Army of the United States were present in the room at his invitation."

Prosecutor Ladon remained convinced that Hotelling was guilty of worse, but somehow his wild schemes to free and arm German soldiers on U.S. soil, recruiting trips, and attempted codebreaking didn't amount to trying to organize an uprising. It did, however, disturb military morale. On July 6th, with Kissman in the first month of his 25-year term, the court sentenced Hotelling to six months at the Disciplinary Barracks. He got out after two in September 1944.[8]

———

A lucky man, he walked out of the Disciplinary Barracks that fall, owing the Army another 269 days of service for "good time lost." He was "restored to duty" and was shipped to rural Tennessee to rejoin Maurer, Drewes, Poehlmann, Nobis, and many of his former mates in the re-named 1800th. All, according to the former 620er Rudi Nobis, still despised the work and the unit's mean life.* Yet, perhaps beaten down by the drama, abuse, and hostility, many of the company's suspected subversives now spoke of "accommodation" with the unit.

Hotelling, who never got Leonhard's intercepted jailhouse instructions for keeping the pro-German flame alive, was one of them. Nobis recalled that he'd dropped his scheming and lowered his profile for the duration. "After having realized there was a purpose for that company," explained Menke Drewes, who

---

* In Maple's and Leonhard's absence, Nobis "attempted to take over the legal requests and rights of members of the organization." Six CIC agents kept the 500 men of the 1800th under tight surveillance into 1945.

had once aspired—jokingly, he swore—to become Gauleiter * of the American West. "I felt that maybe the situation wasn't too bad at all and that eventually we might be reassigned to either our old outfits or similar units."[9]

Hotelling's extraordinary luck held. The Army assigned him to a desk job removed from the ditch digging and road repair his mates were doing. A year later, in November 1945, it abruptly promoted him to private first class, upgraded him to "clerk financial," and sent him to occupied Japan for three months. Hotelling's detail computed air corps data about fuel consumption and recorded engineers' staff hours. Among other benefits, it allowed Hotelling to put "overseas duty" on his post-war resume. The Army, now rapidly demobilizing, discharged him on February 24th, 1946. He went home to his New Jersey family, which a few years earlier had been so frightened that it twice warned the FBI he was a worrisome security risk. With him, he had his honorable discharge papers. The boilerplate language on them testified to his "Honest and Faithful Service to this country."[10]

—•—

Germany was still smoldering in May 1945. Hitler was dead only a few weeks, and the first shocking reports of the horrors at his concentration camps were emerging. In the Pacific, the savage Battle of Okinawa—a massive 82-day bloodletting of 65,000 killed and wounded, many during hand-to-hand combat with some Japanese troops reduced to fighting with shovels and pails of slop—was still raging.

But that month in Washington, Secretary of War Stimson was already forming an "Advisory Board on Clemency" to review all the wartime general courts-martial of U.S. soldiers.

His Board first targeted some 27,000 "serious" cases in which a soldier was serving more than six months in prison.[†] At the war's start, the Selective Service had tried mightily to keep felons out of the military altogether. It tested enlistees and draftees for "criminal tendencies" (then including homosexuality) and classified those likely to commit "heinous crimes" as 4-F, or not draftable. But by the end of 1942, about the time it was segregating those suspected of subversion into misfit units like the 620th, it lowered its standards.

---

* A "gauleiter" was a Nazi party administrator who oversaw and often determined the political activities in German and German-occupied regions.

† The Board assumed longer sentences probably involved felonies and heinous crimes. Some soldiers convicted of misdemeanors, however, also had gotten sentences longer than six months. "Heinous crime" was defined as treason, murder, rape, kidnapping, sodomy, pandering, "sex perversion" or drug use.

It began "to take almost anyone." Civil judges often gave even civilians convicted of certain crimes during the war a choice of serving time or enlisting. And the Armed Forces, desperate for manpower, did induct them. Stimson's new Review Board began re-evaluating the cases of soldiers—like Maple and his mates—who had committed some sort of crime *since* being inducted.

Its actions, one historian claimed, would achieve a "high water mark" of American clemency. In November 1945, about the time Eric Hotelling was being shipped to Japan, recently retired Supreme Court Justice Owen J. Roberts took command of the Board. By the time its work was done, it looked at some 84,245 cases tried during the war, "serious" and otherwise. It remitted or reduced sentences in 85 percent of them.

It wasn't altruism. A War Department consultant in 1944 had outlined the argument that putting soldiers in prison could also effectively be "pampering" them, given that even a dank cell was preferable to the hell of D-Day or Guadalcanal. "One way to conserve manpower and ensure we don't pamper prisoners is to put them back in the foxhole," a National Defense University study later contended. And the armed forces needed manpower to meet the menacing new Soviet military threat.

———

Roberts' group ultimately paroled about 50 percent of those still in custody and returned the equivalent of three full infantry divisions to duty. It reduced the sentences of thousands more and upheld death penalties only for those soldiers convicted of rape or causing loss of life. Commutations sped up, too. Between them, presidents Roosevelt and Truman commuted 34 death sentences in 1945 (up from 10 in 1944). Truman commuted another 28 in 1946 and another 45 through 1949.[11]

And after rethinking the sentences it had handed down, the War Department launched a review of its entire judicial system. A similarly curious or sentimental or honest or uniquely compassionate military reaction had followed earlier conflicts. In 1919 Secretary of War Newton Baker had told Congress he was concerned that court-martial "sentences that may have been appropriate . . . during a time of war [may no longer be] appropriate after hostilities ceased." Congress replied with a Special Clemency Board to review some 5,400 World War I cases. That Board ultimately recommended some form of clemency in the vast majority—4,724—of them.

"The war was over," one historian of the era explained, "and it was time to let society reform these soldiers."

Now, a similar sentiment—emotional, empathetic, practical, and tight-fisted—rose in Washington. "We court-martialed about two million soldiers during World War II," explained retired Col. Fred L. Borch, a faculty member at the Judge Advocate General's School of the U.S. Army in Charlottesville, Va., "and these were long sentences, 25 and 35-year sentences." By war's end, "the Army didn't want to spend the money dealing with these prisoners and thought, 'let's put the war behind us.'"[12]

—•—

As Roberts' board combed through the military's wartime sentences, in 1946, a nine-member War Department committee began a deep-dive review of its whole court-martial system. It looked worn. The Army's judiciary had grown during the war but remained understaffed to dispense justice for a force of nearly eight million people trained to do violence and then abruptly suppress their emotional reactions to their work. Worse yet, many of its lawyers and judges were not, in fact, lawyers or judges.

"The system not infrequently broke down because the courts were frequently staffed with incompetent men," the committee found. Army defense counselors, in particular, suffered from a "lack of experience and knowledge" of military law, much like the two thinly experienced Army men it had assigned to defend Dale Maple.

Commanding officers—who often knew even less law than the soldiers assigned to defend the accused—also dominated the proceedings, and they were military officers, not trained judges. They were more concerned about command than justice. Officers tended "to regard the courts-martial primarily as instruments enforcing discipline by instilling fear and inflicting punishment, and [the commanding officer] does not always perceive that the more closely he can adhere to civilian standards of justice, the more likely he will be to maintain the respect and the morale of troops." That, too, led to inappropriate punishments.[13]

While they instilled discipline and exacted retribution, the sentences began to look very different from civilian courts' then-current sentencing philosophy. Civil courts at least formally aimed to get the prisoner back into society sooner rather than later. Their "rehabilitation" model—which tried to fit the punishment to the criminal and the circumstance rather than the crime—had dominated civil court philosophy since the late 19th century. Soon, in 1949, the U.S. Supreme Court would declare that "retribution is no longer the dominant objection of the criminal law. Reformation and rehabilitation of offenders have become important goals." Civil judges' philosophy would soon begin to change again, this time toward using sentencing as a way to protect society from criminals. But the military, sick of war and anxious to release or reclaim its men and women, was just then catching up with long-established civilian practices.[14]

Not least, the legal theories behind the charges against the men of the 620th sprang leaks.

Some War Department reviewers questioned the very "usefulness" of charging people like Maple, Kissman, and Leonhard with aiding the enemy. For one thing, it was not always clear just what constituted "aid." Prosecutors simply didn't find it a very practical charge.

For another, it was hard to get convictions for it. "Only two cases involving World War II prosecutions in violation of Article of War 81 ever reached the Board of Review level, and both involved offenses committed within the United States," an analysis at Judge Advocate General's School found. Those two, of course, were Maple and Leonhard.[15]

The military's clemency movement began immediately after the war ended. It aimed at nothing less than to speed "the rehabilitation of dishonorably discharged prisoners by returning them to their home communities." Three years after the war's end, Roberts' and two other reform boards studied 3,751 soldiers who had gotten and completed early paroles. The study, begun in November 1948, concluded that the re-integration program was working. A mere 2.65% of the parolees—148 people—had violated their parole terms in some way.[16]

Even notorious prisoners were getting out by late 1948. George John Dasch and Ernest Peter Burger, the German saboteurs who in 1942 had turned their fellow terrorists in to the FBI and got long prison sentences for their troubles, were free by 1948. President Truman released them on the condition they return to Germany, which they did.

And punishments for crimes like the Inner Circle's no longer carried death penalties. In 1948, the House of Representatives amended the Criminal Code to reduce the penalties for treason, rebellion or insurrection, sedition, subversion, and, not least, "activities affecting armed forces during war." Treason still carried the death penalty or sentences of more than five years. During the war, penalties for "false reports or false statements with intent to interfere with the operation or success of the military or naval forces of the United States or to promote the success of its enemies" (among the charges the Inner Circle faced) could include execution. In 1948, with Maple and Leonhard still incarcerated, the sentences were changed to fines and a maximum of 20 years in prison.

Harboring people who disrupted (or even threatened to disrupt) the military's wartime efforts earned fines and not more than ten years in prison.[17]

Not everyone was happy about the military's retreat from capital punishment. Bernard Ladon, who had led the prosecution of Maple, Hotelling, and Kissman, was dubious about them. Almost four years after the war's end, he still believed, "In most instances, I have found the sympathies of the clemency board to have been misplaced."[18]

Intelligence agencies' version of post-war clemency, however, was dramatically more aggressive, drawing close and helpful to many ostensibly reformed Nazis. In April 1945, before the surrender, Allen Dulles—then stationed in Bern, Switzerland with the OSS and destined to lead the CIA—rescued the notorious SS General Karl Wolff from Italian partisans who had surrounded Wolf's villa, looking for vengeance.

By 1948 and 1949, American Intelligence was bankrolling the equally despised Reinhard Gehlen, not too long before Hitler's Eastern Front intelligence chief. He was best known among the Allies for finding Jews and Communists for the SS's death squads and for torturing Russian POWs. Gehlen, who sold himself to the OSS and then CIA as a Soviet expert, soon recruited Dr. Franz Six, one of his wartime death squad leaders, and high-ranking former members of the German High Command for his U.S. spy team. The military, moreover, quickly swept up and put German scientists to work in rocket and weapons development projects.

The civil courts, FBI, and Congress also quickly switched enemies. Congressional committees, attuned as ever to political opportunity, immediately resumed their pre-war pursuit of leftists, union leaders, and others supposedly prone either to treason, disruption, Soviet sympathies, or political opposition. FBI Director Hoover, who earned his political spurs in the first World War's wake by arresting and deporting supposed Reds and anarchists, turned his post-war guns on Communists, dissidents, and gay men.

The civil justice system, too, became progressively more punitive. Case by case, sentencing policies began to steer from prevention and rehabilitation and toward "crime control" and tying mandatory prison stays to the offense regardless of circumstance.[19]

Post-war, civil courts' sentencing immediately grew sterner. The number of "serious" sentences (those longer than six months) handed out in federal and state courts jumped by 15.3 percent from 1945, the last year of the war, to 61,338 in 1946, the first full year of relative peace. They continued their upward trend through the end of the decade. The nation's "incarceration rate"—the number of state and federal prisoners per 100,000 residents—was at 101 when the war ended. It was 10 percent higher by 1951.

Even as the military moved its prisoners out of prison, the country's total prison population thus increased by more than 24 percent from 1945 to 1950. It has not dipped since.[20]

Civil authorities even went after wartime transgressors the military had already freed. In October 1944, as Myron Cramer was writing his then-confounding military recommendation to spare Dale Maple's life, an Air Force man named Martin James Monti walked onto the airfield in Milan. He jumped into an empty plane and flew it to the nearest German base he could find. After the surprised Germans heard his story and untied him, he generously gave the valuable plane and its technology to the Luftwaffe and announced he was defecting. The Nazis soon put him on German State Radio to broadcast—infrequently and reportedly not very skillfully—propaganda messages back to American forces. When the Air Force caught up to him after the war in 1946, it court-martialed him for stealing the plane, sentenced him to 15 years, and then in the spirit not just of mercy and but of replenishing a rapidly shrinking air corps, suspended the sentence and allowed him to re-enlist.

His freedom was brief. The FBI picked Monti up immediately after the military honorably discharged him in 1948. It charged him with treason and got him convicted. He was sent to Leavenworth for 25 years.

Herbert John Burgman got 20. The Army found Burgman, another American citizen who had stayed in Europe to work for the Nazis, in Frankfurt in 1945. His German State Radio show—he called it "Radio Debunk"—blamed Roosevelt and "his Jewish and communistic pals" for starting the war. Almost all Allied soldiers, he added, were carrying sexually transmitted diseases. For that, if for no other reason, he advised German women to shun the invaders emphatically.

But instead of trying him when it found him, the Army hired him as an interpreter. His punishment: report to the military police on his way to work every day. Civilian authorities, however, pounced. They re-arrested him and shipped him to the United States, where he was convicted of 13 counts of treason in 1949 and sentenced to Lewisburg State Prison for up to 20 years. (He died of heart disease, however, in December 1953). Donald S. Day, a *Chicago Tribune* reporter who also broadcast anti-Semitic denunciations from Berlin, was first arrested and released by the U.S. military. Civilian authorities recaptured and charged him with treason in 1949.

All the civilian traitors—people who got the kind of open, civil treason trial Maple had desired—got harsher sentences from civilian courts than they would have from military courts.

Similar postwar punishments befell others civil courts accused, like the Inner Circle, of giving aid and comfort to the enemy. Robert Henry Best, a foreign correspondent who also made propaganda broadcasts for the Nazis, was convicted on 121 counts of treason and was sentenced to life. (He died in prison in 1952). Mildred Gillars, in turn, was a U.S. citizen who had chosen to stay in Germany with her husband in 1941. After her husband fell on the Eastern Front, she couldn't travel home and got a new job as "Axis Sally" on German State Radio, broadcasting anti-American opinion. She was convicted of eight counts of treason and sentenced to 10-to-30 years. Already at Lewisburg was Douglas Chandler, serving a life sentence for ten counts of treason for his German State Radio broadcasts urging Americans to "throw off tyranny" and to embrace isolationism.

The judicial storm reached the Pacific Theater, too. Better known as "Tokyo Rose," Iva Toguri D'Aquino was a U.S. citizen who happened to be in Japan visiting relatives in December 1941 and could not get home. Despite refusing to renounce her U.S. citizenship, she got a job as a typist at Radio Tokyo. In 1943, she was impressed into working with American prisoners of war who, in turn, were being forced to broadcast propaganda. The POWs, who knew her from her dangerous efforts to smuggle food to other prisoners, insisted she take the microphone. She did on the condition that she wouldn't have to criticize the United States. The prisoners who wrote her show complied and gave her scripts that they later claimed were intended as satire to mock Japanese arrogance and culture. Neither the Japanese nor the Americans got the joke. After the war, she was convicted in civil court on one count of treason. Six years later, she was freed only after trial irregularities—including a witness who perjured himself—cast the trial proceedings into doubt.

Nothing enraged civilian critics more than presidential pardons. The presidents of mid-20th century America were in synch with their predecessors after previous wars. President Washington had pardoned two leaders of the Whiskey

Rebellion, both convicted of treason.* The first President Adams pardoned contributors to Fries' Rebellion. Jefferson pardoned deserters from the Revolution and, after him, James Madison freed deserters from the War of 1812. James Buchanan pardoned Brigham Young for his part in the Utah War of 1857–58. Lincoln, Andrew Johnson, Theodore Roosevelt, Warren Harding, and Calvin Coolidge all pardoned both civilians and soldiers convicted of wartime crimes.[21]

But each official act of leniency in the years after World War II was blasted in politics and the press as an example of soft-headed thinking if not outright criminal bribery. Much of it didn't lack for hyperbole.

U.S. Senator Styles Bridges[†] (R-New Hampshire) demanded justice as he flourished the names of 5,856 "outlaws . . . granted pardons or other forms of clemency during the last 20 years." Bridges presented them as evidence of liberal corruption and reckless public security. Most on the list were former bootleggers, "confidence men," bank embezzlers, and income tax evaders. Two had been charged with dealing with the enemy during World War I.[22]

---

* In 1794, President Washington explained to Congress that he thought his Whiskey Rebellion pardons "consistent with the public good . . . to mingle in the operations of Government every degree of moderation and tenderness which the national justice, dignity, and safety permit."

† In 1953, Bridges and Sen. Herman Welker found out that Buddy Hunt, son of Democratic Senator Lester Hunt, had been arrested for soliciting sex from a male undercover officer near the White House. Bridges and Welker, both Republicans, that they'd publicize and prosecute Hunt's son's homosexuality if Hunt did not immediately resign from the Senate and, in effect, thus make the Republicans the majority party in the Senate. The threat of a "morals charge" against his son and the attendant publicity drove the elder Hunt to kill himself in his Senate office in June 1954.

CHAPTER 16

LEFT BEHIND

The world outside their cells, however, remained mostly a fantasy for the remaining members of the Inner Circle. At the Disciplinary Barracks, the determinedly sunny Siering and the intense Leonhard still awaited the outcome of their request for a writ of habeas corpus. If the Federal District Court in Kansas ruled for them, the Army would free them and intern them with other enemy aliens for the rest of the war. After the war, Leonhard planned to head "home" to Germany.

Siering had other plans. First, he'd finally collect on his 1939 "deal" with the INS to trade his Army service for dropping his deportation order. And when the war was over, he was going to get out of uniform and become a citizen of the United States.

Siering had tried again and again to convince various commanding officers that someone—the Army, the immigration service—owed him citizenship. Now, locked up in the Disciplinary Barracks, he took a new tack: Someone owed him a discharge.

He believed his induction at the Chicago draft center became improper and void the moment he refused to line up with the other inductees or take the oath. His transfers—first to Camp Grant for training and then to a 620th made up of "disloyal Americans, Nazi sympathizers, some communists and some Jews who had escaped from Germany" and, lastly, to the Disciplinary Barracks at Leavenworth—thus were not legal.

He and Leonhard had spent much of 1944 working with a local attorney to prepare their case. The first thing the court did was to separate their requests on the grounds that Leonhard's argument for a discharge was different from Siering's.

Leonhard, whose induction fit legal protocols, argued that he should be released because, as an enemy alien, he shouldn't have been allowed to enlist in the first place.

———

Leonhard's bid floundered from the start. In October, Federal District Court Judge Walter A. Huxman denied Leonhard's request. He agreed Leonhard had registered as an enemy alien—meaning he'd been born in Germany and had not been naturalized—in Austin in 1940. He admired many things about Leonhard: how he'd enlisted in October 1941, before the U.S.'s entry into the war, and persisted in try to become naturalized. In February 1942, as he waited for a determination on his most recent citizenship request, Leonhard dutifully complied with a new presidential order that all non-citizens re-register. On furlough in Los Angeles to register, he reported that he was still a German citizen but in the process of becoming an American one.

But Huxman cited the portions of the Selective Service Act of 1940 that said that all males residing in the U.S. between the ages of 18 and 45—whether or not they were citizens—were liable for military service. Leonhard was a resident, and his country of origin didn't matter.

All aliens, Huxman added, were entitled to the protection of the law and the Constitution. But in return "for the rights and privileges they enjoy, they owed allegiance to the country and support for its governments . . . And in war, they share equally with our citizens the calamities which befall our country, and their services may be required for its defense . . ."

Huxman thus sent Leonhard back to Fort Leavenworth to be court-martialed. Leonhard went, but Malcolm McNaughton, a lawyer in Leavenworth, Kansas, quickly appealed.[1]

In December, Siering stood with the same lawyer before the same Judge Huxman in Topeka, 63 miles from the Disciplinary Barracks.

Huxman didn't think Siering's German citizenship was an issue, either, but agreed with Siering's argument. The Selective Service Act, Huxman said on December 24th, outlined three steps to be inducted into the armed forces. Siering had taken two of them: he'd shown up at the Chicago induction center on his assigned date and was found "acceptable" at the Center. But he had refused the third required step, which was to take the oath. His refusal to swear the oath or line up with the other men "resulted in a failure to induct him into the Army," Huxman maintained. "In my view, it does not [have lawful] custody of Siering . . . Then he is not subject to the jurisdiction, control, or orders of military authorities." Siering, therefore, was "entitled to the writ releasing him from custody."

The officers at the Disciplinary Barracks quickly appealed, which sent Siering, like Leonhard, back behind bars, losing hope.[2]

It was June 1945—just as the Advisory Board on Clemency was being formed in Washington—before the court looked at Siering's writ again. This time it formally denied it. Siering could appeal that ruling, but he dithered as the July 13th deadline for filing an appeal came and went.

Eleven days later, the Army set Siering's court-martial for late July.

Surprised, Siering asked for and got the proceedings moved back to August 8th. In the interim, prosecutors called Leonhard, Kissman, and the unpredictable Dale Maple to testify at Siering's trial.[3]

In retrospect, Fritz Siering's crimes were giving people rides. He'd driven his new wife Ana, Schwichtenberg, and Leonhard on their New Year's jaunt at the dawn of 1944. While behind the wheel, he tried to convince Schwichtenberg that Germans lived far better in the United States than they did in Germany. Among many favors for his mates, he had given Maple a ride to Camp Hale's dump to pick up what turned out to be rucksacks. In the law's eyes, Siering then aided and abetted Maple by storing the mysterious objects in his car for two nights. Next, he allowed Maple to park Maple's just-purchased Reo near the rented house in nearby Red Cliff, where Siering's and another Army wife lived.

Then there was the night, in the general alarm over Maple's and the prisoners' disappearance from Camp Hale, MPs swept him, Hotelling, Leonhard, Kissman, and others into the camp's brig for interrogation and, ultimately, arrest. He had been struggling for air ever since.

On August 8th, 1945—the day the U.S. dropped a second atomic bomb, this time on Nagasaki—he found himself in the Disciplinary Barracks' trial room facing five charges under two Articles of War. By taking Schwichtenberg on the New Year's Eve tour of three Rocky Mountain towns, he "harbored the enemy" and violated Article of War 81. When he accepted the rucksacks from Maple at the camp dump and kindly let Maple keep them in Siering's car for two nights, he had helped Maple desert, which violated Article of War 59.[4]

There were many reasons to let him off. His mates' pre-trial statements to Military Intelligence and then to the prosecution consistently alleged he hadn't known what either Maple or the members of the Inner Circle were planning. He had heard rumors about their desire "to try to get back to Germany, so far as I heard, especially Leonhard." But that sounded absurd, and the men of the Inner Circle didn't discuss such things with him much anyway.

He had to be nervous when Maple, apt to say anything, took the stand at Siering's court-martial. "The situation of our company was rather odd," Maple testified. "I might say we were all almost dubious about his disloyalty. All the members of the company were under suspicion, and . . . we were never sure that Fritz could be trusted."

At their courts-martial and then at Siering's trial, Leonhard and Kissman confirmed that the anti-Nazi Siering was never included in any conspiratorial talks and wasn't a close friend. But Siering's reputation as a soft touch for favors was well-established, and many in the company took advantage of it. "The boys," the defendant himself testified, "would ask me to bring a packing box or something back to the train station for them. They know I am good-natured." His role at Rim Rock was to be a nice guy. "Sometimes we went on week-ends in the Black Hills and would bring back boxes for them."[5]

His military prosecutors, on the other hand, turned a dark light on Siering's character, statements, the evidence of his quest for citizenship, and Maple's and Leonhard's testimony. He'd come to the U.S. illegally "by jumping a boat." They flatly denied that Siering had tried to become a citizen in 1940. Despite Maple's testimony, they contended Siering had known what Maple was up to. The proof: Siering had been "apprehensive" when Maple temporarily stored his German rucksacks in Siering's car. If he and Maple weren't co-conspirators, what was Siering doing "in the company of those others" before the February 15th escape? And his understanding of English on the stand failed "only on the points which were pertinent to the case. Does that," they asked, "indicate innocence?"[6]

The court didn't entirely agree. It found him innocent of aiding Maple's desertion and of relieving the enemy by accepting the rucksacks. He was guilty, however, of harboring Schwichtenberg and storing the packs for Maple. For that, they gave him a dishonorable discharge and sentenced him to ten years of hard labor.

On August 14th, 1945—three months after the War Department began investigating and softening punishments—his Board of Review shortened his sentence to five years in confinement. The war over, he was moved from the

Disciplinary Barracks, not to Leavenworth but the Fifth Service Command Rehabilitation Center in Fort Knox, Kentucky* as a general prisoner.

Some found it hard to believe. Rudolph Nobis, who believed Maple's eventual escape from the gallows was the result of cooperating with the FBI, suspected collusion in Siering's case, too. Discharged and working for his father back in Ohio, Nobis contended that Siering won release by turning state's evidence.

He did not stay at Fort Knox for long. The Army discharged him within a year, on May 27th, 1946, and transferred him directly to the immigration service across the river in Cincinnati. No longer a soldier or a civilian, he was jobless and finally about to be deported.

Yet Fritz Siering, whose wife of four years had divorced him[†] and taken his prized car while he was behind bars, stayed doggedly determined to become a U.S. citizen and claim an American future. In the teeth of an Immigration campaign to deport internees and even "de-naturalize" foreign-born citizens, he figured his best remaining chance was to be restored to active military duty as Hotelling had been. Siering, harkening back to another second-language misunderstanding when he'd been sent to Fort Knox, was sure he already had another deal, this time to return into the Army.[7]

In his careful, backward-leaning script, he wrote to describe the situation to the Army's Adjutant General. "During the month of August 1945," he wrote in July 1948, "the writer received a court-martial and was sent to a rehabilitation center in Fort Knox, Kentucky with the understanding [that] good behavior would restore me to active duty. Instead for the good service rendered, he received a [dishonorable discharge] for which I am at a loss to explain."

He enclosed a positive reference from his commanding officer and, "thanking you kindly for any consideration given me in this matter," asked the Adjutant General to review his case.

---

* Fort Knox: The Army had bolted a detention center, called The Rehabilitation Center, onto the what was primarily a training facility in 1944. The training facility had a checkered past. In May 1944, an African-American Air Force Group—the 477th Bombardment Group—was transferred to the adjacent Godman Army Airfield after an airfield near Detroit refused to let the Black airman use the officers' club. The relatively liberal Godman did indeed allow the airmen into Fort Knox's officers' club, but when the men went to eat at its club, Fort Knox denied them entry.

† Siering had married the former Ana Muhr in Chicago in February 1942 and, according to one of Siering's mates in the 620th, she may not have been entirely monogamous. She was alleged to be having an affair with another member of the company.

A lieutenant colonel with the Military Justice Division wrote him back a week later. He explained he didn't have the authority to change a dishonorable discharge order and kindly signed it, "sincerely yours."

Siering replied immediately, arguing in stilted legalese that the officer's letter itself somehow "substantiated" Siering's claims and was enough to win the day in "the majority of cases" like his.

The reply ended up on the desk of another Army lawyer on July 25th, 1946. "This letter appears to need no reply," he noted and filed it away.[8]

Unaware of his appeal's fate, Siering kept writing letters. He appealed to officers up and down the War Department hierarchy and up and down the Immigration service. He went to Chicago to seek the help of his former employer and find the Immigration official who, he believed, had struck the first deal with him. After 17 months, Immigration ran out of patience and, in January 1948, put him on a Pan American Air flight. It took him to San Juan, Puerto Rico, where he switched planes to Buenos Aires. There, he planned to renew his efforts to get back to the United States or, if that failed, try to tempt the odds against setting up a new life in another foreign, this time Spanish-speaking, land.[9]

——

Theo Leonhard's bad luck was lasting even longer. More attuned to both English and the law than his buddy Siering, he appealed Huxman's ruling against him almost immediately. It took until October 1945 for it to reach the U.S. District Court of Appeals in Kansas. There, a three-judge panel handed down a decision that became oft-cited case law for years after that.

Leonhard's induction into the Army had been resoundingly legal, the panel ruled. Resident aliens like Leonhard, the judges said, had "obligations, so long as they reside in the United States, [that] do not differ materially from those of native-born or naturalized citizens."[10] He was also subject to the same laws and standards of behavior.

So, in January 1946, Theophil Leonhard—once an immigrant awed by the "greatness of America," a doctoral student who patriotically enlisted despite having a high draft number, and finally a soldier involuntarily plucked for the 620th from a unit heading into the Pacific—was sent back into the military justice system to be court-martialed. In giving a note to Schwichtenberg to take back to Germany, the Army said Leonhard had corresponded with the enemy, attempted to "relieve" the enemy, and given intelligence to the enemy. He had also tried to contact authorities of the German Reich, assisted in another soldier's desertion, and helped to "harbor and protect" a prisoner of war on the New Year's ride with Schwichtenberg and Siering through Colorado mountain towns. The maximum sentence, once again, was death.

———

Nationwide, the military was methodically reducing or commuting the sentences of some 80,000 soldiers when the familiar cast of characters assembled at the Disciplinary Barracks for Leonhard's court-martial: Intelligence Officer Curran, Kissman, Siering, and FBI agent Donworth Johnson (Bryce couldn't make it). Leonhard's attorneys promised to produce letters and testimonials from people who knew Leonhard before he'd joined the Army.

The Army, in turn, had its witnesses, statements, and documentary evidence of an impressionable boy in Germany who had become bitterly anti-French when French troops expelled his family from its home in Alsace after World War I. As a nine-year-old on a visit with his parents to Nuremberg in 1923, he'd been "thrilled" to glimpse the rapidly ascending Hitler. In 1932, he was 18 when he told a fellow student in the family's Texas hometown that he wanted to be a spy for Germany. While a student, he had visited the German consul in New Orleans and "associated with" Gerhard Wilhelm Kunze, then membership Secretary and later head of the German American Bund. In 1936—the same year he first applied for U.S. citizenship—he sent a letter to Hitler through the consul's diplomatic pouch, apparently applying for officer training in the German Army. He got no answer.

The next year, visiting his family in tiny Stonewall, Texas, Leonhard falsely claimed to be a citizen, apparently to vote in his county elections. While in college at Southwestern University in Georgetown, Texas, he was one of 33 university choir members who annually toured central and east Texas where the FBI's Johnson would tell the court, he "always seemed to have funds" and the time to speak "to young Germans' meetings" in the area. "He was sometimes given the Nazi salute by young people and at one time exchanged the Nazi salute with the German consul before the student body at Southwestern University," the agent added.

Leonhard recalled he'd told school friends at Southwestern that his associations with and letters to German officials were mere requests for documents for his thesis. The German consuls he contacted "were aware that I frequently criticized certain actions of the German government" and thus wouldn't want him as a fellow Nazi. One consul, however, thought he'd get a "warm welcome" in Germany anyway.

He did consider emigrating briefly, but "I felt I had a future in this country." Kunze himself eventually told a congressional committee that, while he'd met Leonhard on a visit to Texas, Leonhard was not a member of the Bund and hadn't seemed interested in becoming one. But the contacts and his not-understated admiration for the German government, however, made him "quite unpopular" at Southwestern and later at the University of Texas. Some students in his political science class complained that he was too sympathetic to the German government. Hence, the perhaps-mocking Nazi salutes.

He'd had a similar reputation among Stonewall's 250-some residents, the majority of them—including his parents—of German heritage. Residents who were children there in the 1930s and 1940s recall Leonhard taking every opportunity to "talk at public events, fish fries, and barbeques, and he'd start going on his talks. It was kind of like ISIS today, where people talk against their own country." It did not sit well with the locals or his family. Margaret Maenius, another Stonewall resident at the time, recalls that Leonhard's father, the local pastor, "was very, very upset" about his son's darkening reputation and, eventually, was "very very against" Theo's behavior at Camp Hale. All were sensitive to inviting a backlash against Germans and German-Americans in the area, many of whose sons were, in fact, then overseas fighting against relatives still living in Europe. "It was kind of bad here," Maenius said. After Theo made headlines, moreover, "we were afraid to talk about it because we were scared the government might be listening in," added Cliff Maenius.*

Leonhard also raised concerns when he joined the Army in 1941. He came under particular scrutiny by merely applying to join the Investigation Branch of the Army's Office of the Provost Marshal General. "The position sought would involve access to classified information, and he admits that he expected to handle the evacuation of aliens on the West Coast," Army investigator Curran told the judges at Leonhard's court-martial. The request raised the kind of suspicion that soon got him transferred into the 620th. "He maintained a good military record until the military authorities knew of his background," an Army parole official later noted. "After being transferred to the 620th and the 1800th, he indicated embitterment toward the United States, particularly her Army."[11]

When he came to the stand, Kissman testified that Leonhard had been there the day Maple had asked him to buy a gun for him. It was the moment

* The government was indeed listening in and had been since the war's beginning. The FBI's San Antonio office kept a close eye on the predominantly German American communities around Fredericksburg and its satellite towns like Stonewall.

Kissman said he had come to understand some of what Maple had in mind. It was probable that Leonhard understood as well.

And on January 9th, 1946, prosecutors at Leonhard's trial called Dale Maple—the one man who could confirm or deny the defendant's role in the events of February 15th, 1944—to the stand.

— —

"If it please the court," Maple said as he took his seat in the witness chair, "I decline to testify at this time." He declined even to take the oath, to tell the truth.

"I don't understand," the court's law member—its guardian of legal procedure—said. Did Maple have a "religious conviction, or what?"

He did not. The trouble, Maple explained, was that the court-martial was not public.

The explanation clarified nothing, and after a recess, the prosecution tried again. Again, Maple demurred. "I morally cannot consent to take part in secret proceedings." Almost two years since his desertion and his arrest, he maintained that his status as a prisoner subject to a military court remained unsettled. And he firmly believed in open trials for everyone, including enemy aliens like Theo Leonhard.

They brought Maple from the prison again the next day, this time with a subpoena, and tried a third time to get him to testify. "No, sir," he said again. His grounds this day were that he was himself going to seek a new trial, preferably in a public, civilian court. His testimony in this secret military one could well be "extremely prejudicial" in a new open trial, especially since he didn't even know what charges he'd be facing in a new trial. Moreover, all his efforts to publicize the "un-American" conditions in the 620th had been kept secret during wartime for "national security reasons." But the war was over now. Now the only possible reason for these secret trials was "to avoid embarrassment to higher authority" responsible for the Army mistreatment he had been trying to protest in the first place. "On those grounds, I refuse to testify."

The prosecutor, angry, reminded him about the 23rd and 24th Articles of War, which required members of the military to take the oath and to testify. Failure to testify or respond to a subpoena was a misdemeanor. Maple said he understood.

They brought him back again the next day, this time for a private talk. Maple's refusal stood. Frustrated, Leonhard's prosecutors gave in. They dismissed him and sent him back to the prison.

A month later, Adjutant General Col. George Connor summarized the three maddening days in a memo called "Misconduct of Dale Maple" for Leavenworth's warden. "Since Maple [now a federal prisoner] is not subject to court-martial jurisdiction, this matter is brought forward for such consideration as you deem appropriate."[12]

There is no record of Maple being punished for refusing to testify, but he might have had other reasons to keep his mouth shut. Testifying against another miscreant violated the prison code. "If you turn rat," Maple's former cellmate Benny Staggs explained, "you get killed."[13]

Leonhard himself didn't take the stand. Instead, lawyer McNaughton told the defendant's story through the voluminous statements Leonhard had given during the Army's investigations during the weeks after February 15th.

There were mentions of his Lutheran minister father, his family's elevated social position, and their sacrifice when Theo's brother Edgar was killed in action over Austria in 1944. There were letters, too, from Texas praising Leonhard's intelligence and community service. A letter from an administrator at Southwestern noted he had been an honor student. "Aside from his Nazi activities, he was a likable chap and very smart." But his legal defense remained that he was a German citizen wrongly put through all this. His parents, both born in Germany, had immigrated to Texas and been married in Galveston in 1911. His father had been called back to Germany during World War I to minister to the Kaiser's Army, was rousted by the French after the Armistice in 1918 and returned to Texas with his wife and sons Edward and Theo in 1923. Though he'd tried, Theo was never naturalized.

No one, however, denied that he went with Schwichtenberg on the New Year's tour, illegally given him an American uniform, had offered his services to the enemy through both Schwichtenberg and Hotelling, and, finally, failed to report Maple's desertion and aid to the enemy. The verdict came in quickly.

He was guilty. Once a Board of Review approved the sentence in October 1946, he was to be dishonorably discharged and join the 15,774 soldiers still confined for one reason or another in the United States. He was to spend the next ten years of his life among some of them, at hard labor at Leavenworth Penitentiary.[14]

Benny Staggs, Maple's cellmate, thought Leonhard "got off easy."[15]

Defeated in both civil and military courts, Leonhard was at a dead-end, much like Siering. He was glum and resentful, "emotional" and "moody" when they took him to the prison after the trial. He'd been "a victim of circumstance," he told the associate warden who met him there. His real crime was that he had known Maple was planning something big. But there had been months of "big talk," and no one except Hotelling had ever actually tried to follow through on it.

A psychologist came to interview him next. Leonhard was "very polite," he reported, but "brusque" and still "in entire sympathy with the German cause, still loyal to Germany and disloyal to the U.S." Nevertheless, he seemed "non-delinquent." He'd probably make a "good general adjustment" to life at Leavenworth.[16]

CHAPTER 17

DEUS EX HARVARD

As Leonhard settled in at Leavenworth, Hotelling—one of the Inner Circle's most active members—was already home in New Jersey, enrolled at Rutgers, and majoring in chemistry. Rudolph Nobis, who had volunteered to keep the spirit of resistance up after the reorganization into the 1800th, had been home in Canton, Ohio, since November 1945. Otto Idelberger, Jr., one of Kissman's best friends in the unit, was discharged in March 1946.

Out in society, life for them and other German sympathizers and even for innocents with vaguely German ties could be dangerous. Few cultures, of course, tolerate enemies and even foreigners in their midst well, and for the already discharged 620ers, caution and rigorous secrecy were often necessary. So was camouflage. The Oxford-educated, Polish-born Menke Drewes and his new wife, for whom he gave up revolution talk back in late 1943, were in Arlington Heights, Illinois, where he was then working as an electrician, bowling[*] and carefully calling himself an Americanized "Mike."[1]

Expulsions, lynchings, and massacres of German speakers were erupting in just liberated Europe and the triumphant Soviet Union. Vengeance in the United States never approached that level of violence, but public bile was high. Popular culture was full of insidious, relentlessly cruel Germans, arrogant and robotically obedient to insane Authority. On the street, loyal American residents of German heritage—especially those with accents—often faced still-resentful neighbors, resistance to buying German goods, and outright social ostracism and violence.

---

[*] "Mike" Drewes won $58.20 in a doubles bowling tournament. He is referred to as active bowler in 1947 in Arlington Heights league. He is elsewhere referred to in conjunction with "Drewes Electric."

Washington greeted peace by angrily deporting many, including Siering, who were neither citizens nor pro-German. One, Max Ebel, fled Germany in 1937 after a gang tried to force him to join the Hitler Youth, and knifed him. Escaping to the U.S., he soon married and joined a family woodworking business. When war arrived, the FBI arrested and interned him as an enemy alien and confined him to at least three internment camps during the next three years.*

"I left Germany because of the Nazis, and I came here, and I was a Nazi," Ebel said. In all, the FBI interned some 11,000 American citizens of German ancestry as well as thousands more German "enemy aliens" during the war in camps in Georgia, Utah, and Texas. The U.S. had exchanged about 2,000 of them for Americans interned in Germany. Now, the war over, it moved to get rid of many of the rest of them.

Former sympathizers faced worse. Immigrant Paul Schlenther of West Haven, Connecticut, for one, was a naturalized citizen who had been a low-level Bund member until Pearl Harbor Day, when he quit and joined the Army. Once in uniform and fearing that "he would be ripped apart from his family," he lied about his past Bund membership. His fear was well-founded. The government had "de-naturalized" a number of Bund members during the war. When the Army found out about Schlenther, it mustered him out and turned him over to Immigration to be interned and, although still a citizen, eventually deported.

Paul Knauer, an insurance broker in Milwaukee, and Wilhelm Hack, a "medical chemist," had both been Bund members and spent the first year after the war trying to get out of internment on Ellis Island to rejoin their American families. Immigration deported both of them in August 1946. Hans Geisler, a soldier, had been court-martialed and sentenced to five years in prison "when he said he thought Germany's cause a just one and that he would not fight against the Japanese because that would amount to fighting Germany." He was still serving his sentence when, the war over, the government revoked his U.S. citizenship and turned him over to Immigration to be deported. Many higher-ranking Bund members—including naturalized American citizens—were in the midst of years of lawsuits to overturn their deportation orders. [2]

---

* It took almost three years to empty all the camps. In January 1947 the U.S. Circuit Court of Appeals in New York finally cleared the way to deport another 305 German enemy aliens from Ellis Island (as well as some 400 Japanese enemy aliens from camps on the West Coast).

Leonhard joined Maple and Kissman at Leavenworth Penitentiary, where they were at least somewhat shielded from the official and public threat other sympathizers faced. They were the only familiar faces he found at the prison. But the Dale Maple who Theo Leonhard encountered there was a different Dale Maple.

He had just finished writing an article for the prison quarterly about "detainer rules," which courts used to keep people confined while they awaited trial. Investigations, crowded court dockets, reviews, and more regularly had been causing long, frustrating, tense waits. Worse yet, delays like Maple's and Leonhard's were often extended by the military's special and often-secret review procedures. The system's thoroughness and caution, done primarily to protect defendants, effectively made the "speedy trial" guaranteed in the Constitution impossible.

To the old Dale Maple, such judicial irony—protecting the constitutional right to a fair trial by muddying the constitutional right to a speedy trial—was another reason to favor strong, unencumbered dictators who powered past niceties and got things done. But the new rah-rah Maple advised his imprisoned readers to adopt a smiling passivity. While prisoners can complain about the overlapping state and federal detainer regulations, he wrote, they should know rules are fixable. "Let's cooperate—All the way!" he urged his audience of hardened criminals. [3]

By then, Maple had gotten his belongings back—his uniforms, books, dress shoes, and more—and a cell to himself. Suddenly a social sort, he sent a copy of an interesting *New York Herald Tribune* article over to Kissman's cell. To Leonhard, for whom he refused to give helpful testimony, he turned "passably friendly." His letters to his mother proposed breeding Chows again if he ever managed to get out of prison. The Andrews Sisters' "Rum and Coca Cola" had become his favorite song of the moment, and he had humbly accepted a "meritorious service" award for work in Leavenworth's education department.

His memory, moreover, had become conveniently selective. He wrote his mother that the war's end in August 1945 was a relief, despite the destruction of the Germany he'd once hoped to prevent.

———

"I'm certainly happy that [surrender] came so much sooner than anyone expected or hoped. Well, it couldn't come soon enough, could it?" His dissatisfactions with the larger world turned considerably more conventional. Politically, he was now most upset by ongoing Republican political losses and especially the round of labor strikes roiling the country after years of wartime wage freezes. "The strike situation is certainly bad—and slightly disgusting," he wrote.[4]

He filled his free time with rummy, checkers, shuffleboard, and a return to the bridge table where, as the victim of a prank at Harvard, he had once become the subject of a *Boston Herald* feature story for being dealt an odds-defying perfect hand of 13 hearts. His taste in humor, at least the kind he'd share with his mother, had veered toward the childish:* "Did you hear the one about the cub bear? He only had three hairs. He wasn't fuzzy, was he?" [5]

He seemingly was everywhere in the prison all at once and, in Authority's eyes, a budding prison star. When the warden put him in the Leavenworth print shop to learn to run a printing press, he not only learned it but quickly developed and printed new "educational accounting forms" for the staff. Soon after that, he was transferred back into the Education Department, where he taught other prisoners shorthand, trigonometry, and algebra. "Since I strongly disapprove of the way algebra is usually taught, I'm trying to make some improvements," he wrote his mother. He taught statistics to a group of teachers. "He learns new skills at a miraculous speed," his supervisor marveled. He did the work of "several industrious and highly trained inmates." On his own, he studied adult reading problems, set up an "experimental" class in that, too, and counseled "subnormal non-reading adult prisoners." He did the accounting for the prison's Education Department and served as a translator for prisoners who spoke little English.

In April 1946, the war in Europe over for almost a year, he was rewarded again. The Army reduced Maple's sentence from life to 10 years, which meant he would get his first parole hearing—if not a parole—decades sooner.[6]

"It seems evident he has repudiated his former ideas," Maple's minder observed. Yet a prison committee still didn't think he was ready for freedom, and five months later, on September 18th, 1946, denied him parole. It did, however, "unanimously reduce his custody from 'close' to 'medium.'" His reputation rose still higher. By the next Spring, his parole reviewer was convinced "he is not a true criminal nor an unstable individual . . . It is felt . . . that if he is returned to civilian life, he will probably not [join] in any treasonable activity and, surely,

---

* His affinity for language jokes was displayed in many letters to his mother. "Grandpa: I sure miss the old spittoon now that it's gone. Daughter: Well you sure missed it while it was there;" "Did you know that a hot-dog is the only dog that feeds the hand the bites it?"

not in any criminal activity . . . On the whole, he offers a fairly good prognosis for future social rehabilitation."

By then, Leavenworth's warden had become as forgiving as some of the Army and FBI interviewers who in 1942 had put Maple's fascism down to schoolboy immaturity. Maple's pro-German views, the warden allowed, were once "common to many very intelligent people who considered the world in quite a mess . . ." Now, "he seems to be as hurt as any normal citizen [by] the revelation of the atrocities, particularly as brought out in the trials of the Nazi war criminals . . . This man is, of course, likely to follow further elusive trails which might lead to a utopia, but it is believed he is normally patriotic and is not likely to offend again."[7]

But the warden feared that, if they ever did let him out, he would be in for the same discrimination other fascist sympathizers and all ex-cons faced. "He may have a great deal of difficulty in making an economic adjustment being forced to have to make a living at some menial kind of task when he is really excellently fitted for teaching." Given Maple's record and dishonorable discharge, the warden figured that getting a teaching job was not likely.[8]

Paul Kissman got an offer to avoid all that in late 1946. The thaw in the military justice system produced an Army offer to reinstate him, erase his dishonorable discharge, and make him eligible for the generous veterans' benefits Congress had begun bestowing on its returning soldiers. But he'd had enough of the Army. When recruiters "inquired of the inmate whether or not he was interested in restoration to duty rather than to be paroled, he stated that he thought he would be better off on parole."

They gave it to him two months later. At 11:17 A.M. on February 15th, 1947, three years to the day after Kissman lied to Sgt. Altman and Dale Maple took off with Schwichtenberg and Kikilius, Kissman walked out of Leavenworth with his convict record into the custody of his parents. He had $25 in his pocket and orders to stay in the western district of Pennsylvania at least until June 12th, 1952.

Statistically, his life prospects were not good. At various points during the next decades, a majority of former prison inmates were re-arrested after their release, and about 40% of them landed back in jail or prison. Other studies found that, historically, only about 12 percent of the nation's employers were willing even to take job applications from people with a prison record. Most ex-cons who got jobs did so through friends or family, and even those people didn't stay employed for long. Only 45 percent of the 740 prisoners in the same study of prisoners' long-term employment outcomes were still employed eight months after being set free.[9]

To the naked eye, Paul Kissman's prospects, in other words, were dubious as his train pulled into Erie the next day. Shortly after that, he started a job as a machine operator at Reed Manufacturing Company, managed by a friend of the family, at 72 cents per hour.[10]

———

Maple's prospects had not brightened but, without much evidence, he turned optimistic that an approaching parole hearing was the one that would free him. And his expectations of what his life might be like after prison, also without much reason, stayed high. The warden feared they had risen well beyond what former prisoners and fascist sympathizers could reasonably expect.

As Kissman's train pulled away without him in February, Maple asked his mother—once a nurse and now married to a well-liked and presumably well-connected merchant in Rhode Island—if she thought Newport Hospital would hire him as a clinical psychiatrist. Perhaps he could get a job teaching at St. George's Academy in Newport? Maple told her he was considering going back into analytical chemistry and, for fun, taking a seat with the Newport Symphony Orchestra. Then again, he might go for a master's degree at Harvard or Boston University in either clinical or abnormal psychology. He asked his mother which school was cheaper. At the time, she was still paying off his loans from Harvard.[11]

His parole hearing did not go well. Though the records have since been destroyed, Maple himself called the hearing "rather curt." He went back to his cell knowing it would be more than a year until he got another one.[12] He was, unlike the increasing numbers of ex-mates and sympathizers, stuck.

Then, from out of the blue, he heard from a former college classmate.

———

In 1948 Charles Orlando Porter was three years out of the Army Air Force, a newly minted lawyer, and an Oregonian with a new job in Boston as associate director of a just-launched organization called Survey of the Legal Profession. The Survey was to be a high-minded, clear-eyed monitor of "what the lawyer does do, fails to do, and ought to do in contemporary America—and against the background of world events." His interest in the topic was not new. An

activist since his first days at Harvard, he'd founded the *Harvard Law Record**
in 1946.

"Its purpose," he later explained with a typical mix of sardonic humor and
social purpose, "was to help egocentric, money-mad law students develop a
sense of citizenship and remind alumni-alumnae that most communities need
lawyers dedicated to informed altruism, at least part of the time."

As a student, he had been a constant in Harvard's political scene, loudly
and emphatically at the other end of the spectrum from Dale Maple, who lived
on the same hall at Dunster House. In 1940, Porter energetically lobbied his
fellow students to help pressure the then-isolationist U.S. to intervene in Europe. "Desiring to help F.D.R. get the United States in the war against Hitler, I
started the Harvard Student Defense League." With that group, he helped stage
the campus's "first public interventionist meeting." His supporters, he recalled
with some delight 50 years later, interrupted the isolationist protesters outside
with "a barrage of snowballs."

Drafted in July 1941, Porter's first assignment was as a correspondent for
Yank magazine in the Panama Canal Zone. He returned briefly to marry Rad-
cliffe grad Priscilla Galassi before being sent to England and the continent to
help produce a book for the 9th Tactical Air Command. Next assigned to be
an "investigator-examiner" in the War Crimes Branch of the U.S. Forces in
Europe, he got back in 1945 to finish law school at Harvard[13]

Now 27, Porter also had just been named to the Harvard Law School Association's council. It was no small honor. Other council members were the
U.S. Secretary of War, a lawyer with the new United Nations, and a judge on
the U.S. Circuit Court of Appeals. In the coming years, he would continue a
career notable—not always affectionately—for its fervent idealism. Soon a U.S.
congressman from Oregon, he would take on an unending succession of often
wildly unpopular causes.

In the name of protecting others' religious freedom, for example, Porter—a
devout Christian—would lead a politically precarious charge to remove a large
cross that loomed above his hometown of Eugene. Outraged by the House
Un-American Activities Committee's red-baiting and its collateral destruction
of typically law-abiding citizens' economic lives, he campaigned to disband the
committee. Porter favored a more responsible investigative body free of posturing. He would champion decriminalized abortion. He'd argue against U.S.
cooperation with dictators like Raphael Trujillo of the Dominican Republic

---

* The *Harvard Law Record* still claims to be "the oldest law school-affiliated newspaper in the United
States."

and Fulgencio Batista of Cuba. (One of his constituents had been murdered allegedly by Trujillo's secret police).

———

On the other hand, he advocated a realpolitik recognition of "Red" China. His vain hope: the newly triumphant Maoist regime would provide some relief for a Chinese populace long beaten down by warlords, aristocrats, colonial powers, and, most recently, Japanese invaders. An advocate for public ownership of health care, banks, and transportation, his liberal *bona fides* were not only impeccable but far ahead of most of the American left.

"Porter's speeches," the Roseburg, Oregon *News-Review* would later write, "sound as if they were made by [Soviet Premier Nikita] Khrushchev." Long before they became widely discussed, he urged policymakers to pay attention "to the multiple impending environmental crises that . . . threaten to make our Earth unfit for human life." After it became a blunt instrument of the Cold War and a prison, he would lobby to return the Guantanamo Naval Base to Cuba. He plumped for publicly funded political campaigns as a way to blunt the influence of lobbyists and private interest groups. The head of Oregon's American Civil Liberties Union would eventually eulogize him as having "a political view on the liberal edge, in many cases, ahead of his time."

He was also impulsive, occasionally combative, and overly enthusiastic, even for his friends' tastes. Despite his "understanding and helpful" wife's pleas not to, he ran for Congress six times during the next three decades and lost four times. He took the rejections with resigned good humor. "My constituents," he wrote after what he swore was his final congressional loss, "insisted on my staying close to them when they voted in what was my fourth unsuccessful attempt in 1972 to return to Congress." Then he ran for the Senate. "Chalked up another loss," he told his fellow Harvard alums in 1981.

"I have one or two mental reservations as to how sound Porter himself is," the director of the like-minded World Peace Foundation* said in 1948, about the time Porter turned his attention westward to Dale Maple.[14]

———

"I hope they shoot the bastard," he thought when he read in 1944 that his former Harvard housemate Maple had been convicted of treason. Still in the military at the time and about to be shipped overseas, Porter felt betrayed.

---

* The World Peace Foundation is now affiliated with the Fletcher School of Law at Tufts University, dedicated to "intellectual leadership on issues of peace, justice and security."

He'd liked Maple and thought him "an exceptional person. He was a friendly, sensitive neighbor of mine . . . His playing of Chopin was like nothing I had heard before. His genius never intruded upon his sense of humor, his modesty, generosity, and good manners." They'd double-dated at least once.

But fresh from the death and horror of the past years, he wondered what had gone wrong in Maple. In Europe, he "brooded about Maple." When he got back to the States in the fall of 1945, his curiosity got the better of him. He contacted the Judge Advocate General's office in Washington to find out what he could about the crime. He learned Maple was in Leavenworth.

In San Francisco to clerk for a federal district judge, he was on a sightseeing trip to Alcatraz when the subject came up again. Someone mentioned that the home for the nation's most violent and despicable characters had moved from Alcatraz to Leavenworth.

Charles Porter's quick-trigger sympathies and liberal antennae awoke. Something didn't make sense. He found it hard to imagine what his Harvard classmate, the brilliant linguist, skilled musician, overly sensitive, and incisive debater Dale Maple was doing at hard-bitten Leavenworth. The Maple he knew was not violent or despicable or probably, despite Maple's well-known collegiate fascist sympathies, a real traitor. And Dale Maple, who as an undergraduate had loved the military life of R.O.T.C., surely would not have become such a defiant soldier without cause.[15]

Porter contacted Maple's mother in Rhode Island and then Maple in Kansas. From Mae Scoville, there was an interested reply. From the prisoner, there was nothing. But, undeterred, Porter traveled down the West Coast from San Francisco to talk to L.G. Maple in San Diego. Maple's father repeated one of his favorite themes: that it was the Army's fault. The Army itself was crazy to put a German sympathizer like Dale Maple in close proximity to German P.O.W.s. Porter, in any case, came away from the visit mistakenly believing the Army had once put Maple next to the flame, doing guard duty at Camp Hale's prisoner stockade.[16]

Long a skilled writer, Porter was hooked and turned to his typewriter. His first published work had been a purple-tinged elegy about a Harvard-Yale football game for his hometown newspaper. "In the days when I read Tom Swift and Horatio Alger books, I regarded the Harvard-Yale football game as the classic of classics. Today I saw Harvard overwhelm Yale in a game that was not a whit less than I dreamed of in those days of boyhood," the teenager wrote. He improved. He would later write for the Law Record and, while at the Survey, would author several handbooks for organizing local bar associations. In the coming years, he would also write for *The Nation, Saturday Review, The New Leader, Coronet,* and *The Northwest Review,* publish "An interview with Fidel Castro" for a North American-Cuban "Friendship Committee," and co-write a book called *The Struggle for Democracy in Latin America.*[17]

And now, in April 1948, he typed a letter to the biweekly *Harvard Alumni Bulletin,* pleading for help in understanding what had happened to his former classmate and support in setting Dale Maple free.

"I write this letter to the Bulletin because Dale's other friends . . . may be interested in joining with me to discover the complete facts about his court-martial and his present state of mind," he wrote. What he'd learned so far warranted action. "Unless facts other than I now possess indicate to the contrary, it is my considered opinion that a petition for clemency in his behalf to the President of the United States is in order if parole is not possible."

He recalled that one of his law professors taught that punishment ought to fit the criminal, not the crime. Porter was sure Dale Maple's punishment just didn't fit Dale Maple, although the misconduct itself was egregious. "Had he been shot, I should not have protested, then or now. Deterrence of treason in the course of a war for survival requires stern measures. However, I would have reproached the Army, as I reproach it now, for inducting him and assigning him to this particular kind of duty . . . Sending him to guard Nazi prisoners was like assigning a known kleptomaniac to duty as a clerk in the Post Exchange." With that in mind, "Leavenworth is no place to rehabilitate the Dale Maple I knew . . . From my recollection of Dale, I cannot believe that he was guilty of any depravity or that subsequently, he has acquired menacing attitudes, but I want to see all the facts before attempting to help him."

He added in the *Alumni Bulletin* letter that the Army wanted Maple's consent and "eighty-odd dollars" (about $900 today) to photostat the court-martial proceedings that might reveal more facts. Helpful input from "competent psychiatrists" would also help, although that obviously would cost still more. "I shall appreciate hearing from anyone who is interested, whether he seeks to confirm or to correct the opinion set forth above."

As legal argument, of course, his reasoning was sentimental and grievously flawed. Maple had never been assigned to guard P.O.W.s. It was also specious. "I knew Maple quite well in college and graduate school," a classmate replied in one of the *Bulletin*'s next issues. "As a friend, he was everything Porter says—humorous, generous, an all-around good fellow." But Porter's argument was "based on the misconception that one cannot be a fine person to one's friends and at the same time a full-fledged Fascist." The writer had known fascists who did not look much like devils. It was wrong to think that, "to be a Fascist one must be the sort of person who steals pencils from blind men and cheats his friends at poker . . . [But] The Fascist, above all people, applies one standard of behavior to his own 'chosen people' and another to the rest of the world."

If his goal in writing the *Alumni Bulletin* piece was to rally Ivy League support to reconsider Maple's fate, Porter did not succeed.* He got a disappointing total of eight responses to his *Bulletin* piece. One, however, was from Dale Maple.

——— • ———

So, in September 1948, after Porter returned from San Francisco to Boston to work at the Survey, he stole a day from his wife and growing family to interview Mrs. Scoville in nearby Newport. Either out of his own or Mae Scoville's pocket, he also collected the record of Dale Maple's court-martial proceedings.

In them, something else caught his eye. Porter decided that, if Maple really had intended to defect to Berlin during the war, he would have taken two German officers from Camp Hale with him, not two lowly enlisted men. It all seemed highly suspicious.[18] He wrote Maple again.

——— • ———

Porter's letters were censored before Maple got them, and Maple's replies went through a "release" process before hitting the mail. The process left the surviving correspondence between the prisoner and his would-be savior almost chatty. Porter joshed about family, trying to build rapport before asking questions. Maple replied as openly and warmly as censorship and a four-page limit on letters would allow. "Congratulations, by the way, on your happy marital status," he wrote. They did discuss why Schwichtenberg and Kikilius wouldn't wear the civilian clothes Maple had bought for them during the escape. ("If they were apprehended in civilian clothes, they would be charged with espionage," a capital offense.) He explained the books he allegedly kept too long from Harvard's library ("I was partly amazed and partly amused by the charges"). He'd been coy

---

* It would not be the last time Porter sought help in freeing prisoners or the last time he'd be disappointed. In later years he went to Cuba to interview the newly triumphant Fidel Castro and to try to free political prisoners there. Hoping to put a deal together, Porter broke from his talks with Castro to call Robert F. Kennedy, then U.S. attorney general directly from Cuba. The deal he had in mind apparently was never consummated.

with his fellow soldiers about his plans, he said, because "I simply didn't want my intentions to become known until I announced them publicly myself."[19]

With another parole hearing approaching and Porter working for his release on the outside, Maple turned again to dreaming about life after prison. His ideas, once again, were drastically divorced from the reality of what convicted traitors and ex-cons could expect. He considered teaching comparative philology, although now he envisioned getting his doctorate at Harvard instead of the University of Berlin. Chemistry was set aside, but he still liked the idea of becoming a clinical psychologist. And, if worse came to worst, he could see himself "working in his father's business [the defense contractor National Steel and Shipbuilding] perhaps in a traveling capacity."

Hoping it would help get him back into Harvard, he spent his free time working on "a psychological monograph on the identification and analysis of reading difficulties among adults." He enlisted the help of his godfather, a professor at the University of Chicago, but it was never published.

Another taste of the treatment convicted traitors could expect after prison: Harvard's Graduate School of Arts and Sciences turned him down. After "consulting faculty members and others who would be involved," it decided the *magna cum laude* Maple "wasn't Ph.D. material." Also, he was in prison for an indeterminate period. [20]

The idealistic rookie lawyer Porter figured Maple's best chance for a pardon was the psychological case he had mentioned in his *Bulletin* plea for help. It might prove some sort of insanity during the events of 1944, reveal a mitigating childhood deprivation before that, or, better yet, portray him as a safe behavioral bet for peaceful rehabilitation. On his own and at his own expense, Porter proceeded to recruit an all-star list of psychologists to evaluate the prisoner. He pitched the idea to Kenneth Tillotson, head of psychiatry at McLean Hospital and a psych instructor at Harvard Medical School, and Karl Menninger of the Menninger Clinic, then based in Topeka and home to both a large sanitarium and a renowned School of Psychiatry. Both were interested.

———

At 11:35 P.M. on August 3rd, 1948, correctional officer J.W. Cantrall made his regular rounds through the darkened cell block at Leavenworth, checking to make sure prisoners were where they belonged. At one cell, there was scurrying. He investigated and found Dale Maple was "in bed with inmate [REDACTED]. Maple had an erection and was putting his penis back in his shorts when I threw the flashlight beam in the cell. Maple was sitting up on the pillow by [REDACTED's] head."[21]

The tryst—memorialized in Maple's prison record as "a degenerate act"—earned Maple 30 days of restrictions and a moratorium on his correspondence with Porter. His next letter to the lawyer was not until September 10th. In an age when many families, courts, employers, most of the straight world, and even parts of the hounded gay community itself cast homosexuality as a psychological problem, Maple grew dubious about basing his parole case on a psychological profile that risked exposing his sexual orientation. It was already strongly suggested in his still-private military, FBI, and "sanity" records. Opening those records to outside psychologists, a clemency board, potential employers, or even Charles Porter would be a dangerous risk.

His caution was prudent. The Army, among other institutions, still considered homosexuality a "psychopathic personality disorder." The government, believing gay men and women "vulnerable to blackmail," still considered homosexuality a security threat. The State Department fired 31 gays in 1947, 28 in 1948, and, even as Porter considered bringing psychiatrists into the case, another 31 in 1949. For whatever reason, Maple neglected to mention the incident and tried to steer Porter in a different direction.

"Let's just forget about that one, please," he wrote Porter of the psychology plan. "Actually, I am wondering if things may not be going slightly at a tangent. As I see it, the heart of the matter is concerned with the Army situation and much less with me personally."[22]

Porter never would fully abandon the idea, but before he got Maple's latest letter, he came up with another idea to win Maple's release. He'd make him a star.

CHAPTER 18

YOUR BOY'S HALO

On September 2nd, 1948, Porter wrote to yet another Harvard man, 32-year-old Ely Jacques Kahn, Jr., a reporter for the *New Yorker*. He made an offer few reporters could refuse: a wealth of the documentary materials and insights and sources about "the only American soldier ever convicted of treason." In his letter, Porter introduced himself as the lawyer for this still-unnamed client (he later explained that anonymity was needed until the magazine agreed to do the story). And the client, he swore, "is a genius—I use the term to mean a man who scores in a certain range on standard intelligence tests. He was my friend and classmate at Harvard. He was stupid, however, in some respects but never treasonable."

The deal was sweet. Porter would send Kahn a "suitcase" full of the materials about a brilliant traitor and his trial, just about everything a writer would need. It included the $80 record of Maple's court-martial and letters the client had written his mother while in the Army. Porter also had some news clippings. He hoped, "an article by you could pave the way to a pardon . . ." Still, "I'd be willing for you to write it as you saw it."[1]

After checking with his editor E.J. Kahn, Jr. grabbed the offer. Kahn was an elegant writer, a dogged reporter, and, later, a well-known book author. "Kahn," his obituary in the *New Yorker* eventually noted, "was a short, strongly built man with a smiling face. Underneath this Hildy Johnson* exterior, though, he was a

---

* "Hildy Johnson" was one of two lead characters in the 1928 Ben Hecht/Charles MacArthur comedy "The Front Page." Johnson was a fictional Chicago reporter who, about to quit the frantic world of tabloid newspapering to get married and find a "respectable" job, accidentally gets an exclusive story-of-a-lifetime covering and then trying to save a wrongly convicted escaped murderer. After numerous successful runs on Broadway, it was made into movies alternatively called "The Front Page," "His Girl Friday," and "Switching Channels."

man of deep feeling and private generosity. He loved tennis, backgammon, and crossword puzzles. His major at Harvard had been Latin and Greek, which is evident in his writing style: superbly classical, terse, graceful, and lyrical with detail." His work for his articles about Maple in the magazine was indeed artful and exhaustive.

"Flattered" by Porter's offer and "delighted beyond words with the over-whelming amount of background material you sent me," Kahn nevertheless proceeded during the next months to verify everything. He contacted Maple's former high school, his college teachers, classmates, pastors, Army buddies, parents, his prosecutors, and his defense lawyers. Almost all—with the excep-tions of Maple's father and subsequently Maple himself—proved willing to cooperate, sometimes in long narrative letters and sometimes by submitting to interviews.

Many of Kahn's sources offered theories about Maple's confounding jour-ney, about Maple's parents, about sanity, treason, military officers, the FBI, and, not least, homosexuality. Before he finished collecting it all, Kahn ended up a friend of Porter and his wife Priscilla, trading good-natured complaints about staying up all night with newborns. As Kahn interviewed people, Porter continued to find more sources for Kahn to meet.[2]

He organized some of them for a dinner with Kahn in Boston that Kahn later referred to as "The Symposium." Around the table with Porter and Kahn were Joe Clawson, another Dunster alum; Raymond Dennett (who had won-dered about Porter's "soundness") of the World Peace Foundation; and Dr. Kenneth Tillotson, one of the psychiatrists Porter was trying to interest in examining Maple. Each member of the group had definably illustrious careers. The first of Clawson's books, *Psychology in Action*, had just been published; he was to become a well-known innovator in consumer research and a consultant to many large corporations. Dennett was a co-editor of an academic handbook on negotiating with the Russians and would continue what already had been a high-flying career in foreign affairs at MIT, the Council on Foreign Relations, Columbia, and the American-Scandinavian Foundation. Harvard's Tillotson was chair of McLean Hospital's psychiatry and neurology unit.

The convivial evening, set in a hotel restaurant, featured much bantering about Harvard life and, as the talk turned to Maple, a thick bog of multi-syllabic theorizing. The men started happily enough with their memories of Maple's student days. Of Maple's musical skills, Clawson—himself a pianist—judged his former housemate "good in the sense that Harry Truman [an enthusiastic and cheerfully self-described piano hack] is good." Of the Hitler bust Maple had kept in his room at Dunster House and his disruption of Harvard's German Club, Clawson joked, "The only place this guy could have got away with what he did without psychiatric observation was in the Harvard Yard."

Tillotson saw an opening to claim, on a more clinical note, that there was "a psychological background for treason." And, just as Maple feared when talk about him turned to psychology, the subject careened to Maple's homosexuality. Kahn's notes of the discussion recorded that Clawson "never thought him (Maple) a queer, but a little effeminate . . . His roommate, oddly enough, though a triumph of masculinity, was pursued by queens." Tillotson, who had never met or examined Maple, diagnosed him anyway.[*] "Egotistical homosexuality" explained the "psychodynamics of the situation . . . maternal attachments are important in paranoid cases, also in homosexual cases."[3]

Kahn was intrigued. Looking for some meaning in this Harvard alum's strange behavior, Tillotson's proposed link between homosexuality, treason, and Nazism[†] seemed to hold some promise.

In a letter to one of his sources, Kahn conceded that the *New Yorker* would never allow him to write about Maple's sex life or a possible relationship to Maple's crime. But "you are probably more aware than I am of Maple's own leanings in that direction. I've been told that Kissman and Hotelling, among others in Maple's company, were also conspicuously non-heterosexual in outlook, and it is my hunch that Maple's abnormal (in the pre-Kinsey sense of the word) or non-existent sex life may have been a determining factor in his espousal of Nazism."

---

[*] Sex was on Tillotson's mind at the time for other reasons. The married Tillotson had been having an affair with a nurse, who, in trying to quit the liaison the prior year, had filed a complaint with the Massachusetts State Department of Health that "Tillotson's amorous attentions were endangering her health." The doctor "asked" her to leave her job after she filed the complaint. But a Middlesex County (Massachusetts) grand jury indicted both of them—because of their previous affair—on morals charges including adultery, "illicit relations" and "alleged lascivious acts." Tillotson thus resigned his posts with the hospital and Harvard's medical school just the month before "the symposium." Both nurse and doctor would be found guilty of "moral turpitude" in May 1949. The nurse's fate is unknown, but Tillotson was fined $750 and had his license suspended for three months. He later opened a private practice from his home, where four years later, one of his patients was the young novelist Sylvia Plath. Tillotson recommended that Plath, who was in acute distress and had begun to cut herself and speak of suicide, take sleeping pills, and get a job "to take her mind off her troubles." Plath did later work at a local hospital. She hated the job, and one biographer thinks her experience informed a scene in *The Bell Jar*, her best-known book, in which the main character Esther Greenwood's mother suggests Esther find a job helping unfortunate people as a way to combat depression.

[†] The ties between "maternal attachments" and homosexuality were an oft-cited, if unproven, truism of the age. In a 1944 article called "Mothers . . . Our Only Hope," J. Edgar Hoover blamed "parental neglect"— including women working outside the home—for "perversion."

Kahn also asked his source, who, as a prosecutor had interviewed the two German prisoners, if he thought the Germans were involved with each other. Did he think "Maple was partly motivated in taking off with Schwichtenberg by a close affection for the man?" His correspondent Bernard Ladon, who was by 1948 in private practice in Texas, did "not get the impression of homosexuality in the relationship between Kikilius and Schwichtenberg. As a matter of fact, such thought never entered my mind; however, now that you have mentioned it, such may have been the case. I am a rather naïve bastard, and things like that never entered my mind."[4]

Kahn's questioning never did yield much support for the theory and only mixed agreement about Maple's orientation. At a lunch with Julian Sobin, formerly of the German Club and Maple's ROTC unit as well as an officer at Fort Bragg when Maple was there, Kahn asked if Sobin thought Maple a "homo." Sobin "never heard any of that kind of talk about him" and, at least before the troubles, also considered him to be a loyal American and an excellent soldier.

Porter's assessment was similarly heterosexual. In a letter to Porter, Kahn again speculated that Maple "seemed to admire the superman type, though; his latent, or more than latent, homosexuality, may have had something to do with his admiration for Nazis if he admired them." But Porter shrugged the idea off. He and Maple had double-dated at Wellesley. Maple "seemed to like girls, but not to be overly interested in them." Porter recalled "a good deal" of gay life at Dunster House, "but no hints from Maple."[5]

Kahn lost some of his reportorial nerve when he tried to bring the subject up with Mae Scoville, Maple's mother. In a jovial note after visiting her, Kahn reminded Porter of Tillotson's contention that "the clue to everything might be Maple's masturbation habits in his boyhood . . ." Kahn confessed, "I could not bring myself . . . to ask Mrs. Scoville Dr. Tillotson's big question."

———

His interview with Maple's mother, however, was a turning point in Kahn's feelings about Dale Maple. "Mrs. S was extremely kind to me," he told Porter. "I'm sorry to have to say that some of the stuff I did learn doesn't exactly put a halo on your boy's battered head." The final collapse of any sympathy Kahn might have had for Maple came when Kahn ran across Maple's jailhouse note to Kissman in the court-martial transcripts about using "the abused Americanism angle" and laying it on thick.

Porter agreed Maple's note to Kissman looked terrible. But the point, he added, wasn't Maple's crime or his notes. It was that he didn't still belong behind bars.

Hungry for material that might outweigh the note's unflattering impression, Porter again went back to Maple, pressing him for details that could shed a softer light on the case for setting him free. Perhaps because he didn't have more information to give, Maple's letters to Porter became less frequent. By November 1948, Porter was "a bit uncomfortable" that he wasn't hearing from Maple's father or much from Maple anymore. He'd sent the prisoner some more questions and a friendly note about Porter's cherished Harvard-Yale football game. Its prose was only a shade less sentimental than his 1937 column about his first game.

Maple replied the next month, answering Porter's questions and reminding his lawyer not to recruit psychiatrists on his behalf. "I do hope you won't put out too much about the psychiatric matter," he said. He signed off by adding, "Wish I could have been with you to see Yale take their beating." [6]

Porter wrote back, but two weeks, three, four passed without a reply. Concerned, he reached out to Maple's mother and, still exploring his initial idea, asked more experienced lawyers if they thought he could win a pardon using psychiatrists' testimony exclusively. He wrote Kahn that one advised him, "that the parole board might well see value in the psychiatric report I propose, but that there is 'nothing in the record that will make out a *prima facie* case to support your contentions.' Ow."[7]

Kahn, seemingly always polite, replied but was busy at home organizing his notes for the story. Into the late winter of 1948-1949, he eventually knitted some 30,000 words together and submitted them to the magazine and its opaque publishing schedules. In one of his memoirs, Kahn wrote a "glossary" to explain what editing and publishing guidance writers could expect to hear from legendary *New Yorker* editor William Shawn:

What Shawn Says	**What Shawn Means**
Good	Dubious
Very Good	Marginal
Great	Passable
"We're going to run this in . . . the next issue"	"I'll be revising the schedule soon and plan to keep you in mind."
". . . this month"	"This year if all goes well"
". . . very soon"	"Sometime, probably, but don't count on it."
". . . soon"	"Never"[8]

The story, in any case, was off to the magazine's deliberate fact-checking department. For Porter and Maple, Mae Scoville, the dozens of people Kahn had interviewed, and Kahn himself, the manuscript effectively disappeared.

In their shared state of suspension—Porter waiting for some word from Kansas and hoping Kahn's article would do some good; Kahn waiting to see if his article would come out—the two men kept in touch. In February 1949, the lawyer told the writer Maple's mother wanted her materials back and to see the manuscript before publication. Kahn agreed to retrieve the materials from the fact-checking department but turned down Mae Scoville's request to see the manuscript before publication. She had indeed mentioned something about seeing the draft during their interview. Kahn, however, had explained he probably couldn't do that and confessed to Porter that he'd more or less let the matter drop without answering her more definitively.

Kahn was not immune to her feelings, however. "I hope that my piece will not cause Mrs. Scoville any undue additional suffering, but I am afraid that her son, regardless of what you or I might or might not do, has already committed her to many years of suffering, perhaps to a lifetime of it . . . Tragedy," the Greek major Kahn added, "is always sad, and the people unwittingly involved in a tragedy are the most pitiable of all."

Others were waiting, too. In May, a reader from Chicago wrote Shawn, saying she'd heard the magazine was preparing an article about the infamous Maple and asking if it'd been published. She enclosed postage for him to send it to her. Someone at the magazine replied only that, "One of our writers has been doing some researching into the matter of Dale Maple, with a possible story in mind. Whether the story will be completed and acceptable, we can't tell you now or even give an approximate date. We will, however, send your note to our writer. Very truly yours, The NEW YORKER." [9]

Meanwhile, the determined Porter kept grinding. He resolved to go ahead without the publicity and without the prisoner if need be. Months after Maple's correspondence with him tailed off, he partnered with Maple's mother to submit paperwork applying for a pardon on Maple's behalf.

"It was turned down by a form letter," he wrote Kahn that February. Maple, moreover, had gone entirely silent. "Nothing new to report. No letters, nothing. Guess I'm not his Valentine, which I suppose is just as well. However, I feel like a dud as his counsel—he won't even write to me."[10]

Kahn finished his Maple draft and left for Washington, D.C. to start what would become a two-part series about New York Sen. Jacob Javits for the magazine. But in July 1949, still awaiting proofs of his Maple article, Maple's overwhelming silence during the prior six months abruptly changed from seeming curious to feeling suspicious.

Someone else, Kahn learned, was on the story's trail. And someone—Maple, Maple's father, even the impatient Porter—would have to be cooperating with the mysterious writer. The family could well be looking for someone promising a more sympathetic version of the story and, with it, a better chance at freedom. And if the interloping story—even a brief or superficial one—appeared sooner than the *New Yorker's* glacial editing process allowed, Kahn's editors could well cancel his story altogether.

"By the way," Kahn wrote Porter with what seemed to be elaborate nonchalance, "when I was in Washington last week, as I was on another story, I heard that another reporter is doing a Maple story, too—for *Collier's*, I was told. Have you heard anything about it, or is it just a rumor designed to make me nervous?"

He had reason to be nervous. *Collier's* was a significant competitor, a 60-year-old weekly that, like the *New Yorker*, had a proud history of sophisticated journalism and quality fiction. It was also far bigger than Kahn's magazine. The *New Yorker's* paid circulation in 1946 was about 300,000. Despite a slow post-war decline then accelerating by competition from television and a Madison Avenue perception that its readers were older and conservative, *Collier's* in 1950 still boasted one of the highest circulations in the country, just under four million readers[11]

Porter dismissed the threat—"I have heard nothing about another reporter on the Maple trail"—and changed the subject.

He had another idea. His petition for parole denied, his publicity plan on hold, and his "client" gone silent, he was going to go Leavenworth to confront Maple himself. At the Survey's expense, Porter was scheduled to go to an American Bar Association meeting in St. Louis in September and would somehow get one state over to meet with his client. He'd see him in person for the first time since Harvard. He'd re-earn his trust, set him straight, and prepare one last and best appeal for freedom before Maple would end up serving his whole term.

Getting from St. Louis to Leavenworth, however, was expensive. Now 30 years old, not truly practicing law yet, and with two young children, Charles

Porter mentioned his intent to Mae Scoville, who, also still hoping to spring her son, offered to pay Porter's way to Kansas. Excited, he wrote to Leavenworth's warden to schedule his heart-to-heart with Maple.

———

Warden Walter Hunter's reply was waiting for him when he checked into the Statler Hotel in St. Louis. "Our files," Hunter said, "fail to disclose that you are an attorney for him, and we find no evidence where he has requested you to perform legal services for him. To our knowledge, you are not his attorney . . ."

Hunter added another reason to bar Porter. "In your correspondence with [Maple], we have noted that apparently you are making an effort to publicize this case. This is definitely against the policy of the Bureau of Prisons. Under the circumstances, it is not possible to grant your request for a visit. Very truly yours . . ."

Porter, shocked, called Hunter immediately. On the phone, he protested that he was indeed Maple's attorney. "'Ask him,' I said [to Hunter]," he wrote Kahn, "and, finally, he said he would."

And Hunter did. After checking with inmate Maple, the warden sent Porter a telegram. It arrived at the hotel on Sunday, September 4th:

> RE TELEPHONE CONVERSATION HAVE CONTACTED
> DALE MAPLE. INFORMS ME YOU ARE NOT HIS
> ATTORNEY AND HAS NO MATTERS FOR YOU TO
> HANDLE FOR HIM[12]

———

The financially struggling bleeding-heart Charles Orlando Porter was crushed. Unbidden and mainly at his own expense, he had been actively writing and meeting and campaigning for Dale Maple for well more than a year. It was not the ending he'd anticipated.

In his hotel room, the discouraged Porter wrote Mae Scoville. "It may be that Dale acted under duress," he said, enclosing the money order she had sent him to get from St. Louis to Leavenworth. "However, for the record, I have been repudiated by him as his counsel and have no choice but to cease all efforts on his behalf. I regret this turn of events. Perhaps someday we shall know what happened behind those walls."

Confused and perhaps embarrassed, Scoville wrote her son to ask what had happened and then sent Porter an apology and an explanation. Her son had told her that only family members could visit prisoners. "Of course he can come as my attorney of record," Maple wrote his mother, "except that he isn't on the record that way and I don't want to put him on for various reasons, among them being that he couldn't write [to Maple] then except under special circumstances pertaining to business. When he [Porter] gets back to Boston, I'll write and try to explain it all."

He never did. Maple, moreover, would never write or thank his would-be savior.

Kahn reached out to console the jilted Porter. "The disaffection of your erstwhile client puzzles me, too, and I am sorry that it should have turned out this way for you, after all the work you have done on his behalf."[13]

The jilted Porter wrote Kahn back, thanking him for his thoughts. They soon met for lunch in New York. Kahn, as condolence, paid for the lunch, "including cocktail and cigars." Their subject remained imprisoned in Kansas.

PART FIVE

APRES FASCISM

One day in the mid-1960s, a young girl in Erie, Pennsylvania, is sorting through family photos with her mother and comes across one of her father in his U.S. Army uniform. She turns the photo over and frowns at the word written on the back. "Mom," she asks, "what does 'censored' mean?"[1]

CHAPTER 19

EDITS AND PAINT JOBS

As Maple moldered, Fritz Siering was in Argentina. Now 32, he more or less re-assumed the position he'd occupied in Chicago in the late 1930s: working as a mechanic, living as a refugee with limited local language skills, and still hoping to become a U.S. citizen someday. He was married again, too. In 1949, he wed the 39-year-old Frieda Paula Leibrecht, herself a native of Germany. Some things had changed, of course, since the '30s. Where Ana Siering, his second wife, was rumored to be less than monogamous during their marriage, Frieda Siering was allegedly outgoing and loyal.[1]

Siering's path to citizenship remained as unlikely as any deported, dishonorably discharged soldier's dreams of building a new life in America. In addition, he was an ex-con. All ex-cons confront confusion—new technologies, customs, language, cultures—and more debilitating still, unemployment, housing discrimination, alienation, under-staffed support groups, and a lack of marketable skills. Their families change or perhaps divorce them. The few who successfully manage all that follow disciplined project lists that include re-education and renewed—or brand new—attention to nurturing healthy families and support networks.

In general, rehabilitation specialists agree that creating "a life of stability" is the overarching goal and that it requires unusual fortitude. One rehabilitation professional, himself a former drug dealer and murderer, observed that all freed prisoners ultimately must struggle up steep, slippery psychological ladders: acknowledging the damage done, atoning, repairing and, not least, finding "permission to forgive myself."

The men of the Inner Circle—like their country in the aftermath of war—had daunting emotional and psychological tasks in front of them. The men of the Inner Circle, however, skipped some.

Guilt ordinarily would be one of them. All suffered the judicial kind of guilt: the stern reaction to violating some objective moral or legal rule or custom. But guilt's other face, according to psychiatrist Herant Katchadourian of Stanford, is the personal one: regret, shame, embarrassment, and the disgust one feels about one's own actions. Like Lady Macbeth's futile attempts to wash herself of her and her husband's murders and crimes, he says, feeling guilty can long outlast and sometimes bite more deeply than a society's punishments for legal transgressions. Escaping that kind of guilt and restoring meaning to one's life requires introspection and, not least, brutal honesty. Those were not strengths of most of Dale Maple's Army buddies.[2]

———

By the time E.J. Kahn, Jr. caught up to him in 1948, Eric Hotelling already had an abridged, finely polished, and guilt-free version of his previous life. His misadventures at Columbia were deleted. His misadventures in the Army, he contended, were mere fictions concocted by one "contemptuous" and "contemptible" officer who was out to get him.

"The charge(s) of treason, inciting a mutiny and abetting a desertion made against me publicly by the camp commander, Lt. Col. John Chase, were later dropped," he told Kahn. There had not been "a shred of evidence" connecting him to a mutiny. "I was ultimately cleared completely by the military intelligence authorities, sent overseas, and granted a commission."[3]

Which was true, although hardly the whole story. He skipped the parts that might have required regret, much less atonement. There were his Nazi agitations at Columbia, his researched military plans, maps and letters; his preparations for mutiny; the Rim Rock designs to recruit mutineers at other camps and then a guerrilla army to kill American soldiers and, by extension, civilians; his parents' alarmed reports to the FBI about his pro-German activities; his scribbled efforts to decipher Naval code; his masked invitations to soldiers at Fort Leonard Wood in Missouri to join and, not least, his unwavering pro-fascist reputation among the 33 fellow soldiers Army intelligence officers interrogated in the weeks after Maple's escape.

Instead, Hotelling jumped ahead to the part of the story where he found himself briefly back with the 1800th in Tennessee, where he described himself as "resigned" to being in a labor unit. As a desk-bound "clerk general," he apparently avoided most of the ditch-digging, hog pond cleaning, road work, brush-clearing, and other manual labor the rest of the unit's soldiers were doing.

Kahn either neglected to record Hotelling's account of his relatively privileged duty in his notes, or Hotelling left that part out too.[4]

On the strength of his mysterious honorable discharge, Hotelling had made progress re-integrating into distinctly non-Nazi postwar America by 1946. His first try at re-joining polite society was to apply to Columbia, where his dad had been a key faculty member. His famous father had moved to a new position at the University of North Carolina, and, perhaps still smarting from Eric's dorm disruptions and Nazi propagandizing five years before, Columbia turned him down.

Eric then enrolled at Rutgers in September 1946, where he did well. He was finishing up a bachelor's degree at Rutgers University in 1948 when Kahn interviewed him. To keep bed and board together, he also did clerical work in three-month stints at the pharmaceutical company American Cyanamid and a Connecticut company specializing in oilfield supplies. Still more in line with his new ambitions, in 1948 and 1949 he also worked (probably part-time) as a chemist at Merck Rahway, another pharmaceutical company. Academically, he squeezed in four graduate-level courses in chemistry, achieved Phi Beta Kappa status, and was admitted to the Sigma Xi science research honor society. He joined the campus ROTC unit and, perhaps oddly for a native-born former fascist sympathizer who conceivably might be self-conscious about his past, the campus German Club.[*] Now, he was preparing to move on to graduate studies at the University of Michigan, where he hoped to get master's and doctoral degrees in chemistry.[5] Eric Hotelling was the first veteran of the Inner Circle to defy the seemingly inevitable downward arc of post-prison life.

———

The *New Yorker* finally published Kahn's story about Dale Maple in 1950. Called "The Philologist," it appeared in four parts in March and April issues, 18 months after Charles Porter first enlisted Kahn in his cause. The rumored *Collier's* story that had worried Kahn so much never materialized, the victim of a change of editors at the magazine the previous Spring.[6]

The *New Yorker* didn't publish any letters about the story, and if other re-action to the public reappearance of Maple—once the focus of a sensational national manhunt—existed, it was muted. Other periodicals and newspapers took no notice of the story or Maple and wouldn't for another eight months. Neither L.G. Maple and Mae Scoville, his parents, nor Ruth C. Maple and

---

[*] Rutgers' German Club, like even Harvard's German club before Maple joined, was apolitical and dedicated to studying language.

Edwin Scoville, his stepparents, commented in any publicly available correspondence or communication. Some former Harvard classmates sent Kahn congratulations for an impressive article, but the public remained steadfastly uninterested. A Theodore Donay—a civilian, convicted of treason, who had once helped a German POW escape—vanished in a rented motorboat off Catalina Island soon after the Maple articles appeared. He was last seen in the vicinity of a mysterious submarine. Even that, however, did not return Maple to the national conversation.

The *New Yorker* project did alarm Maple's jailers, especially the evidence that Maple corresponded with Porter. "During the past year [Maple] . . . had considerable correspondence with a Charles O. Porter, who apparently is making a serious effort to have his story published and also to secure him favorable consideration from the Parole Board," they wrote in April 1949. In response, the board deferred a recommendation to schedule another parole hearing for Maple. Warden Walter Hunter, still stewing about it, denied Porter's visit to Leavenworth a few months later.[7]

A half-year after that, when the article appeared, *The New Yorker's* Spring, 1950 issues seem to have skipped Kansas. Parole records from 1950 no longer exist, but Maple's prison reports leave both the magazine and the series' appearance unmentioned. The publicity that Porter had worked so hard to generate, in sum, didn't materialize.

But by 1950, Maple himself was also one of the relatively few World War II soldier-miscreants that the military's ongoing sentencing reviews and clemency reforms had not yet freed. Prison officials, moreover, were concerned about the costs of taking in the growing numbers of prisoners the increasingly punitive civil authorities were sending them. Their deliberate probation process had already been grinding for more than five of the ten years that Maple's shortened sentence demanded. Not least, the newly compliant Maple had long become one of the Leavenworth administration's favorites.

"He is considered to be well disposed," his 1948 progress report found. It also noted he "is a Catholic convert who has been helping out with the organ and choir, and attending Sunday services, but not quite as regularly as he should." In return for "above average" work in the Education Department, administrators began giving him "good time"—essentially sentence reductions—at the rate of two days per month. Warden Hunter had become a big fan. "This extremely intelligent and versatile inmate is apparently humble," Hunter wrote. "He is not forward. He never complains. He cooperates. He has the respect of inmates and officers." Even his "degenerate act" of August 1948 was not enough to significantly alter his superiors' view of him. Just before the incident, they increased the rate at which he accrued "good time" again, from two to four days of "good time" per month. With each accrual, he moved four days closer to release. Just after the incident, he was put on 30 days of restriction. The incident was forgotten as soon as the restrictions expired, and skipping the standard regression after punishment, Maple began to accrue four days a month again.[8]

They waited until June 1950, two months after the final installment of Kahn's story about him appeared, to do another annual review of Maple's record. Forgetting how they had rejected the persistent Charles O. Porter in mid-1949, they still cited Maple's contact with Porter as a reason to keep him at Leavenworth. His review noted, inaccurately, that he was still in touch with Porter, but given his awards, recognitions, and the "good time" he'd earned, his release date moved from the original March 1954 to November 1950.

A short month later, on July 13th, his parole committee decided that whatever threat Maple had once posed to the United States' war effort, to other U.S. soldiers and the nation's communications and transportation was a mistake that had been rectified. The United States Board of Parole issued a Certificate of Conditional Release, allowing Dale Maple, Inmate 61364-L, to return to the world. With still more good conduct time deducted from his sentence, he was to leave Leavenworth—draw his first breaths outside of custody since February 1944—at 9:30 A.M. on October 8th. Officials handed over the $31.62 Maple had left in the prison bank after six and a half years, and the former prisoner headed for San Diego. There Maple was to be met by Glenn A. Dempsey, a one-time Ford salesman who was by then a veteran federal probation officer "prominent in prisoner-aid activities." His father and his new stepmother would also be there. "His father," his parole board noted, "reported that he would help Maple obtain employment at his father's place of work."[9]

October 8th, 1950, was a Sunday, church, and movie day at Leavenworth. Maple's former Camp Hale confederate Theo Leonhard, once self-appointed *Standortenfuhrer* of the Gestapo section of the SS, was fully recovered from some minor surgery earlier in the year but was still smarting from the Army's latest denial of clemency. He was still communicating with a few of his former mates, but while some of them would indeed re-assemble in the coming years, there is no record of Leonhard and Maple ever seeing each other again.

J. Edgar Hoover found out about Maple's parole 15 days later. It would be the second-to-last entry in his version of Maple's file. No one seems to have bothered to tell Charles Porter about the release.[10]

———

As he arrived in San Diego at 2:31 P.M. on October 10th, 30-year-old Dale Maple still did not know much about the civilian difficulties before him. His contacts with the outside world since his capture six-and-a-half years before had been short, censored, and infrequent. He had, it's true, seen movies, read newspapers, and heard radio news. But he had had only eight visits from outsiders at Leavenworth since May 1944. Five involved his mother, sometimes with his stepfather, and sometimes with his aunt in tow. His aunt had visited by herself once. Most visits were in one-hour increments, although there had been a 90-minute meeting with two parole board officials from Kansas City in 1948 and a 15-minute meeting in February 1946 with William Humphrey Biddle, the defense attorney Maple's father had hired for his 1944 trial. He had corresponded by letter with his aunt (twice), his godfather (once in 1945 and another time in 1948), Porter (three times), and Miss Helen Fugera Pirzynski, a friend in Fall River, Massachusetts (twice). Correspondence with his mother was more frequent. The prison's Mail Record showed five letters sent to his mother, although Kahn's notes suggest there were more. All his other personal interactions during the most recent fifth of his life had been within the restricted, culturally segregated, and occasionally violent society of what was then the nation's most notorious prison.

Outside, of course, the world had turned over. Maple had last been in San Diego during the summer of 1941. At the time, he was still loudly broadcasting his new Nazi notoriety and reeling from narrowly missing out on Herbert Scholz's promised trip to Berlin. Ryan Aircraft, a defense contractor, had just withdrawn a job offer. Around him at the time was a nation darkly conflicted over its fears of the seemingly immutable approach of war.

In the fall of 1950, by contrast, Maple was let off into what was then the most powerful and prosperous society on Earth. It was, moreover, an unrecognizable culture. Scholars describe it as worried about communism and nuclear war but enjoying a fundamental optimism that had been mostly missing from American life since the Depression's start in 1929. Total income was 50 percent higher than it had been in 1935. A flood of new products was rising, soon to vastly expand the boundaries and understandings of what a consumer culture meant. Consumer spending alone was up by 60 percent in the five years after the war. Some 151 million Americans had bought 21.4 million cars, 20 million refrigerators, 5.5 million stoves, and 11.6 million televisions.

In each year since the war's end, Americans filled over a million new housing units. Political culture included a bully assumption of expansive global power that was very different from the angry, punitive, and nationalist withdrawal from foreign affairs that had immediately followed the first world war. Nationally marriage and birth rates, after a century of slow decline, were spiking. Both men and women were marrying at earlier ages than they had since 1935. Something better—something prosperous and more convenient and different from every place else—surely was coming. A vast wave of educational benefits for veterans and new college facilities presaged the arrival of a historically talented workforce. A new National Science Foundation spoke of an ongoing commitment to discovery and a core belief in progress.

Where in 1941, Maple disdained Washington as the seat of weak and dithering democracy, in 1950, he was to join a citizenry that judged it in often-heroic terms. In its popular culture and schools, the government—its military, spies, bravest jurors, teachers, sheriffs, and senators—were the good guys, intervening to assure the best possible results. "Few Americans doubted the essential goodness of their society," one historian recorded. "[They] trusted their leaders to tell them the truth, to make sound decisions . . . For a while, the traditional system of authority held."

But this, some historians maintain, was also the beginning of an "age of acquiescence." It was a vivid contrast to the near rebellions against corporate power stretching back to the Gilded Age and the opposite of the skepticism of, even insolence toward, authority traditionally touted as a proud American virtue. Instead, class tension over resources and wealth mainly became seen as un-American, at least to the majority-white Americans. Now voter turnout rebounded in both off-year and presidential elections, which is to say engagement and belief in the government were strengthening. Voter turnout stayed high throughout the decade. Society remained rigidly segregated, but for the lucky daily life's focus seemed to be on business, on family, and on achieving a personal stability that had been unattainable for many during the prior two decades. Perhaps because of a peak in union bargaining power and the fantastic technological gains during the war, dramatic increases in worker productivity were widely shared and turned in part into real wage gains for all segments of the population.

Assuming they followed a straight and narrow path, people in Dale Maple's generation, born in the 1920s, ultimately would have a 90% chance of out-earning their fathers. Real income itself began an upward turn during the 1950s, even for the population's bottom 40 percent. (The middle class's share would stay stable at about 55 percent of the nation's wealth. The top 10 percent of the country's earners' share declined marginally to something just under three-quarters of total U.S. income).

Corporations, widely hailed as the fount of prosperity, also carried their share of the burden. Corporate taxes accounted for six percent of the gross domestic product. (Congress began transferring that corporate burden to individuals in 1953. By 1983, the corporate tax share would fall below one percent).

There was opportunity, much of it starting with little more than a feeling. By the time of Maple's release, for example, several of the members of the 10th Mountain Division had returned to Colorado, where they started a small ski run at the mostly abandoned mining town of Aspen. (In a few years, two others would repeat the trick in a sheep meadow that was also in Camp Hale's vicinity, starting the Vail ski resort). In many quarters, it was also the start of an age of solidity, perhaps an instinctual post-traumatic pursuit of order and security, structure, and relatively peaceful conformity. Sociologists would eventually document the rise of a commercially aggressive but hierarchically compliant and family-oriented "Organization Man," the move of the American dream to planned suburban communities and, for the expanding numbers of white middle-class women, a mostly domestic and economically dependent role. On the radio, much spoke of stability, sentiment, and contentment.

In contrast to the tight music, throaty horns, and melancholy songs of unbridgeable longing that Dale Maple wrote his mother about from prison during the anxious war years, most of 1950's top songs were slow and often soothing. They were Nat King Cole's "Mona Lisa" and Doris Day's "Bewitched, Bothered & Bewildered." The Andrews Sisters, famous during the war for the jumping "Boogie Woogie Bugle Boy of Company B," were in 1950 singing "I Can Dream, Can't I?" Through much of the decade, the new medium of television generally offered sanitized versions of history, diversions, and news. All shared a perspective of an honest and trustworthy government, basically beneficent business, grabby unions, and a foreign policy nobly dedicated to assuring freedom abroad and at home.[11]

Maple's San Diego County also was dramatically different. When he was last there, it was the nation's 43rd biggest city, with 200,000 souls living on the tuna industry, the aircraft industry, a Naval base, and tourism. By Maple's return in 1950, it was the United States' 31st largest city. Its in-city population of 334,000 swelled with the rising American demand for tuna, one of the city's major industries, and by defense spending.

Military families who had been stationed there during the war, liked what they found and stayed. Including its suburbs, San Diego had more than doubled in size in a decade. Maple found himself among more than half a million county residents, joined periodically by another 40,000 off-duty sailors and Marines. All struggled with a terrible housing shortage that would soon make the area one of the nation's most profitable real estate markets and one of its next examples of suburban sprawl. Convair, an aviation company of 32,000 employees, was the city's biggest single employer. It was still home to the U.S. Navy Training Center, which was far bigger than in the pre-war summer of 1941.

———

The father who met Dale Maple, moreover, was in some ways a stranger. Father and son had not seen each other for six years. L.G. Maple had never visited him in Leavenworth and wrote him sparingly if at all. Dale had sent him three letters over the years.

Joining his father had rarely come up during most of those years in exile. Almost all of Maple's dreams of life after prison had him going east, to Rhode Island, to live near his mother, not west to his father's California. Maple remained in touch with both parents but, although inmate phone records either were not kept or have not survived, his father was mostly absent from the mails and even conversation until the end of his son's prison term approached.[12]

Nevertheless, Maple arrived in San Diego prepared to move in with his father and his dad's second wife, Ruth, who he may never have met before. Their home was at 6530 Scimitar Drive, some six miles from National Steel and Shipbuilding, where L.G. Maple was a division manager. The elder Maple was by his first wife's account a tough and controlling man. By Kahn's notes, he was "an angry man." By a report in the *San Diego Union* in 1944, he was also a fiery man ready to shoot the escaped German POWs if they had shown up at his door during the four-day national hunt for them and his son. But, pursuing a life after professional death and, perhaps, some structure, Dale Maple went west. Portrayed in clinical, legal, and more than a few windy dinner conversations as an oppositional, truculent, attention-seeking, somewhat obnoxious, "psycho" narcissist, Dale Maple arrived to take cover in the rewarding, seductive new conformist consensus he had once so spectacularly flaunted.

The notorious son's arrival gathered even shorter-lived notice than the four-part series about his conviction in *The New Yorker*. It was four months later, in February 1951, that the *San Diego Union* picked up a War Department notice about his release. The headline, buried on page 10, was "U.S. Frees Maple; Aided Nazis' Escape." The reporter called L.G. Maple, who confirmed that Dale—who the reporter recalled had "a brilliant and promising career in which young Maple, with straight 'A' grades from San Diego High School, won a scholarship at the age of 16"—had been back in town since October. L.G. added that Dale was living with him but offered little else. It was to be the last public reference to Dale Maple's wartime experience for the next 50 years.

True to his word, L.G. Maple got his son a job at National Steel and Shipbuilding. The company, a manhole-cover manufacturer, now rising rapidly on the postwar tide of prosperity and enjoying a lucrative portion of the emerging military-industrial complex, was a near-perfect mirror image of its age. Not long before called California Iron Works, it had grown into National Iron Works and then National Steel and Shipbuilding. By Maple's first day of work, it was a diversified operation that fabricated steel and built tuna boats, boilers, and military barges. Navy work—mostly boats and radar equipment—had recently become its biggest revenue generator. Its steel fabrication plant, meanwhile, took it into farm equipment and many kinds of commercial construction. Long past its days of family ownership, it was then owned by a joint venture of a steel company and a construction firm. During the next decades, it would continue to assume the evolving shapes of corporate America. It would be a buyout target, a management-controlled employee stock company, a giant with a name reduced to an otherwise nonsense stock ticker word (NASSCO), and, soon, a substantial part of a massive international conglomerate.

L.G. Maple rose with it. In 1953, he engineered a process that cut the company's cost of removing mill scale from steel by 30% and, among other things, won an admiring story and portrait in the newspaper. In 1956, his steel went into the largest Navy ship ever constructed in San Diego. By the end of the decade, he was developing buildings around San Diego for a local conglomerate, and he and his wife Ruth had begun to subdivide eight lots they had bought around their neighborhood. In all, the elder Maple rode the company into the expanding white upper-middle class of the 1950s. He was an inventive, productive, and successful executive. His wife was a fine social asset, serving on multiple committees of the San Diego Woman's Club—tea hostess, decorations committee chairwoman, planner of the Young Woman's Christian Association's Christmas Party (which held a "promise of unusual charm"), program manager for "Patriotic Days" (done up in flag colors, featuring a brief historical quiz as lunch was being served)—with the wives of subcontractors, corporate superiors, clients and Navy purchasing officers.[13]

And as senior executives can do, the job L.G. Maple got for his wayward son was a good one. Dale found himself working for one of the company's brightest stars.

Alfred A. Brosio was NASSCO's general manager. His resume included graduating with honors from the University of California at Berkeley, engineering experience, designing and managing dams, ships, and shipyards for the Army Corps of Engineers as well as market-driven companies, and managing hundreds of workers at various stops along the way. Brosio and the ex-con, moreover, hit it off. When Brosio left NASSCO in 1953 to start not one but two companies of his own, he took Maple with him.[14]

So, Dale Maple, now 32, became office manager of A.L. Brosio Co, which soon grew into a lucrative—Maple himself would later claim it as the biggest—insurer of California's vast fleets of commercial, industrial and pleasure ocean-going vessels. Maple, of course, did well in orderly, predictable environments like Leavenworth and, before that, at basic training, in school and ROTC. It was when the world grew unpredictable and disorderly, when he caused the chaos himself at Harvard or when the Army "shanghaied" him, that he seemed to go wide off the rails. But whether it was structure, a newfound social conscience, exhaustion from swimming against the current for so long, or the sheer peace of swimming with the cultural current for a change, Dale Maple, seemingly against all the odds, began to prosper like his one-time friend Eric Hotelling.

In business, he at first foreswore Harvard's potent professional network, including Porter and others who could help him get back on his feet. Aside from more frequent bulletins about promotions and marriages, members of each Harvard class sent chatty updates about their families, their accomplishments, their travels, and even their politics to a hardbound "Class Notes" book Harvard produced for each class every five years after its graduation. For Maple's class of 1941, Porter, for one, regularly submitted sober analyses of social issues as well as often-entertaining essays. While Maple was in prison, his classmates' entries chronicled storybook Harvard-esque ascensions through the military, government, science, family businesses, commerce, the arts, the professions, and society.

But the shamed Dale Maple did not return a questionnaire in 1946 for the first edition of the Class of '41's *Class Notes*. The only entry was the address of his mother's house in Newport, gleaned from old school records and rendered in one line. It was not until the 1956 edition, six years after his release from Leavenworth, that Maple finally returned a *Class Notes* questionnaire. It, too, was only one line, this time showing his father's address.[15]

Out of his classmates' sight, he was trying to fit himself into the professional and personal mold of a more conventional and conventionally secure man. For one thing, he had his mother near him again. Mae and Edwin W. Scoville, his stepfather, had been doing well in Newport, also beneficiaries of the nation's expanding prosperity. Edwin himself had gone back into business for himself after the war, and by 1948 had a well-established appliance store in town. While Mae Scoville gave herself over to fundraising for the Community Chest, the YMCA and church charity events, Edwin was an officer of the local Kiwanis Club and, with Mae, an active member of St. John's Episcopal Church. Business was good enough for them to move the appliance store to a new building sometime in 1953 or 1954, which is when their luck seemed to turn.

On October 7th, 1954, ghost-like, Edwin Scoville "appeared suddenly" on a Newport street before the car of a Mrs. Caroline B. Lemly, 28. She hit him, injuring his right leg and back and, unable to flag down help, got him into her car to take him to Newport Hospital. Then, several months into his recovery, burglars broke into his new store. Entering through a small window one night, they got away with a mere $3 in change, but the two events apparently amounted to something of a last straw. Edwin, whose life had been spent entirely in the northeast, threw caution to the wind. Later in 1955, he and his wife sold everything and moved to San Diego to be near Mae Scoville's still-loved son, Dale.[16]

And he was taking risks again. Though neither his father's nor his mother's reaction was recorded, he found a life partner. How or exactly when remains a mystery, except that Maple and John Frank Kucera (listed occupation: seaman, but at the time he may have had half-interest in a local restaurant) were together either tending or living on a farm on Route 2 in rural San Diego County. Then, in a series of transactions from August 1957 through April 1958, Dale Maple "an unmarried man" and John Kucera "an unmarried man" jointly bought a 10-year-old, two-bedroom, one-bathroom 1,587 square foot house at 10216 Hawley Road for $10,000. Ownership was split 50/50.

On what was then a gently curving dirt road, the only neighborhood restriction in the legal documents was that the new owners were prohibited from operating a hog farm on the property. "There was nothing out here . . . it was a very secluded place," Kucera's nephew recalled years later. Dale was a changed man again. He was beginning to do much better financially. Being "office manager" at A.L. Brosio Co. had come to comprise more than administrative duties, for Maple was now negotiating with clients and selling insurance policies. He did have at least one run-in with the law. On October 22nd, 1955, either shortly before or shortly after his mother moved to San Diego, police arrested him. The charge was "drk," which police officials today interpret as relating to drinking, and the fine was $10.* Alcohol, a relative later recalled, would continue to play a role in his life. [17]

In the 1950s Southern California, given Maple's sexual orientation, it needed to be secluded. His homesteading carried more than the financial and emotional risks that all nesting homebuyers take. He was in the bosom of a conservative family, in a church that doctrinally damned homosexuality and living in a conformist, socially punitive time. Sodomy was still a crime in all the 48 states. Being gay was still described as an illness in much medical literature. In business, it was mostly a profound professional handicap. Had he been in government, Dale Maple would legally be a traitor, this time because of his sexuality. Two months after Maple's return to San Diego, a report contending gays were "security risks"—"depraved" and thus particularly vulnerable to blackmail—was distributed in the U.S. Senate. In 1953, President Dwight Eisenhower issued an executive order that forbade the federal government and its contractors to employ homosexuals. Gays didn't have much help to call on. Despite the tenuous existence of two secretive support groups (one called the Mattachine Society, the other the Daughters of Billitis), gay life in San Diego remained widely demonized by the straight world and repressed for decades.

In many cities, gay men's social lives were often confined to what were mostly seedy and furtive bars. To protect themselves from ongoing police extortion and entrapment, some forbid kissing and overtly "effeminate" behavior. Others didn't. In 1952 San Diego's Cinnabar, one shocked magazine reported, employed "prancing misfit" waiters "in peekaboo blouses" who "make love with sailors." "For those in a hurry, jobs are performed in the men's rooms and telephone booths." Police bar raids and street arrests of men deemed to have a "woman's hairdo" or be wearing "flamboyant" clothes were common. In 1959, the U.S. Supreme Court overturned California's relatively new "sex registration law" that required gay people to register their addresses with the

---

* San Diego Police Department arrest records for most transgressions are purged and destroyed after 20 years. Maple's 1955 arrest appears in an FBI notation, not in police department records.

state. However, the next year San Francisco's "Gayola" case detailed how police were still demanding payoffs to protect gay hangouts from more police raids and arrests. San Diego would not have a formal LGBTQ community center until 1971, and then it initially consisted of an answering machine hidden in a utility closet.

Nevertheless, at age 38, ex-con Dale Maple moved into an arrangement—buying and sharing a home with another unmarried man—that in 1958 was as daring a high-wire act as being pro-German was in 1941.[18]

Staying on the wire required balance, discretion, and a bit more anonymity than Maple could manage. None were qualities that, despite his bravura performances at Leavenworth and at A.L. Brosio, came naturally to him.

He began to fall away from them as the decade ended, not only in his legally risky personal life but in increasingly frequent bids for public attention. In the aftermath of his real estate purchase, he became something of a boldface name in at least one newspaper column. Frank Rhodes authored a *San Diego Union* gossip column typical of the time. It reduced press agent tips to one-line quips and event listings separated by ellipses from snide political and cultural criticisms (e.g., about actress Dorothy Malone: "in a role that requires genuine emoting, Miss Malone turns to concrete").

Out of nowhere, "insurance man" Maple began to appear among the ellipses in January 1960. "Remember the doctor who insured his wife against having twins?" Rhodes wrote. "Insurance man **Dale Maple** reports she didn't . . ." Four months later: "Insurance man **Dale Maple** never knew he had civic pride until he placed a call from the Beverly Hilton to San Diego the other night. 'One moment,' said the L.A. phone girl, 'I'll give you the suburban operator . . .'" Later: "**Dale Maple** and Bill Gordon, a couple of insurance men," co-chaired an auto show. They expected 30,000 people.

He offered himself as an expert news source, too. As "office manager for A.L. Brosio Co., San Diego agent for Lloyd's of London," he told a reporter why insurance companies forbid ships to carry nuclear fuel. (Ships could carry much more fuel than airplanes and therefore, he said, an ocean-going accident would be more environmentally toxic than a plane crash). He walked another reporter through the need for what laypeople might think to be exotic business insurances. One was for rainfall, which he said was "actually inexpensive as insurance goes." Another was for outdoor events like school carnivals, golf tournaments, and—a special interest of Maple's—auto races. He'd recently insured a car rally at Torrey Pines for what was then a newsworthy $25,000.[19]

At work, his specialty was "marine insurance," covering the vast commercial tuna boat fleets that, in combination with four big canneries and scores of small support businesses, represented San Diego's third-largest industry in the 1950s, sixties, and seventies. The boats themselves, called "seiners," were ever-more expensive and technologically complex vessels that used speedboats and helicopters to herd tuna into vast nylon nets. The nets, in turn, could close on hundreds of tons of tuna at a time, haul them up to be frozen and then trans-port them back to the onshore canneries that packed and distributed them.[20]

Bosio himself was known as an expert tuna boat designer, but by the middle of the tumultuous 1960s, formerly independently owned boats themselves were being out-fished or being folded into larger corporate organizations. Maple, too, moved into the more corporate environment of American National General Agencies, a giant insurance firm based in Dallas. For ANGA, he initially became "national marine insurance director," working the entire West Coast industry. Soon after that, he was promoted to corporate vice president and president of ANGA's big San Diego office. When not traveling the state, he worked out of an executive office in the landmark Home Tower building downtown.

Dale Maple was prosperous. His father was, too. By 1960, L.G. had also gone corporate. He worked at the Westgate-California Corporation, a con-glomerate owned by "Mr. San Diego" C. Arnholt Smith. Smith owned United States National Bank, the region's largest bank, which in turn held 53% of Westgate-California. As such, Smith had significant investments in silver mines, transportation companies, and, not least, Dale Maple's tuna industry. Politically, he was a Republican force: a prominent financial backer of Richard Nixon and, by many accounts, was the man who broke the cannery unions by moving some of the business to Peru and investing heavily in high-tech seiner boats. Many local family tuna enterprises soon closed, while Smith occupied the center of city economic and political power. He unilaterally shut down the street in front of City Hall to build his Westgate Hotel across the way. According to legend, "No politician or bureaucrat dared ask whether Smith had received a permit." L.G. Maple was by that time "bank properties and construction manager" for Smith's U.S. National Bank. For Westgate, L.G. built bank branches, hotels, and industrial properties from the Mexican border north into Orange County

L.G. had other titles within the company, some less than legitimate. Smith sometimes called him and other executives into his office to sign papers listing them as officers of companies that held loans from Smith's bank. None of it was legal. Maple, for example, was "vice president" of Excalibur Engineering of Los Angeles, which had supposedly bought 160 acres of southern California farmland with $600,000 of U.S. National Bank money. On another day, Smith asked him to sign as "vice president" of Kingsburg Oil Co. The promissory note amount that time was $750,000. The money from the loans to fake businesses went to Smith himself, sometimes to pay off previous debts. Neither Maple nor any of the bank executives who later testified in various civil suits around what soon became the largest bank failure of the time had ever heard of Excalibur, Kingsburg, Woodlake Farms, Balboa International S.A. or any of the other companies before Smith told them to sign documents as their executives. They did it, Maple and his executive colleagues testified, because their boss had told them to. All the notes listed the bank as both trustee and beneficiary.[21] All were counted among the increasingly illusory assets of C. Arnholt Smith's collapsing empire.*

Before L.G.'s employer went south, these were Dale Maple's best times. His home on Hawley Road was nice, steadily increasing in value as a subdivision, and schools grew around it. Inside, the decor centered on a wall of Dale's books, many in foreign languages, and a piano that he played both for relaxation and for what Kucera's nephew—who lived with them during his high school years—recalled as frequent parties. His free time, Maple himself would say, was spent pursuing his "continued interest in matters musical and an active interest and participation in sports car activities, including membership on the board of various coordinating councils."

The sports car activities were events with clubs devoted to individual models (Maple was president of the Jaguar Club for a time) and, according to some, a magnet for southern California's gay community. "All of these people seemed to be gay, too. Not all of them, but they would have events around the cars and at different people's houses." On Sundays Maple, who Kucera's young nephew considered an uncle, would play the organ at the nearby Catholic Church. They also took the boy to visit L.G. Maple, whose relationship with his son was "good, okay." The devoted Mae Scoville, living not too far away, did not appear to be on the regular cycle of family gatherings for the clan on Hawley Road. [22]

And now, at last, Maple felt confident enough to reach out to his alma mater. His 1961 *Class Notes* entry remained a mere one-line address, but in 1966, some 16 years after returning to San Diego, 22 years after he deserted from Camp Hale and 24 years after he unceremoniously stopped showing up in Cambridge, he finally sent a more meaningful response to Harvard's *Class Notes*.

---

* Neither L.G. Maple nor his fellow executives apparently profited individually or drew penalties for the false filings, which violated several Federal Deposit Insurance Corporation and banking regulations. Smith himself was accused of bank fraud, income tax evasion and making illegal campaign contributions. He was eventually convicted of embezzling $8.9 million from the bank and his other companies. He ultimately served eight months "tending roses at a county honor camp in 1984." He died of congestive heart failure at home at age 97 in 1996.

Like Hotelling, he was not entirely forthcoming. He gave the impression to his classmates that the second act of his adult life had begun without the benefit of a first act. All his grad school schemes, pro-Hitler declarations, provocative press clippings, arrangements with Nazi spy-runners in Boston, his plans to go to sabotage school in Germany, his Army segregations and humiliations, his terrorist plans, his desertion, his escape with and harboring of two German prisoners of war, his capture in northern Mexico, his court-martial, his death sentence, and his five and a half years in prison went un-mentioned.

Instead, his first words to classmates were, "Subsequent to disentanglement from the armed services in 1950, I joined the staff of National Steel & Ship-building Corporation as assistant to the general manager." Without describing when or how, he reported he'd gone to the A.L. Brosio Company, become a specialist in marine insurance, and followed "an ever-widening interest in the various aspects of insurance . . . to my association in 1964 with the American National General Agencies, an insurance managing general agency dealing with all types of insurance, including marine insurance."[23]

And so, by 1966, "subsequent to disentanglement," impulsive risk-taker Dale Maple admitted to finding a professional home in risk management, the often-profitable discipline of carefully examining experience to predict the results of future behavior.

Like most of the former conspirators in the 620th Paul Kissman had entirely deleted his past experiences from his, his acquaintances' and his new family's memories. Now earning "good money" as the popular foreman at a large factory in Erie, he was the father of two girls. They were never told anything about Leavenworth or his Army experiences.[24] In San Diego, the teenager who lived with Maple and John Kucera never heard a word about his adopted uncle's court-martial or death sentences or arguments that bad dictatorships were better than good democracies. In New Jersey, Eric Hotelling, building on a past purged of wrongdoing and the supposedly seductive displays of Nazi flags, was settling into an important new job of his own and, in his spare time, starting work on a book. Fritz Siering was back from Argentina.

All, now stripped of their histories, kept the pasts blank or unrecognizable. Where all that was headed was unclear, and it remained to be seen if even those who cleansed themselves of history were doomed to repeat it.

CHAPTER 20

THE REBEL AFTERLIFE IN THE LAND OF PLENTY

Hotelling thought Theo Leonhard "the heart and soul of the pro-German element" in the 620th, and the teacherly, intense Leonhard was indeed fiercely attached to his German heritage. He did not often stray far from any of his principles before his induction, while he was in the Army and, not least, when he was struggling to escape the Army. His inflexibility often cost him dearly in the years during and probably after the war. Though details of his life after his release into the historic prosperity and cultural tumult of postwar America are scarce, Leonhard was the only member of the Inner Circle who apparently did not erase, whitewash or reconstruct his strange Army experiences.

While the other Camp Hale rebels accommodated themselves to life in the new 1800th labor battalion or as federal prisoners, Leonhard was doggedly pursuing his legal options at the Disciplinary Barracks. He had appealed the federal district court's 1944 rejection of his application for a writ of habeas corpus, which would have removed him from the Army's jurisdiction in 1945 and probably put him into an internment camp for the war's duration. But the war was over by the time the appeals court ruled against him, and the court returned him to the military's embrace. The military, in turn, didn't get Leonhard into the court-martial room at the Disciplinary Barracks until January 1946. It was September before it finished reviewing and approving his sentence. The sentence: 10 years and a dishonorable discharge.[1]

With room at the prison scarce, moreover, Leonhard couldn't be transferred to the penitentiary at Leavenworth from the Disciplinary Barracks until October 1946, nearly two years after Maple and Kissman. His behavior at the

Barracks after his conviction began much like Maple's, committing minor acts of defiance. Another prisoner, for example, kicked a barrel that had a beehive in it down a hill, and Leonhard defied an order to leave it and the honey inside alone. He got 15 days of restrictions. He got another 15 days when a guard found a compass—considered contraband—in the wastebasket in his cell. Soon enough, again like Maple and Kissman, he began racking up "above-average work reports."[*]

Unlike Maple and Kissman, however, he did not overtly renounce his Nazi sympathies or deny his past. But "no acts have been observed which might be considered as indicating bitterness toward this country." Personally, "he displays no bitterness; on the contrary his attitude is wholesome, humble, diligent and gracious." He worked hard. "Although Leonhard is a well-educated man, there is no task in the institution so menial that he will not cheerfully and skillfully . . . perform it." On Sundays, he directed the choir in the Protestant chapel. During the week, perhaps working with Maple, he taught reading to men who were "slow learners." As a teacher, "he is masterful. Also teaches high school English and social studies." By 1949, he was earning meritorious "good time" and $5 per month[2]

His progress toward release was as deliberate and grudging as Maple's. His parole committee turned him down in February 1949 despite his good behavior and an agreement with former 620 mate Rudolph Nobis. Nobis, now living in Ohio, offered to take him in whenever he might be released.

"If paroled, [Leonhard] wished to avoid returning" to Texas "where his father is a clergyman because he thinks he might embarrass his father." Nobis, whose family in Canton had a decorating business, promised Leonhard a room at his house and, first, a job as a paint sprayer. It would be a considerable drop in occupational status for the former doctoral candidate and political science instructor at the University of Texas, where his heart seemed to be.

Even at the depths of his legal troubles in 1944, he could instantly wax sentimental about the university. His interrogator at the Disciplinary Barracks, himself a graduate of the University of Texas, had tried to loosen the "died-in-the-wool Nazi" Leonhard's tongue by condemning him "for bringing disgrace to the University and particularly to Dean Taylor, who was the head of the College of Engineering. In this manner, I worked on his loyalty as a Texas Ex,

---

[*] Leonhard's only other black mark was for talking in the mess line in May 1950, when he walked "double" with another inmate. He got a week's worth of restrictions.

and he burst out crying and advised me that he hated the United States, but he was loyal to Texas."[3]

In August 1950, the parole committee denied leniency again, this time despite acknowledging that Leonhard's sentence was running too long. It pointed out that Maple, confined in one way or another for the same length of time as Leonhard, was about to be released. It did change his custody from "close" to "medium" (something granted to Maple four years before) and then shortened Leonhard's sentence to eight years, from 10. But it was not until the next August that the Army's reformed judicial branch finally agreed to forgive the rest of his sentence. After finishing some paperwork, he finally left Leavenworth at 9:45 A.M. on September 1st, 1951. He arrived in Canton that night with $32.82 in his pocket.[4] The last of the misfit unit's rebels to be sentenced, he was also the last to enter the new world.

———

Leonhard's wall-painting career was either short or never started, for he soon was doing the accounting for the Nobis Decorating Company of North Canton. The company itself was vastly smaller than Maple's NASSCO but no less a reflection of postwar prosperity. Rudi, another of the budding successes of the postwar 620th, took over the company, founded by his immigrant father Fred, sometime in the mid-fifties. He added a successful stained-glass window operation that eventually became the company's best-known asset. Its windows are still in place throughout the Midwest, including churches in Michigan and Ohio. After a fire, Rudi moved the business to Florida in the 1970s, where the firm continued to expand.

Theo Leonhard, though, had moved on long before, although perhaps not without visiting Paul Kissman 50 miles away in Erie. One of Kissman's daughters, then a young girl, remembers being introduced to a "Mr. Leonhard," although she doesn't know that it was the same man. By then, however, Kissman was in active contact with at least two other 620 veterans[5]

Leonhard, in any case, soon caught on as personnel manager at a construction firm in Chicago Heights, Illinois, where Drewes also was then living. Chicago's substantial German community at the time was treading carefully. "German Americans," a Chicago historian found, "kept their ethnicity to themselves, and they were not very eager to revive it in the 1950s and '60s."

Leonhard, much as he had in college and in the 620th, soon won some prominence within the community. In his off-hours, he became president of the Chicago Heights German American Club, by then a social organization hoping "to deepen and further the ties and friendship between the United States and Germany, and to keep alive German traditions and cultural traditions" among most of its relentlessly assimilating members. He was one "Theophil" or "Leonhard" among the area's vast German ethnic population who did not change his name to "Ted," "Tom" or "Leonard." Members of his and other such clubs attended "international fairs" of foreign-made goods, card parties, holiday dinners, turkey shoots, concerts, and dances. There were also programs like the discussion about a former Wehrmacht lieutenant and POW who escaped from a stockade in North Carolina in 1945, "faded into anonymity in Chicago" and turned himself in to the FBI in 1959. ("I was broke," he told a reporter, "and decided to give up running.")

The Chicago Heights club's political sympathies at the time were not publicized, but some other German American social clubs managed to preserve their pre-war Bund roots. The Bund disbanded in 1941, and many former members regrouped in German "singing societies" in Hudson County, New Jersey, as the Springfield Social Club in Detroit and at *Haus Veterland*, the Bund's former Chicago headquarters. In Erie, Paul Kissman's Siebenbuerger Club, founded in 1898 and still a social center of the local German community, celebrated Hitler's birthday at least into the 1960s.[6]

The ex-con Leonhard also preached, delivering a speech called "Martin Luther" at the Walther League, a Lutheran youth organization, and another titled "Luther the Man" at Immanuel Lutheran Church in Chicago Heights.

———

His luck did not hold. In 1965, doctors told Leonhard he had bladder cancer. It was not a good diagnosis. Weakened, his revered father dead eight years, he at last felt safe enough to venture back home to Texas without causing embarrassment.

In Fredericksburg, he took an apartment either near or with his widowed mother. He was soon moved 240 miles to MD Anderson Hospital in Houston on April 19th, 1966, and, after 20 days, died at 5:10 A.M. on May 9th. He was 52, the last member of the Inner Circle to be freed and the first to die.

The funeral notice in the Fredericksburg paper neglected to mention Leonhard's war, prison records, or dishonorable discharge. No one else mentioned them, at least publicly. His mother, 77, had lost one son over Austria and shared her husband's community embarrassment over Theo. Burying him, she checked the box on Theo's death certificate that said he'd never served.[7]

A Mrs. Gertrude Karas, described as "a close friend of the late Theophil Leonhard" from Chicago Heights, hurried to Texas for the funeral. She was late. A train accident in Illinois delayed her arrival in Fredericksburg until about an hour after the service ended. Kathe Leonhard, Theo's mother, was touched that someone came all that distance to bid Theo goodbye and offered to put Mrs. Karas up. A reporter for the local paper soon came over to interview the big city visitor. She remembered how fondly Leonhard had spoken of the area. "Theophil had always told [their co-workers] of the pretty hills here, but they had pictured it as flat, uninteresting country." But he'd been right. His country, she marveled, was beautiful.

Leonhard had effectively exiled himself from the area to avoid causing his family embarrassment, but ultimately news of his transgressions found its way there. In July 2020 documents from as his 1946 court-martial showed up at his gravesite in Fredericksburg, Texas. An organization that tends seemingly unvisited veterans' graves placed them there, making Theophil Leonhard the only member of the Inner Circle whose past caught up to him even in death.[8]

———

Paul Kissman, in turn, parlayed his first post-prison job into a return to the social class from which he sprang. Thirty-two when he got back to Erie from Leavenworth in 1947, Kissman moved back in with his parents and took a job on the factory floor of what was then 51-year-old Reed Manufacturing, a well-regarded manufacturer of patented vises, pipe tools, and cutters. (Its older vises and devices, now deemed "classic" by collectors, are still traded online at this writing). The company was a community pillar, notable for supporting public causes and, not least, its apparent willingness to give a second chance to someone as compromised as Paul Kissman. The ex-con Kissman's job sponsor was, in fact, a scion of the Wright family, which had owned the company since 1902.

He found a city much transformed since he'd left it at the tail end of the Great Depression. Erie had become a prosperous, smoke-belching Great Lakes industrial hub turning out forges, locomotives, radio parts, refrigerators, valves, rubber and brass products, paper, stoves, and more. Reed Manufacturing was one of its most stable companies. Another was the automotive wheel division of the Malleable Iron Company, whose chief clerk was Kissman's parole adviser.

Better yet, his family—his network—was more or less intact. His parents were still living in Paul's boyhood home. He was particularly close to his father who, retired but still active in various lodges, may have helped land him at

Reed. One brother was a "structural electrician" in Santa Monica, starting his own family, and another—the seemingly less settled Herbert—was still in Erie. Herbert, a family member recalled, "was a heavy drinker and a bit of a ne'er-do-well, flitting from job to job." But the family regularly took both Herbert and Paul with them to visit older brother Clayton in California.

To all appearances, the Kissmans remained a textbook example of family unity until the mid-seventies. After decades of upheaval in domestic life—the financial displacements and altered gender roles of the Depression and war years, the vast migration of populations from south to north, the erratic union challenges to corporate power and, certainly not least, the death or crippling of much of a generation of young males in the war—Americans were creating what one scholar called a "surge in family life." In the loveless language of sociology, it was about building security and emotional safety in a threatening nuclear and rapidly changing world. Statistically, it was an interruption of previous trends. Up to that point in the 20th century, birth rates had been declining as both marriage age and divorce rates rose. [9]

Paul prospered at Reed, rising to become foreman and spending his free time singing with church and social club groups, when he fell for Gladys Elma Schroeder, who worked in Reed's front office. They married, moved into a house near Kissman's parents, and began a family. One daughter, Lisa, was born in 1952, after which Gladys Kissman left Reed and remained a homemaker for the next 22 years. A second daughter, Lori, arrived in 1958.

He never really gave up his interest in either "the optical trade" or conservative politics. "If he had to live his life over, he would become an ophthalmologist," he would tell his youngest daughter. He promised to donate his eyes to science. "His mother had glaucoma later in life. Dad would always be the one to put drops in her eyes."

———

Their home life seemed warm for a time. When they played cards or Scrabble or dominos, "he always won." He joked about his size-13 shoes, and "was very strong, both mentally and physically. He was outgoing and friendly . . . When we would go to church, my father's powerful voice would overtake the entire congregation while singing hymns. I would be so proud as I stood next to him as a young child." At home, he collected coins, watched football and played piano. Lori's favored her dad's renditions of "Fly Me To The Moon" and "Edelweiss."

German music and German culture were ubiquitous in the house. "We grew up in a German house. We didn't have a swastika or anything, but he did celebrate Hitler's birthday," sister Lisa recalled. "He loved America and he loved Germany. That's who my dad was. Very intelligent, very outspoken. Very outgoing."[10]

Politically, Paul and Gladys Kissman were "staunch conservatives," and then some. "My parents fought hard to keep our constitutional rights," daughter Lori explained. They campaigned for like-minded candidates—Barry Goldwater was a favorite in 1964—and would "go door-to-door with petitions and place fliers on cars in parking lots. [Gladys] also cared deeply about environmental and health issues." That, in part, meant taking to the front lines in Erie's long fight over fluoridating the city's water supply.*

Sometimes, the kids went along. In the early 1960s Lisa, the oldest daughter, tagged along with her father to a local bookbinding shop. "I was in charge of putting blue binders on all these books." The adults met in the back. "I asked my dad what they were doing back there, and he said, 'It's a secret society.'" She was at a chapter meeting of the John Birch Society, founded in Indiana in 1958 initially to fight what it claimed were conspiracies by Moscow, bankers, and liberal politicians to replace the American republic with a communist, collectivist government.

Kissman's days of thinking the free market was responsible for the Depression he'd toured in the 1930s and his affinity for "socialism" upon returning from his short stay in Germany in 1940 were long gone. The Birch Society was often cast as "proto-fascist," maintaining that the United States was founded as "a republic, not a democracy." It insisted that expanded voting rights and the "coddling" of criminals, multi-nationalists and liberals were successfully subverting the country. By the late 1950s, Society founder Robert Welch saw it as a nation rife with traitors. They included President Dwight Eisenhower, "a conscious, dedicated agent of the communist conspiracy," supporters of the United Nations, the Council on Foreign Relations, the United Auto Workers, Robert Kennedy and, not least, the civil rights movement. The "Negro Revolutionary Movement" was no less than "the flaming front of the whole proletarian revolution."

---

* The Kissmans opposed it. Voters already had rejected a 1954 proposal to treat Erie's water supply with fluorine—the goal was to improve local dental health—by an overwhelming 4:1 margin. But as more cities in the state adopted it and pressures from the state's Department of Health and the medical and dental societies mounted, in March 1964, the City Council, mayor, and head of Public Works simply announced that fluoridation would start as soon as July 1st. Within a week of the announcement, a "Citizens Opposed to Fluoridation" group formed to cancel the plan and put it on the November ballot. Though they failed to get enough signatures, City Council put it on the ballot anyway when the group said it would seek an injunction. In November, voters rejected fluoridation again, this time by a 3:1 margin.

The Society sought to impeach Earl Warren, chief justice of the U.S. Supreme Court, hoping to reverse court rulings on police reading people their rights upon arrest and, not least, school desegregation. On a local level, it fought to end sex education, to defeat women's rights groups threat from trying to "bring on the complete breakdown of family life" and, among scores of other causes, halt the fluoridation of local water supplies

The blue bindings that Lisa Kissman was putting around printed materials were probably copies of the Society's latest literature, which typically featured patriotic, blue covers.

———

She accompanied her dad on trips to Buffalo, too. "We went frequently, very frequently . . . I don't know why we went. I think it must have had something to do with the John Birch Society." Everybody had families with them. The kids would play while the adults did whatever adults did. There was the Newcomber family, the Geer family, and, among others, the family of Otto Idelberger, Jr., his mate from the 620th who'd once accompanied Eric Hotelling on his recruiting trips to Denver and Camp Carson in Colorado Springs. By then, he was a business owner in Parsippany, New Jersey [11]

And she vaguely remembers a man named "Leonhard" visiting them in Erie, although she could not say it was her dad's former Army pal.

Eric Hotelling also dropped in.

"He became a life-long friend to my parents and sent them postcards from his world-wide travels," daughter Lori recalled. Her sister Lisa "met him a lot of times." Hotelling came to Erie often and, while there, even dated Gladys Kissman's sister "off and on. Aunt Betty said, 'he was rather dull.'"

Nevertheless, two years later, Eric, with Harold Hotelling in attendance, married someone else 130 miles away, in Pittsburgh.[12]

———

By now Eric Bell Hotelling was, like Kissman, swimming in the rushing economic mainstream of American postwar life. His pro-German mates on the periphery of 620th's Inner Circle were also doing well. Otto Idelberger Jr. was in the heating oil business in New Jersey. Hugo Opton had stayed in the military, gone to Korea, and was about to re-enlist again. This time, it was with the Air Force, where he became a career officer.

Rudi Nobis was ascending to leadership of the family decorating business in Ohio. Menke Drewes, after serving as an executive at the Berkeley Company (a welding equipment manufacturer for the aviation and automotive industries in Danville, Illinois), was living in upscale suburbs on Chicago's North Shore and working at Martin-Marietta's Chicago offices. Still married to the organist he'd fallen for in 1943, he came to develop at least one patent for a coupling needed for space travel simulations. He was also a community pillar. In 1958 he was named "Worthy Grand Patron" of the Order of the Eastern Star of Illinois, a 15,000-member chapter of "the world's largest philanthropic fraternity that admits both men and women to membership."[13]

Hotelling, with his bachelor's degree from Rutgers in hand, migrated for graduate work to the University of Michigan. He earned a master's in 1951 and spent the next years pursuing his doctorate as a William S. Merrill Fellow in Pharmaceutical Chemistry, which paid him some $1,100 a year (about $10,300 in today's dollars). The years in Ann Arbor seemed to be almost drama-free, although in August 1953, five months before getting his doctorate, he abruptly resigned the Merrill fellowship.

His reasons remain a mystery. Campuses were in an uproar—especially at Michigan—over persistent demands to fire faculty members. Sometimes with the help of Hoover and the FBI, Wisconsin Senator Joseph McCarthy was regularly accusing faculty with having some real or imagined affiliation with communist, socialist, liberal, or labor groups. Michigan's president eventually bent to the pressure, banishing three faculty members the next year. It sparked street demonstrations and, soon, some big-name professors to move on to more receptive campuses. But, given his previous avowals, Hotelling's support of left-ists even in the name of academic freedom seems unlikely. He may well have finished his coursework and, already affiliated as a research chemist with the Consolidated Coal Company of Pittsburgh, could have been able to get by without the Merrill money.[14]

———

Around 1 A.M. of a cold morning in late 1953, Milton Adams of 5359 Youngridge Drive in Pittsburgh was awakened by faint noises coming from the apartment above him. To Adams, who by day was an FBI agent, they sounded like "weak signals appearing to be short wave radio transmissions." They were "either weak wireless transmissions or possibly reception of signals." Another apartment neighbor called them "dit-dah" sounds. The signals "continued for several minutes."

Moreover, the man in the apartment above Adams "appeared very secretive, kept his shades drawn at all times, and associated with no one except a Chinese chemist who lived nearby." It was also at a time when the United States was at war—officially, it was a "police action"—with the Chinese and North Korean military on the Korean peninsula. The "Chinese chemist" certainly could be an American of Chinese heritage or, to a suspicious mind during wartime, an enemy. It was enough for the FBI to launch yet another investigation of Eric Bell Hotelling, the man in the apartment above Adams.

Adams noted that Consolidated Coal, Hotelling and the chemist's workplace, was not a "key facility," but the FBI began looking into Adams' neighbor just in case. It checked to see if Hotelling had a license to operate a short-wave transmitter. In its files, it quickly re-discovered his pro-German activities at Columbia, the worried calls from Hotelling's parents, the mutiny reports from Rim Rock, and the statements of soldiers he'd talked to on his Denver recruiting trips. Washington, D.C. agents began investigating Muriel Burrows Hotelling, Eric's sister. The Pittsburgh office ratcheted up its surveillance, documenting Hotelling's activities and associates in and around Consolidated Coal. "Discreetly," it contacted sources at the University of Michigan. [15]

Then the FBI reviewed the record of Professor Harold Hotelling, Eric's father, then at the University of North Carolina.

———

The FBI's findings about the younger Hotelling were either lost or destroyed. Most of the documents that the FBI and the Navy's Criminal Investigative Service ultimately declassified were about the much more famous, accessible, and politicly progressive elder Hotelling.

There were records, easily dismissed in any other age but the McCarthy 1950s, that hinted at liberalism. The FBI found Harold Hotelling's signature on a statement from the late 1940s deploring the "outside spokesmen of hysteria" who had convinced Queens College to revoke the student charter of American Youth for Democracy. In 1941, he'd signed a petition to reinstate a City College tutor who was a former communist and member of the Anti-Fascist League. (The long-time tutor, openly leftist, had told a congressional committee he could think of only three communists at the college. The college fired the tutor after another faculty member, whose definitions of communism were more flexible, told the same committee there were a more threatening 50 "supposed communists" on campus.)

Another reason to suspect Harold Hotelling was his open-mindedness. In 1943, he'd agreed to be a reference on the job application of someone an anonymous source once named as "an underground member of the [Communist

Party] in Washington, D.C." The professor had also been a member of the National Council of American Soviet Friendship, a celebrity-studded group formed in 1943 to promote a permanent united front alliance against fascism. By the rabidly anti-communist early 1950s, McCarthy branded it a subversive organization.

In the end, the FBI—rarely accused of having nuanced views of ideologies in those Red-baiting days—also put positive estimates of Harold Hotelling into the file. The FBI's New York office reported he was "'liberal' in that he favored broader Social Security, government spending in economic emergency, and international exchange of scientific information up to the point where the best interests of the country would deem such expedient." In the dis-interred Harold Hotelling files, an agent quoted a source in Columbia's Economics Department calling the professor "a humanitarian and liberal in his views on racial tolerance and his interest in the fate of people of foreign countries."[16]

— —

In its surveillance of his son, meanwhile, the FBI either missed or neglected to report that Eric Hotelling was then courting Berenice* Ann Heinz, the 26-year-old daughter of a machinist at one of Pittsburgh's big copper rolling mills. The couple married in October 1956. The rigorously tolerant Harold Hotelling, who had once accused his extremist right-wing son of subversion and had him tailed by the FBI, served as Eric's best man.[17]

The other fruits of the FBI's investigation in 1953 and 1954 either were not recorded or are lost like many of the parts of Eric Hoteling's life. It was not the first time the government investigated him, and it would not be the last. In all the instances, however, Eric Hotelling himself remained unscathed. Other than his short stay in the Leavenworth Disciplinary Barracks in 1944, he was never affected by or fired from a job for political reasons.

Instead, his career took off. Michigan published his dissertation and, even as the Navy began a new investigation of him, he left Consolidated Coal in 1958 to win increasingly responsible corporate positions. His next was at Stein-Hall & Co., a New York maker of industrial glues and chemicals for the paper, corrugated cardboard, and textile industries. He went to and stayed for two-year stretches at American Machine & Foundry (AMF), Virginia Chemicals, and General Foods before he landed as a senior vice president at the Yoo-Hoo Beverage Company in 1966.

---

* Her name was alternately spelled as "Berenice" and "Berenece."

He already owned parts of at least three patents when he and Berenice moved to Stamford, Connecticut to take the job at AMF. They'd be among about 40 he'd develop. AMF manufactured tobacco production and bowling equipment while building a thickening book of defense contracts. Though the Department of Justice files do not explain them, it is conceivable that the subsequent FBI investigations of Eric Hotelling were background checks for participating on AMF teams doing Defense Department work. [18]

But it was at the Yoo-Hoo Beverage Company, at least to outside eyes, that Hotelling fully achieved the kind of family stability and professional security that ex-cons are said to need. His family grew to include son Eric H., born in 1959, and daughter Brenda, born in 1964.

Yoo-Hoo itself, decades old by the time Hotelling joined it, was becoming ever-better known for its chocolate soft drink. Its ads featured New York Yankees catcher Yogi Berra chirping "It's Me-He for Yoo-Hoo!"

Hotelling's role at the company was less public than Berra's but not invisible. His research was devoted mainly to developing "high protein drinks" for foreign markets, where the company marketed them as low-cost, nutritional foods that would ease hunger in poorer countries. "Soft drinks with high-protein soybeans have had a good reception in the Far East, but they have failed in other parts of the world where the taste of soy is not common," Hotelling explained to a wire service reporter. But Yoo-Hoo's "soft drink with a milk protein base" had recently been "successfully" tested in Chile and Cyprus, and the firm would soon open a bottling plant in Sierra Leone. Muslims in Africa, he observed, "would prefer chocolate and banana" ingredients to the fish and other animal proteins the company included in other markets. Life was good.* [19]

He traveled the world, sending the Kissmans postcards from Yoo-Hoo's foreign outposts. His research bore fruit, winning him new patents. With his wife, he nested in a series of upscale communities in New England and Pennsylvania. Meanwhile, in print, he became the dashing Dirk van Kirk.

Writing under the pseudonym of Phelps Jay Phelps, Hotelling wrote a thriller called *The Lost Treasure City of Tlaxu*. Published in 1969 by Vantage, then the nation's dominant "vanity press," it featured the adventures of Dirk van Kirk, a Rutgers graduate much like the once-blond Hotelling. Hotelling

---

* Berra, officially the company's "vice president for promotion," had a 15-year contract with the company that included a raise "after each winning Yoo-Hoo season." To a *New York Times* reporter interviewing him about the arrangement, the catcher admitted, "I don't know everything about franchising and stuff, but I sure know how the money's moving."

had an unfailingly adoring view of van Kirk. Dirk was "a strong, lean, well-knit young man with blue eyes, a blond crew cut, brilliant mind, sympathetic by nature and far above average in appearance."[20] He soon enlists an old buddy "stuck in the dullest office the world has ever produced, learning the insurance business," although he allowed that his buddy's boss "can't be all bad if he reads Spengler."* Also on board is his buddy's butler, James Poop.

Dirk, Poop, and his buddy overcome "firefish," giant condors, and cunning bad guys to explore the remote headwaters of the Amazon River, looking for a storied emerald mine. They find instead a mysterious city built over the mine, ruled by evil priests carefully bred from their Inca roots—Inca people, one character explains, "have a much lower scale of civilization"—to become Caucasian. They do so by kidnapping, enslaving, and impregnating white women. By the time Dirk arrives, all the women are beautiful sex objects. The beauties include the princess who has been unfairly denied her rightful place on the throne of Tlaxu.

Kerfuffles, gruesome tortures, and wild orgies follow. The orgies are fueled by aphrodisiacs which the beautiful princess, who otherwise offers no hint of lab experience, identifies by their chemical names: cantharides and yohimbine. She shares author Hotelling's familiarity with chemistry at another point. The princess knowingly attributes Tlaxu's animals' large size to eating a plant that "produces a steroid substance chemically related to the pituitary hormones."

At the last minute, Dirk saves the princess from being forced to join the orgies, and she falls for Dirk. The evil priests apparently have no choice but to kill her, Dirk, Poop, and Dirk's buddy, who has secretly found and married a beautiful woman of his own. The chase goes through tunnels, into mammoth storehouses full of emeralds, around huge snakes, into roaring underground rivers, over precipitous waterfalls, and into a last confrontation with the firefish. Dirk and the princess finally make it back to New York, where they marry. After the ceremony, Dirk regrets that his new bride will never get to assume her rightful place as Tlaxu's queen. "My dearest Dirk," she replies, "this morning

---

* Oswald Spengler's *Decline of the West* directly informed Hitler's National Socialism, the notion of "culture" as "race," and "foreign" races that threatened the German "race." It was a favorite of Nazi sympathizers like Maple, who often quoted from it and who, perhaps coincidentally, was in the insurance business at the time Hotelling's book appeared. *Decline of the West*, originally published in Germany in 1923 and derived from the American Eugenics movement of the early 20th century, argued that a population becomes a "race" when it was united in outlook. He foresaw a final struggle between capitalism and socialism, which represented "the will to call into life a mighty politico-economic order that transcends all class interests, a system of lofty thoughtfulness and duty sense." He added, "A power can be overthrown only by another power, not by a principle, and only one power that can confront money is left. Money is overthrown and abolished by blood."

I received the title which I would rather possess than any other in the whole world—that of Mrs. Dirk van Kirk. Do not try to fob off any lesser one on me."

In his self-written "About the Author" note on the back cover, the often-secretive Hotelling/Phelps Jay Phelps revealed a little more of himself. "Under his own (classified) name he has earned degrees . . . at Rutgers & Michigan. A war veteran, a teacher of chemistry, an inventor and businessman, he is a world traveler." He also "owns more than forty patents of one sort or another."

He sent an autographed copy of the book to the Kissman family in Pennsylvania. [21]

———

Yoo-Hoo's sales began a steep upward climb soon after Hotelling got there, and in an age of fevered corporate mergers and acquisitions, soon attracted the attention of a heftier competitor. Pepsi-Cola agreed to buy the company in 1964, but the government sued, claiming a combined company would violate anti-trust laws. Defending Yoo-Hoo was William Rogers, soon to become U.S. Secretary of State under President Nixon. Nixon, then practicing law between campaigns, was the Pepsi attorney defending the acquisition.

Together, Yoo-Hoo and Pepsi and their lawyers lost. Yoo-Hoo stayed independent for the time being. But it grew no less. Its output expanded dramatically from 400,000 cases about the time Hotelling joined it to 6.5 million cases and $17 million in sales in 1973.

But the 1970s were not always kind to Hotelling. His wife Berenice died in 1972 at the age of 42, apparently of cancer. That same year, he continued a second unusually combative campaign to join the school board of Kennelon, N.J. The local paper editorialized against him as "a loser." The town's mayor, as a group of Republicans had done five years earlier, endorsed the Democratic candidate instead. Hotelling, he said, was an "arch-conservative." Then, in December of 1973, his father Harold died. He would carry on alone for a long time [22]

———

In Erie, Kissman often took his family to the Siebenbuerger Club for dinner on Friday nights. His wife Gladys and his youngest daughter Lori would go home afterward, but Paul and his oldest daughter Lisa would stay. Paul would play Euchre, dominos, pinochle, and bridge. He kept up with the world through *U.S. News & World Report.* Lisa would spend as much time as she could with her father. She'd often go over to Reed Manufacturing to meet him for lunch—"it was the only time I'd get to see him"—and tag along on his trips to Buffalo and local John Birch Society meetings. Lisa counted herself as her father's favorite, while Lori was her mother's favorite.

There came a day when Lori and her mother were looking through photos, and Lori "saw a picture of dad with 'censored' on the back. She asked what does 'censored' mean? And Mom told her, 'There was a little bit of a problem with your dad when he was in the Army.'"

Paul Kissman had rarely, if ever, mentioned the "problem" or much else about the mistakes of 1944. As for talk of his Army days, Lisa Williams remembered "none, none, none."

There never would be. Instead, as the '70s unfolded, daughter Lisa remembers Paul as retreating from his family. (Sister Lori denies he did.) Long after his brother Clayton died on the West Coast in 1962, Lisa also recalls her dad going out to California for long weekends. "I don't know if he just loved the weather or if he met someone." (Lori disputes that, too.)

The one night a week at the Siebenbuerger Club with his family, moreover, "trended toward two and three and four nights a week" on his own, Lisa said. He began drinking more. And he spent a lot of time at his parents' house. "I know it sounds strange, but he was there more than he was home. I know it hurt my mom." By the early 1970s, "we hardly saw him. That hurt my mom. That hurt all of us."

———

Around them, like many cities in what then was rapidly becoming the Rust Belt, Erie itself was listing. An exodus of manufacturing jobs accelerated, heading like increasing numbers of companies nationwide at the time to the south toward cheaper labor. Louis Marx & Company, in the 1960s a wildly successful manufacturer of Rock 'em Sock 'em Robots and Big Wheels, shut down in 1978. General Electric, the city's biggest employer, invested $300 million on robots to replace some humans in its locomotive plant. It was also losing money, thanks to its moribund nuclear power division and an organizational structure that struggled to manage its far-flung enterprises efficiently. Corporate raider Carl Icahn pressured it to trim the workforce. GE soon entirely phased out its appliance business, costing another 10,000 jobs nationwide, about 1,000 of them in Erie. Blessed with two superhighways—Interstate 90 in 1960 and Interstate 79 in 1970—its suburbs sprawled, retail business and population migrated to them, and an increasing percentage of residents in the hollowing city itself sank toward poverty. And, like many other cities in the 1970s, Erie's resources were stretched thin by the ongoing demand for city services and the shrinking of its tax base. Its sales tax rose, driving more people out. [23]

The Kissman family began to fray with it, and Paul and Gladys ultimately divorced in 1974. Three years later, Paul retired from Reed. A year after that, he moved away to Escondido in southern California without explanation. "I asked him why he went there," his oldest daughter said. "He said, 'the weather.' Maybe it was to go to meetings. Maybe it was to meet someone. It was all very, very vague." His ex-wife Gladys went to work on the cafeteria tray line at St. Vincent Hospital, which, in the absence of the metalworking, paper, and other heavy industries leaving town or cutting back operations, had become one of Erie's major employers. Daughter Lisa had married and moved away, and Gladys remained very close to Lori. Long after her mother's death in 2002, Lori still referred to her as "my best friend [24]

Her father, however, grew still more distant. "He kept in touch through letters every now and then," his daughter Lori Layden said. He supported her until she was 18, and "he was very generous to my mother after their divorce. The only possession he took was his piano." But then, "The letters between us become more and more infrequent. I ultimately lost touch with him."

He returned to Erie only twice during the next 11 years, and even the purpose of those visits was vague. He called Lisa, but not Lori. He gave Lisa money.

In Escondido in March 1988, a biopsy revealed a small cell carcinoma in his right lung. Three months later, doctors found fluid collecting around his lungs, and in November, suffering from chest pain and shortness of breath, he moved to a facility closer to Escondido's Palomar Hospital. A couple of months later, in early January 1989, his older brother Herbert, still in Erie, passed away, and Paul himself seemed to know his own end was near. From his death bed, he wrote his ex-wife a letter, which was the first his family knew of his illness. Daughter Lori "thought I had time to write him. I did not. I did not have a relationship with him at the time of his death. It is, sir, one of my deepest regrets!"

Paul Kissman drew his last breath at 1:40 P.M. on January 24th, 1989, a week after his final letter arrived in Erie. He was the second to fall of the five men the Army punished after Dale Maple's escapade. By the next day, the un-embalmed corpse of the former National Socialist, U.S. Army corporal, Maple shopping companion, and Camp Hale confederate was signed over to the University of California at San Diego's School of Medicine for study. His death certificate, like Leonhard's, claimed he had never served in the military.[25]

Eric Hotelling was the next to fall, but not before extending his career and his family. He remained at Yoo-Hoo for another seven years after Berenice's death, eventually becoming vice president of research and technology before taking a job as regional market director at the Beech-Nut Nutrition Corporation. In 1982, he moved to the Philadelphia area to become director of marketing and research at Steenland Lithography.

He'd been single for 14 years when he met Elizabeth Mary Green, an Englishwoman who, upon coming to the United States, had adopted an alias (Betty Meyers) and fungible ways of referring to herself (Betty, Betty Mary, and eventually Elizabeth Mary Hotelling.). Not least, she'd had three previous marriages. Her married name immediately before marrying Hotelling in May 1986, was Elizabeth Mary Jackson.* (On her death certificate, she was Elizabeth Jean "Betty" Jackson). Together, they moved into a 50-year-old three-bedroom, one bath, 1458 square foot home on a two-lane street in Croydon in Bucks County Pennsylvania, where they also may have owned or rented out an apartment.

By all appearances, Hotelling's life had turned as personally opaque and outwardly indistinct from the rest of America's. Outside, crises (energy, drug, educational, budget, hostage, crime) had long before obliterated memories of Eric Hotelling's putative rebellion and, until recently, his ideas about class warfare, "racial purity," authoritarian government, and total war.

He had become—like Dale Maple and Paul Kissman, Fritz Siering, and Theophil Leonhard—a fully forgiven, fully assimilated, comfortable, and rewarded member of the society he had once sought to destroy.

Which is how he ended. On January 2nd, 1992, Eric Bell Hotelling died in Philadelphia. The cause of the rigorously private Hotelling's death remained as confidential as many things in his life, but he was 68 and, according to his Social Security records and the Veterans Administration, an honorably discharged member of the United States Armed Forces.[26]

---

* There was no wedding announcement in the local papers and the surviving children of all the Hotelling and Jackson marriages declined to comment for this work.

CHAPTER 21

MAPLE AT SEA

There was no public reckoning, either, on January 24th, 1957, when Fritz Siering returned to the country he had wanted to adopt him ever since he fled the Nazis 21 years earlier. This time he entered with permission as a legal alien with an Argentinian passport. He had his third wife, Frieda, with him, too. They set up house in Miami and, within a month, filed a petition with the federal district court stating he aimed, at last, to become a naturalized citizen of the United States as soon as possible.[1]

Five feet, 3 inches tall, 170 pounds, and with a distinguishing scar on his left cheek, he landed in a growing support network. There were soon other Sierings living nearby; some, like his immigrant mother, the former Hedwig Sophie Weber, were fresh from Germany. And he arrived with a full head of steam. He first listed himself in city directories as a mechanic, and within seven months of his arrival, he was part of the new General Stamping & Manufacturing Company. Within a year, he and his new wife bought a single-family, 12-year-old house in Miami, and by 1960, he had become vice president of the company. The Sierings also turned into active real estate investors, buying and selling properties in Hialeah, Miami, Miami Shores, Coral Gables, and Lake County, Florida. Sometimes the deals were in Friedrich's name, sometimes in Frieda's, sometimes in conjunction with Heinrich G. Siering, a relative, and Heinrich's wife, Anna.

Among the properties they eventually owned was General Stamping's light industrial building in Hialeah. Within ten years, he was president of the company. In 11 and late in life (they were both in their fifties), the Sierings had a daughter, Marlene, in 1971.

The die-making and metal-working shop turned out fittings for boats, door hinges and towel bars. Most notably: it also manufactured and distributed "Magic Fingers," the bed vibrator that enjoyed a brief vogue in high-end resorts before becoming a staple in low-end hostelries that rented their rooms by the hour.

Then even that market faded. The "Magic Fingers" coin box, it seems, had become a popular magnet for thieves. "They'd smash the nightstand, so the hotels took them out," Siering told *The Miami Herald*. But one night when daughter Marlene, then three years old, couldn't sleep, he "took the vibrator and put it under her crib. She fell asleep." For a while, it looked like it might become a hit. One of Siering's employees told the *Herald* in introducing the product that Adrienne Barbeau, a well-known author and actress of the day, had already bought "several" home versions as Christmas gifts.

"There's always a sexual connotation," the employee added, "but most people enjoy it because it's relaxing. [2]

And 26 years after first asking the immigration service to be naturalized. Friedrich Siering finally became a U.S. citizen in September 1966. Frieda Siering took the oath in December 1970. There's some evidence that either work or wanderlust took them temporarily to Wisconsin and Colorado, but property and business records indicate south Florida was their permanent home.

They prospered even as Fritz Siering, aging, began to pull back from the business in the early 1990s. he began to transfer corporate power to his daughter, now in her early twenties, and Cherlynn Wetzel, a long-time employee. They sold the company in 1994, and on April 16th, 1999, Friedrich Siering, by then a widower for five years, passed away at age 81 at South Miami Hospital. The cause of death was not listed, although his cremation was.

To the question about whether he had ever served in the U.S. armed forces, a former neighbor in Coral Gables checked, "yes." He apparently had told her all about it.[3]

And so almost all of the veterans of the mistakes at Camp Hale in 1944 passed, meeting quiet, anonymous, and unceremonious endings that couldn't be imagined when they roiled the nation's media and military justice system. The more conventional their lifestyles had become, the less the world took notice until it took none.

Some of them, of course, had still actively sought attention. Jelly Bryce, the sharply dressed and legendary FBI marksman who had interviewed Dale

Maple in New Mexico, left the bureau in 1958. Then, after legally changing his name to "D.A. Jelly Bryce," he threw his hat and his new name into a crowded Oklahoma gubernatorial race as an independent. (Though it was unclear that "oil companies and the major construction companies" had offered to donate to his campaign, he loudly refused to take donations from them. Running on an anti-corruption platform that he swore would save the state $20 million a year, but he came in third with slightly more than six percent of the vote).

He and his wife retreated to Mountainview, Oklahoma, where Bryce did some private detective work, hunted, fished, and ran a ranch. His wife died in a car crash in 1973, and, at an Oklahoma City hotel for a reunion of former FBI agents the next year, Bryce himself had a fatal heart attack. Decades later, several authors and law enforcement bloggers still wrote about him, repeating even the most fanciful stories about him often enough that many have acquired the force of truth.[4]

On Friday May 27, 1994 E.J. Kahn Jr.'s wife ran a Holyoke, Massachusetts stop sign, and piled into a pickup truck in the intersection. All three of the passengers in the Kahns' car were hurt badly. Kahn himself, 77 and with a heart condition, listed to his side. "Several" bones were broken, one of his lungs collapsed and, along with his wife and a passenger in the back seat, he was rushed to Holyoke Hospital. He lasted less than a day there. "His heart," his son reported, "gave out."

In death, the non-military people in this tale got far more attention news-papers than the Inner Circle. Kahn had authored 27 books, and what he once estimated were millions of words for the *New Yorker*. He had reported for it from Korea, South Africa, and elsewhere. He'd written about Japanese soldiers who had hidden in jungles, unaware that World War II was over. His reporting covered the Coca-Cola Company. He wrote stories about State Department experts driven from office for offering advice the government ultimately didn't take and about senators, cultural heroes, baseball players, and tycoons. Among all his creations, there was no mention in the obituaries and retrospectives of his long-ago series about the only United States soldier convicted of the military equivalent of treason on U.S. soil during World War II.[5]

Kahn's one-time source Charles Orlando Porter also stayed in the public eye and kept calling journalist friends to the very end. Even as he insisted on racking up electoral losses, he kept diving into largely unwinnable liberal causes as he built a successful law practice in downtown Eugene.

His youngest son remembers him talking openly to family members as well as journalists about any subject that presented itself but couldn't recall a mention of the names of Dale Maple or E.J. Kahn. Hearing how his father, mistaking it to be a hard-luck story, threw his energies into Maple's cause, Sam Porter laughed. "It sounds like something my dad would do."

His father, he added, threw himself headfirst into causes all the time. His life-long concern about U.S. Latin American policies began upon hearing of the 1956 abduction and gruesome murder of a Columbia University professor by or at the order of Dominican Republic dictator Rafael Trujillo. Such concerns sent him to Cuba and violent societies around the world, sapped his wealth and turned him into a life-long right-wing target.* †

His last failed run for office was in 1980, but he kept his hand in by calling Paul Neville, a columnist at the *Eugene* (Oregon) *Register-Guard*, each week. He railed about what Neville termed his "latest passionate cause." Neville's newspaper once described Porter as "brash, glib, witty, smarter than hell, younger than springtime, a political disaster, a martyr who won't stay dead, a chronic meddler, a thick-skinned egomaniac who's lovable as a puppy, persistent as a bulldog, optimistic as a bride, moral as a preacher, imaginative as a mad scientist and beneath it all, where it really counts, an authentic American hero."

But in 2001, he encountered what Porter himself called a "dark visitor," Alzheimer's disease. "I was shocked," he told Neville. "I had to come to grips. But after I thought about it a while, I realized that I'm ahead of most people who never had any fun." His wife Priscilla died the next year, and Porter eventually moved to an assisted living center. He died in 2006, on New Year's Day, at the age of 87.[6]

Dale Maple had been dead for five years by the day Charles Porter died and been absent from the public's memory for even longer. Slipping from memory,

---

* An Asian fact-finding trip in 1959 and Porter's criticism of Chiang Kai-shek, Taiwan's (then called Formosa) leader and a long-time hero of *Time* magazine owner Henry Luce, earned then-congressman Porter a scathing report in *Time*. His trip "created more embarrassment and consternation than a plague of gooney birds." The writer (the article, like all *Time* pieces of the period, was unsigned) also blasted Porter's supposed closeness with Fidel Castro and hostility toward the American ally Trujillo in the Dominican Republic. Porter suffered the first of his electoral defeats the next year."

† The Columbia professor was Jesus de Galindez, who had authored a scholarly paper entitled "The Era of Trujillo." He was kidnapped and brought to the Dominican Republic by Robert A. Maheu & Associates, a security firm the CIA often hired for such activities. Galindez was subsequently murdered, as was the naïve pilot who had flown Galindez to the Dominican.

too, were his and his confederates' considerable intellectual gifts and talents, their serial blunderings, gravely adult crimes, betrayals, and, by the time of their deaths, even the once civilization-shattering meanings of his war.

In the early 1970s, he still worked for the giant insurer American National General Agency (ANGA), brightly reporting he was president of the "American National Agencies'" office in suburban Flinn Springs. By 1976, he was "national marine director" for "Insurance General Agency." He described it as "part of ANGA" and as ""the largest underwriter of marine insurance in California."

He was busy. His job, he told readers of Harvard's *Class Notes* of 1976, entailed "a great deal of business travel." He also had "a large dog and a hobby as an organ builder (as well as church organist and choir director) which have helped make up for the lack of wife, children, and grandchildren!"[7]

But by then, the region's tuna industry—the most lucrative part of his and ANGA's marine insurance practice—was in a rapid decline. In the years after World War II, it speedily evolved from being a business of tuna boats owned mostly by generations of Portuguese, Italian, and Japanese American families into substantial corporate enterprises that themselves were now changing again.

Maple's boom began to fade in the late 1960s not because of wavering demand for tuna but because of what was amounting to mass slaughters of dolphins, the mammals who often swam and were killed with tuna in industrial seiner fishing. Regulations passed in 1972 to protect the dolphin then pushed the tuna boats to waters farther and farther away. The same regulations required the city's dozen or so canneries to stop accepting seiner-captured fish, and foreign companies began buying the canneries and moving them as well as the cannery jobs overseas.

By the middle 1970s, the 250-some seiners based in San Diego had dwindled to 45. Many of those, moreover, began to dock elsewhere and were being put up for sale. Reading the change, ANGA itself pulled out of the market. In 1978, a mere two years after describing himself as national marine director of a thriving ANGA subsidiary, Dale Maple officially "retired" at age 58 from the insurance business.[8]

Publicly, he portrayed the move as a successful man's idyllic respite. "Since retiring from day-to-day active business pursuits in 1978, I have followed a less rigorous regimen of business consultation (when anyone wants to listen). This has permitted pursuit of far more useful activities such as vegetable gardening."

But money worries soon followed. John Kucera did not work much, and Maple's parents had left him with a disappointing inheritance. His mother, who had not worked outside the home since at least the late forties, apparently had little to leave. She died in 1969 and her second husband, Edwin Scoville, the breadwinner, soon moved 150 miles away and remarried two years later. L.G. Maple, meanwhile, was professionally orphaned by C. Arnholt Smith's banking and real estate empire when it drowned under waves of criminal prosecutions.

Dale had stayed close to his father through those years, spending most family occasions with him at L.G.'s Maple's house and then taking care of him through the illness that killed him in March 1979. "He left something to Dale, but not much compared to what he had," Kucera's nephew recalled. "Maybe the will wasn't done the way it should have been."

The bulk of the inheritance and property went to Dale's stepmother Ruth, with whom Dale's relationship was "fine, but she was really religious." So, too, was Ruth's sister, who had moved in with the elder Maples years before. After Ruth's death in 1999, the remaining estate went to the Catholic Church that L.G. Maple used to disparage.

His earnings reduced and his cupboard un-replenished, Dale Maple's professional life declined into dabbles. In 1984, he claimed to have "set up a computerized business consulting firm and have been kept out of other mischief by the problems of establishing databases and programming systems." The business, however, was never registered and may have never been more than an idea as close to happening as going to grad school in wartime Berlin. Soon he was working some blocks down on Hawley Road, managing a convenience store "just for something to do [9]

Otherwise, Maple and Kucera did "not much. They drank. They drank too much, I know. Neither one of them worked very much, and they probably should have. In their later life, they let things go down." Many years later, after Maple and then Kucera passed away, nephew Greg Nudera—by then a contractor with his own family—inherited the house on Hawley Road. "The place," he recalled, "was a shambles."

Nudera loved his uncle John Kucera and, despite their shuffling ends, considered Dale Maple an uncle, too. They were, in fact, his supportive on-site parents during his school and high school days. "He taught me a lot, and I really cared for him." But Dale kept his secrets close. He never told Nudera about the dramas of his first act: his flirtations with the Gestapo agent at the German consulate in Boston during his Harvard days; his Army past; his time in Leavenworth, his death sentence. When told about it, Nudera laughed. He could readily imagine the way the young Maple had abruptly disrupted the university's strenuously apolitical German Club. "He could open his mouth," he said. "If he didn't like something, he told you." Socially and in business and at home, Nudera remembered the mouth that had once upended Dale Maple's, Theo Leonhard's, Paul Kissman's, Eric Hotelling's, and Fritz Siering's lives as one of Maple's more endearing qualities.

Maple began complaining of a persistent cough and shortness of breath in the spring of 2001. Treated for pneumococcal pneumonia, however, his condition soon worsened, and his physician amended the diagnosis to acute respiratory distress syndrome. It is one of those diseases often associated with cigarette smoking and heavy alcohol use, and it leaves the victim breathing rapidly and struggling for oxygen. Blood pressure falls. Organ failure frequently follows. So, it did weeks later when on May 28th, Dale Maple, 81, bedridden for days at the city's Alvarado Hospital, succumbed to respiratory failure.

He chose to be cremated, and on June 4th John Kucera helped scatter his ashes at sea off the coast of San Diego. Kucera, either out of consideration or simply because he did not know Dale Maple's full story, apparently never told anyone about his partner's wartime alliances. On Maple's death certificate, he checked the box that claimed his partner's military career—and his attempts to hobble the American war effort, mount terrorist strikes, and spirit away German POWs—had never happened at all. [10]

THE FRAGRANCE ON OUR HEELS

"Forgiveness is the fragrance the violet sheds on the heel
that has crushed it." —Mark Twain

As Dale Maple's memories and ashes sank into the Pacific on June 4th, 2001, so did a few more pieces of the 34 wars the United States fought during the 20th century. In the deep, they joined the soaked and forgotten memories of the young America's military wars of the late 18th century and the constant 58 American wars of the bellicose 19th.

Victors usually let transgressions like the Inner Circle's fade from memory faster than the defeated, and punishments seem to be even shorter. Wars, of course, span the 140 and as many as 300 millennia since *homo sapiens* evolved on Earth and, some millennia later, rose to the top of its food chain.

We are a violent breed, although hardly the only one. Thousands of termites will mass against each other, sometimes sending in the equivalent of suicide bombers that fill themselves up with toxic blue crystals, explode in their enemies' midst and spray them with poison. Bonobo monkeys, humans' closest remaining genetic relatives, will organize their forces to attack other groups of bonobos. Like us, lions, hyenas, wolves, cheetahs, and the red colobus monkey also join in "the cooperative killing of rivals" of their own species. Watching ants battle in a Malaysian rain forest, a *Scientific American* correspondent reported, "the raging combatants form a blur on all sides. The scale of the violence is almost incomprehensible, the battle stretching beyond my field of view. Tens of thousands sweep ahead with a suicidal single-mindedness. Utterly devoted to duty, the fighters never retreat from a confrontation even in the face of certain death. The engagements are brief and brutal. Suddenly, three soldiers grab an enemy and hold it in place until one of the bigger warriors advances to cleave the captive's body, leaving it smashed and oozing."[1]

Adolph Hitler's war was not altogether different, founded as it was on a grim, zoological view of the world. Human races, Hitler believed, differed in the implacable way species differed. Their conflicts sometimes were about resources and sometimes land or maybe even love but, whatever the soon-forgotten reasons, they were always inevitable. The only "morality" involved was in which "race" survived. Eat or be eaten. All the niceties of human philosophy—faith, peace, empathy, evidence, and cooperation among them—were wasteful distractions that, in the end, made it harder to win. So did refinements like treaty obligations, religion, and ideologies built on anything other than inevitable conflict. In National Socialist eyes, tribes with such beliefs were weak and the easiest to defeat. For humans as well as other species, the alternative to winning was extinction.

Then again, Hitler's races—everyone's races—are biological myths. Much of the breathtaking horror of World War II was based on imaginary, unsupportable, and daresay stupid ideas sprung from illusions out of someone's damaged psyche. There are no organic, no real biological differences between any of Earth's human tribes. Races are political, social, made-up distinctions we choose to draw. Generally, they cause only heartbreak, something else all our tribes share.

No wonder we are anxious to forget what we've done.

———

Not a few psychologists would argue that Dale Maple, Theo Leonhard, Eric Hotelling, and Paul Kissman chose sides in their era's global slaughter for other reasons. All were angry and professionally abused, notably by the Army itself. Of the four—we're excusing Fritz Siering, the fifth man, whose opposition to fascism as well as the Inner Circle's plots was never in question—only Leonhard and Kissman had even tribal ties that might pull them toward favoring Nazis. Hotelling and Maple simply pursued their own made-up identities all the way into their troubles.

The admittedly less-suspenseful, but probably a more important part of their stories, is how neither Maple nor his mates suffered the normal life-long consequences of what today would be criminally liable terrorist activities. Their real success was wiping their memories clean no less.

———

I, for one, was initially attracted to the tale in part for its ironic contrast between the Inner Circle's deadly serious plans and their ultimately banal adult lives. In one light, their conspiracies were not far removed from modern-day jihadist commanders—some acting out the affectations of middle-class boys with confected identities—now jailed or assassinated without trial for warring or even talking about warring with the United States. Many of those still imprisoned for decades at Guantanamo at this writing are merely suspected, like the Inner Circle, of preparing to blow up innocents.

The disloyal Americans' suffering, needless to say, was dramatically different and dramatically shorter. These four men, all born to accomplished families, rapidly found acceptance and prosperity when their suffering ended. It might well be a function of their color or their parents' economic class. As one legal scholar put it, "having successful parents would lead to a lot of youthful indiscretions being forgiven in ways that would not work if you were poor."[2]

Working class and non-participant Friedrich Siering was the one who suffered longest, unjust incarceration and then a nine-year exile.

Maple and his remaining crew seemed to change less than the society they rejoined in the late 1940s and early '50s. Their successes came as progress for most classes of Americans began to slow and regress to pre-war levels. People born between 1910 and 1930 had better than a 90 percent chance of out earning their parents. By the 1984, American babies had less than a 41 percent chance of out earning their parents. In the interim, changes in technology and increases in trade had inexorably "closed off traditional sources of middle-income jobs."[*]

Paul Kissman, son of a railroad engineer, was among the last American postwar blue-collar generations to make a comfortable living. Around him, overall economic mobility slowed during the century's second half despite the growth of vast, lucrative new industries. The new industries were increasingly service industries that required wholly different skills and training. The policies that supported the new industries, moreover, were "reducing the rewards society generates for those of different abilities."

Rewards thus increasingly flowed to those already reaping them. A former head of the Council of Economic Advisors called it the "Great Gatsby Curve," a mathematical proof suggesting that every one percent increase in one family's

---

[*] The same researchers who measured social mobility also modeled what effect higher economic growth rates during the period had on the ability to move up in status. They found that, short of decades of sustained hyper-growth, it would have made no difference. For, regardless of how dramatically the country's gross national product grew, it would have been distributed through the same increasingly inflexible channels back to the wealthy.

income slowed the social mobility—the chances for a generation to advance economically—of another family earning less.

Scholars have found the same surnames in the same elevated economic classes for generations at a time, sometimes for hundreds of years. As the blessings of prosperity pooled above, the classes below seemed to thicken and stall in a pattern not unlike that of late 18th-century France.

———

Or perhaps the 620ers' recoveries happened because the world simply forgot their transgressions. During their post-prison lives, as television began to shrink our attention spans, we learned to shape a world increasingly without context and history.

Our "typographic mind" consumed information in a logical, straight line. It plowed through a subject, modifier, verb, and object to find news, sensation, meaning, and explanation.

It seems to have been overwhelmed. Linear thought has given way to a "telegraphic mind" that consumes bite-sized, telegraphic signals, rapidly arriving without evidence, context, or nuance.

The men of the Inner Circle left prison at the start of the television age. Everything—news, sensation, evidence, analysis, facts, music, opinion, even relationships—came in ever-increasing volumes and velocities of images, all loudly re-shaped into their most entertaining, commercial, dramatic forms. We accept those ginned up presentations as Truth. The context of past behaviors, be they crimes or inventions, are overwhelmed and sometimes too time-consuming to think about. By now, we're left to understand the present by only the most recent exaggerated things we saw or heard.

Memories of these soldiers' specific crimes and even their wars were no match for the new crises, conflicts, and daily images that followed. They were remembered at first as abstractions—injustice, anger, horror, regret—and then rationalized and then, if remembered at all, fictionalized. The United States, for example, was at war with somebody—typically as the aggressor—for 221 of its first 243 years but remains convinced it is a just and peace-loving nation. Its citizens forgot, and they forgave. They forgave, moreover, whether the founding transgression was the result of social fraying, territory, food, money, natural disaster, sex, some leader's primitive drive for more or even innocence.

———

Yet the forgiveness and renewal that the men of the Inner Circle enjoyed is exactly what traditionally differentiated warlike humans from the planet's other warlike creatures. Humans' biological relatives also kill or abandon or ostracize their outliers, but they parole no one, and move on seemingly without regret. While there are many examples of other animals sharing food, reviving a fellow monkey, communicating warnings, and expressing affection and support for each other, the notions of imprisonment and re-acceptance into the herd and what we'd call mercy seem to be exclusively human.

So, too, are the agreements—also destined to be forgotten—not to repeat history. Without reading too much into the arc of Dale Maple and his Inner Circle, it's possible to see something frustratingly eternal in whatever drives both the good and destructive in us. The lessons of our follies and cruelties, our treasons, delusions, and our wars shrink and, finally, fade to gray.

ACKNOWLEDGEMENTS

Many friends, colleagues, new acquaintances and generous souls have contributed to this project. Among them are my interviewees: kind souls who trusted a stranger with their time and remembrances of loved ones, even loved ones whose youths were not always well-spent. While some of the resulting material about misbehaving relatives and acquaintances may prove disquieting for them, I hope they will find the material respectful and accurate.

There were scores of others: the excellent Lori Cox-Paul of the National Archives at Kansas City; Kevin Morrow in Washington, D.C; Eduardo Adam-Rabel in Florida; Fred Borch of the U.S. Judge Advocate Law School; Albert Alschuler, late of the Northwestern University School of Law; Judge Morris B. Hoffman of the Denver, Colorado District Court; Tom McAnear of the National Archives at College Park, Maryland; Derek Moses of the San Diego Public Library; Liz Hicks and Evelyn Weinheimer of the Gillespie County (Texas), Historical Society; John Ulrich at Harvard; Romeo Valdez of Insurance Jour-nal; Jocelyn Wilk of the Columbia University Archives; the whole caring crew of the Stephen H. Hart Library and Research Center at History Colorado (Laura Ruttum Senturia, Sarah Gilmore, Patrick Fraker and Melissa VanOtterloo); Emily Swenson and Margaret Leary of the University of Michigan's Bentley Historical Library; Claire De Witt; Sue Barlow; Mark Springer; the preternaturally patient staff at the San Diego County Clerk & Recorder's office and at the San Diego State University Library; Charles Brown of the University of Michigan and, certainly not least, a generous and helpful researcher named Carolyn Rogers met amid the maze-like digital hallways of Ancestry.com. Whether they knew it or not, Todd Neff, Mark Springer and Dr. Steven P. Ringel were my much-appreciated beta readers.

Speaking of support, there is none more meaningful or warmer, generous, or sweet than that of my wife Edie, who I now publicly forgive for being correct about everything.

NOTES

FOREWORD

1   In the new America, the Bureau of Justice Statistics found that only 12.5% of employers would accept an application for someone with a criminal record. Les Lovoy, "Life After Prison: Es-Felons Often Struggle to Find a Job", WBHM (Birmingham, Ala), June 25, 2014, https://news.wbhm.org/feature/2014/life-after-prison-ex-felons-often-struggle-to-find-a-job/, accessed Jan 26 2017.

PART ONE: ESCAPE
CHAPTER 1: WHERE IS HE?

1   Least desirable duty: U.S. War Department. Army Service Forces, Opinion of the Board of Review. U.S. v. Maple, June 22, 1944, HC-Vol I, FF10.

2   Altman, Kissman: National Personnel Records Center, National Archives St. Louis. [Record of Trial] U.S. v. Siering, 31,

3   National Archives at Kansas City. Record Group 129, Testimony of Sgt Alexander V. Altman.

4   The Military Intelligence Service wrote the order creating the 620 and two similar units on October 3, 1942, and immediately proceeded to start transferring men from their current units into the new company. Robert Lee, *Fort Meade and the Black Hills*. (Lincoln: University of Nebraska Press, 1991), 223-24.

5   Subversive word a day: James J. Weingartner, *A Peculiar Crusade: William M. Everett and the Malmedy Massacre*, (New York: New York University Press, 2000), 17.

6   Meeting in the boiler room: E.J. Kahn, Jr. "Interview with Rudolph F. J. Nobis," HC C Box 2. FF56, 125.

7   Secret stills, swimming pools: David R. Witte, *World War II at Camp Hale: Blazing a new trail in the Rockies*. (Charlotte, N.C: The History Press, 2015), 166; Awesome swimming pool: Glebo, Blog post, Feb 19, 2011. professionalsoldiers.com/forums/archive/index. php/t-32459.html. Accessed 10-26-15; Selling to civilians: Kahn, 127; Mattress warehouse: Letter to the Editor from (Mrs.) Jeanne Rockwell Noonan, *The New Yorker*, March 13, 1950, HC C Box 2 FF55; Kahn, 115.; WAC love letter: National Personnel Records Center, National Archives St. Louis. Re: Siering Friedrich, Statement of Friedrich W. Siering, 22 March 1944, 10.

8   Emotional reaction: Statement of Theophil J Leonhard, Pvt., Court Martial Materials— [Report of Investigation, cont] 1944 HC FBIM–Box 1 FF4, Exhibit E, Items 620-621.

9   You're in the 620th, "Heil Hitler" greeting: National Archives St. Louis, [Record of Trial] U.S. v. Siering, 59, 75; Frozen laundry: Testimony of Dale Maple, Court-Martial Records [Record of trial], HC-Vol II FF2, 182; Pariahs: Letter Eric Hotelling to E.J. Kahn, Jr. December 29 1948, HC C Box 2 FF42, 3.

10 E.J. Kahn, Jr, "Who Wants To Go To Germany In Wartime?" *The New Yorker*, April 1, 1950, 68. Shopping trip: Court-Martial Records HC-Vol. I FF1, 9; "Sort of a hurry": Teletype to Director, SACs, 2-17-44, 7:18pm, FBIM HC Box 1 FF 10; License: Testimony of Fritz Owen, Court-Martial Records [Record of trial], HC-Vol II FF2, 74.

11 Resentments: U.S. War Department, "Why I Covered Maple's Escape Temporarily."
Statement of Paul Kissman, HC FF4; Kissman Statement, FBIM HC Box 1 FF10, Items
490-504,; Active hostility: "Maple Testimony," [Record of Trial} HC FF2; Maple abuse:
Letter Hotelling to Kahn,, December 29 1948 HC C Box 42; *ibid.*, 151. Porcupine quills:
Records of the Bureau of Prisons, U.S. Penitentiary, Leavenworth, U.S. v. Kissman, [Record
of Trial]; Inmate Case Files, 1895-1952, National Archives Identifier: 571125.
12 Verge of riot, targeting officers: War Dept., Kissman, HC-Vol 1., Item #512.
13 New commander: Court-Martial Records [Record of trial], HC FF2, 27; Search for Maple:
Altman Testimony, HC-Vol II, FF2, 84.
14 Meeting Maple], Testimony of Earhard Schwichtenberg,, Court-Martial Records [Record
of trial HC-Vol II, FF2, 171; Passport: The document belonged to POW Eduard Mueller.,
ibid. HC FF2 168; Maple expect two German prisoners—a Walter Boesel and an Egon
Muschick—to join them. "Memorandum for the Officer in Charge. Subject: Dale Maple,
Pfc.," Court-Martial Records [Report of Investigation, cont.] 25 February 1944, HC-Vol
IV EXHIBIT B Item 581.

CHAPTER 2: AN IMMENSE, STAGED LIE OF A PLACE
1 Shopping trip: Court-Martial Records, HC-Vol I FF1, 9; "Sort of a hurry:" HC FBIM
– Box I Teletype to Director, SACs, 2-17-44,, HC FF 10; The license: Testimony of Fritz
Owen, Court-Martial Records [Record of trial], HC-Vol II FF2, 74.
2 Sort of a hurry: FBIM – Box 1 Teletype to Director, SACs, 2-17-44, HC FF 10; The
license: Owen Testimony, Court-Martial Records [Record of trial], HC FF2, 74.
3 Getting to Germany: Schwichtenberg Testimony, FF2 164, 169; Kahn, "Germany In
Wartime," 68. Belief in victory: A U.S. Army Chaplain, "PWs: Nazis in U.S. Prison Camps
Are Arrogant and Sturdy but Far from Being Supermen." *Life* Magazine, Jan 10, 1944,
47-48.
4 Statement of Fritz Wilhelm Siering, HC FBIM–-Box 1 FF17, Items 529-543; Denver
guesses: Down in Denver. Statement of Kurt F. Schoen 6 March 1944, Court-Martial
Records HC FF3, item 462.
5 Mutiny, sabotage plans: Memorandum for Mr. Ladd. Feb 25, 1944, HC FBIM-Box 1 FF14
Items 422-433.
6 Kikilius background: Testimony of Heinrich Kikilius, Court-Martial Records [Record of
trial], HC FF2, 175; Motion picture Nazi: Ladon to Kahn, HC C FF44; Schwichtenberg
background: Schwichtenberg Testimony, 169.

CHAPTER 3: PANIC
1 Dawson's day: Court-Martial Records [Record of trial]: HC FF2 26-28.
2 Siering Statement, 2-28-44—2/29/44 FBIM-Box 1 HC FF17. Items 529-543
3 Statement of Paul Kissman, HC, FF16, Items #521-527.
4 Prisoner escapes: Associated Press. "Escape tunnel Found at War Prisoners' Camp at
Trinidad." *Denver Post* Nov 8, 1943, 1; Capture at the train station: Karl-Heinz Schmidt
"Escape from Camp Trinidad" *Denver Post Empire Magazine* March 14, 1954, 9. Weapons
search: Associated Press. "Trinidad Nazi Camp Searched for Missing Army Weapons."
Denver Post, April 1, 1944, 1.
5 Private went AWOL: Memorandum, D.M. Ladd to J.C. Strickland, 15 February 1944.
HC FBIM Box 1 HC FF6; Ladd: Athan G., Theoharis Ed., *The FBI: A Comprehensive
Reference Guide.* (Westport, CT: Greenwood Publishing Group, 1999). 338.; Army &
FBI link Maple to POW escape: J.M. Curran, Subject: Dale Maple, Pfc, et. al., Report
of Investigation, 15 March 1944. Memorandum for the Office, March 31, 1944,

Court-Martial Records [Report of Investigation] HC FF4, Item 542. Curran was chief of the Army's Intelligence Branch at the 620's headquarters in Omaha.

6   Kissman Statement, HC, FF16, Items #521-527.

7   Opinion of the Board of Review, Court-Martial Records HC-Vol 1 – April 17, 24,25,26,27,28 and May 8 1944.

8   Breakdown in New Mexico: Testimony of John H. Breen, Court-Martial Records [Record of trial], HC-Vol. I, FF2, 134-137; Opinion of the Board of Review, Court-Martial Records HC FF1.

9   In the desert, Kunze: Teletype to SACs, HC FBIM Box 1 FF10; Statement from [REDACTED), HC FBIM Box 1 FF16 Items #521-527.

CHAPTER 4: A COLLECTION OF REBELS

1   Hotelling:: Memorandum for Mr. Ladd, Feb 25 1944 HC FBIM Box 1, FF 14 item #422-433; Denver meeting: FBIM Box 1 HC FF15, items 350-360 & FBIM Box 1 HC FF14 items 346-349; Quartermaster: Letter Bernard Ladon to E.J. Kahn, Jr., January 5, 1949, HC C FF 44, Items 260-276; Paul Kissman, "A Statement Of My Relations With Certain Members of the 620th Engr. Co," Feb 25 1944, HC FBIM Box 1, FF14; Hotelling politics: Interview with Rudolph F. J. Nobis, Kahn notes and queries re Dale Maple. HC C Box 2 FF56, 117.

2   Second Denver recruiting meeting: "Statement Made by [Redacted]" February 25 and 26, 1944, FBIM Box 1, FF15 items 350-360.

3   Camp Carson visit: *ibid.*

4   First schemes: Leonhard Statement, Feb 24, 1944 HC FBIM Box 1 FF13 items 434-445. Siering's car: Testimony of Fritz Wilhelm Siering, Court-Martial Records [Record of trial], HC FF2 128, 133
    Leonhard's Mexico trip: Letter to J. Frank Dobie from Theophil J. Leonhard., Jan. 3, 1943, Frank Dobie Papers, Harry Ransom Center, University of Texas, file 129. 8.

5   Testimony of Fritz Wilhelm Siering, Court-Martial Records-Vol II-Dale H Maple [Record of trial] HC FF2 120-

6   Visit to the dump: Siering Testimony, HC FF2, 127

7   The right to sell property: "Leonhard Statement" Feb 24 1944 HC FF13 Box 1, 434-445; "Did for spite:" United States v. Private First Class Friedrich W. Siering, 36 702 841, Court-Martial Records [Record of Trial] National Personnel Records Center, National Archives St. Louis. Re: Siering Friedrich, 60.

CHAPTER 5: JEWISH REFUGEES SEEKING FREEDOM

1   The Reo, abandoned: Testimony of John H. Breen, Court-Martial Records [Record of trial] HC-Vol II FF2, 134-137.

2   Publicity: *Salt Lake Tribune*: HC-Box 1, FF10; FBI alerts: Telex to JC Strickland, Hoover, *et. al.*, Fr D.M. Ladd, Feb 16 & 17, 1944, FBIM Box 1, HC FF10; Quite wealthy: Testimony of Paul Kissman, HC-Vol I, FF2; L.G. Maple's suspicions, HC FBIM Box 1 FF12, Items 588-590. Memorandum for the Officer in Charge. Re: interview with L.G. Everett Maple, Fr: James L. Sloan, Captain/Officer in Charge,"February 23, 1944. HC FF12.

3   Bryce: Michael Newton, *The FBI Encyclopedia.* (Jefferson, NC: McFarland & Co., 2003), 157. David LaPell, "D.A. 'Jelly' Bryce: the F.B.I.'s first Sharpshooter" 3/21/12. guns.com. http://www.guns.com/2012/03/21/da-jelly-bryce/ Accessed Nov. 11, 2015; Ron Owens, *Legendary Lawman: The Story of Quick-Draw Jelly Bryce* (Nashville: Turner Publishing Company, 2010), 492.

4   POWs in Texas: Arnold P. Krammer, "When the Afrika Korps Came to Texas," *The Southwestern Quarterly*, Vol. 80. No. 3, (January 1977), 248.

5   Kissman confesses: Paul Kissman, "Why I Covered Maples Escape Temporarily," Court Martial Records [Report of Investigation], Feb 27, 1944, HC FF4, item 675.

6   "No." *Ibid*, Items 490-504.

7   Crossing into Mexico: Schwichtenberg Testimony, Court-Martial Records [Record of trial], HC FF2 169.

8   Memorandum for Mr. Ladd. From E A Tamm, Feb 25, 1944, HC FBIM Box 1 FF 14, Items #422-433.

9   Arrested: Testimony of William F. Bates, Court-Martial Records [Record of trial] HC FF2, 154. Heading to Germany: Testimony of Jose Magnana Zaragoza, Court-Martial Records [Record of trial] HC FF2 146, 148 ; Testimony of Medardo Martinez Mejia, Court-Martial Records [Record of trial] HC, FF2 139-140.

10 At the Palomas customs house: *ibid.,* FF2 146, 148; Mejia Testimony, HC FF2, 139-140.

11 The Reo, found: Breen Testimony, HC-Vol II, FF2, 136; Bates Testimony, HC FF2, 151-154; At the Palomas customs house;: Magnana Testimony, HC FF2, 146, 148.

PART TWO: INFIDELITY
CHAPTER 6: THE GRAD SCHOOL PLOT OF 1940–1941

1   Dress like Hoover: "FBI Special Agent, Delf A. 'Jelly' Bryce (1934-1958)" Historicalgman. com, accessed Jan 2, 2016.

2   Not our war: "Maple Testimony" Court-Martial [Record of trial] HC FF2, 190; German-American Bund: United States Holocaust Memorial Museum, Washington, D.C. http:// www.ushmm.org/wlc/en/article.php?ModuleId=10005684 accessed Nov. 16, 2015.

3   Campus opinions: Richard D. Edwards, "Harvard Views the War" *The Album 1941*, Vol LII, Cambridge, Mass: The Album Board, Harvard University, 255-56. Lindbergh's radio address: Susan Dunn, *1940: FDR, Willkie, Lindbergh, Hitler—the Election amid the storm.* (New Haven: Yale University Press, 2003) Excerpted in *The Atlantic*, July 8, 2013. http:// www.theatlantic.com/national/archive/2013/07/the-debate-behind-us-intervention-in-world-war-ii/277572/ accessed Nov. 21, 2015; Lindbergh on Jews: Candace Fleming, *The Rise and Fall of Charles Lindbergh*, (New York: Schwartz & Wade: 2020) 247-253; Steven J. Ross. *Hitler in Los Angeles*. (New York: Bloomsbury, 2017), 205. Arnie Bernstein, *Swastika Nation*. (New York: St. Martin's Press, 2013), 9. U.S. House of Representatives 75th Congress, Investigation of un-American propaganda activities in the United States, https://archive.org/ stream/investigationofu194114unit/investigationofu194114unit_djvu.txt accessed Jan 10, 2016; Mark D. Van Ellis, "Americans for Hitler – The Bund" America in WWII. http:// www.americainwwii.com/articles/americans-for-hitler/ accessed Feb 28, 2018.

4   Rise in power: Hans-Adolph Jacobson & Arthur L. Smith, Jr., *The Nazi Party and the German Foreign Office* (New York, Taylor & Francis Group, 2007), 23; Conant (footnote pg. 47) "Harvard goes to war" *The Harvard Gazette* Nov. 10, 2011, https://news.harvard. edu/gazette/story/2011/11/harvard-goes-to-war/

5   Full meaning of the term: "Statement of Dale Maple," HC FBIM Box 1, February 20, 1944, HC FF10.; Rise in power: Jacobson & Smith, 19.

6   Prosperity: Mark Weber, "How Hitler Tackled Unemployment and Revived Germany's Economy" Institute for Historical Review. http://www.ihr.org/other /economyhitler2011. html accessed 10-19-15. The "institute," one should understand, is a Holocaust denying organization. Based on similar transcripts published at worldfuturefund.org—a research institute—the author's belief is that the Hitler speech quotations are accurate; "What Did the Fuhrer Give You" Poster displayed at the Topography of Terror Museum, Berlin.

7   Jew Deal: Bernstein, 55; Third-worst recession: Douglas Irwin, "What caused the recession of 1937-38?" VOX CEPR's Policy Portal, Sept 11, 2011 http://www.voxeu.org/article/what-caused-recession-1937-38-new-lesson-today-s-policymakers Accessed Nov 16 2015.

8   Kissman's trip to Germany: Kissman Statement, Items 490-504.

9   Atlanta: "Spy Suspect Held by Atlanta Police" *New York Times*, May 24, 1940, 12; Texas arrests: United Press, "Father and Son Held in Texas" *New York Times*, May 26, 1940; Shipyard incidents "Dies Hearing Bares Shipyard Sabotage" *New York Times,* October 2, 1940, 1,12; Hotelling: Telex: Director, FBIM, Fr Milton K. Adams: to SAC New York Re; Pittsburgh letter to Director 3/16/54.

10 Bull sessions at Harvard: Letter John O. Felker to E.J. Kahn, Jr, Nov 10 1948, HC C HC FF40.

11 Three ideas about the war:. Edwards, 256-57.

12 Residents on Maple: HC FBIM Box 1 FF 6; Bookish: Memorandum for the Officer in Charge. James L. Sloan. Feb 23 1944 FBIM Box 1 FF12 Item 588-590; "Weeping": Testimony of Mae Scoville, Court Martial Records [Report of Investigation] HC-Vol III, FF3 233; Before her marriage Maple's mother—then Mae Cleo Harris—herself had "quite a reputation in the neighborhood [near San Bernadino} as a pianist." "Moonlight Ceremony at Rubidoux Cross" *San Bernadiono Daily Sun*, July 21, 1915, 6; Club memberships: Emily R. Breslow, "Harvard to Treason;". Porter, "Dale Maple," *Harvard Alumni Bulletin*, April 10, 1948, 542.

13 "Brain": Letter Paul Maiss to E. J. Kahn, Jr. November 16, 1948 HC C HC FF45; Ugly Duckling: Letter Edwin F. Self to E.J. Kahn, Jr. 26 Nov 8, 1948, HC C HC FF52.

14 Letter Alexander Boeker to E.J. Kahn Jr., Dec. 31, 1948, HC C Box 2 HC 37; Emotionally unstable: "Report of Investigation," HC FBIM Box 1 FF 7.

15 Academic freedom: "Browder Is Facing City College Ban" *New York Times* Dec 3, 1939, 34; "Topics of The Times," *New York Times*, Oct 10, 1940, 24; "Manning Renews Fight on Russell" *New York Times* March 13, 1940, 20; "Post For Russell Cut From Budget At Mayor's Order." *New York Times*, April 6, 1940, 1, 19; "Teachers Seen Tied to Red Party Line" *New York Times* March 4, 1941, 25. 31.

16 German political theory: "Statement of Julian Sobin," March 3, 1942, HC FBIM FF7; Liberal German Club: *The Album* 1941, Vol LII, (Cambridge, Mass: The Album Board, Harvard University), 155; Roosevelt: Dunn, *1940: FDR, Wilkie, Lindbergh, Hitler* http://www.theatlantic.com/national/archive/2013/07/the-debate-behind-us-intervention-in-world-war-ii/277572/ accessed Nov. 21, 2015.

17 Disrupting the German Club: "Sobin Statement" HC Box 1 FF12.

18 Hittite studies: Letter Dale Maple to Chas O Porter Sept 25 1948, E.J. Kahn, Jr., HC C FF35.

19 Acquire a reputation: "Maple Testimony" Court-Martial Records [Record of trial], HC FF2, 189.

20 Letter Maple to German Club Oct. 14, 1940, FBIM HC Box 2 FF7.

21 Intense belief: E.J. Kahn, Jr . "Notes" Undated. HC-Box 2 FF56, 49.

22 Crimson mentions: YARDLING GETS 13 HEARTS. "Freshmen from Everywhere Win Scholarship Awards—Names Listed Below," *The Harvard Crimson*, May 4, 1938; "University Honors 114 Undergraduates with No-Stipend Harvard Scholarships," *The Harvard Crimson* November 14, 1940: The Hearts miracle: Letter Richard B. Wolf to E.J. Kahn, Jr. October 7, 13, 15, 1948 HC C Box 2 FF52.

23 "The Making of a Nazi" *Time* magazine [Education] (October 28, 1940)., 48. Reputation: "Maple Testimony," Court-Martial Records, [Record of Trial] HC Box 1 FF2,190.

24 Maple at the *Crimson*: Statement of Julian Sobin, May 23, 1942, HC FBIM Box 1 FF 12; "Fourth Year Military Science Student Ousted By Department From Course For Nazi

Views" *The Harvard Crimson*, November 14, 1940; Possibly psycho: Interview with Maj. Henry D. Jay, HC, FBIM Box 1 FF7.

25 Associated Press, "Harvard Student Quits R.O.T.C.," *New York Times*, Nov. 15, 1940, 9.

26 First Fruit, Ear Operations: "Maple Testimony," HC FF2, 190; ROTC uniform: John O. Felker letter, HC C FF40.

27 First Scholz contact: Guy Hottle, SAC Washington Field Office, "Memorandum to Mr. Hoover," May 16, 1946, FBIM, HC FF33.

28 Scholz in Boston: "SS-Oberfuhrer Dr. Herbert Sholz, Lieselotte 'Lilo' Scholz." Axis History Forum. http://forum.axishistory.com/viewtopic.php?t=165588 accessed Nov 22, 2015; "So Handsome, so charming," *Pittsburgh Post-Gazette*, June 19, 1941.

29 Welfare Association: "Memorandum for Mr. Ladd," Feb 25 1944 FF14, #426.; Financing Moran: Addie Diradoorian, "BC priests connected to Nazi and British espionage during WWII." http://thetab.com/us/bc/2015/09/30/bc-priests-connected-to-nazi-and-british-espionage-during-wwii-485, accessed Nov 23, 2015; Implicated in conspiracy: "SS-Oberfuhrer Dr. Herbert Sholz, Lieselotte 'Lilo' Sholz." Axis History Forum. http://forum.axishistory.com/viewtopic.php?t=165588 accessed Nov 22, 2015. The reference was made in an April, 1946 column by syndicated columnist Walter Winchell.

30 Robert A Miller, "A True Story of an American Nazi Spy: Willliam Curtis Colepaugh" https://books.google.com/books?id=ndSkplZUUh8C&pg=PA43&lpg=PA43&dq=German+consulate+Boston+1940&source=bl&ots=H_08gw_w7a&sig=2ubplj2E1E6cc3p9dvguKuQgdgQ&hl=en&sa=X&ved=0CC8Q6AEwA2oVChMIxM7xi7LHyAIVBORjCh18jQw2#v=onepage&q=German%20consulate%20Boston%201940&f=false. Accessed Oct. 21, 2015.; Operation Elster: "William Curtis Colepaugh" Wikipedia https://en.wikipedia.org/wiki/William_Colepaugh accessed Oct. 21, 2015.

31 Sausman: "Memorandum for Mr. Ladd." Feb 25 1944, FF14, #422-433; Maple told Bryce that Sausman had "a considerable' impact on him. Letter M.C. Sosman, M.D. to E.J. Kahn, Jr. January 8, 1949. HC.C FF52.

32 "James": "Memorandum from for Mr. Ladd," Feb 25 1944, #422-433.

33 Frank J. Kluckhohn, "Fifth Column Curb: Reich Activities Here Are Found Inimical to U.S., the Note Declares." *New York Times*, June 17, 1941, 1,3; Boston consulate: *Boston Globe*, Oct. 15, 1940, Kahn, Notes., 50.

34 Scholz' on leaving: "Fifth Column Curb, *New York Times,* June 17, 1941, 3.

35 Grad students, Hittite collection: Letter Edgar Sturtevant to E.J. Kahn, Jr. 5 November 1948 HC C Box 2 FF52.; Consolidated Aircraft: "Maple Testimony," HC Box 1, FF 2, 190.

36 "In a country at war: "Opinion of the Board of Review," Court-Martial Records, HC-Vol 1 , FF1, 4. Opportunity: Maple Testimony, HC FF 2, 191.

37 *Ibid,*. Military research (footnote): "Harvard goes to war" *The Harvard Gazette* Nov. 10, 2011, https://news.harvard.edu/gazette/story/2011/11/harvard-goes-to-war/

Detainees: *WW2 Internment in the United States. Chronology—Suspicion, Arrest, and Internment* ©Fallon/Jacobs 1996 http://www.foitimes.com/internment/chrono.htm accessed Nov 29, 2015; Hoover and Biddle (footnote): United States Senate, "Select Committee to Study Governmental Operations with Respect to Intelligence Activities," May, 1976, 420-421.

Maple Testimony, HC, Box 1, FF 2,191.

Ibid., 191.

Nazi salute: Memorandum for Mr. Ladd. Feb 25, 1944, HC FBIM-Box 1, FF 14 #430. Facility with English: Testimony of D.A. Bryce, Court-Martial Records [Record of trial], FF2 158. German accent: "Office Memorandum, 2-1-49 To Mr. Nichols From: M.A. Jones," HC FBIM FF34

38 Atlanta: "Spy Suspect Held by Atlanta Police" New York Times, May 24, 1940, 12; Texas arrests: United Press, "Father and Son Held in Texas" New York Times, May 26, 1940; Shipyard incidents "Dies Hearing Bares Shipyard Sabotage" New York Times, October 2, 1940, 1,12; Hotelling: Telex: Director, FBIM, Fr Milton K. Adams: to SAC New York Re; Pittsburgh letter to Director 3/16/54

39 Lost job: Opinion of the Board of Review, HC-Vol I, FF1.

40 Ibid,, 191.

CHAPTER 7: "HIS MAD CAREER"

1   Nazi salute: Memorandum for Mr. Ladd. Feb 25, 1944, FF14 #422; Facility with English: Bryce Testimony, FF2 158.

2   Accent: Office Memorandum, 2-1-49 To Mr. Nichols, HC FBIM FF34.

3   Mueller's life story: "Bryce Testimony," Court-Martial Records, HC FF2,158; Fingerprints: Memorandum for Mr. D.M. Ladd, February 19, 1944, HC FBIM FF10.

4   Maple confession: "Bryce Testimony," Court Martial Records, HC FF3, 261.

5   "Memorandum For Mr. D.M. Ladd, February 19, 1944, HC FBIM Box 1 FF10.

6   Stopping the interview: "Bryce Testimony," Court-Martial Records HC-Vol II. FF2, 158; Admission: Teletype from Morley, Feb 19,1944. HC FBIM Box 1, FF10.

7   Office Memorandum to Mr. Tamm Fr D.M. Ladd, February 19, 1944, HC FBIM Box 1 FF10.

8   Memorandum for the Officer in Charge, 25 February 1944. Court Martial Records HC Vol IV. EXHIBIT B, 587.

9   Write his own statement: "Bryce Testimony," Court-Martial Records HC-Vol II, FF2, 158; "Examination of D.A Bryce," Court Martial Records [Report of Investigation], HC, Vol III Box 1 FF3, 258.

10 E.J. Kahn, "Interview with Mae Scoville" Undated, Notes, HC C FF 56, Box 2, 73.

11 Disharmony: Maple Statement, Feb 20, 1944 HC Box 1 FF10.

12 'Adolescent snobbishness: Letter Harry Jones to E.J. Kahn, Jr. Oct. 29, 1948. HC C Box 2, FF43; German teacher: Letter Lawrence W. Carr (La Mesa, CA) to Lawrence Boydstun, San Diego High School. Nov 1, 1948 HC C Box 2 FF36; No idea: Letter Robert H Pfeiffer to E.J. Kahn Jr, Jan 8 1949. HC C Box FF48.

13 Maple enlists: Maple Statement. Feb 20, 1944, HC Box 1 FF10; Maple Testimony, Court-Martial Records HC-Vol II FF2, 191; Concentration camp: "Tent Town Built for Aliens at Fort Devens" New York Times, April 2, 1942, 23

14 Maple's oath: Maple Statement, FBIM—Box 1 HC FF10.

15 Library puzzle: Letter Dale Maple to Charles O Porter, Sept. 10, 1948, HC C Box 2. FF35; Letter Pfeiffer to Kahn, HC C FF48; Departing Harvard: HC FBIM – Box 1 HC FF 7; Library hooks: HC FBIM—Box 1 FF6.

16 Resentment: His monitor was a Sgt. Leslie Price. "Maple Testimony," Box 2 FF2, 191.

17 CIC investigations: "Counter-Intelligence Corps: History and Mission in World War II" The Counter-Intelligence Corps School, Fort Holabird, Baltimore, Md. Army War College, Carlisle Barracks, PA .https://fas.org/irp/agency/army/cic-wwii.pdf, accessed November 30, 2015, 14; Commanding officer: Letter Charles O Porter to E.J. Kahn, Jr. October 1, 1948. HC C Box 2 FF49. 'Pre-Nazi' ideas: Report of Capt. A.J. Martin, June 1942. Court-Martial Records [Report of Investigations] HC FBIM – Box 1 HC FF7.

18 Sense of hostility: Letter to J. Edgar Hoover from [Redacted], Special Agent in Charge, Atlanta. June 12, 1942; Telex J. Edgar Hoover to SAC, Atlanta, July 8, 1942. Contradictory spirit: Report to J. Edgar Hoover from SAC Savannah, August 7, 1942. All in HC FBIM – Box 1, FF7; ROTC: "Maple Statement," Box 1 FF10; "Maple Testimony," HC Vol II FF2 191.

19 Ft. Meade transfer: Maple Testimony, HC FF2 191; No positive information: HC FBIM
    Box 1 FF 7; "Aloof:" Report of Wesley R. Hurt, CIC, January 15, 1943. HC FBIM Box 1
    FF9.
20 Maple's sexual orientation: *ibid,*, HC FF9; Call to German embassy: E.J. Kahn, Jr. "The
    Philologist," *The New Yorker,* March 25, 1950, 35. Happy: Statement of James L. Sloan,
    February 23, 1944, FBI Materials—Box 1 HC FF12, Item 588.; Maple Statement,
    February 20, 1944. FBIM, FF1. This much I do know: Letter Dale Maple to Mrs. Edwin
    Scoville, March 23, 1943. E.J. Kahn, Jr., "Notes" Undated, HC C Box 2 FF56, 34.
21 Peculiar treatment: "Maple Statement," FBIM Box 1 FF1.

CHAPTER 8: SHANGHAI CAMP

1   "Erie Man Who Aided Escape Was Bundist." *The Kane Republican,* March 11, 19443-11-
    44, 1. Kissman Statement, FBIM – Box 1, FF16. Opinion of the Board of Review, HC-Vol.
    1 FF1,5.
2   *Ibid.,* Siering Testimony": HC-Vol II FF2, 123. Arboitsbund: Siering Statement
    FBIM—Box 1, FF17 Items 529-543. Second War Powers Act of 1942: Wikipedia, https://
    en.wikipedia.org/wiki/War_Powers_Act_of_1941, accessed July 30,2020.
3   Leonhard background: Board of Review Opinion, Court Martial Records HC Vol. I, FF5;
    Patriotism: Leonhard Statement, Feb 24, 1944" HC-Vol IV, FF4 Exhibit E Item 614;
    Leonhard Statement. FF 13, Item 44; Lyndon Johnson: Author interview of Ms. Margaret
    Maenius, May 17, 2016; German consul: "Memorandum for Mr. Hoover July 8 1944 Fr:
    Dwight Brantley." HC FBIM—Box 1 FF30. Texas Pro-German activities: Ernest B Skinner,
    "Review of the Record of Trial" [Clemency Data] Judge Advocate Notorious Offenders Series
    28 January 1946, Inmate 63453-L Theophil J. Leonhard. U.S. Penitentiary, Leavenworth
    Kansas. Textual Reference (RDT2); Leonhard's background: "Leonhard Statement," Court
    Martial Materials [Report of Investigation, cont] 1944 HC Exhibit E, Item 614 and FBIM–
    Box 1 FF4, 614-16: "Theophil Leonhard Rites Held Here Today" *Fredericksburg Standard*
    (Fredericksburg, Tx) May 11, 1966, https://www.newspapers.com/image/86030559/?ter
    ms=Theophil%2BLeonhard&match=2, accessed Dec 22 2015; "Southwestern University
    Choir To Be Here Sunday," *The Bryan Eagle,* April, 13 1935,.2 (https://www.newspapers.
    com/image/48161587/?terms=Theophil%2BLeonhard accessed Dec 22 2015; "F.H.S. Echo"
    Fredericksburg Standard, 7 Jan 1937, pp 6 https://www.newspapers.com/image/8807860
    8/?terms=Theophil%2BLeonhard accessed Dec 22 2015; Dies committee: U.S. House of
    Representatives. 75th Congress "Investigation of un-American propaganda activities in the
    United States. Hearings before a Special Committee on Un-American Activities, https://
    archive.org/stream/investigationofu194114unit/investigationofu194114unit_djvu.txt,
    accessed Jan 10 2016.
4   Drewes: "State OES Officer Who Is Native of Germany to Be Owen Scott Guest," *The
    Decatur* (Illinois) *Herald.* Aug. 3, 1958, 38; Statement made by S/Sgt Menke Drewes 10
    March 1944, HC FBIM–Box 1, FF23, Items 393, 395.
5   Leuth: Letter Dale Maple to Chas O Porter, December 5, 1948, HC C FF35.
6   Detentions, internal deportations: WW2 Internment, http://www.foitimes.com/
    internment/chrono.htm accessed Nov 29 2015; Jan Jarboe Russel, *The Train to Crystal City:
    FDR's Secret Prisoner Exchange Program and America's Only Family Internment Camp,* (New
    York: Simon & Schuster,2015), 4; "Crystal City Internment Camp" https://en.wikipedia.
    org/wiki/Crystal_City_Internment_Camp, accessed March 14, 2016.
7   Measures will be instituted: "Memorandum from Director of Intelligence, Dec 28,
    1942 to CIC, Fort Meade, Maryland," HC FBIM Box1 FF8. Subsidiary investigation:
    "Memorandum from Director, Intelligence Division, Fourth Service Command, January
    1943, to CIC, Fort Meade, Maryland," HC FBIM Box1, FF7.

8   Where I am right now: Letter Dale Maple to Mae Scoville, April 6, 1943, E.J. Kahn, Jr. Notes, HC C Box 2; Unit make-up: "Maple Testimony," H C-Vol II FF2, 192.
9   Disgusted: "Drewes Statement" 10 March 1944 FF27, Item 395.
10 Mail, furlough, letdown: Kissman Testimony, HC-Vol II FF2 104, 105, 110.
11 Leonhard's embarrassment: Leonhard Testimony, HC Vol II, FF 2, 53; Dissatisfaction: Maple Testimony, , HC-Vol II FF2, 192; 57; Letter Hotelling to Kahn, Dec 29 1948, HC C FF42, 3.
12 Kissman's parents: Kissman Testimony, HC-Vol II FF2 104; People of influence: Leonhard Testimony, HC-Vol II FF2, 41.
13 Showing up at the front: Maple Testimony, HC-Vol II FF2 ,193; Alienated: Maple Statement, FBIM – Box 1 HC FF10; Leonhard Statement, HC-Vol IV FBIM-Box 1 FF4, Exhibit E, 621; No intention of staying: Opinion of the Board of Review, HC-Vol I, FF1, 6.
14 German accent: Maple Testimony, HC-Vol II FF2, 192.
15 Social activities, taste for violence: "Leonhard Statement," HC Vol IV FBIM – Box 1 FF4, Exhibit E, Item 617-18; Camp Norland: Report by Walter C. Hoteling, Court-Martial Records [Report of Investigation] March 28, 1944. FBIM – Box 1. HC Vol II FF2, 7; Hotelling: Letter Milton K. Adams to Director, Federal Bureau of Investigation, March 16, 1954, FBIM-Box1 FF34; Source, footnote #1: Letter Jones to Kahn, HC C FF43. Source, footnote #2: Opinion of the Board of Review, Court Martial records – Vol I – Dale H. Maple – Box 1 HC FF 1.
16 Rim Rock "closer group: Statement made by John F. Schumacher, 14 March 1944, Court-Martial Records [Record of Investigation] HC FBIM – Box 1, EXHIBIT H, Item 427; Interview with T/5 Frank X. Hofmann, March 14, 1944. Court-Martial Records [Record of Investigation] HC FBIM – Box 1, FF3, EXHIBIT F, Item 421; Form an organization: Statement made by Carl Chiaramida, March 10, 1944, Court-Martial Records [Record of Investigation] HC FBIM – Box 1, Vol III, FF23 EXHIBIT F, Item 409; "I stopped him right there:" Statement made by Eugene Ricci, March 14 1944, Court-Martial Records [Record of Investigation] HC FF25 EXHIBIT G, Item 423; Court-Martial Records, [Record of Investigation] HC FBIM-Box 1, FF3 EXHIBIT G, Item 423; "By education or by force:" Statement of Arthur I. Luck, March 16 1944, Court-Martial Records, [Record of Investigation] HC FF 26 Item 440-441.
17 Chiaramida and Hotelling: J.M. Curran, Interviews with Eric B. Hotelling, Pfc., ASN 12076330 and Otto Idelberger Jr., Pvt, ASN 32457934 , March 15, 1944, Court-Martial Records [Report of Investigation] HC.-Vol V Box 1 FF25, Item 753, 6;. Disrupt the war: Maple Statement. Feb 20, 1944 FBIM Box 1 FF10; "Subversive Meetings, Rim Rock Lodge, Canyon, Spearfish S. Dak." Memorandum for the Office, March 31, 1944, Court-Martial Records [Report of Investigation] HC-Vol IV Box 1, FF4
18 Rim Rock: War Department. Military Intelligence Division, "Report of Investigation. Subject: Dale Maple, et.al." 15 March 1944. HC FF25, Item 542, 2; Drewes' recruiting: Siering Statement, February 28, 1944, National Archives St. Louis, 11.
19 Rim Rock rhetoric: Walter C Hoteling, Report to J.M. Curran, March 28, 1944, Court-Martial Records [report of investigation] HC FBIM–Box 1 FF27, 2, 5. Normal soldiers' complaints: Drewes Statement, March 10 1944, F22, Item 397.

CHAPTER 9: MUTINY
1   Car wreck: Memorandum for Mr. Ladd Fr: J.C. Strickland, February 24, 1944. HC FBIM—Box 1 HC FF6; Letter Dale Maple to Mae Scoville, August 6, 1943, E.J. Kahn, Jr., HC Notes, Box 2 FF55, 35.
2   Lindbergh, Ford, Coughlin: Luck Statement, HC-Vol III FF26, Exhibit J, Items 443-444.

3   Mass desertion: Letter Hotelling to Kahn., December 29, 1948, HC C HFF42; Sabotage plan: "Examination of D.A Bryce," HC-Vol III FF3, 258-29.
4   K.J. Arrow and E.L. Lehmann, "Harold Hotelling, 1895-1973" National Academy of Sciences., 2005. http://www.nasonline.org/publications/biographical-memoirs/memoir-pdfs/hotelling-harold.pdf accessed Jan 7 2016.
5   Telex: To Director, FBI New York Re: Pittsburgh letter to Director March 16, 1954 HC FBIM FF34; Enlistment: U.S. World War II Army Enlistment Records, 1938-1946 Ancestry.com Operations Inc, 2005. National Archives and Records Administration. accessed Dec 24 2015.; "Molesting" report: Telex: Adams to Director, FBI, March 16, 1954, Federal Bureau of Investigation, Record Management Division, Re: FOIA 1345492, Sept. 22, 2016 HC FF34; Mountain Lakes warning: Letter Col. C.V Constant from P.E. Foxworth April 27, 1942, Re: FOIA 1345492.
6   Arrest, October warning, Nazi tendencies, Provost warning: Letter Frank D. Fackenthal (Provost, Columbia University) to Federal Bureau of Investigation (Foley Square office), October 2, 1942, FOIA 1345492; November warning: *ibid*, "Memorandum Att: Special Agent (FBI) R.R. Granville (New York) Re: Eric Bell Hotelling, Espionage, From 'CMJ'" November 19, 1943, FOIA 1345492..
7   Eric as "subversive:" Letter to Col. C.V Constant (director, Security and Intelligence Division, Second Service Command, Governors Island, New York) from E.E. Conroy, SAC, FBI, NY,. February 17. 1944 FOIA 1345492; German tutor:, Telex: Director, FBI Fr:, SAC New York Re; Pittsburgh letter to Director March 16, 1954; Evasive phone calls: *ibid*, Memorandum for the file, Eric Bell Hotelling, November 22, 1943.
8   Countrymen: Maple Statement, February 20, 1944. HC Box 1, FF10; "Pro-Nazi ideas": Memorandum for Ladd, Feb 25, 1944 HC FBIM – Box 1 FF14, Items #422-433;
9   Poehlmann , Waldman: Hoteling, Report of Investigation ,March 28, 1944, Vol II FF27, 6; New Year's Eve: Memorandum for the Office, March 31, 1944, Box 1, HC-Vol. IV Box 1, FF4; Loaned uniform: Leonhard Statement, Vol IV FF4 Exhibit E Item 621. Now do you believe: Kahn, Notes, Undated. HC C Box 2. FF 56, 88, 89
10 Leuth: E.J. Kahn, Jr., Interview with Eric B. Hotelling, Notes, HC C Box 2 FF56, 153; Disappeared: Nobis Interview" Kahn, Notes HC C Box 2 FF 56, 118; Maple reassigned as punishment: Letter Dale Maple to Chas O Porter, November 5, 1948. HC C Box 2 FF35.
11 Real motive. Letter Hotelling to Kahn, December 29, 1948. HC C Box 2 FF42, 4-5.
12 Prisoners escape: Leonhard Statement, HC FBIM – Box 1 HC FF4 Exhibit E, Item 618.
13 Leonhard, Maple's plans: Curran, Report of Investigation March 15, 1944. FF4 Item 545, 4.; Sensational: Leonhard Testimony, HC FF2, 42-43.
14 Real motive. Letter Hotelling to Kahn December 29, 1948, HC C Box 2. FF42, 4-5.
15 Hotelling plan: J.M. Curran, "Report to Chief IB, S&ID, 7th SC, Omaha, Nebr.," March 15, 1944. Court-Martial Records [Report of Investigation], HC Box 1 FF4 Item 749, 2; Marshal Tito: Leonhard Statement, HC FBIM—Box 1 FF4 Exhibit E, Item 614.
16 Hotelling recruiting: Curran, Interviews with Hotelling and Idelberger," HC. Box 1 FF4, Item 752, 5; Complete plan: Letter Ladon to Kahn, January 5, 1949, HC C FF44, 2.

PART THREE: NOOSE
CHAPTER 10: "THE BIGGEST CASE OF IT'S TIME"
1   Jurisdiction, Bryce Testimony, HC FF3, 256-262.
2   Federal Bureau of Investigation "History of the FBI World War II Period: Late 1930's—1945" https://www2.fbi.gov/libref/historic/history/worldwar.htm accessed Nov 27 2015.
3   Rumrich: Federal Bureau of Investigation, "Byte Out of History: Spies Caught, Spies Lost, Lessons Learned," December, 2007, https://www.fbi.gov/news/stories/2007/december/

espionage_120307 accessed Nov 27 2015; Turrou's contracts: Francis MacDonnell, *Insidious Foes: The Axis Fifth Column and the American Home Front* (New York: Oxford University Press, 1995) 49-50; Embarrassment: FBI, Byte Out of History.

4   Abwehr history: Peter Duffy, *Double Agent: The First Hero of World War II and How the FBI Outwitted and Destroyed a Nazi Spy Ring* (New York: Scribner, 2014); Military secret: It was called the "Norden bombsight". Sherryl Connelly, "New Yorker risks life as double agent in Nazi underground," *New York Daily News*, July 12, 2014 http://www.nydailynews.com/news/world/new-yorker-risks-life-double-agent-nazi-underground-brings-duquesne-spy-ring-new-book-article-1.1864628 accessed Nov 27, 2015.

5   Grumman: *ibid.*

6   Duquesne Ring: Duffy, 86-89; Connelly, *New York Daily News*, July 12, 2014

7   World War II: German Saboteurs Invade America in 1942, HistoryNet, June 12, 2006 http://www.historynet.com/world-war-ii-german-saboteurs-invade-america-in-1942.htm accessed Nov 27, 2015.

8   Napoleon: Curt Gentry, *J. Edgar Hoover: The Man and His Secrets* (New York: W.W. Norton & Company, 1991), 289; Sabotage case: HistoryNet, June 12, 2006; George John Dasch and the Nazi Saboteurs, https://www.fbi.gov/about-us/history/famous-cases/nazi-saboteurs, accessed December 1, 2015; "Deplored the Gestapo;" Lewis Wood, "Nazi Saboteurs Planned to 'Blow' TVA and Hell Gate, Clark Reveals," *New York Times*, November 8, 1945, 10; German saboteurs executed in Washington. http://www.history.com/this-day-in-history/german-saboteurs-executed-in-washington accessed December 1, 2015.

9   Biddle: Gentry, 291.

10 Moving the case out of civil court: Fred L. Borch, "Sitting in Judgment: Myron C Cramer's Experiences in the Trials of German Saboteurs and Japanese War Leaders" *Prologue Magazine*, Summer, 2009, Summer, 2009, Vol 41, No. 2, 34+

11 *New York Times,* November 1, 1945, 10. Hoover and *Newsweek*: Gentry, 291. *Life* magazine: Newton, 57.

12 FBI counter-intelligence investigations: Weingartner, 20.

13 Civilian participation: *ibid.* Maple's Statement, HC FBIM Box 1, FF11, 2; Jurisdiction: Delmar Karlen and Louis H. Pepper, "The Scope of Military Law," *Criminal Law, Criminology and Police Science*, September-October, 1953, Vol 43, No. 3., 291.

14 MID jurisdiction: Weingartner, 20-23; Hoover and Donovan: Gentry, 266-68, 294-95.

15 OSS and NKVD: *ibid,* 312-16.

16 "Keep it quiet," D.M. Ladd, Memorandum for Mr. Tamm, February 19, 1944. HC FBIM–Box 1 FF11.

17 Civilian participation: Tamm, Memorandum, February 21, 1944. FBIM—Box 1, FF11, 1.

18 ibid.

19 ibid.

20 ibid.

21 Hale's intelligence officer: Memorandum for Ladd, Feb 25 1944, HC FBIM-Box 1, FF 14, Item #422-433; Custody: J.M. Curran, "Subject: Dale Maple, Pfc, *et. al.*," Court-Martial Records [Report of Investigation], 15 March 1944. Memorandum for the Office, March 31, 1944, HC Box 1, FF4, Item 543; No use wasting time: Memorandum for Mr. Ladd, Feb 25 1944, HC FBIM-Box 1 FF 14, items #422-433.

22 Compelled to release: "Army Will Try S.D. Soldier in Treason Case" *San Diego Union,* Feb 23 1944, 4:3. HC Box 2, FF56.

23 Fight to the Last: Memorandum for Ladd, Feb 25, 1944, FBIM-Box 1 HC FF14, Items 423.

24 Curran, Memorandum, March 31, 1944, HC Box 1, FF4, Item 550, 9. Maple possessions: Admission Memo, Office of the Supervisor of Prisoners, United States Disciplinary

Barracks, Ft. Leavenworth, Kansas, 27 February 1944. Inmate 61364-L-Dale H Maple, National Archives at Kansas City. Record Group 129, Records of the Bureau of Prisons. Dept of Justice. Bureau of Prisons. U.S. Penitentiary, Leavenworth. Inmate Case Files, 1895-1952. National Archives Identifier: 571125.
25 El Paso: Memorandum for Ladd, Feb 25, 1944. FBIM Box 1, HC FF 14 Item #433.

CHAPTER 11: THE DESIGNED-TO-FAIL PLOT

1 "Father of soldier hits treason charge," *Washington Star,* Feb. 21, 1944, A-13.
2 Angry man: Kahn., Notes, FF56, 6. Name changes: E.J. Kahn, Jr., Interview with Mrs. Scoville. Undated. HC C FF56, 75; Ralph Maple shot: "Colton Police Officer in Duel with F. Watts," *San Bernardino County Sun,* Sept. 17, 1916, 1,5; Letter Orson P. Jones to E.J. Kahn, Jr. Dec 9, 1948, HC C FF43; Personnel office: James L. Sloan, Captain/Officer in Charge, "Memorandum for the Officer in Charge. Re: interview with [REDACTED]. February 23, 1944." HC FBIM – Box 1, FF12, Items 588-590.
3 Too smart: Scoville Testimony, 236-37.
4 Maple Testimony, 194, 198.
5 Trying to get caught *ibid.,* 195-198.
6 Open trial: *ibid.,* 199.
7 Hotelling's background: National Archives and Records Administration. *U.S. World War II Army Enlistment Records, 1938-1946* [database on-line]. Provo, UT, USA: Ancestry.com. accessed Dec 24 2015; Violent revolution: Curran, "Report of Investigation," March 15, 1944, HC-Vol V FF4 Items 748, 752; High I.Q.: Office Memorandum to Nichols, Jan. 26, 1949 HC FBIM-Box 1 FF34, 3; Crackpot: Statement of BLANK {Otto Idelberger], 2/28/44—2/29/44, HC FBIM—Box I C FF 17 Items 274-276; Delusions of grandeur: Statement made by Wilhelm C. Poehlmann Pfc. 9 March 1944, Court-Martial Records [Record of Investigation] HC-Vol II EXHIBIT K, Item 456.
8 Not in Inner Circle: United Press, "Ten U.S. Soldiers, 2 WACs Accused of Dealing With Nazis," *The Daily Clintonian* (Clinton, Indiana) 10 March 1944, 1; United Press, "8 U.S. Soldiers Held For Aiding in Nazi 'Break'" *The Times* (San Mateo, California) 10 March 1944, 6; United Press, "Three Admit Charges, Camp Hale Commander Says; WACs Sentenced for Love Missives," *The News-Herald* (Franklin, Pennsylvania), 10 March 1944, https://www.newspapers.com/image/54167944/?terms=Theophil%2BLeonhard, accessed Dec 22, 2015; Not pro-German, "defensive" mutiny: Curran, "Report of Investigation, 15 March 1944," HC-Vol IV FF4 Items 748, 753, 6; M.A. Jones to Mr. Nichols, "Office Memorandum, Feb 1, 1949" HC FBIM FF34.
9 He knew: "Kissman Statement, 27 February 1944" HC FBIM – Box 1, FF15, Items 490-504.
10 Just didn't care: Leonhard Statement, Feb 24 1944, HC FBIM – Box 1, FF13, Items 443;
11 Hotelling sentence: Memorandum to Nichols, Jan. 26, 1949," HC FBIM – Box 1 FF34.
12 Leonhard Gestapo letter : Memorandum for Hoover, July 8 1944," HC FBIM-Box 1 HC FF30.
13 "Ridiculous:" Memorandum for Mr. Nichols Fr: Clyde Tolson. March 7, 1949. HC FBIM – Box 1, FF21 12; Intercepted notes:. Letter Ladon to Kahn, December 27, 1948., HC C FF44. 2.
14 Can't prove anything: Opinion of the Board of Review, 22 June 1944, Court-Martial Records HC-Vol I FF1; They wanted a story: E.J. Kahn, Notes, Interview with Scoville, HC C FF 56, 73. Unduly worried: Letter Dale Maple to Mae Scoville, March 11, 1944, E.J. Kahn Jr., Notes, Undated. HC C FF56, 36.

15 Kogelman: Statement made by Hugo Opton, 17 March 1944 Curran, Report of Investigation, FF2 Item 416; Transfers from unit: Summary Report of Interviews 3 March 1944-16 March 1944. 28 March 1944, Court-Martial Records HC-Vol II FF2, 9.

16 Italians: Memorandum for the Officer in Charge. Interview with Pvt. Renato Mazza, March 16, 1944, HC-Vol II, FF2, 9; Drewes Statement, HC-Vol II FF2, Items 400, 402; Kogelman's refusal: "Opton Statement," FF2, Item 414.

17 Maple's plan: Memorandum for the Office, March 31, 1944, HC-Vol IV Box 1, FF4, 23, Item 564.

18 "Lay it on thick:" Letter E.J. Kahn, Jr. to Charles O. Porter, 1 November 1948, HC C FF49.

CHAPTER 12: IN COURT

1   "Testimony of L.G. Maple," Court Martial Records [Report of Investigation] 1944, HC-Vol III, FF3, 240

2   Judges, witnesses, exhibits, lawyers: Court-Martial Records [Record of trial], HC FF2, 1-2, 24; Biddle: Lt. Col Bernard R. Brown, "Opinions and Reasons Therefor," May 22,1944, Board of Review Findings, HC FF1, 16.

3   Expect the extreme: Letter Humphrey Biddle to E.J. Kahn, Jr. Oct. 11 1948, HC C Box 2 FF37.

4   Executions in 1944: National Archives – Supreme Commander of the Allied Powers, Reg 331, Stack 290, Rm 9, Comp 31, Shelf 1, File: "Execution Report," http://www.deathpenaltyinfo.org/executions-military accessed Dec 26 2015. Biddle: Michael Collins Piper and Ken Hoop, "A Mockery of Justice – The Great Sedition Trial of 1944. http://www.solargeneral.org/wp-content/uploads/library/ADL/a-mockery-of-justice-the-great-sedition-trial-of-1944.pdf accessed March 16 2016.

5   Charges: Board of Review Opinion], HC-Vol I Box 1 FF 1.

6   Parents in the anteroom: *ibid.*, 70.

7   Maple takes lead: DM Ladd, "Memo to J.F. Buckley April 28 1944," HC FBIM-Box 1, FF29; L.G. as co-counsel: Kahn, Germany In Wartime, 70; Afraid of Dale: Kahn, Scoville interview, Notes, HC C FF56, 72.

8   Schwichtenberg Testimony, HC-Vol II FF2 167-172. Kikilius Testimony, HC-Vol II FF2 176-177.

9   Correcting his mother: Mae Scoville Testimony, HC-Vol III FF3 238.

10 1937 at Harvard: Letter Mae Scoville to E.J. Kahn, Jr. October 25, 1948, HC C FF52.

11 Domestic discord: Mae Scoville Testimony, HC Vol III FF3, 231.

12 L.G. Maple Testimony, HC-Vol III FF3 239, 241-243, 249.

13 Lawyer's upset: Memorandum to EA Tamm Fr: D.M. Ladd, May 4 1944, HC FBIM Box 1, FF29.

14 Terrorist commonalities: R. Borum, *Psychology of terrorism.* (Tampa: University of South Florida, 2004) https://www.ncjrs.gov/pdffiles1/nij/grants/208552.PDF accessed Dec. 14, 2015.

15 Effeminate, harmless: Letter Theodore F. Whitmarsh to Kahn, November 8th, 1948. HC C Box 2 FF52; Not unpopular: Letter Jones to Kahn, Oct. 29, 1948. HC C FF43; Strange walk: "Interview with Edward Greer," E.J. Kahn, Jr., Notes. Undated. HC C FF56, 78; "Bitterly Anti-Catholic" father: Mrs. Scoville Interview, HC C FF 56, 70; Letter Jones to Kahn, Dec 9, 1948, HC C FF43; Reaction vs. father: Interview with Roger Oresman, E.J. Kahn Jr., Notes, Undated. HC C FF 56,45.

16 Testimony of Erwin S Chappel, Capt., Medical Corp, Court Martial Records [Report of Investigation], HC-Vol III FF4 274-277.

17   Misjudged temper: "Testimony of Major Thomas I Metzger, M.D.," Court Martial Records
     [Report of Investigation], HC-Vol III FF3 271-272; Physical at jail: "Memorandum for the
     Officer in Charge. Subject: Dale Maple, Pfc., 25 February 1944, HC-Vol IV FF4 EXHIBIT
     B, Item 587; Nazi leaders' intellect: Kahn, "Germany In Wartime?" *The New Yorker*, April
     1, 1950, 71.
18   Stephen P., Karns, J.D., "Military Trial Procedures," http://www.usmilitarylawyer.com/
     military-legal-procedures.asp accessed January 6, 2016
19   Worry about verdict: Letter Biddle to Kahn, J Oct. 11 1948, HC C Box 2. FF37.

CHAPTER 13: TANGLED WEBS THEY WEAVE

1   Death sentence guessed: *ibid.*
2   The: E.J. Kahn, Jr., "Interview with Frederick Bernays Wiener," Undated. HC C Box 2,
    Notes, FF56, 94.
3   Disbanding the 620th: General Order Number Four "Disbandment of 620th Engineer
    General Service Company and General Order Number 5, Activation of Company "A",
    1800th Engineer General Service Battalion, National Personnel Records Center, National
    Archives St. Louis. Re: Siering Friedrich; Name change: Letter Rudolph Nobis to Charles
    O Porter October 19 1948, HC C FF46; "Sadistic": *ibid.* Fight in Tennessee: Kahn, Nobis
    Interview, HC C Box 2 Ff 56, 115. Letter Rudolph Nobis to E.J. Kahn Jr October 29 1948
    HC C FF46.
4   Implicating Siering: "Summary of Expected Evidence," Trial of Friedrich W. Siering.
    Memorandum from Carl D. Ganz, JAGD to Commanding General, Seventh Service
    Command, National Personnel Records Center, National Archives St. Louis. Re: Siering
    Friedrich 3.
5   Siering citizenship: United States v. Siering, National Archives St. Louis. Re: Siering
    Friedrich, 53-54; Deportation, induction proceedings: Friedrich W. Siering, Petitioner v.
    William S. Eley, Col, U.S. Disciplinary Barracks, Fort Leavenworth, Kansas, Respondent.
    District Court of the United States for the District of Kansas, First Division, National
    Archives St. Louis. Re: Siering Friedrich.
6   Induction bargaining: U.S. v. Siering, 68, 66.
7   "Bitter:" *ibid*, 68; Refuse the oath: "Opinion of the District Court," Siering v William S.
    Eley, District of Kansas, First Division. December 23, 1944, National Archives St. Louis.
    Re: Siering Friedrich, 2; Citizenship promise: Record of Trial, National Personnel Records
    Center, National Archives St. Louis. Re: Siering Friedrich, 68; "No action:" Siering v Eley,
    Opinion of District Court, 2.
8   Habeas corpus: United States of America War Office, *A Manual for Courts-Martial U.S.
    Army,* revised April 19 1943, 192.; "Judge Studying Soldiers' Cases," *Lubbock Morning
    Avalanche,* 18 Oct 1944, 9. https://www.newspapers.com/image/9453631/?terms=The
    ophil%2BLeonhard, accessed Dec 22 2015; Leonhard v. Eley. No. 3175. Circuit Court
    of Appeals, 10th Circuit, October 16, 1945, https://casetext.com/case/leonhard-v-eley,
    accessed Dec. 22 2015.
9   Letter Ladon to Kahn, Jr., December 27, 1948, HC C FF44.
10 Witnesses: "Summary of Trial." Inmate #61423-Paul Kissman. National Archives at Kansas
    City. Record Group 129, Records of the Bureau of Prisons. Dept of Justice. Bureau of
    Prisons. U.S. Penitentiary, Leavenworth. Inmate Case Files, 1895-1952. National Archives
    Identifier: 571125.
11 Witnesses, swastikas: *ibid.* Bund membership, refusal to sing: "Erie Man Who Aided Escape
    Was Bundist," *The Kane Republican*, 3-11-44, 1; High school German Club: *New Castle
    High School Yearbook, 1939.* Accessed on Ancestry.com, April 30, 2016.

12 Nov 28 1944: Board of Review Opinion, GCM Order, 103, E.J. Kahn Jr., Notes, HC
    C Box 2 FF56, 103; Fred L Borch III, "Tried for Treason: The Court-Martial of Private
    First-Class Dale Maple," *The Army Lawyer*, Nov 2010, DA PAM 27-50-450, 8; Inmate
    Record—Dale Maple. Inmate #61364-Dale H Maple National Archives at Kansas City.
    Record Group 129, Records of the Bureau of Prisons. National Archives Identifier: 571125;
    Board of Review Opinion: Kahn, HC C Box 2 FF56, 103.

PART FOUR: DESERTS, JUST & OTHERWISE
CHAPTER 14. ON THE SCAFFOLD

1   Danielson's order: War Department Summary, Nov. 28, 1944, Inmate 61364-L – Dale H
    Maple, National Archives at Kansas City.
2   Cramer: Borch, "Sitting in Judgment" *Prologue Magazine*, Summer, 2009; Cramer's
    recommendations: Office of the Judge Advocate General, Board of Review Holdings,
    Opinions and Review, 1944, p 7, 15, 29, 43, 63; Interview with Frederick Bernays Wiener,
    HC C Box 2, 92.
3   Military executions in 1944: National Archives (I) – Records of Far East Command,
    Supreme Commander of the Allied Powers and United Nations Command 1945 – 1957,
    Provost Marshall Section, Reg 554, Stack 290, Rm 50, Comp 7, Shelf 3, Entry 156;
    National Archives (II) – Supreme Commander of the Allied Powers, Reg 331, Stack
    290, Rm 9, Comp 31, Shelf 1, File: "Execution Report. http://www.deathpenaltyinfo.
    org/executions-military, accessed Dec 26 2015; Lincoln's mass pardon: Matt Ford. "The
    Limits of Obama's Clemency" *The Atlantic*. Dec 18, 2014. theatlantic.com/politics/
    archive/2014/12/the-limits-of-obama-mercy/383870/, accessed Feb 15 2016; Military
    executions 1930s, '40s and '50s: Margarete Werner Cahalan, and Lee Ann Parson, *Historical
    Corrections in the United States, 1850-1984* U.S. Department of Justice, Bureau of Justice
    Statistics (Rockville Md::Westgate Inv,1986), 23.
4   Letter Dale Maple to Mae Scoville: May 17, 1944, Kahn, Notes, 36; Recipes: *ibid.,* June 18
    1944; Postwar celebration, Red Sox, Dewey, Joan Davis: Letter Maple to Scoville NOTES.
    Undated. HC C Box 2 FF 56; "Mrs. Scoville Interview," Undated. Kahn, Notes, HC C Box
    2 FF56, 68-76; Dreading: Letter Maple to Scoville, December 6, 1944. Kahn, HC C Box 2
    F 56, 38.
5   Cramer memo: Borch, *The Army Lawyer*, 9; Memorandum for Major General Edwin M.
    Watson, The White House, Washington, D.C. Subject: Private First-Class Dale Maple
    (11048476), Company A. 1800th Engineer General Service Battalion." From: Myron C.
    Cramer, Major General, 25 October 1944. HC-Vol III FF63.
6   Commutation Document. Nov 15, 1944 HC-Vol III FF62, Item 5153; Commutations:
    "Petitions Granted – Commutation" http://clemency-by-us-president.silk.co/page/1945,
    accessed Jan 6 2016.
7   Could have been worse: Letter Dale Maple to Mae Scoville, December 6, 1944. Kahn,
    NOTES. Undated. HC C Box 2 FF 56, 38.
8   Transfer: Inmate Record—Dale Maple. Inmate #61364-Dale H Maple National Archives at
    Kansas City; Admission interview: Admission Summary, Jan. 4, 1945. Maple, Dale 61364-
    L Inmate Records, U.S. Penitentiary, Leavenworth, Kansas. National Archives at Kansas
    City, Record Group 129, Inmate Case Files, National Archives Identifier: 571125.
9   Newspapers: Associated Press. "President Commutes Death Sentence Given Deserter"
    Washington Star, Dec 11, 1944; *San Diego Tribune-Sun*, Dec. 8, 1944. *Boston Times-Herald*,
    Dec. 12, 1944; Fertile soil for disloyalty: Board of Review Opinion, HC-Vol I FF1.
    Astonished: Hotelling Interview, Kahn, C Box 2, 151. Kahn, Frederick Bernays Wiener

Interview, HC C FF56, 94; L.G Maple's influence on verdict: Letter Joseph A. Hartman to E.J. Kahn, Jr. Oct 27, 1948 HC C FF42.

10 Author telephone interview with Fred L. Borch, (Col. Ret), February 19, 2016.

CHAPTER 15. FIRST DRIPS FROM A FROZEN HEART

1 Admission Summary, January 18, 1945, Inmate #61423-Paul Kissman. National Archives at Kansas City. Record Group 129, National Archives Identifier: 571125. "Current Population Reports, Consumer Incomes, U.S. Bureau of the Census, March 2, 1948, Series P-60, No. 2. http://www2.census.gov/prod2/popscan/p60-002.pdf, accessed March 5, 2016.

2 Prison life: Interview with Arthur (Benny) L. Staggs by E.J. Kahn, Jr. Undated. HC C Box 2 FF56, 65.

3 Disloyalty error: "Special Progress Report, December 1945," United States Penitentiary, Leavenworth, Kans. Inmate #61423-Paul Kissman. National Archives at Kansas City. Record Group 129. National Archives Identifier: 571125.

4 Documentary evidence arrested: Curran, Report of Investigation, March 28, 1944, HC-Vol V FF4, Item 752, 5; FBI summary: Adams, Synopsis of Facts, HC FBIM-Box 1.

5 Hotelling interview: Letter Bernard Ladon to E.J. Kahn, Jr., January 5, 1949. HC C Box 2, FF44.

6 Charges, trial dates: Office Memorandum to Mr. Nichols, Fr: M.A. Jones, Feb 1, 1949 HC FBIM FF34, 3; Articles of War: "The Articles of War, Approved June 4, 1920-September, 1920." (Washington: Government Printing Office: 1920), accessed June 21 2016 http://ibiblio.org/hyperwar/USA/ref/AW/index.html, 19, 25, 27-28. Hotelling denials: Curran, "Report of Investigation," Items 748 - FF4 Item 753, 6; E.J. Kahn, Jr., Interview with Eric B. Hotelling, Notes, HC C Box 2, Item 152.

7 Crackpot: Memorandum. Jones to Nichols, HC FBIM FF34, 3. Batty: Schoen Statement, of 6 March 1944 HC-Vol III, FF16, Item 465; Utter abandon: Leonhard Statement, HC-Vol IV Box 1 FF4 Exhibit E, Item 618.

8 Conviction: Adams, HC FBIM-Box 1; "Dead earnest," Letter Ladon to Kahn, January 5, 1949, HC C Box 2, FF44.

9 Bar fight: Kahn, "Nobis Interview," K, HC Box 2 C Notes FF 56, 115; "Drewes Statement," HC-Vol II FF4, Item 402.

10 Restored to Duty: Adams, HC FBIM-Box 1; Army records: *U.S. World War II Army Enlistment Record,* ,Enlisted Record and Report of Separation, Honorable Discharge, Hotelling, Eric B, 24 February 1946. Ancestry.com Operations Inc, 2005, accessed Dec 24 2015.

11 Changing induction standards: Karlen and Pepper, *Criminal Law, Criminology and Police Science*, 290; High water mark, put soldiers back in foxholes: Col. James J Smith, U.S. Army "Military Clemency and Parole: Does It Work?" Executive Research Project 1993. National Defense University, Fort McNair, Washington, D.C, 6-7; Commutations: "Petitions Granted – Commutation" http://clemency-by-us-president.silk.co/page/1945, accessed Jan 6 2016; The number of general courts-martial was variously reported as 63, 876, resulting in 60 110 convictions. Andrew Jackson May, *Investigations off National War Effort, U.S. House of Representatives Committee on Military Affairs*, (Washington, D.C: U.S. Govt Printing Office, 1946), 22-23.

12 Clemency after World War I: Smith, "Military Clemency," 6-7; Incarceration cost: Borch, Interview, February 19, 2016.

13 System breakdown: Report of U.S. War Department Advisory Committee on Military Justice, 13 December 1946, 4; High water mark: Smith, Military Clemency a 6-7; "David

Hasenritter and Steven Andraschko, "The Army Clemency and Parole Board" *Corrections Today*, May 1, 2013. http://www.readperiodicals.com/201305/2984463671.html, accessed March 5 2016.

14 Albert Alschuler. "The Changing Purposes of Criminal Punishment: A retrospective on the Last Century and Some Thoughts About the Next" *University of Chicago Law Review*, Vol 70, No. 1 (Winter 2003), 7, http://chicagounbound.uchicago.edu/cgi/viewcontent.cgi?artic le=1893&context=journal_articles, accessed July 19 2016

15 Treason: Kevin Goszlola, "Aiding the Enemy: The Unprecedented Prosecution of Bradley Manning." ShadowProof. https://shadowproof.com/2013/07/25/aiding-the-enemy-the-unprecedented-prosecution-of-bradley-manning/, accessed Dec 29, 2015

16 Parole successes: Herman L Goldberg and Frederick A. C. Hoefer, "Army Parole System," *Journal of Criminal Law and Criminology* Summer 1949 Vol 40 Issue 2, 159; Combined clemency boards: Smith, "Military Clemency," 17.

17 Lesser treason penalties: Treason, Sedition and Subversive Activities, Title 18—Crimes and Criminal Procedure Part I—Crimes, 18 USC Ch. 115, https://uscode.house.gov/view. xhtml?path=/prelim@title18/part1/chapter115&edition=prelim, accessed 7/30/2020.

18 Misplaced sympathies: Letter Ladon to Kahn, December 27, 1948. HC C FF 44.

19 Alschuler. "Changing Purposes," 7-10,

20 Sentencing, incarceration trends: Cahalan and Parson, "Historical Corrections," 2-3.

21 Presidential pardons: Thanks to Northwestern University law professor Albert W. Alschuler for sharing an excerpt from an unpublished journal article that included a short history of presidential wartime pardons. Washington: James D. Richardson, *Messages and Papers of the Presidents* (Washington, D.C: Government Printing Office 1896), 184.

22 Bridges: Walter Trohan, "Tear Secrecy Off Truman, F.D.R. Pardons; Clemency Granted to 5,856 Outlaws" *Chicago Tribune*, Aug 30, 1953, 1 http://archives.chicagotribune. com/1953/08/30/page/1/article/tear-secrecy-off-truman-f-d-r-pardons, accessed Jan 6, 2015; Bridge's failed blackmail of a fellow senator (see footnote: David K. Johnson, The Lavender Scare: *The Cold War Persecution of Gays and Lesbians in the Federal Government*, (Chicago: University of Chicago Press, 2004), 141.

CHAPTER 16. LEFT BEHIND

1 Certificate, John E. Buehler, Trial Judge Advocate, Fort Leavenworth, Kansas, 8 August 1945; Judge Studying Soldiers' Cases," *Lubbock Morning Advance*, 18 Oct 1944, 9. https:// www.newspapers.com/image/9453631/?terms=Theophil%2BLeonhard, accessed Dec 22 2015; Circuit Court of Appeals, Tenth Circuit.151 F2d 409 (10th Circuit 1945) Leonhard V. Eley No 3175; Disloyal Americans: National Archives St. Louis. Re: Siering Friedrich.

2 Failure to induct: the precedent was *Billings v. Truesdale*. Opinion draft responding to motion to dismiss, in Fredrich [SIC] W. Siering v William S. Eley. Opinion of District Court, National Archives St. Louis. Re: Siering Friedrich, 2-3; Writ: Siering v. Eley, U.S District Court, District of Kansas, Dec. 23, 1944. Ruling on writ, "*Worksheet Memorandum*," National Personnel Records Center, 14 August 1945, National Archives St. Louis. Re: Siering Friedrich.

3 Trial date: *ibid.*.

4 Charges: Board of Review, General Court-Martial Order No. 947. 14 August 1945 National Personnel Records Center, National Archives St. Louis. Re: Siering Friedrich.

5 Germany rumors: Siering statement, Box 1 HC FF17, Items 529-543; Trust: Maple Testimony: U.S. v. Siering, 19; Good-natured: U.S. V. Siering, National Archives St. Louis, 59, 63-64, 70; Fort Knox: www.knox.army.mil "History of Fort Knox", accessed May 17, 2016

6 Prosecution arguments: Record of Trial. U.S. v. Siering, 78-79.

7   Release: General Court-Martial Order No 542, 27 May 1946. U.S. v. Siering; Affairs
    (footnote): Marriage license {09EE6CC9-05AA-4C9D-B623-A80E3C3FB73B, File
    1721305, Cook County Genealogy Records (Marriages); Kahn, Nobis Interview, HC C
    Box 2, FF56, 115.
8   Letters: To Adjutant General, United States Army, Washington, D.C. from Friedrich
    Siering, July 8, 1946.; Letter Lt. Col. Chester D. Silvers to Friedrich W. Siering, July
    16, 1946; To Lt. Col. Chester D. Silvers from Friedrich Siering, July 19, 1946. National
    Personnel Records Center, National Archives St. Louis. Re: Siering Friedrich.
9   Deportation; Series Title: Passenger and Crew Manifests of Airplanes Arriving at San
    Juan, Puerto Rico, 01/01/1942 – 06/30/1948; NAI Number: 2945867; Record Group
    Title: Records of the Immigration and Naturalization Service, 1787-2004; Record Group
    Number: 85 The National Archives at Washington, D.C., accessed 5-22-16.
10 Leonhard's suit: "Judge Studying Soldiers' Cases," *Lubbock Morning Avalance,* 18 Oct 1944,
    9. https://www.newspapers.com/image/9453631/?terms=Theophil%2BLeonhard, accessed
    Dec 22 2015; Court of Appeals decision: LEONHARD V. ELEY. NO. 3175. CIRCUIT
    COURT OF APPEALS, TENTH CIRCUIT. OCTOBER 16, 1945. https://casetext.com/
    case/leonhard-v-eley, accessed Dec. 22, 2015.
11 Heart and soul: Kahn, Notes, HC C Box 2, FF56 152; Nazi contacts: Skinner, "Clemency
    Data," Record of Trial 28 January 1946 Inmate 63453-L Theophil J. Leonhard. U.S.
    Penitentiary, Leavenworth Kansas. Notorious Offenders series. Textual Reference (RDT2);
    Staying in the U.S: Leonhard Statement, HC-Vol IV Box 1 FF4 Exhibit E, Item 615;
    Kunze visit: United States House of Representatives, "Investigation of un-American
    propaganda activities in the United States." Hearings before a Special Committee on Un-
    American Activities. 75th Congress https://archive.org/stream/investigationofu194114unit/
    investigationofu194114unit_djvu.txt, accessed Jan 10 2016; Unpopular: Admission
    Summary, October, 1946, Inmate 63453-L Theophil J. Leonhard, U.S. Penitentiary,
    Leavenworth Kansas. Notorious Offenders series. Textual Reference (RDT2), 2; Stonewall
    speeches: Author interviews with Margaret Manius, May 17, 2016 and Cliff Manlius, May
    26, 2016; Embitterment: Skinner, "Clemency Data." 28 January 1946.
12 Maple at Leonhard's trial: "Memorandum for Warden," Federal Penitentiary, Leavenworth,
    Kansas. 21 February 1946 and Extract - Record of Trial, Leonhard, Theophil J. 9 January
    1946. Bureau of Prisons. Inmate Case Files, 1895-1952. National Archives Identifier:
    571125 National Archives at Kansas City.
13 Rat: Kahn, Staggs interview, Undated. HC Box 2 C FfF56, 67.
14 Parents' return to U.S: Margaret Maenius interview May 17, 2016; Sentence: "Record of
    Court Commitment" 8-16-51, Inmate 63453-L Theophil J. Leonhard. U.S. Penitentiary,
    Leavenworth Kansas. "Notorious Offenders" series. Textual Reference (RDT2); Likeable
    chap: Admission Summary, 3; Prisoner-soldier population, Smith, 8.
15 Got off easy: Kahn, Staggs interview, 67.
16 Moody: Admission Summary, 2, 5.

CHAPTER 17. DEUS EX HARVARD
1   Nobis: U.S., Department of Veterans Affairs BIRLS Death File, 1850-2010 [database
    on-line]. Provo, UT: Ancestry.com, accessed July 11, 2016; Drewes: "Arlington Bowlers
    Win 21 of 24 Doubles Prizes" *Arlington Heights Herald,* Apr 4 1947, 9. Idelberger: U.S.,
    Department of Veterans Affairs BIRLS Death File, 1850-2010 [database on-line]. Provo,
    UT, Ancestry.com, accessed Dec. 13, 2016.
2   Vengeance in Europe: Tara Zahra, "A Brutal Peace: On the Postwar Expulsions
    of Germans," *The Nation,* Nov. 29, 2012. https://www.thenation.com/article/

brutal-peace-postwar-expulsions-germans/, accessed June 4, 2017; Max Ebel: Sara M. Earle, "Germans, Too, Were Imprisoned in WWII" *Concord (N.H.) Monitor*, January 23, 2000. Enemy aliens: Karen E. Ebel, "WWII Violations of German American Civil Liberties by the US Government" *The Freedom of Information Times*, Feb 24, 2003. http://www.foitimes. com/gasummary.htm, accessed May 12, 2017; "Court Lifts Bar to Deporting 700 Axis Aliens" *Chicago Tribune* Jan 3, 1947, 3; "Schlenther Admits Talk With Kunze" *Hartford Courant*, Jan 3, 1945, 2; "Stay Is Denied In Deportation Of Two Aliens" *Chicago Tribune*, Aug 8 1946, 22; "Dr. Willumeit Asks Court Rehearing in Loss of Citizenship" *Chicago Tribune* Nov 8 1946, 7; "Willumeit Asks U.S. Court of Appeals to Restore Citizenship" *Chicago Tribune*, Jul 31, 1949, 4

3   Dale Maple, "The Detainer System," *The New Era,* Winter 1945 cited in Kahn, NOTES Undated. HC C Box 2 FF56, 5.

4   V-J Day: Letter Maple to Scoville, Kahn, Notes HC C Box 2 FF 56, 39-40; "Passably friendly:" Staggs Interview, Kahn, Notes, HC C Box 2 FF56, 65. Politics: Kahn, Letter Maple to Scoville, FF56, 39, 41,42.

5   Activities: Scoville Interview, HC C Box 2 FF56, 68. Corny jokes: Letter Maple to Scoville, HC C Box 2. FfF56, p 39, 41,42.

6   Algebra: *ibid,* 41. Miraculous speed: "Recommendation for Exceptionally Meritorious or Outstanding Service Award" April 26, 1948, Records of the Bureau of Prisons, Inmate Record—Dale Maple. Inmate #61364, National Archives at Kansas City. Record Group 129, Bureau of Prisons. U.S. Penitentiary, Leavenworth. Inmate Case Files, 1895-1952. National Archives Identifier: 571125; Clemency denied: *ibid,* "Parole Progress Report," July 1947.

7   Repudiated ideas, custody: "Special Progress Report. Maple Dale 61364-L, August 17, 1946," "Special Progress Report," September 4, 1946; Well-disposed: "Special Progress Report," May 1948; all in Inmate Record—Dale Maple, National Archives at Kansas City. Record Group 129, Records of the Bureau of Prisons. Dept of Justice. Bureau of Prisons; Good time: "Recommendation for Exceptionally Meritorious or Outstanding Service Award," March 8, 1948 and Director, U.S. Bureau of Prisons, Memorandum to Warden, Leavenworth, June 7, 1948. Warden a fan: Walter A. Hunter, "Recommendation," April 26, 1948; "Meritorious Record of Prisoner," April 8, 1949 and "Industrial Record of Prisoner," October 1950, .all in .Inmate Case Files, 1895-1952. National Archives Identifier: 571125

8   Economic adjustment: "Special Progress Report." August 17, 1946.

9   Recidivism: Lawrence A. Greenfield, "Prisons and Prisoners in the United States." U.S. Dept. of Justice, *Bureau of Justice Statistics Bulletin*, April 1992, NCJ-137002, 21; Job Applications: Lovoy, "Life After Prison;" Christy Visher, Sara Debus and Jennifer Yahner, "Employment after Prison: A Longitudinal Study of Releases in Three States" *Urban Institute Justice Policy Center, Research Brief*, October, 2008. http://www.urban.org/sites/ default/files/alfresco/publication-pdfs/411778-Employment-after-Prison-A-Longitudinal-Study-of-Releasees-in-Three-States.PDF accessed Jan 26 2017.

10   Kissman parole: The United States Board of Parole, Washington, D.C., Certificate of Parole. Feb 3, 1947; "Release Progress Report" February 15, 1947; "Record of Court Commitment," all in Inmate #61423-Paul Kissman. National Archives at Kansas City. Record Group 129, Records of the Bureau of Prisons. Dept of Justice. Bureau of Prisons. U.S. Penitentiary, Leavenworth. Inmate Case Files, 1895-1952. National Archives Identifier: 571125

11   Post-prison plans: Letter Maple to Scoville, February 27, 1947, March 9, 1947, April 1, 1948 , HC C Box 2, FF56, 42-44; Harvard loan: Kahn, Notes, HC C Box 2, FF56, 76.

12   "Rather curt:" Letter Maple to Porter, Sept 10, 1948. HC C FF35.

13 Money-mad students: *Harvard College Class of 1941, Fiftieth Anniversary Report*, (Cambridge, Ma: Harvard University, 1991), 449; FDR, snowballs: *ibid*, 448, 450; War record: *Harvard Class of 1941, Sixth Anniversary Report*, (Cambridge, Ma: Harvard University,1946), 244-45.

14 Survey of Legal Profession: "Law Survey Takes Graduate of E.H.S." *The Eugene Guard*, Feb 8 1948, 5; Robert M. Segal, "Lawyers in the National Economy" *American Bar Association Journal*, October, 1956 Vol 42, 920, https://books.google.com/books?id=8vZy3GSGV1gC &pg=PA920&lpg=PA920&dq=Survey+of+the+Legal+Profession,+Boston,+Mass.,&source= bl&ots=xkeuqmrlbj&sig=hjz9 MAVzHzIehPyFcoYUQRpdboQ&hl=en&sa=X&ved=0ahUKEwia94PHvKzKAhU Pz2MKHaEvBk4Q6AEIOzAG#v=onepage&q=Survey%20of%20the%20Legal%20 Profession%2C%20Boston%2C%20Mass.%2C&f=falsel, accessed Jan 15, 2016; Public ownership: Sam Porter, "Democratic Party of Lane County," Facebook entry, January 1, 2016; Liberal causes: "Charles O. Porter," *Harvard College Class of 1941, Fiftieth Anniversary Report*, 450; Ahead of his time: William G. Robbins, "Charles O Porter, (1919-2006)" *The Oregon Encyclopedia*. https://oregonencyclopedia.org/articles/?q=Charles%20 O.%2C%20Porter; Harvard Law Association: "Local Man Gets Post," *The Eugene Guard*, June 19, 1947, 19 and *The Berkshire County* Eagle, June 4, 1947, 14; Khrushchev: "Contrarian Congressman Charles O. Porter, 86," *The Washington Post*, January 6, 2006, http://www.washingtonpost.com/wp-dyn/content/article/2006/01/05 /AR2006010502166. html, accessed Feb 3, 2016; Trujillo: Author interview with Samuel C. Porter, July 19, 2016; Campaigns: *Harvard College Class of 1941, 25th Anniversary Report*, , 1024-1026; Political losses: *Harvard College Class of 1941, 35th Anniversary Report*, 184; "Soundness:" Letter Raymond Dennett, (director, World Peace Foundation) to E.J. Kahn, Jr. October 4, 1948, HC C Box 2.

15 Alcatraz: *ibid*.

16 Ibid.

17 Northwestern: Samuel Porter interview, July 19, 2016; "Chas. Porter One of Editors of 'Collegiate Review." *The Register-Guard*, Eugene Oregon, 24 October 1938, 10; Harvard-Yale game: Dick Strite, "High Climber" *The Eugene Guard*, Nov 30 1937, 8. Journalism credits: *Class of 1941, 25th Anniversary Report*, 1966, 1024-1026.

18 Bulletin plea: Charles O. Porter, "Dale Maple," Letter to the Editor, *Harvard Alumni Bulletin*, April 10, 1948, 542-43; Refuting Porter: E. Mott Davis, Jr., Letter to the Editor. "Dale Maple," *Harvard Alumni Bulletin*, May 29, 1948, 658-59; Kahn, "First Chat," 5. Kennedy call: (footnote) Porter interview, July 19, 2016.

19 Congratulations: Letter Dale Maple to Chas O Porter, Sept 10 1948; Civilian clothes, books, secrecy: Letter Dale Maple to Chas O Porter, Sept 25 1948; Letter Dale Maple to Chas O Porter, November 5 1948 All in HC C Box2 FF35.

20 Harvard application: Interview with Payson Wild, George Adams and William Pinkerton, Kahn, Notes, undated, HC C Box 2 FF56, 53.

21 Tryst: Violation No. 2139, in "Special Progress Report. Maple, Dale. April 1949," Bureau of Prisons. U.S. Penitentiary, Leavenworth. Inmate Case Files, 1895-1952. National Archives at Kansas City identifier: 57112.

22 Gay personality disorder: Alan Berube, *Coming Out under Fire: The History of Gay Men and Women in World War II*, (Chapel Hill: University of North Carolina Press, 2020), 12. State Department firings: Jill Lepore, *These Truths* (New York: W.W. Norton and Sons, 2018), 550. Tangent: Letter Dale Maple to Chas O Porter, December 5 1948 HC C Box 2 FF35.

CHAPTER 18: YOUR BOY'S HALO

1   Porter's offer: Letter Charles O. Porter to E.J. Kahn, Jr., September 2, 1948, HC C Box 2 FF49; Withholding name: Charles O. Porter to E.J. Kahn, Jr., September 8, 1948. HC C Box 2 FF49; Samuel Porter interview, July 19, 2016. (Porter may have contacted Kahn at the suggestion of Harry Frank, a former *New Yorker* reporter who had been Porter's superior in the military).

2   Obituary: Bruce Bliven, "E.J. Kahn, Jr" *The New Yorker*, June 13, 1994, 12; Delighted: E.J. Kahn, Jr. to Charles O.Porter, 14 September 1948. HC C FF49.

3   "The Symposium:" Kahn, NOTES, October 1948 HC C Box 2 FF 56, 56-58. Elaine Tyler May, *Homeward Bound: American Families in the Cold War Era*, (New York: Basic Books, 2008), 73.

4   Kahn's speculations: Letter Ladon to Kahn, December 27, 1948. HC C Box 2 FF44; Letter Ladon to Kahn, January 5, 1949. HC C Box 2 FF44.

5   Julian Sobin, Lee Dimond lunch: Kahn, NOTES undated HC C Box 2 FF56.

6   Tillotson's question; halo: Letter, E.J. Kahn, Jr. to Charles O. Porter, 1 November 1948. HC C Box 2 FF49.

7   Communication flags: Letter Porter to Kahn, November 8, 1948. HC C Box 2 FF49. Letter Maple to Porter December 5 1948, HC C Box 2 FF35.

8   Shawn's glossary: E.J. Kahn, Jr., *About The New Yorker and Me* (New York: Penguin Books, 1979), 118.

9   Mae Scoville's materials: Letter Kahn to Porter, 19 February 1949. HC C Box 2 FF50; Undue suffering: Letter Kahn to Porter. 29 September 1949, HC C Box 2 FF50; Wait for the story: Letter to The New Yorker from Carol Heidt, May 4, 1949. HC C FF42; Letter to Mrs. Carol M. Heidt from "The New Yorker" May 9, 1949, HC C Box 2 FF50.

10 Nothing new: Letter Porter to Kahn, February 14, 1949. HC C Box 2 FF50.

11 Competition at Colliers: Letter Kahn to Porter. July 12, 1949. Porter's reply, July 13, 1949, HC C Box 2 FF50; Collier's circulation: William H. Young and Nancy K. Young, *The 1950s*, (Westport, CT: Greenwood Press, 2004), 152. New Yorker circulation: Steve Rothman, "The Publication of 'Hiroshima' in The New Yorker," Jan. 8, 1997, http://www.herseyhiroshima.com/hiro.php, accessed June 6, 2016.

12 Not Maple's attorney: Letter Walter A. Hunter, Warden, United States Penitentiary, Leavenworth, Kansas, to Charles O. Porter. September 1, 1949. HC C Box 2 FF50; Behind those walls: Letter, Charles O. Porter to Mrs. Scoville, September 12, 1949. HC C Box 2 FF50; Letter Mae C. Scoville to Charles O Porter. September 19, 1949. HC C Box 2 FF50.

13 Letter E.J. Kahn, Jr. to Charles O Porter. 13 September 1949. HC C Box 2 FF50.

PART FIVE: *APRES* FASCISM

1   One day in the mid-60s: Email, Lisa Williams to William Sonn, Dec. 9, 2016.

CHAPTER 19: EDITS AND PAINT JOBS

1   Infidelity: Kahn "Nobis Interview," HC C Box 2 FF 56; Leibrecht: Florida Naturalization Records, 1847-1995. The National Archives at Atlanta; Atlanta, Georgia, USA.; Petitions for Naturalization, compiled 1913 – 1991; National Archives Publication: 578688; Record Group Title: Records of District Courts of the United States.

2   Guilt: Herant Katchadorourian, *Guilt, The Bite of Conscience*. (Stanford, Ca: Stanford University Press, 2009), 3,9,21.

3   Cleared: Letter Hotelling to Kahn, December 29, 1948 HC C Box 2 FF42.

4   Kahn, "Hotelling interview" HC C Box 2. FF 56, 151.

5   Rutgers: Adams, "Synopsis of facts" HC FBIM FF34; ROTC: Email Erika Gorder (Rutgers University Libraries) to William Sonn, July 20, 2016.
6   Colliers drops story: "Office Memorandum To: Tolson, Fr: Nichols," April 8, 1949, HC FBIM FF34.
7   Deferred parole: United States Bureau of Prisons, U.S. Penitentiary, Leavenworth, Kansas; Against prison policy: Letter Walter A. Hunter (Warden) to Charles O. Porter, September 1, 1949. HC C Box 2 FF50.
8   Dept of Justice. United States Bureau of Prisons. U.S. Penitentiary, Leavenworth. Inmate Case Files, 1895-1952. National Archives Identifier: 571125, "Admission Summary," Jan. 4, 1945; Repudiated ideas: ibid, "Special Progress Report," 17 August 1946, 2.
9   United States Board of Parole, Certificate of Conditional Release, July 13, 1950; U.S. Penitentiary Leavenworth, Kansas Oct. 6, 1950; "Inmate's Release Schedule," and "Release Progress Report," Dale Maple, October 8, 1950; Obituary: "Glenn A. Dempsey," *San Diego Union* 2-19-1979, B-5.
10 Hoover told of release: Memorandum for Mr. Hoover from SAC Kansas City. October 23, 1950, HC FBIM FF34.
11 Marriage rates: May, *Homeward Bound,* 3, 158. Voter turnout: R.K. Landers, "Why America doesn't vote." *Editorial research reports* (Vol. I) (Washington, DC: CQ Press 1988). library.cqpress.com/cqresearcher/cqresrre1988021900, accessed May 30, 2016; Off-year turnout: "Voter Turnout," FairVote. www.fairvote.org/voter_turnout#voter_turnout_101, accessed May 30, 2016; Society's goodness: David Halberstam, *The Fifties.* (New York: Villard/Random House, 1993) IX-X; "Acquiescence:" Steve Fraser, *The Age of Acquiescence: The Life and Death of American Resistance to Organized Wealth and Power,*)New York: Little, Brown and Company, 2015), 4-5; Earning power: "The Fading American Dream: Trends in Absolute Income Mobility Since 1940,"Raj Chetty, David Grusky, Maximilian Hell, Nathaniel Hendren, Robert Manduca, Jimmy Narang, "Trends in Absolute Income Mobility Since 1940," National Bureau of Economic Research Working Paper No. 22910, 2016; Income distribution: Holger Apel, "Income Inequality in the U.S. from 1950 to 2010" *Real-World Economics Review,* Issue no. 72, 30 September 2015, 2, http://www.paecon.net/PAEReview/issue72/Apel72.pdf, accessed May 30, 2016; Popular songs: Rock Music Timeline.com www.rockmusictimeline.com/1950s.html, accessed May 30 2016.
12 Leavenworth contacts: US Bureau of Prisons, United States Penitentiary, Leavenworth, Kansas, Penal and Correctional Institutions "Visit Record" and "Inmates Mail Record," Inmate—Dale H. Maple.
13 L.G. Maple's innovation: "Shipbuilder Using New Process Here" *San Diego Union* May 10, 1953, 50; Ruth Maple social life: "Reciprocity Day of S.D.W.C. Slated Tuesday" *San Diego Union* March 6 1949, 65; Irene M. Clark, "Mrs. Heilman Re-elected 'Y' President" *San Diego Union,* June 30, 1949, 17; "S.D.W.C. Plans to Install at May Luncheon." *San Diego Union,* May 21 1950, 63; "Dramatic Artist To Be Heard By S.D.W.C." *San Diego Union,* May 1, 1952; "'Patriotic Days' Motif for Party" *San Diego Union,* February 9, 1953, 15; Kathryn Steffan, "Youngest Leads of Woman's Club Tells of Plans" *San Diego Union,* April 17, 1957, 18
14 Obituary "A.L. Brosio Dies; Noted Engineer" *San Diego Union* July 27, 1984, B-4.
15 Responses: Class Notes, Harvard Class of 1941, Sixth Anniversary Report, (Cambridge, MA: Harvard University, 1946,) 205; Class Notes, Harvard Class of 1941, 15th Anniversary Report, (Cambridge, MA: Harvard University, 1956, 172.
16 Scovilles in Newport: Email from Kirby Lee (Newport Public Library) to William Sonn, March 28, 2016. Auto accident: "Pedestrian Felled.*" Newport Daily News,* Friday Oct 8.,

1954, 2; Break-in: "Police Investigate Breaks in Two Local Stores." *Newport Daily News*, Wed Jun 1, 1955, 20; Move to California: Kirby email.

17 Farm, seclusion: Author interview with Gregory T. Nudera, July 12, 2016. Deed of Trust, Block 53 of the subdivision of the "S" Tract of Rancho El Cajon in the County of San Diego. August 6, 1957; Deed of Trust September 20, 1957; Grant, Ed Fletcher Company, April 29, 1958; Full Reconveyance, Union Title Insurance Company, June 9, 1958.

18 "Employment of Homosexuals and Other Sex Perverts in Government," cited in *Milestones in American Gay Rights Movement*, www.pbs.org/wgbh/americanexperience/features/timeline/stonewall/, accessed July 5, 2016; Randy Dotina, "Running a Gay Bar in the 1950s," KPBS, May 13, 2011. http://www.kpbs.org/news/2011/may/13/running-gay-bar-1950s/, accessed July 5, 2016; Cinnabar: *USA Confidential*, referenced in "Gay Chronicles: California" http://gayinsacramento.com/Chron1-Calif-page.htm, accessed July 5, 2016.

19 Dorothy Malone, auto show: Frank Rhodes column, *San Diego Union*, May 18, 1969, 31. Frank Rhodes column, *San Diego Union*, Jan. 28, 1960, 20. Twins: Frank Rhodes column, *San Diego Union* May 12, 1960, 20; Nuclear fuel: Jack MaGee, "Nuclear Fuel Must Go by Air" *San Diego Union*, 7-26-1961, 10; Complex insurance matters: Joe Brooks, "How Could I Know It Would Rain?" *San Diego Union*, May 26, 1963, 73.

20 Arnold Fernandes, "The Rise and Fall of the Tuna Industry in San Diego" West Coast Tuna History http://www.westcoasttunahistory.com access July 14 2016; John D. Cramer, "Sun Sets on Fleet: San Diego Tuna Fisherman Squeezed by Economics, Environment" October 7, 1990. *Los Angeles Times*. http://articles.latimes.com/1990-10-07/local/me-2779_1_san-diego, accessed July 13, 2016; Roger Showley, "Tuna: A San Diego fish story" *The San Diego Union-Tribune*, June 16. 2012. http://www.sandiegouniontribune.com/news/2012/jun/16/tuna-san-diego-fish-story/, accessed July 13 2016.

21 "Bank Adds New Orange Country Unit" *Los Angeles Times,* March 4, 1956, 124; "Bookkeeper Signed Loans She'd 'Never Heard Of," *San Bernardino County Sun*, Sept 3, 1976, 21; Mel Baughman, "Smith's Bank linked to many sales in Kern" *The Bakersfield Californian*, Jan 20, 1974, 7-8; "C. Arnholdt Smith" https://en.wikipedia.org/wiki/C._Arnholdt_Smith, accessed Dec 22, 2016; "San Diego Tycoon C. Arnholt Smith Dies" *Los Angeles Times*, June 10, 1996, http://articles.latimes.com/1996-06-10/news/mn-13551_1_san-diego, accessed Dec 22 2016.

22 Wall of books: Nudera interview, July 12, 2016. Responses to Harvard: *Class Notes, Harvard Class of 1941, 20th Anniversary Report*, (Cambridge, MA: Harvard University, 1961), 174; *Class Notes, Harvard Class of 1941, 25th Anniversary Report*, (Cambridge MA: Harvard University, 1966), 848; Sports car activities, church organist: Nudera interview, July 12, 2016.

23 Class Notes, 20th Anniversary Report, 174; Class Notes, 25th Anniversary Report, 848.

24 "Good money:" Author interview with Lori Layden, Nov. 10, 2016.

CHAPTER 20: THE REBEL AFTERLIFE

1 Heart and soul: Kahn, "Hotelling Interview," HC C Box 2 FF 56, 153; Sentence: General Court Martial Order Number 111, September 6, 1946, Headquarters, Fifth Army, Chicago, Illinois.

2 Beehive: Paul Roberts, S/Sgt "Disciplinary Report" May 27-1946, Office of the Supervisor of Prisoners, United State Disciplinary Barracks, Fort Leavenworth, Kanas, 29 May 1946 Inmate 63453-L Theophil J. Leonhard. U.S. Penitentiary, Leavenworth Kansas. "Notorious Offenders" series. Textual Reference (RDT2); Compass: T. Beltman, "Disciplinary Report," July 28, 1946, Notorious Offenders series. Textual Reference

(RDT2); "Conduct Record—Theophil J. Leonhard, 63453-L, Department of Justice, U.S. Penitentiary, Leavenworth, Kansas; Work reports: "Special Progress Report." November 1947, "Notorious Offenders" series. Textual Reference (RDT2); Politics: "Special Progress Report." November 1948, "Notorious Offenders" series.

3   1949 hearing: Letter Nobis to Kahn, January 9, 1949 HC C Box 2 FF46. Job promise: "Parole Progress Report." August 1949, Notorious Offenders series. Textual Reference (RDT2); Texas Ex: Letter Ladon to Kahn, December 27, 1948, HC C Box 2 FF 44, 3.

4   Sentence shortened: "Record of Court Commitment" 8-16-51, Notorious Offenders series. Textual Reference (RDT2}; Clemency denied, 1950: "Special Progress Report." April 1951, Notorious Offenders series. Textual Reference (RDT2]; Released: Adjutant General, Dept of the Army, 10 August 1951, Notorious Offenders series. Textual Reference (RDT2); Inmates Release Schedule—Theophil J. Leonhard, August 31, 1951, U.S. Penitentiary, Leavenworth, Kansas.

5   Nobis Decorating: "Michigan Stained Glass Census" www.michiganstainedglass.org/ collections/studiosartist.php?id=17-82-97, accessed July 11, 2016;: Untitled, The Evening Independent (Massillon, Ohio) Aug 3, 1963, 9; "Fred Nobis Dies," *Akron Beacon Journal* (Akron, Ohio) July 30 1987, 16; Accounting: Release Progress Report" September 1 1951 Notorious Offenders series. Textual Reference (RDT2)]; Kissman reunion: Lisa Williams interview, December 13, 2016.

6   German ethnicity: www.encyclopedia.chicagohistory.org/pages/512.html, accessed Feb. 13 2017; Gerald T, McJimsery, ed., *Documentary History of the Franklin D Roosevelt Administration,* Vol 32, "Roosevelt, J. Edgar Hoover and Domestic Surveillance 1939-1942," 481; German-American club(s): "German-American Club Organized," *Forest Park Review* (Forest Park, Illinois), December 10, 1959, 2; "German American Club Will be Established" *The Decatur Herald* (Decatur, Illinois) May 29, 1961, 14; Programs: "Foreign-Made Items Viewed" *Decatur (Il) Herald*, April 25, 1963, "Habich Lades Win Div in G.A. League," *Blue Island (IL) Sun Standard*, May 27, 1954; "German-American Club Turkey Shoot Huge Success," *Blue Island (IL) Sun Standard*, Nov. 21, 1957, 7, "German POW, Free in U.S. 14 Years, Gives Self Up To FBI" *Southern Illinoisan* (Carbondale, IL) May 11, 1959, 1; Siebenbuerger Club, Hitler's birthday: Lisa Williams interview, December 13, 2016.

7   Preaching: *Chicago Heights Star*, Nov 1 1962, 19. Leonhard's Death: Death certificate: Texas, Death Certificates, 1903-1982 [database on-line]. "Theophil Leonhard Rites Held Here Today" *Fredericksburg Standard* (Fredericksburg, Tx) May 11 1966, Ancestry.com, 11www.newspapers.com/image/86030559/?terms=Theophil%2BLeonhard&match=2, accessed Dec 22 2015.

8   "Mrs. Gertrude Karas" *Fredericksburg Standard*, 18 May, 1966, 7 www.newspapers.com/ima ge/86030616/?terms=Theophil%2BLeonhard, accessed Dec 22 2015.

9   New job: "Parole Progress Report, Paul A. Kissman, 61423-L" January 1947 United States Penitentiary, Leavenworth, Kansas, 1. Parole adviser: *ibid*; Father, Herbert: Letter Lori Layden to William Sonn, Oct. 27, 2016; "Paul B Kissman dead at 90" *New Castle News*, (New Castle PA), Aug. 24, 1964; Herbert was married once to Gladys G. Burnside in 1929, but they separated two years later and were divorced on the grounds of desertion several years later. *New Castle News*, November 21, 1933, 11. Santa Monica brother: "Clayton Kissman" *Erie Daily Times*, May 28, 1962, 55; Surge in family life: May, *Homeward Bound*, 6.

10   Optical interests: Letter, Layden to Sonn, Oct. 27, 2016; Kahn, *The New Yorker*, April 1, 1950, 68.

11   Lisa Williams interview, December 13, 2016; Chip Berlet, *Right-Wing Populism in America*: "The Pillars of U.S. Populist Conspiracism: The John Birch Society and the Liberty Lobby," 9; Letter to the Editor from D.C. MacLean, *Lebanon Daily News* (Lebanon, Pa), 10-9-1961,

4; "Scott Rejects Support of John Birch Society" *Standard Speaker* (Hazelton, Pa), Aug 15 1964, 1; Arthur Krock, "Dirksen Cites Chief Birch Candidate Was a Democrat" *Pittsburgh Post-Gazette* Oct 5, 1965, 9; Mary Kay Quinlan, "John Birchers: 'I Told You So' *Democrat and Chronicle*, (Rochester NY), Nov 18 1973, 196; Molly Ivans, "Some Mormons consider ERA a threat to the family" *Democrat and Republican* (Rochester, NY) Nov 27 1979, 15.

12 Life-long friend: Letter Layden to Sonn, October 27, 2016; Hotelling visits, dating: Lisa Williams interview, December 13, 2016.

13 Bureau of Vital Statistics, State of Florida, Otto Idelberger Jr. Death Certificate, Amended Oct 14 1994; Opton: "Return from Korea" *Daily Chronicle* (Centralia, Washington) 5-16-51, 11; U.S., Department of Veterans Affairs BIRLS Death File, 1850-2010 [database on-line]. Provo, UT, Ancestry.com 2011; Drewes: Patent # 3044275, July 17, 1962; "State OES Officer Who Is Native of Germany to be Owen Scott Guest." *The Decatur Herald*, Decatur, Il, Aug 3, 1958, 38; "1,200 Delegates Salute Leaders of Eastern Star" *Chicago Tribune,* Oct 7, 1958, 29.

14 Bachelor's degree: Granted January 31, 1948. Email Erika Gorder (Rutgers University Libraries), to William Sonn, July 20, 2016; Fellowships: University of Michigan. Board of Regents, *Proceedings of the Board of Regents (1951-1954)*, 14, 260, 508, 635, 891; Work history: Adams, 6; "Eric Bell Hotelling," *American Men & Women of Science, 1992-93.* 18th Edition, Volume 3, G-I. (New Providence, New Jersey: R. R. Bowker Database Publishing Group).

15 Adams, 3, 10, 15, 19-20.

16 Harold Hotelling reports: Memorandum to Special Agent in Charge, New York re: Eric Bell Hotelling, Espionage—X, September 7, 1954; Adams, 17. "Schappes" petition: "Dreams and Fighters: The NYC teacher purges" http://www.dreamersandfighters.com/schappes/inter_schappes.aspx, accessed July 26 2016; "Liberal:" Telex: Director, FBI, Fr: SAC New York Re; Pittsburgh letter to Director March 16, 1954.

17 Obituary "Howard E. Heinz," *Pittsburgh Post-Gazette* (Pittsburgh, Pa) May 17, 1965, 22; Engagement, *Pittsburgh Post Gazette* (Pittsburgh, Pa), 2-2-56, 12; Best man: "Heinz-Hotelling Wedding" *The Pittsburgh Press* Oct 8, 1956.

18 Stein-Hall: "Stein-Hall Names Director," *New York Times*, March 3, 1956, 23; Hotelling's patents: Wet tobacco: Andrew Eugene Carmellini, Mount Vernon, NY, and Eric Bell Hotelling, Wesport, Conn, assignors to American Machine & Foundry Company United States Patent Office 2,949,117 August 16, 1960; Plasticizer: Eric Bell Hotelling and Thomas Edward Kelly, Westport, "Method of making a smoking product" United States Patent Office US 2957478 A Oct 25, 1960, assignors to International Cigar Machinery Company, 'Inc., New Jersey No Drawing. Filed Sept. 30, 1959, Ser. No. 843,376; Heat and chemical degradation: William Kwo-Wei Chen, Stamford, and Howard Martin Halter, South Norwalk, Conn., Eric Bell Hotelling, Portsmouth, Va., and Clayton Andrew Wetmore, Norwalk, Conn, assigners to American Machine & Foundry Company, New Jersey. United States Patent Office 3,257,334, June 21, 1966; AMF: "American Machine & Foundry Company, List of Deals," Lehman Brothers Collection—Contemporary Business Archives, Baker Library, Harvard University, www.library.hbs.edu/hc/lehman/company.html?company=american_machine_foundry_company, accessed July 27 2016; Research interests: *American Men & Women of Science,*: Children: Email Carolyn Rogers to William Sonn, April 9, 2016.

19 Children: *ibid.*; Yogi Berra's deal: "Ball Player Sold" *New York Times*, March 4, 1961, 28; Robert M. Lipsyte, "Yogi Berra Works Out With a Management Team" *New York Times*, November 17, 1962 29,31.

20 Would-be authors would pay "vanity presses" to publish their books. Such businesses are now firmly replaced by self-publishing technologies.

21 Phelps Jay Phelps. *The Lost Treasure City of Tlaxu.* (New York; Vantage Press, 1969);
Autographed copy: Lori Layden to William Sonn, October 27, 2016.

22 "Yoo-Hoo Beverage Expands Worldwide," *Asbury Park Press* (Asbury Park, New Jersey)
Sept 27 1970, 72; Prosperity: Bill D. Ross, "Yoo-Hoo: A Carlstadt Success Story" *New York
Times*, March 2, 1975, 73; Obituary: "Berenice Hotelling," *The Pittsburgh Press* (Pittsburgh,
Pa) July 27, 1972, 4; "Harold Hotelling, a Developer Of Biometrics, Is Dead at 78.," *New
York Times*, Dec. 27, 1973, 40.

23 "Louis Marx and Company" en.wikipedia.org/wiki/Louis_Marx_and_Company, accessed
Jan 6, 2017; Interstates, suburban sprawl, GE: Behind The Marker" ExplorePAhistory.
com, http://explorepahistory.com/hmarker.php?markerId=1-A-C1, accessed Jan. 6, 2017;
Appliance business: Peg Thomas and Michael L. Walden, *Battleground: Business* (Westport,
CT: Greenwood Press, 2007, 282); GE: "General Electric Company" (International
Directory of Company Histories. (Farmington Hills, Mi: Thomson Gale, 2006).

24 Family life, hints of Army "problem:" Lisa Williams interview, Dec. 13, 2016; Letter Layden
to Sonn, Oct. 27, 2016; Ex-wife's death: "Gladys E. Schroeder Kissman. Worked for Reed
Manufacturing" *Erie Times News.* Sunday Aug 18, 2002.

25 Herbert Kissman died on January 6 1989, Erie Public Library Research, August 9, 2016;
Kissman in California: "Paul A. Kissman" *Erie Daily Times*, January 30, 1989, 74; Letter
Layden to Sonn, Oct. 27, 2016; Lisa Williams interview, Dec. 13, 2016; Certificate of
Death. Paul A. Kissman, State of California, County of San Diego. 38937 (Registration
District) Certificate Number 001147.

26 Carolyn Rogers email, April 9, 2016. "Elizabeth Mary Hotelling," Ancestry.com; Provo
UT Death records: Veterans Burial Card, Ancestry.com. U.S., Social Security Death Index,
1935-2014, Provo, UT.

CHAPTER 21: MAPLE, AT SEA

1 The Sierings' arrive: Passenger Manifest, Braniff Airways, Inc. Jan 24, 1957. The National
Archives at Washington, D.C.; Washington, D.C.; Series Title: Passenger and Crew Lists
of Vessels and Airplanes Arriving at Miami, Florida.; NAI Number: 2771998; Records
of the Immigration and Naturalization Service, 1787–2004; Record Group Number: 85;
"Declaration of Intention No. 11,937," U.S. Immigration and Naturalization Service,
Southern District of Florida; Naturalization petition: The National Archives at Atlanta,
Atlanta, Georgia, USA; *Petitions for Naturalization, 1913–1991*; National Archives
Publication: 578688; *Declarations of Intention for Citizenship, compiled 1913—1990*,
National Archives Publication: 578685; Record Group Title: Records of District Courts of
the United States; Record Group Number: 21.

2 Florida Dept. of State Division of Corporations, General Stamping Document #225608
search.sunbiz.org; First home mortgage: Lots 14-16, Block 47 Brickell Estates (now
770 SW 21st Road) Miami-Dade County Clerk's Office, Miami-Dade.com; Real estate
purchases 1960-1985: Miami-Dade County Clerk's Office, Miami-dade.com; Siering's
professional titles: *Polk's Miami Suburban Directory*, 1961-64, 1966, (1966: R. L. Polk &
Co., Publishers); *Polk's Miami City Directory*, 1976 (1976: R. L. Polk & Co., Publishers);
Products: ads in *The Miami Herald* FUN IN FLORIDA Magazine 2/21/60, 44 and *Miami
Herald*, 3/10/72, 10/15/72, 10/18/72, 10/20/72, 10/22/72, 10/24/72, 10/28/72. Magic
Fingers: Amanda Marques Gonzales. "'Magic Fingers' reach for home sales." *Miami Herald*,
July 22, 1990, 3,4.

3 General Stamping & Manufacturing Corporation Annual Report, 1994, Florida Dept. of
State, April 25, 1995; Frieda's death: Social Security Death Records, Ancestry.com. Provo,

UT, accessed Sept. 20, 2016; Obituary, "Siering, Frieda P.," *Miami Herald,* July 19, 1994, 48; Death, military service: State of Florida, Bureau of Vital Statistics, Certificate of Death for Friederich Siering, April 19, 1999.

4   Gene Curtis, "FBI agent's gun skills off mark politically," *Tulsa World,* June 13, 2007; "FBI Special Agent, Delf A. "Jelly" Bryce (1934-1958)" Historicalgman.com, accessed Jan 2, 2016; Newton, *The FBI Encyclopedia,* 157); LaPell, http://www.guns.com/2012/03/21/ da-jelly-bryce/, accessed Nov. 11, 2015; "Interview with Jelly Bryce," WKY- KTVY TV—KFOR, 1958 News Can # 636. http://51297323.domainhost.com/JellyBryce/ about_real_jelly_bryce.htm access August 12, 2016; 1958 vote: Arrell Gibson, *Oklahoma, a History of Five Centuries,* (Norman, OK: University of Oklahoma Press, 1981), 246; Heart attack: Charles Benne, "Legendary Lawman Jelly Bryce," June 3, 2000, Officer.com. http:// www.officer.com/article/10233523/legendary-lawman-jelly-bryce, accessed August 12, 2016.

5   Richard D. Lyons, "E.J. Kahn, Jr., 77, Writer For the New Yorker. *New York Times,* May 29, 1994 http://www.nytimes.com/1994/05/29/obituaries/e-j-kahn-jr-77-writer-for-the-new-yorker.html, accessed August 3, 2016; AP News Archive, "E.J. Kahn Jr., New Yorker Writer, Dead at 77" May 28, 1994, http://www.apnewsarchive.com/1994/E-J-Kahn-Jr-New-Yorker-Writer-Dead-at-77/id-dc3bf45d8a9a19ff8a78116567ff7f76, accessed August 3, 2016.

6   (Footnote source): David Talbot, *The Devil's Chessboard* (New York: HarperCollins, 2015), 320-327. Porter's last years: Author interview with Sam Porter, July 19, 2016; Paul Neville, "'Dark visitor' hasn't gotten best of Charlie Porter" *Eugene Register-Guard* (Eugene, OR) Aug 8 2004, 11. Right-wing target: "The Scrutable Occidental" *Time,* Nov 30 1959, 16.

7   Harvard College Class of 1941, 35th Anniversary Report, (1976: Cambridge, Ma. Harvard Class Report Office,) 152-53.

8   Tuna industry: Fernandes, "The Rise and Fal ," West Coast Tuna History http://www. westcoasttunahistory.com access July 14 2016; John D. Cramer, "Sun Sets on Fleet: San Diego Tuna Fisherman Squeezed by Economics, Environment" October 7, 1990. *Los Angeles Times.* http://articles.latimes.com /1990-10-07/local/me-2779_1_san-diego, accessed July 13, 2016; Roger Showly, "Tuna: A San Diego fish story" *The San Diego Union-Tribune,* June 16. 2012 http://www.sandiegouniontribune.com/news/2012/jun/16/ tuna-san-diego-fish-story, accessed July 13, 2016.

9   Retirement, gardening: "Dale H. Maple," *Harvard College Class of 1941, 40th Anniversary Report,* (Cambridge, Ma. Harvard University,1986), 134; Mother's death: "Mae Scoville" Ancestry.com. U.S., Social Security Death Index, 1935-2014 [database on-line]; Maple's inheritance: Nudera interview, July 12, 2016; Computer consulting: *Class of 1941,*138; Convenience store: Nudera interview, July 12, 2016.

10   "They drank:" *ibid;* Death, cremation: County of San Diego, Vital Records, "Dale H. Maple Certificate of Death," June 4, 2001.

AFTERWORD

1   David Gutiérrez, "Humans are not the only animals" *Natural News,* March 26, 2014. http://www.naturalnews.com/044451_war_, accessed Dec. 3, 2015; Malaysia: Mark W Moffett. "Battles among Ants Resemble Human Warfare" *Scientific American,* December 2011. http://www.scientificamerican.com/article/ants-and-the-art-of-war/, accessed Dec 3, 2015.

2   Youthful indiscretions: Email Charles Brown (Labor economist; University of Michigan) to William Sonn, Jan. 24, 2017.

BIBLIOGRAPHY

Alschuler, Albert. "The Changing Purposes of Criminal Punishment: A Retrospective on the Last Century and Some Thoughts About the Next" *University of Chicago Law Review*, Vol 70, No. 1 (Winter 2003), Accessed July 19, 2016. http://chica gounbound.uchicago.edu/cgi/viewcontent.cgi?article=1893&context=journal_articles.

The Album 1941, Vol LII Cam bridge, Mass: The Album Board, Harvard University, 1942.

American Men & Women of Science, 1992-93. 18th Edition, Volume 3, G-I. New Providence, New Jersey: R. R. Bowker Database Publishing Group.

———. 18th Edition, Volume 3, G-I. New Providence, New Jersey: R. R. Bowker Database Publishing Group, 1994.

Ardman, Harvey. "World War II: German Saboteurs Invade America in 1942." HistoryNet. Accessed Nov 27, 2015. http://www.historynet.com/world-war-ii -german-saboteurs-invade-america-in-1942.htm.

Arrow, K.J., and Lehmann, E.L. "Harold Hotelling, 1895-1973" *National Academy of Sciences, 2005.* Accessed Jan 7, 2016. http://www.nasonline.org/publications /biographical-memoirs/memoir-pdfs/hotelling-harold.pdf.

Articles of War, Approved June 4, 1920-September 1920. Accessed June 21, 2016. http:// ibiblio.org/hyperwar/USA/ref/AW/index.html.

Beatty, Jack. The Rascal King: The Life and Times. of James Michael Curley. Boston: Da Capo Press, 1992.

Borch III, Fred L. "Lore of the Corp. Tried for Treason: The Court-Martial of Private First Class Dale Maple." The Army Lawyer, Nov 2010.

Borum, R. (2004). Psychology of terrorism. Accessed Dec. 14, 2015. Tampa: University of South Florida. https://www.ncjrs.gov/pdffiles1/nij/grants/208552 .PDF.

Breslow, Emily R. "Harvard to Treason." The Harvard Crimson Magazine. March 2, 2011. Accessed Oct 4 2015. https://www.thecrimson.com/article/2011/3/3 /maple-german-prisoners-club/.

Cahalan, Margarete Werner and Parson, Lee Ann. Historical Corrections in the United States, 1850-1984. Rockville Md: U.S. Department of Justice, Bureau of Justice Statistics, 1986.

Christenson, Ron, ed. "Joseph E. McWilliams and Far-Right Leaders." Political Trials in History: From Antiquity to the Present. New Brunswick, N.J: Transaction Publishers, 1991.

Counter Intelligence Corps: History and Mission in World War II. Accessed November 30 2015. https://fas.org/irp/agency/army/cic-wwii.pdf. The Counter Intelligence Corps School, Fort Holabird, Baltimore, Md. Army War College, Carlisle Barracks, PA.

DeAngelis, Tori. "Understanding Terrorism," Monitor on Psychology, American Psychological Association, Nov 2009. Accessed Dec 14, 2015. http://www.apa.org /monitor/2009/11/terrorism.aspx.

Ebel, Karen E."WWII Violations of German American Civil Liberties by the US Government" The Freedom of Information Times, Feb 24, 2003. Accessed May 12, 2017 http://www.foitimes.com/gasummary.htm.

Ellis, Robert B. See Naples and Die: A World War II Memoir of a United States Army Ski Troop in the Mountains of Italy. Jefferson, North Carolina: McFarland Publishing, 1996.

Encyclopedia of Chicago History. http://www.encyclopedia.chicagohistory.org/pages /512.html. Accessed Feb. 13, 2017.

Federal Bureau of Investigation. "A Byte Out of History: Spies Caught, Spies Lost, Lessons Learned." Accessed December 2007. https://www.fbi.gov/news/stories/2007 /december/espionage.

Fort Knox Cultural Resources Office. "Fort Knox History: World War II Axis POWs" https://mybaseguide.com/installation/fort-knox/community/world-war-ii-prisoner -of-war-camp-established-at-fort-knox/.

Frensch, Thomas. The FBI Files on John Steinbeck. New Delhi: New Century Books, 2002.

"General Motors: Mark of Excellence." Ann Arbor Sun. April 5, 1974.

Gutiérrez, David. "Humans are not the only animals that engage in war" Natural News. March 26, 2014. Accessed Dec. 3, 2015. http://www.naturalnews.com /044451_war_chimpanzees_animal_behavior.html.

Harbin, Julie Poucher. "Psychology of a Terrorist: Experts Go To The Source," Islamic Commentary, Nov. 6, 2014. Accessed Dec 14, 2015. http://islamicommentary.org /2014/11/psychology-of-a-terrorist-experts-go-to-the-source/.

Harvard Class of 1941, Sixth Anniversary Report, Cambridge, Mass: Harvard University, 1946.

Harvard College Class of 1941, 15th Anniversary Report, Cambridge, Mass: Harvard University, 1956.

————, 20th Anniversary Report, Cambridge, Mass: Harvard University, 1961.

————, 25th Anniversary Report, Cambridge, Mass: Harvard University, 1966.

————, 30th Anniversary Report, Cambridge, Mass: Harvard University, 1971.

————, 35th Anniversary Report, Cambridge, Mass: Harvard University, 1976.

————, 40th Anniversary Report, Cambridge, Mass: Harvard University, 1981.

————, 45th Anniversary Report, Cambridge, Mass: Harvard University, 1986.

————, Fiftieth Anniversary Report, Cambridge, Mass: Harvard University, 1991.

"Investigation of un-American propaganda activities in the United States." Accessed Jan 10, 2016.

Irwin, Douglas. "What caused the recession of 1937-38?" VOX CEPR's Policy Portal, Sept 11, 2011. Accessed Nov 16, 2015. http://www.voxeu.org/article/what -caused-recession-1937-38-new-lesson-today-s-policymakers.

J. Frank Dobie Papers, Harry Ransom Center, University of Texas, file 129.8

Karns, Stephen P., J.D., "Military Trial Procedures," U.S. Military Law. Accessed January 6, 2016. http://www.usmilitarylawyer.com/military-legal-procedures.asp.

Krammer, Arnold. "When the Afrika Korps Came to Texas" Invisible Texans: Women and Minorities in Texas History. New York: McGraw-Hill, 2005.

Krear, H. Robert. "The Journal of a US Army Mountain Trooper in World War II." Western History Collection, 10th Mountain Division Room, Denver Public Library.

Kruse, Megan, "Harold Hotelling, 1895-1973" American Statistical Association. Accessed Jan 7, 2016 http://www.amstat.org/about/statisticiansinhistory/blocks /dsp_biosinfo.cfm?BioID=7&pf=yes.

Lee, Robert. Fort Meade and the Black Hills. Lincoln: University of Nebraska Press, 1991.

Metropolitan State University Denver. "Greetings from Camp Hale, Top of the Nation." https://archive.org/stream/investigationofu194114unit/investigationof u194114unit_djvu.txt.

———. "Camp Hale History." Accessed Nov 1, 2015. https://www.msudenver.edu /camphale/camphalehistory/.

Miller, Robert A. "A True Story of an American Nazi Spy: Willliam Curtis Colepaugh. Accessed Oct 21 2015. https://books.google.com/books?id=ndSkplZUUh8C&pg=PA 43&lpg=PA43&dq=German+consulate+Boston+1940&source=bl&ots=H_08gw_w7 a&sig=2ubplj2E1E6cc3p9dvguKuQgdgQ&hl=en&sa=X&ved=0C8Q 6AEwA2oVChMIxM7xi7LHyAIVBORjCh18jQw2 - v=onepage&q=German consulate Boston 1940&f=.

Moffett, Mark W. "Battles among Ants Resemble Human Warfare" Scientific American Dec 2011. Accessed Dec 3, 2015. http://www.scientificamerican.com /article/ants-and-the-art-of-war/.

Moore, John Hammond. The Faustball Tunnel: German POWs in America and their Great Escape New York: Random House, 1978.

National Archives (I) – Records of Far East Command, Supreme Commander of the Allied Powers and United Nations Command 1945–1957, Provost Marshall Section, Reg 554, Stack 290, Rm 50, Comp 7, Shelf 3, Entry 156.

National Archives (II) – Supreme Commander of the Allied Powers, Reg 331, Stack 290, Rm 9, Comp 31, Shelf 1, File: "Execution Report. http://www.death penaltyinfo.org/executions-military, access Dec 26 2015.

National Archives and Records Administration. Electronic Army Serial Number Merged File, 1938-1946 [Archival Database]; ARC: 1263923. World War II Army Enlistment Records; Records of the National Archives and Records Administration, Record Group 64; National Archives at College Park. College Park, Maryland, U.S.A.

The New York Nazis of 1938. Accessed Oct 22, 2015. https://www.nowtheendbegins.com /?s=New%20York%20Nazis%20of%201938&sort=oldest.

Newton, Michael. The FBI Encyclopedia. 2003. Jefferson, NC: McFarland & Co, 2003.

Peckham, H. H. The Making of the University of Michigan, 1817-1992. 175th anniversary ed., [Corrected printing] Ann Arbor, MI: University of Michigan, Bentley Historical Library, 1997.

Phelps, Phelps Jay (Eric Hotelling pseudonym). The Lost Treasure of Tlaxu. New York: Vantage Press, 1969.

"Porter, Charles Orlando, (1919-2006)" Biographical Directory of the United States Congress https://bioguideretro.congress.gov/Home/MemberDetails?memIndex =P000439.

RallyPoint, The Professional Military Network. https://www.rallypoint.com/answers/ww2 -discharge-papers-what-does-days-lost-for-article-of-war-aw-107-mean, accessed 6-20-2016.

The Reporters Committee for Freedom of the Press. Covering courts-martial: Finding the docket. Accessed Feb 14 2016. https://www.rcfp.org/wpcontent/uploads/imported /MILDOCWP.pdf.

Robbins, William G. "Charles O Porter, (1919-2006)" The Oregon Encyclopedia. Portland, OR: Oregon Historical Society. https://www.oregonencyclopedia.org /articles/porter_charles_o_1919_2006_/#.X-ifJC1h3Aw.

Shimo, Cedrick. "The 1800th Story: A student exiled to the 1800th." Accessed Oct 26, 2015 Japanese American Veterans Association. http://www.javadc.org/1800th _story%20Shimo.htm.

Smith, Col. James J. "Military Clemency and Parole: Does It Work?" Executive Research Project 1993. Fort McNair, Washington, D.C: National Defense University,1993.

Special Committee on Un-American Activities. House of Representatives, 75th Congress.

"SS-Oberfuhrer Dr. Herbert Sholz, Lieselotte 'Lilo' Sholz." *Axis History Forum.* Accessed Nov 22, 2015. http://forum.axishistory.com/viewtopic.php?t=165588.

Theoharis, Athan G. *The FBI: A Comprehensive Reference Guide.* Boston: Greenwood Publishing Group. Oryx Press, 1999.

University of Michigan, Board of Regents, Proceedings of the Board of Regents (1951-1954).

Van Ellis, Mark D. "Americans for Hitler – The Bund" America in WWII. Accessed Feb 28, 2018 http://www.americainwwii.com/articles/americans-for-hitler/.

Weber, Mark. "How Hitler Tackled Unemployment and Revived Germany's Economy." Institute for Historical Review. Accessed Oct 19 2014. http://www .ihr.org/other/economyhitler2011.html.

Weingartner, James J. A Peculiar Crusade: William M. Everett and the Malmedy Massacre, New York: NYU Press, 2000.

Williamson, Eileen. "Camp Hale Military Munitions Remediation Project." Accessed Nov 1, 2015. https://www.army.mil/article/132165/military_munitions _remediation_at_camp_hale_the_project_the_history_the_public.

Willing, Richard. "The Nazi spy next door." Accessed Oct 16, 2015. http://usatoday30 .usatoday.com/news/nation/2002/02/28/usatcov-traitor.htm.

Witte, David R. *World War II at Camp Hale: Blazing a new trail in the Rockies.* West Columbia, SC: Arcadia Publishing, 2015.

Worhmoth, Eric. "History of the FBI World War II Period: Late 1930's—1945." USHAP 2016=17 (Blog). Accessed Nov 27 2015 https://www2.fbi.gov/libref /historic/history/worldwar.htm.

WW2 Internment in the United States. Chronology—Suspicion, Arrest, and Internment. Accessed Nov 29 2015. ©Fallon/Jacobs 1996 http://www.foitimes.com/internment /chrono.htm.

"Yoo-hoo" Wikipedia entry. Accessed Jan 11, 2016 https://en.wikipedia.org/wiki/Yoo-hoo.

DOCUMENTS
Certificate of Death. Paul A. Kissman, State of California, County of San Diego. 38937 (Registration District) 001147 (Certificate Number).

Cook County, Illinois Marriage Index, 1930-1960 [database on-line]. Friedrich Siering. Provo, UT, USA: Ancestry.com Operations Inc, 200.

Eric B. Hotelling. Records of the Chief of Naval Operations and Record Group 319: Records of Army Staffs. Record Group 38:

Fredrich W. Siering v William S. Eley. Opinion of District Court of the United States for the District of Kansas, First Division. December 23, 1944. National Personnel Records Center, National Archives St. Louis. Re: Siering Friedrich.

Friedrich Siering. National Personnel Records Center, National Archives St. Louis. Re: Siering Friedrich.

Inmate Record #61364-Dale H Maple. National Archives at Kansas City. Record Group 129, Records of the Bureau of Prisons. Dept of Justice. Bureau of Prisons. U.S. Penitentiary, Leavenworth. Inmate Case Files, 1895-1952. National Archives Identifier: 571125.

Leonhard v. Eley. No. 3175. Circuit Court of Appeals, Tenth Circuit. October 16, 1945. Accessed Dec. 22, 2015, https://casetext.com/case/leonhard-v-eley.

National Archives and Records Administration. Inmate 63453-L Theophil J. Leonhard. U.S. Penitentiary, Leavenworth Kansas. "Notorious Offenders" series. National Archives Textual Reference (RDT2).

———. *U.S. World War II Army Enlistment Records, 1938-1946* [database on-line]. Paul A. Kissman. Provo, UT, USA: Ancestry.com Operations Inc, 2005.

———. *U.S. World War II Army Enlistment Records, 1938-1946* [database on-line]. Eric B. Hotelling. Provo, UT, USA: Ancestry.com Operations Inc, 2005. Accessed dec 24 2015.

Petitions for Naturalization, compiled 1913—1991. Friedrich Siering. National Archives Publication: *578688*; Record Group Title: *Records of District Courts of the United States,* The National Archives at Atlanta; Atlanta, Georgia, USA.

Porter, Charles O. "Letter re: Dale Maple." Harvard University Archive 1948-1949 *Harvard Alumni Bulletin* v. 51 Box 54 Cambridge, Mass: Harvard Alumni Association, 1910-1969.

Record of Trial. United States v. Private First Class Friedrich W. Siering, 36 702 841, National Personnel Records Center, National Archives St. Louis. Re: Siering Friedrich.

Texas, Death Certificates, 1903–1982. Theophil J. Leonhard. Provo, UT, USA: Ancestry. com; Operations, Inc., 2013.

U.S. City Directories, 1822-1995 [database on-line]. *Dale H Maple.* Provo, UT, USA: Ancestry.com; Operations, Inc., 2011.

———. [database on-line]. Paul A. Kissman. Provo, UT, USA: Ancestry.com; Operations, Inc., 2011.

U.S., Social Security Applications and Claims Index, 1936-2007 [database on-line]. Eric B. Hotelling. Provo, UT, USA: Ancestry.com Operations, Inc., 2015.

U.S., Social Security Death Index, 1935-2014 [database on-line]. Paul A. Kissman Provo, UT, USA: Ancestry.com Operations Inc, 2011.

United States Department of Justice, Immigration and Naturalization Service. Friedrich W. Siering. #11,937 Feb. 25, 1957.

United States of America, Bureau of the Census. *Sixteenth Census of the United States, 1940.* Eric B. Hotelling. Washington, D.C.: National Archives and Records Administration, 1940. T627, 4,643 rolls.

INDEX

ABOUT THE AUTHOR

BILL SONN is an author (*Paradigms Lost: the life and deaths of the printed word*, Rowman & Littlefield, 2006) and long-time writer whose work has appeared in *Outside/Mariah*, *Chicago* magazine, *The Progressive*, *Columbia Journalism Review*, *Boston Globe*, *Bild*, *Westword* and more. A former news and communications executive, he has edited several healthcare periodicals as well as *The Straight Creek Journal*, co-founded a news company and served as a consultant to various healthcare companies. He lives in Denver with his wife Edie, not too far from two daughters, their kids, and an abundance of local sisters- and brothers-in-law.

www.ingramcontent.com/pod-product-compliance
Lightning Source LLC
Chambersburg PA
CBHW031242090426
42742CB00007B/276